COMBATING TRANSNATIONAL CRIME

ISPAC

International Scientific and Professional
Advisory Council
of the United Nations
Crime Prevention and Criminal
Justice Programme

ISPAC – The International Scientific and Professional Advisory Council of the United Nations Crime Prevention and Criminal Justice Programme has been established in 1991. Its secretariat is located in Milan at the Centro Nazionale di Prevenzione e Difesa Sociale. The tasks of the Council were defined as 'channelling to the United Nations professional and scientific imput and creating a capacity for the transfer of knowledge and exchange of information in crime prevention and criminal justice drawing on the contributions of non-governmental organizations, academic institutions and formulation and implementation in ths field'.

For further information, please contact:

International Scientific and Professional Advisory Council (ISPAC)
c/o Centro Nazionale di Prevenzione e Difesa Sociale
3, Piazza Castello – 20121 Milano, Italy.
Phone +39/02/86460714
Fax +39/02/72008431
E-Mail:cnpds.ispac@iol.it

COMBATING TRANSNATIONAL CRIME

Concepts, Activities and Responses

Edited by

PHIL WILLIAMS

University of Pittsburgh

DIMITRI VLASSIS

Center for International Crime Prevention
United Nations

FRANK CASS
LONDON • PORTLAND, OR

First published in 2001 in Great Britain by
FRANK CASS PUBLISHERS
2 Park Square, Milton Park, Abingdon,
Oxon, OX14 4RN

and in the United States of America by
FRANK CASS PUBLISHERS
270 Madison Ave,
New York NY 10016

Transferred to Digital Printing 2005

Copyright © 2001 Frank Cass Publishers

Website: www.frankcass.com

British Library Cataloguing in Publication Data

Combating transnational crime
  1. Transnational crime 2. Transnational crime – Prevention –
International cooperation
I. Williams, Phil, 1948 – II. Vlassis, Dimitri
  364.1

ISBN 0-7146-5156-7 (cloth)
ISBN 0-7146-8175-X (paper)

Library of Congress Cataloging-in-Publication Data

Combating transnational crime/editors, Phil Williams, Dimitri Vlassis.
    p.cm.
Includes bibliographical references and index.
ISBN 0-7146-5156-7 – ISBN 0-7146-8175-X (pbk.)
    1. Transnational crime 2. transnational crime – Prevention –
International cooperation
I. Williams, Phil, 1948– II. Vlassis, Dimitri.

HV6252. C65 2001
364.1–dc21   00-065935

This group of studies first appeared as a special issue of
Transnational Organized Crime, Vol.4, Nos.3&4,
Autumn/Winter 1998 (ISSN 1357-7387), published by Frank Cass.

Contents

PART 3: RESPONDING TO TRANSNATIONAL ORGANIZED CRIME

Introduction and Overview

PHIL WILLIAMS and DIMITRI VLASSIS

The rise of transnational organized crime in the last decades of the twentieth century was as unexpected as the end of the Cold War, if far less dramatic and abrupt. In some respects, however, the challenges posed to national and international governance and international security by criminal organizations could prove more enduring, more complex and, in some respects, more difficult to manage than the relationships of the nuclear arms race era. It has to be acknowledged that the failure to manage the transnational organized crime challenge would appear to have much less destructive consequences than those of a failure to manage superpower crises. Nevertheless, these consequences would be far from negligible, especially in the medium and long term.

In order to avoid these consequences, the international community must elevate the struggle against transnational organized crime to one of its highest priorities in terms of both resource allocation and the development of appropriate strategies, and must do so in a sustained and consistent manner. The task is arduous and commitment must be nurtured and maintained in an environment where success of the most evident type might not be guaranteed and progress might appear frustratingly slow. The emergence of transnational criminal organizations is both a symptom and a result of changes in international relations. It is also a development that will help to intensify some of these changes and exacerbate the difficulties of managing globalization.

Another concern is the tardiness of some governments in recognizing the severity of the challenge and in coming to terms with the new features of organized crime. From a contemporary perspective, Al Capone and other American gangsters of the prohibition era in the USA were little more than small-time criminals with merely local reach and limited ambitions. The organized criminals of the 1990s and of today are a totally different breed, combining corporate and criminal

1

cultures, conducting criminal business not only with ruthlessness but also with a degree of business skill worthy of many Chief Executive Officers (CEOs), and accumulating enormous wealth. Transnational criminal enterprises, like licit firms, have exploited the globalization of trade and finance, the revolution in information and communications and the existence of large consumer markets for illegal products, to develop a degree of wealth and power that has posed enormous problems for governments, especially those in developing countries and countries with economies in transition.

Even where governments have recognized the seriousness of the challenge posed by transnational organized crime, they have not found it easy to develop an effective and sustained response. In recent years, however, some progress has been made by states and international organizations in developing measures to combat criminal enterprises that, in James Rosenau's felicitous term, are 'sovereignty-free' actors. This volume can be understood as a snapshot of these efforts to combat transnational organized crime. It is divided into three sections: conceptual analyses relating to various facets of the problem; some examples of transnational organized crime and illegal markets in operation; and papers looking at various initiatives that governments and international organizations have taken and/or need to take.

The papers were first delivered at a conference organized in Courmayeur, Italy, in the autumn of 1998 by the International Scientific and Professional Advisory Council (ISPAC), an umbrella organization bringing together non-governmental organizations and the professional and scientific community, and contributing to the work of the United Nations (UN) in crime prevention and criminal justice. The papers have since been updated.

As well as seeking to explain the rise of transnational organized crime, the papers in the first section of this volume also explore the nature and meaning of transnational organized crime, its operations in illegal markets and the various ways in which it is organized. The relationship between organized crime and ethnicity is explored, as is the involvement of Chinese criminal entrepreneurs – rather than the formal Chinese triad organizations – in alien trafficking and heroin smuggling.

The papers in the second part offer a few case studies of specific criminal activities, such as maritime fraud, as well as analyses of trafficking in women and children and the black market in light weapons.

In the third part of the volume the focus changes to the political, juridical and law enforcement responses, with attention given to Interpol's approach, developments in the European Union – third pillar and Europol – and the International Atomic Energy Agency's response to nuclear material trafficking. In addition, the requirements for a more coordinated and comprehensive strategy are identified. A key component of any such strategy is the UN's effort to develop a Convention against Transnational Organized Crime. The initiatives that led to this effort and the continuing discussions are outlined in a succinct analysis that highlights both the progress made and the difficulties encountered. The papers as a whole offer a sense of the progress made by the international community but also highlight the difficulties that still have to be overcome in what will be an enduring challenge.

PART 1
CONCEPTUAL ISSUES

The Dynamics of Illegal Markets

PINO ARLACCHI

THE NATURE OF ILLEGAL MARKETS

An illegal market is a place or principle within which there is an exchange of goods and services, the production, selling and consumption of which are forbidden or strictly regulated by the majority of states and/or by international law. The very existence of illegal markets is considered a threat to human dignity and the public good. Markets in hard drugs, in armaments sold outside official agreements, in human beings reduced to economic or sexual slavery, in capital of criminal origin are typical of this category of exchanges.

In view of their origins in an array of formal juridical prohibitions, illegal markets are, to a large extent, artificial creations. They have grown in parallel both with the functions of the modern welfare state, and with the development of international law in the wake of the two world wars. Multilateral treaties on the protection of human rights, international conventions on slavery, narcotics and psychotropic substances, the outlawing of violence in interstate disputes, more restrictive domestic and international regulations on the use and trade of arms, are some of the basic examples of legal provisions that have contributed to the creation of today's illegal markets.

Such markets, therefore, cannot just be analysed from an economist's standpoint as the simple result of an increase in supply and demand for some particular goods and services. They must also be examined as an undesired consequence of the effort to protect the 'human and natural substance of society' from the destructive effects of the very same market forces.

To some extent, illegal markets are governed by normal economic forces. There are buyers and sellers, wholesalers and retailers, importers and distributors, and so on. There is a 'retail' sector, composed of numerous small and medium sized, semi-independent firms supplying goods and services to final consumers.

Upon close examination, however, some of the dynamics of criminal markets are substantially different from those that drive legal markets.

Illegal enterprises can resort to the use of violence and intimidation against their competitors and opponents that results in the easy establishment of local monopolies. They also corrupt those who should uphold the law and those who are in positions to manipulate public institutions.

While the core of their activity is to supply illegal goods and services, illegal enterprises are also extensively involved in legitimate business, allowing them to launder money and appear respectable.

The cost of doing business within the illegal economy is much higher than in the legal economy – which is reflected in the market price of most illegal goods. This largely is due to additional costs incurred in the attempt to minimize the risks of being caught. For this reason, illicit markets are often built upon personal relationships – groups based on ethnic, political or religious solidarity. This minimizes the risk of exposure and, in turn, reduces the transaction costs.

THE ROLE OF CRIMINAL ORGANIZATIONS

At first glance, many criminal organizations appear as legal enterprises. However, it is more accurate to say that they tend to imitate their legal counterparts. They move the focus of their activities from one sector to another – from trafficking in stolen goods to counterfeiting, from drugs to trafficking in human beings, and so on – with an ease not known in the past.

The rise of this brand of predatory capitalism has led to an increase in the demand for criminal labor. Consequently, organized criminals have established links with ordinary and juvenile crime – which is clearly seen in the establishment of drug distribution chains that require a whole range of operators – including the recruitment of small-time gang members or prostitutes.

Those who support the legalization of drugs fail to recognize these developments. They naively believe that if countries legalize drugs, organized crime will be seriously damaged – and the public will enjoy the double benefit of a reduced demand for drugs and a decrease in the amount of crime. Unfortunately, this is wishful thinking. We have recently seen several leading mafias lose their slice of the international drug market without disruptive effects on their structure and power. Take the Sicilian Cosa Nostra. When its transatlantic heroin network was dismantled in the late 1980s, it simply shifted the center of its activities from narcotics to extortion and corruption. Other criminal constellations have moved toward more sophisticated businesses such as money laundering. Others have moved towards the new forms of slavery – trafficking in human beings.

SHATTERING THE MYTH OF INVINCIBILITY

In spite of its growth and global spread, it should be remembered that organized crime is a historical phenomenon like others. It has a life cycle, which has a beginning, a development and an end. My personal experience and research have taught me that there is nothing metaphysical in the nature of the mafia. Indeed, every time a criminal cartel has been challenged with the appropriate level of resources, legal tools and political determination, it has been defeated.

It is not true that efforts to fight organized crime at the national and international levels have failed. Even with the limited resources deployed until now, significant breakthroughs have been achieved. Indeed, the single most important accomplishment in the last 15 years in fighting organized crime was to challenge and destroy the myth of invincibility of criminal cartels.

In the 1990s, the Colombians dismantled two of the most powerful criminal coalitions that ever existed. The Medellín and Cali cartels are over – thanks to the formidable drive by the best part of the Colombian state and civil society. Their success has also led to a substantial reduction in the amount of drug money in the Colombian economy. According to a recent study, earnings from the export of all illicit drugs have dropped by half – from a record high of US$4 billion in 1984 to US$2 billion in 1996. This means a drop from the equivalent of 97 per cent of legal exports to 21 per cent, and from 11 per cent to 2.6 per cent of gross national product (GNP).

Similarly in Bolivia, the drug cartels of the 1980s have been dismantled, resulting in a decrease in the coca economy from 9.2 per cent of Bolivia's gross domestic profit (GDP) of the late 1980s to the three per cent of the late 1990s. Whereas drugs constituted the equivalent of 87 per cent of legitimate merchandise exports, that proportion is now under 15 per cent. In Southeast Asia some of the most famous drug lords of the former Golden Triangle have negotiated their withdrawal from the drug trade with governments. In Italy, too, a ten-year effort by the authorities and civil society succeeded in destroying – at least temporarily – the almost mythical Sicilian Cosa Nostra.

In many of these examples, however, we see the space occupied by the big criminal cartels of the 1980s being filled by an array of smaller, less visible organizations. These smaller players are even more difficult to identify and combat than their brazen predecessors. They adopt a low-profile strategy in their relationship with public opinion and the authorities. They are more inclined to manipulate and corrupt than to shoot and bomb. Nevertheless, even with new actors on the scene, the myth of invincibility that for decades has been glamorized and perpetuated in the media has collapsed. Progress has been made.

THE CONVENTION AGAINST TRANSNATIONAL CRIME

So, what next? The next step must be to attack the structural underpinnings of major crime groups worldwide. We need a new global strategy that takes into account the changes just described. The vehicle for it is the Convention Against Transnational Organized Crime. For many of us, this is the fruition of a long-sought vision. For myself, this process means the fulfilment of a proposal I conceived in the early 1980s. In the last sentence of my 1985 book, *Mafia Business*,[1] I called for a global strategy – the linchpin of which was an international convention against large-scale crime. This process, leading to the Convention, is synthesizing the best experiences of the past 20 years on combating the most dangerous aspects of organized crime.

Co-operation Among Countries

The Convention should open the doors for much better co-operation among countries. Until now only a few states have developed sufficient networks of agreements that allow them to work with other countries. Even with these in place, differences between the bilateral agreements create procedural discrepancies that, in practice, make co-operation very difficult. So, for many countries, this Convention will provide the basis for working together in a uniform and co-ordinated manner when building a case. The result will be an easier exchange of information and a more rapid transfer of prisoners and proceedings.

We must ensure that we ultimately achieve a structure that allows for easy and fast responses – for practical tools that practitioners can use. Moreover, the Convention should bring about the harmonization of laws among states on a number of issues, such as participation in a criminal organization or conspiracy.

Preventing Money Laundering

Harmonized laws should also make money laundering a criminal offence. Without money laundering organized crime would not flourish as it has. Preventing criminals from transforming dirty money into what appears to be clean wealth will destroy one of the main purposes of their activities: profits – profits that the International Monetary Fund (IMF) estimates to be two to five per cent of the world GDP. The flow of this money into the legitimate economy also harms economic growth.

Financial havens are increasingly used by criminals to launder money. The lack of harmonized rules among countries jeopardizes efforts to prevent dirty money entering financial systems. Also bank secrecy and a lack of transparency in financial transactions prevent investigators from identifying criminals and their schemes. We must use the opportunity of this Convention to address these issues.

Witness Protection

The Convention should also address the issue of witness protection schemes. Only if witnesses are sufficiently protected can we expect them to provide valuable information to prosecuting agencies and evidence at trial. The concrete experience of some countries demonstrates that a member of a powerful criminal gang who is induced to co-operate with the authorities – a turncoat – is worth between five and seven years of normal investigations.

PROPOSED PROTOCOLS

The proposed protocols of this Convention contain strong measures to address trafficking in women and children, smuggling in migrants and the illicit manufacturing of and trafficking in firearms.

Trafficking in Human Beings

Illegal smuggling in migrants is estimated to be a US$5–7 billion a year business – but the suffering of the tens of millions of people who are victims cannot be measured in monetary terms. Some are initially attracted by the dream of a better life; however, many are taken from their homes and villages by force and deception. Large numbers of them are then exploited, either under the direct threat of violence or to pay their alleged debts. Some are forced into prostitution, others to work long hours in sweatshops or private homes or an array of other activities. Women and children are particularly vulnerable.

Trafficking in people requires a level of resources that can only be offered by elaborate criminal organizations. The travel and false documentation needed to enter illegally the country of destination is the first step. Close ties to the new country's underworld are then necessary to ensure access to the various outlets that use black-market labor and to red light districts.

The international community must counter this scourge, regardless of how people may ultimately be exploited. A forward-looking Convention must cater to the possible scenarios of exploitation.

Organized crime groups have expanded their scope, impacting the destinies of countries. It is the role of the UN to assist governments with creating stable, independent criminal justice systems based on the rule of law. This is a prerequisite for the success of any agenda for development.

NOTES

1. Pino Arlacchi, *Mafia Business: The Mafia Ethic and the Spirit of Capitalism* (Oxford: Oxford University Press 1985).

Transnational Crime: Definitions and Concepts

GERHARD O.W. MUELLER

INTRODUCTION

The concept of 'transnational crime' is exactly a quarter of a century old. The then United Nations (UN) Crime Prevention and Criminal Justice Branch coined the term in order to identify certain criminal phenomena transcending international borders, transgressing the laws of several states or having an impact on another country. In pre-Congress documentation and the Report of the Fifth United Nations Congress on the Prevention of Crime and the Treatment of Offenders, Geneva, 1975, we identified the following categories of transnational crime: crime as business: organized crime, white-collar crime and corruption; offences involving works of art and other cultural property; criminality associated with alcoholism and drug abuse; violence of transnational and comparative international significance; and criminality associated with migration and flight from natural disasters and hostilities.[1]

It must be noted that the term 'transnational crime' did not have a juridical meaning then, and it does not have one now. It is a criminological term, under which may be lumped what is variously and differently defined in the penal codes of states, but with the common attribute of transcending the jurisdiction of any given state. We also observed then that, almost invariably, transnational criminality is organized criminality, although it is entirely imaginable that a single person can engage in transnational crime.

The term 'transnational crime' has been generally accepted as a working concept by criminologists around the world, although it has yet to find a place in the great dictionaries, including the *Oxford Dictionary* or *Webster's*, perhaps because the term or concept is relatively amorphous.

In order to provide greater precision, in 1994 the Secretariat engaged in a bold effort to assess the prevalence and extent of transnational crime, as part of the *Fourth United Nations Survey of Crime Trends and Operations of Criminal Justice Systems.*[2] Transnational crime then was defined as 'offences whose inception, prevention and/or direct or indirect effects involved more than one country'.[3] The Secretariat, from the very outset, was aware of the difficulty of any such effort. Nevertheless, it succeeded in identifying 18 categories of transnational crime, as follows:

1. money laundering (1);
2. illicit drug trafficking (14);
3. corruption and bribery of public officials as defined in national legislation and of party officials and elected representatives as defined in national legislation (17);
4. infiltration of legal business (16);
5. fraudulent bankruptcy (15);
6. insurance fraud (9);
7. computer crime (10);
8. theft of intellectual property (4);
9. illicit traffic in arms (5);
10. terrorist activities (2);
11. aircraft hijacking (6);
12. sea piracy (7);
13. hijacking on land (8);
14. trafficking in persons (12);
15. trade in human body parts (13);
16. theft of art and cultural objects (3);
17. environmental crime (11);
18. other offences committed by organized criminal groups (18).[4]

Serious discussion of the 18 categories is handicapped not only by the lack of precision in definitions, but especially by the difficulty of gauging the extent – or cost – of the criminality involved. Consider that, as national statistics do not contain our 18 categories, no quantification (as to prevalence or cost) can be derived from government figures. Consequently, this analysis suggests alternative means of assessment.

1. Money Laundering

This category has been ranked number one by the Secretariat, because of its massive impact on the global economy. Proceeds from the illicit drug trade alone are estimated to reach a US$400–500 billion figure annually. Add to that income on which taxes are illegally withheld and proceeds from other criminal activities, including bribery and governmental corruption. Most of these funds must be 'laundered', that is, sent on a route from which they emerge as clean, usable assets.

2. Illicit Drug Trafficking

The illicit trade in narcotic drugs constitutes a global shadow economy, rivalling the legitimate economy of many nations. Not only is it the principal generator of money laundering (from which many states derive legitimate income), but it also brings in its wake warfare, murder and every other conceivable criminality. The overall cost far exceeds the estimated US$500 billion annually, though no precise information can be constructed or obtained.

3. Corruption and Bribery

Even when corruption or bribery is not seen as a contributor to money-laundering criminality, it has become largely transnational simply because the economy of nations has become transnational – by acquisition of assets, resources and manufacturing opportunities abroad – and increasingly global in character. Unhappily, the cost of doing business in many parts of the world includes bribery of those (mostly in government) in charge of granting access, franchises or rights of exploitation. No price tag can be placed on the cost of corruption, although Transparency International must be credited for ranking countries in terms of corruption costs and in terms of the percentage of bribes in relation to overall cost. Such figures are based on business surveys. The method also points the way to assessing the cost and extent of other forms of transnational criminality.

4. Infiltration of Legal Business

The cash money-laundering cycle ends with the infiltration of legal business, whether it be the purchase of stocks and bonds, the acquisition of businesses or buying one's way into profitable government operations. Evidence on means and methods is sporadic. Merely by way of example, it is known that the vast money-laundering cycle operated by a Mexican 'drug baron', ultimately resulted in the purchase of auto dealerships in Mexico and of a Blockbuster Video outlet in Houston, Texas, as well as securities investments. Quite frankly, we do not know how many of the businesses we frequent daily have been infiltrated, or are actually owned, by transnational organized crime groups. The prospect is nothing but frightening, however quantification of this phenomenon is impossible at this time.

5. Fraudulent Bankruptcy

The globalization of commerce has turned the once local crime of fraudulent bankruptcy into a transnational crime. Once again, anecdotal evidence suggests that this form of criminality is linked to the money-laundering phenomenon. Washed funds may be used to acquire a business for the purpose of bankrupting it at considerable profit. Currently, no quantification is possible, although there is room for several doctoral dissertations looking at the transnational aspects of seemingly local, but large, international bankruptcies.

6. Insurance Fraud

Just as the transnational criminal phenomenon of fraudulent bankruptcy was spawned by globalization, so is the category of insurance fraud. Insurers operate globally, especially through reassurance, so as to spread the risk of loss globally. No worldwide figures on the extent of insurance fraud have been computed but, for the USA alone, the industry has put its loss figure at US$100 billion annually, which obviously includes foreign, that is, transnational, losses.[5]

7. Computer Crime

Computer crime is, by definition, transnational, since most computers are linked through the World Wide Web. With the legitimate global use of computers goes equal access for illegitimate purposes, whether for espionage (including industrial espionage), sabotage, fraud, extortion or any other criminal activity. The British Banking Association, in the mid-1990s, estimated the annual loss from computer crime to be US$8 billion, which was probably an underestimate.[6]

8. Theft of Intellectual Property

This category includes the unauthorized use of the rights of authors and performers, and of copyrights and trademarks. The perpetrators range from local cottage industries to sophisticated transnational criminal enterprises. It is a no-cost, high-profit form of criminality, hard to assess in monetary terms. However, in the mid-1990s the US Software Publishers Association estimated US losses as US$7.5 billion or more annually – and they have increased since then. In 1998, the annual report of the Business Software Alliance and the Software Publishers Association put global software losses from piracy at around US$11 billion.[7] In this area, however, criminologists once again have to rely on industry to supply the information.

9. Illicit Traffic in Arms

The illicit traffic in arms, including nuclear materials, takes place in a shadowy world virtually beyond the reach of research scholars. Although frequently aided or perpetrated by governments themselves, the trade is performed by an apparently small group of wholesalers, assisted by larger groups of retailers, located at relatively few illicit arms-trading hubs. As regards nuclear materials, obviously, few figures are available. Evidence indicates, however, that although most seizures have involved radioactive junk only a few transfers have included very small quantities of weapons-grade material.[8] Moreover, the problem is not going away. Indeed, the demand for weapons and ordnance of all kinds continues to be high in many parts of the world. And the supply is there.

10. Terrorist Activities

While some terrorists operate locally or nationally (for example, the abortion clinic bombers, the self-styled militias or the so-called Unabomber in the USA), much terrorist activity is transnational. The point needs no belabouring. There may not be a global command structure, yet terrorist organizations of regional outreach have cooperated to act interregionally. The topic is vast, has led to transnational military responses and, in every way, threatens global security. Most of the transnational terrorist organizations have been identified and transnational terrorist acts have been chronicled for some time. Global, regional and intergovernmental initiatives to deal with terrorism are in place. Yet, much experience has shown that only the removal of the terrorists' (sometimes justified) grievances can bring about a real amelioration of the problem.

17

11. Aircraft Hijacking

This term includes the destruction of aircraft in flight – a form of terrorism. While hijacking of planes has decreased significantly as a result of international cooperation (including conventions), destruction of aircraft in flight remains a problem awaiting both intergovernmental and industrial solutions.

12. Sea Piracy

A phenomenon thought to have ended in the nineteenth century, sea piracy resurfaced in the 1970s in the Caribbean, the roadsteads of several West African ports, the Malacca Straits and in South American ports. Piracy, usually perpetrated by locally organized groups, has seriously affected maritime commerce and caused considerable property damage with negative economic fallout, as well as loss of human lives. While not yet under complete control, the problem has been somewhat ameliorated thanks to the efforts of the International Maritime Bureau (IMB), in cooperation with other inter-governmental and trade organizations.[9] Nevertheless, the instantaneous re-emergence of piracy in separate parts of the world is a most interesting phenomenon from a criminological perspective. There clearly was no centralized global command structure (although regionally there were); rather, this form of transnational crime directed against global sea transport emerged from local conditions – similar in different parts of the world. While most of the incidents of piracy have been chronicled by the IMB, the overall cost to international shipping and the general economy is hard to assess.

13. Hijacking on Land

Once a purely local phenomenon, the hijacking of trucks became transnational with the lowering of border restrictions and the consequent expansion of road transportation of cargo, especially across the European continent and into the former Soviet Union. Figures are not readily available, but it is known that European police authorities are cooperating to deal with this form of transnational, and largely organized, crime.

14. Trafficking in Persons

In 1997 the International Scientific and Professional Advisory Council (ISPAC) organized an entire congress around this topic.[10] The international community is less concerned with the efforts of individuals seeking to enter another country illegally than with the exploitative activities of organized groups smuggling large numbers of people, at high risk but with high profit, into countries of legal or illegal asylum. The efforts of the international community to deal with the problem have been fully discussed in the ISPAC report and shall not be reiterated here.

14. Trade in Human Body Parts

Surely one of the most shocking transnational crimes is the trade in human body parts (lungs, kidneys, livers, hearts, etc.), often from 'donors' virtually slaughtered for that purpose, for the benefit of recipients who can afford such illegitimate transplants. This 'trade' appears to be internationally organized. Yet the line between legitimate and illegitimate organ transplant agencies is a hazy one. After several revelations in the early 1990s, information about this form of transnational crime has dried up – although this does not necessarily mean that the phenomenon itself has disappeared.

16. Theft of Art and Cultural Objects

No country is safe from the activities of organized gangs stripping cultural sites (or stealing from museums) and the heritage of a nation, in order to sell *objets d'art* on the lucrative arts and antiques markets of the world. In the process of stripping, entire cultural and historical sites are destroyed by dynamite and sledge hammers. For fine arts alone, an estimated US$4.5 billion of stolen objects wind up annually on the international market, 2,000 objects are stolen monthly and the international data base lists 45,000 stolen objects.[11] With increased cooperation among national governments, auction houses, art and gallery associations, it would seem that the problem is manageable – except for countries lacking the capacity to guard their sites of national heritage.

17. Environmental Crime

Few topics of transnational crime have received as much attention as has that of environmental crime. The Earth, its waters, its stratosphere, are but a single unit. Damage done locally will affect the whole. There is no need in this paper to go into detail. The UN Secretariat was wise to include environmental crime in its 18 most-wanted list.

18. Other Offences Committed by Organized Criminal Groups

This category was meant to be a catchall. At this moment, however, it seems to include principally the vibrant transnational trade in stolen motor vehicles. For the USA alone, it is currently estimated that 300,000 stolen automobiles are being exported annually, mostly by cargo vessels bound for destinations in developing countries or countries in transition. The figure for Western Europe is likely to be much higher (though much of the European illegal transport is by road). The economic impact is considerable, for owners, for insurance companies and even for recipient countries. It is understood that international police cooperation, especially through Interpol and Europol, has led to some successes in dealing with this phenomenon.

These are the United Nations' 18 categories of transnational – and mostly organized – criminality. The number may drop as a result of the efforts of global, regional and national authorities to come to grips with problems. The number may increase as transnational criminals figure out even more new ways of criminally exploiting globalization. Although the international community has had some success in dealing with various forms of transnational crime, much more remains to be done, especially in two sectors: (1) defining transnational criminal activities, especially by analogizing the concepts of national penal codes in order to arrive at common concepts and definitions that would facilitate the work of international police cooperation, globally and regionally; (2) gauging the prevalence, cost and extent of the various forms of transnational crime, so as to devise cost/benefit strategies. In most instances this can be done only through, or in cooperation with, affected industries. In light of all this it is useful to conclude with an assessment of the past and a look into the future.

The past is marked by local crime, as jurisdictionally defined by local penal codes, and as recorded in local and national crime statistics. With the onset of globalization, it was felt that, often, local crime was being impacted by events outside the local or national jurisdiction (drug criminality is an obvious example). We then witnessed the transnationalization of many criminal activities, largely arranged by transnational criminal elements who, just as their legitimate counterparts, cashed in on globalizing markets. We are currently in the process of reacting to transnational crime (a pro-active approach would have been preferable) and appropriate steps are being taken through international cooperation, including the United Nations Office for Drug Control and International Crime Prevention, Interpol, Europol and other agencies, including non-governmental ones such as the

International Maritime Bureau. However, the ingenuity of transnational criminal organizers and organizations might well outrun our contemporary efforts. Ultimately, we need a certain globalization of law enforcement and criminal justice efforts in order to deal with globe-threatening criminal activities.

The world has just created the Permanent International Criminal Court – so far with limited jurisdiction over the most awesome crimes against the peace and security of mankind. Yet, evolution proceeds inexorably, and some day this court will have to exercise jurisdiction over other crimes, transnational in character, which, by treaties and conventions, have already achieved the status of *international crimes* (25 in all!). I hope to live long enough to see the day.

NOTES

1. Department of Economic and Social Affairs, *Fifth United Nations Congress on the Prevention of Crime and the Treatment of Offenders*, report prepared by the Secretariat (New York: United Nations, 1976), A/CONF./56/10, Sales No. E.76.IV.2.
2. A.CONF. 169/15/Add. 1, 4 April 1995.
3. Ibid., para. 9.
4. As it turned out, the 'catch-all' group 18 currently consists mainly of a lively trade in stolen motor vehicles, from West to East and North to South. Note: the categories have been rearranged by this author, with old UN sequential numbers in parentheses.
5. National Insurance Crime Bureau, personal communication by fax 29 July 1996.
6. Larry E. Cutoria, 'The Future of High Technology Crime: A Parallel Delphi Study', *Journal of Criminal Justice*, Vol.23 (1995) pp.13–27.
7. Natalie d. Voss, 'Crime on the Internet', *Jones Telecommunications and Multimedia Encyclopedia*, Drive D:\Studio, Jones Digital Century, 1996. For more recent figures see the report found on http://www.siia.net/piracy/news/ipr98.htm
8. For a scholarly assessment, see Phil Williams and Paul H. Woessnar, *Nuclear Material Trafficking: An Interim Assessment* (Pittsburgh: Ridgway Center for International Security Studies, 1995).
9. Eric Ellen, 'The Dimensions of International Maritime Crime', in Martin Gill (ed.), *Issues in Maritime Crime: Mayhem at Sea* (Leicester, UK: Perpetuity Press, 1995), pp.4–11; see also Gerhard O.W. Mueller and Freda Adler, *Outlaws of the Ocean: The Complete Book of Contemporary Crime on the High Seas* (New York: Hearst Marine Books, 1985).
10. See Alex Schmid (ed.), *Migration and Crime* (Milan: ISPAC, 1998).
11. From Reuters, 'High Tech Art Sleuths Snare Thieves', *C.J. International*, Vol.9 (1993), pp.4–6.

Globalization and Transnational Crime: Effects of Criminogenic Asymmetries

NIKOS PASSAS

International white-collar crime and illegal markets, commonly described as 'organized crime', are not new phenomena.[1] We have been hearing about drug trafficking, smuggling of various commodities, environmental pollution, exploitation of Third World countries by transnational corporations and other kinds of misdeeds for a long time.[2] However, the global age is accompanied by a rise both in the risk of transnational crime and in official concern about it. This rise is fuelled chiefly by the fast integration of world markets and speedy conclusion of transactions thanks to technological advances, the gradual loss of border controls and the lack of appropriate normative and regulatory frameworks. Since the end of the Cold War and in the context of the proliferation of new states, new nationalisms and threats posed by fundamentalism, some forms of crime are regarded as national or global security threats.[3]

Yet, the significance and implications of globalization processes are not fully explored. Most analyses concentrate on the mounting problems in controlling certain types of cross-border misconduct (for example, the drug trade, political violence or corrupt practices) rather than seeking to understand better the nature of the more general problem. Explanations of even spectacular disasters, such as the Bank of Credit and Commerce International (BCCI) scandal or the Barings Bank collapse, focus on corrupt, inept or greedy individuals out of control. Such explanations cloud the systemic causes of the problem.[4] These causes need to be understood before giving serious consideration to certain calls for controversial measures, such as the use of privacy-piercing methods and assigning a law-enforcement role to intelligence services. The task of this analysis is to pave the way for a better understanding of systemic crime problems that result from the processes of globalization.

In brief, the thesis put forward here is the following: at a general level, the causes of corporate offences and illegal enterprises can be traced to 'criminogenic asymmetries', defined as structural disjunctions, mismatches and inequalities in the spheres of politics, culture, the economy and the law. Asymmetries are criminogenic in that (1) they generate or strengthen the demand for illegal goods and services; (2) they generate incentives for particular actors to participate in illegal transactions; and (3) they reduce the ability of authorities to control illegal activities. In the global age, such asymmetries are multiplied and intensified. In addition, the criminogenic potential of other asymmetries is now more easily activated. At the same time, control capacities are seriously undermined. As the world shrinks and becomes a global village, as the connection between society and nation state becomes looser, controllers remain constrained by their divergent domestic rules and limited within their jurisdiction.

Asymmetries are largely the work (direct or indirect) of agents of nation states. In some cases the states are complicit; in other cases they are unable or unwilling to take remedial action. Systemic sources fuelling the demand for illicit goods and services are thus traced back to nation states. As national autonomy is eroded, so is the ability of national authorities to protect their citizens from serious crime. Collaboration is essential, but it is only practiced on a selective and *ad hoc* basis, thereby generating legitimation deficits and new asymmetries. International arrangements are therefore indispensable, but there is no appropriate international normative framework, law-making process or regulatory mechanism with real enforcement power. Efforts to develop international standards are hampered by actions of national authorities. This normative vacuum allows offenders to slip through the gaps of municipal laws and enforcement. In this process, control agencies are often unable to contain even domestic law violations. In the end, just as new crime opportunities arise, cosmopolitan offenders can get away from parochial regulators with ease. Unless this circle is broken or interrupted, illicit business will become attractive to additional actors who see that crime pays.

INTERNATIONAL ASYMMETRIES AND ECONOMIC CRIME

First of all, crime is here defined as misconduct that entails avoidable and unnecessary harm to society, sufficiently serious to warrant state intervention, and similar to other kinds of misconduct that are criminalized by the states concerned or by international law.[5] Any complete explanation of crime requires an account of illicit opportunities, of the motives of leading actors to take advantage of available opportunities, and of control problems. International asymmetries cause illegal markets and corporate misconduct by contributing to all of the above.

One type of illegal opportunity is linked with demand – supply asymmetries, which are necessary conditions for all sorts of smuggling, price gouging or other acts of exploitation (for example, the black markets that develop during war and prolonged regional conflicts). Asymmetries generate the demand for goods that are illegal, unethical or embarrassing. Illegal markets follow the rules of supply and demand, sometimes even more strictly than legitimate markets – because the latter often enjoy protective measures introduced by nation states or groups of states. Whenever there is a gap between local demand and supply, cross-border trade is likely to develop. If the goods or services happen to be outlawed, then illegal enterprises will emerge to meet the demand. In this respect, there is no difference between conventional and criminal enterprises. Very often, when the business is illegal all that changes are some adjustments in *modus operandi*, technology and the social networks that will be involved. In some cases, we have a mere re-description of practices to make them appear outside legal prohibitive provisions.

This is what happened with the slave trade, which continued despite prohibitive legislation introduced by a number of states and which illustrates how irrelevant the legal qualification is to the mechanics of trade.[6] The criminalization of 'commodities' in demand was associated with a clash of ideologies, legal prohibition and the needs of fledgling capitalism. The demand for slaves remained high in line with the needs of the growing American economy, slave prices rose because of the prohibition and the possible profits were quite tempting. As the ideology that legitimated the exploitation of Africans did not vanish overnight, the slave trade would not have given traffickers and corrupt controllers many troubles with their conscience for doing something morally wrong.

Asymmetries in environmental regulation offer a more current illustration of criminogenesis. Increased awareness about serious health and environmental hazards in industrial countries has led to legislation protecting the environment from industrial pollution, even if that might narrow the profit margin of affected corporations. For example, companies have found themselves constrained by laws regulating the disposal of toxic waste they generate. Instead of drastically reducing the risk of improper treatment of toxic waste, however, such regulation brought about asymmetries that gave rise to an illegal market for waste disposal. Within the USA, the rules defining what is 'hazardous' and subject to regulation differed from state to state. This created an opportunity to get rid of hazardous waste in those states that were most permissive about such substances. The large differences in the cost of disposal created incentives to engage in cross-border trade of waste exported to states that left particular substances unregulated. Furthermore, there was a severe shortage of appropriate facilities to deal with the volume of toxic waste generated by the industry. In the end, this shortage and concerns about profit maximization brought in 'organized criminals' whose state-licensed companies illegally dumped the waste for the benefit of the chemical industry, which could save up to 80 per cent of the disposal cost.

Controls were undermined by several asymmetries. By exploiting the cracks between the diverse state rules, companies could commit 'crimes without law violation'. Corporate actors and controllers 'on the take' could rationalize that the national economy would be harmed if the new rules were strictly enforced, as many corporations would go bankrupt owing to the costs of proper waste disposal.

In addition, the power of corporations to influence lawmaking greatly exceeded that of environmental groups. The industry successfully lobbied for the non-regulation of production methods, which could have been altered in order to generate less waste. The industry also succeeded in avoiding criminal liability in the event their waste was discovered to be illegally dumped by their cheap hauling contractors. Furthermore, control agencies, underfunded and plagued by incompetence or corruption of employees, did little to remedy the situation. Corporations effectively externalized the blame, while reaping substantial benefits from nominal regulation and 'organized crime'.' So, rule asymmetries created crime opportunities, price asymmetries provided incentives to take advantage of these opportunities, while power and law enforcement asymmetries weakened social controls.

Similarly, at the international level, regulatory discrepancies along with substantial economic and political asymmetries have given rise to an enormous market for toxic waste. Many Third World countries either did not regulate toxic waste or did so much less rigorously than industrialized states. This provided the opportunity for companies to get rid of their dangerous waste in areas where rules were lax or non-existent. Rich and 'filthy' countries shipped their waste to other countries, less able to adequately deal with the ultimate disposal of such imported 'goods'.[8]

The huge financial and competitive advantages that could be gained by regulatory and cost asymmetries were a strong incentive to profit from the illicit opportunities. Subsequently, additional companies might join in because their competitors did it and their survival was at stake. Power and economic asymmetries led recipient countries to allow all this to go on because of their dependence on foreign investment, the need for cash in order to service external debt and the desire to create jobs. Economic and knowledge asymmetries shaped the motivation of local participants in this questionable trade, too. The decision to go along reflected their lack of full understanding of the extent or nature of the hazard, their desperate need for additional income, or corruption.

Asymmetries contributed in complex ways to the absence of adequate controls. In some cases there are simply no controls at all. When no local rule prohibits or regulates the handling of toxic waste, companies commit crimes without law violation. Technological and knowledge asymmetries are again at play, as local expertise or resources to recognize the risks and deal with the waste are in short supply. Political and power asymmetries play their role when people notice the negative effects, but oppressive regimes disallow protests and ensure that poisoning practices continue unimpeded.[9] Bribes may be paid to ensure that officials' eyes remain blind to the injustice and exploitation that takes place in their jurisdiction. Even when governments of affected countries seek redress and international instruments to remedy the situation, powerful Western governments undermine corrective actions (for example, see the disagreements over the language in the Basle Convention).[10]

Many criminal practices are both the result and a cause of asymmetries that make things worse. This creates a vicious circle where neither illegal markets nor particular offences are independent from each other. In fact, many offences are derivatives or accessories to other crimes (for example, money laundering, capital flight, corruption). Corruption, for example, is a conservative force that maintains or increases asymmetries. In the developing world, it has seriously hampered social, economic and political progress. Through the transfer of illicit payments to the West, corruption undermines economic development. This, in turn, leads to political instability as well as poor infrastructure and social services, lower education standards and the non-completion of projects. Funds are allocated unfairly and inefficiently, which frustrates skilled and honest citizens and increases the general population's level of distrust. As a consequence, much foreign aid disappears, productive capacity is weakened, administrative efficiency is reduced and the legitimacy of political order is undermined.[11] Political violence and other conflicts are likely to spring in such contexts, which then give rise to illegal weapons markets and possible connections with drug trafficking as a source to finance arms purchases.[12] Corruption also directly contributes to illegal markets by playing a facilitative role. Criminal enterprises operate best with the collusion of authorities. Corruption is the abuse of official power for direct or indirect gain, from the point of view of the corrupted. From the point of view of the corruptor, it can also be defined as a 'control of social control agencies'. No reasonably well-organized criminal enterprise can afford to disregard the need to neutralize administrative, legislative and police organizations – just as legitimate companies use lobbying and political campaign contributions to achieve the same end.

Many crimes are related to corruption in the sense that they either facilitate the commission of malpractices, aid the processing of illegal proceeds or constitute a cover-up of the initial crime. These offences include the maintenance and use of slush funds, aiding and abetting, conspiracy, accounting offences, falsification or forgery of documents and the laundering of illicit proceeds.

Corruption, on the other hand, is also a consequence of asymmetries. Companies operating in countries with slow and inefficient administrations will be tempted to pay 'speed money' in order to 'get the job done'. In other cases, a company may lose contracts if it is squeamish about matching the bribes offered by other companies. The more societies are unequal and not based on merit, the higher the preparedness of individuals to pay bribes in order to secure a job or other favours.

In that process, controls are weakened: widespread rationalizations of bribery as a necessary evil will ease the minds of corporate managers. Diverse interpretations of the public interest may turn a corrupt practice into a patriotic act.[13] Economic asymmetries foster attitudes justifying corruption as functional to local economies and as a way of redistributing wealth (for example, in some underdeveloped regions of the European Union (EU), the fight against EU fraud and money coming from Brussels is not a very high priority).[14] The more generalized a clientelist system is, the less participants will feel that they are doing something objectionable. Moreover, legal asymmetries provide a shield against the discovery or sanctioning of corruption. The funds may end up in a secrecy jurisdiction with anonymous accounts. Additional protection is offered by the differential treatment of bribes to foreign officials. In some countries they are a serious offence, while in others they constitute tax-deductible business expenses. This makes it easier for people to think of their corrupt practices as 'technical violations'. At worst, we have another example of 'crime without law violation'.

GLOBALIZATION AND ECONOMIC CRIME

The argument here is that criminogenesis increases significantly as a result of the dynamic of globalization, which multiplies, intensifies or activates asymmetries. Globalization undermines the sovereignty and autonomy of nation states, which are less able to regulate cross-border business transactions. Nevertheless, nation states are far from irrelevant to the understanding of crime facilitation. Indeed, it is through policies decided on and carried out at the national level that asymmetries materialize their criminogenic potential. It is a combination of globalization and the uncoordinated action by nation states that the planet has become 'fraudster-friendlier'. The analysis looks first at the processes of globalization and their consequences with respect to economic misconduct, then examines the central role played by states in these processes.

Globalization refers to a transformation of the world order through the multiplication and intensification of linkages and interconnectedness. One may debate whether the driving force is capitalism,[15] technology,[16] politico-military conditions – the presence of a hegemon,[17] or a combination of such factors.[18] There is no dispute, however, over the fact that capital, goods, services, people and ideas cross borders with increasing speed, frequency and ease. Actions in one country have consequences and significance in distant places. Local events and destinies can hardly be interpreted and understood without looking beyond national boundaries. The world is being reconstituted as 'one place' with global communications and media, transnational corporations, supranational institutions, integrated markets and a financial system that trades 24 hours a day.[19]

As the world is shrinking, both space and time are 'compressed'.[20] The time–space compression is most visible in the economic domain, especially in finance and manufacturing. It has enhanced the global mobility of capital and led to a new international division of labour. We now have 'for the first time, the formation of a single world market for money and credit supply'.[21] Further, globalization extends and intensifies the linkages of the local with the global, thereby leading to a conflation of 'presence' with 'absence'. Social relations no longer require simultaneous presence in a single location.[22] Giddens has pointed to the intensified process of 'disembedding' social relations, which are taken out of local contexts and reconstituted across space and time.[23] In the sphere of business, the internationalization of capital can be conceptualized as 'territorial non-coincidence of capital'.[24] The fall of trade barriers and technological advances enable the expansion of transnational corporations and financial networks that seek to take advantage of regions with low production costs and new markets in an increasingly competitive environment.

Cultural identities also become disembedded as a result of easy travelling and global consumerism. The more global media networks spread and promote foreign styles and images, the more identities become detached from specific time and space.[25] This process is illustrated by the TV series 'Hercules' and 'Star Trek'. Typically American ways of thinking, manners of speech, manicheism, virtues, flaws and weaknesses are projected well into the past and the future. 'Hercules' reconfigures age-old mythological personalities, while 'Star Trek' suggests that the future of Earth will look very much like the core of 'good' US values. Both series thereby effectively universalize things American as they are shown to a world audience.

In the process of globalization, the nation state is being increasingly transcended and considered inadequate as the basis for social analysis.[26] Society and nation state are becoming conceptually distinguishable. Moreover, the independence, sovereignty and autonomy of nation states are systematically undermined by external actors and supranational bodies. Monetary and fiscal policies in one country deeply affect those in other countries. Decisions that constituted and symbolized sovereign powers now have to be shared and coordinated. Even the most powerful of nation states (G7) have felt the need to do so by means of regular meetings of their finance ministers and leaders.

Regional and international organizations are emerging as major players who foster further expansion of global capital and a degree of homogenization in world markets. The World Bank, the International Monetary Fund, the Organization for Economic Cooperation and Development, and the European Union exemplify agents of harmonization. The EU more clearly illustrates the process of 'pooling of sovereignty' among interdependent nation states, as powers and functions are transferred to supra-national institutions.[27]

The operations of transnational corporations further undercut the autonomy of nation states that are less able to handle even domestic problems as a result of actions taken far away. Domestic welfare, balance of payments, employment, even foreign policy, have come to depend greatly on decisions by transnational corporations (TNCs) to invest, establish production units and set up branches or subsidiaries in particular countries or regions. In many cases, both economic and political stability hinges on such TNC decisions and performance. National governments, administrations and legislatures cannot afford to neglect the interests of TNCs in domestic polices and practices.

In short, the number of areas in which national agencies have exclusive jurisdiction is falling, while the number of areas beyond the control of nation states is rising. As a corollary to these processes, the regulatory ability of national authorities is weakened. Tendencies resisting the 'withering' of nation states, universalization and homogenization also develop in the complex dynamics of globalization.[28]

All these developments have inherent criminogenic consequences. Just as globalization serves well the needs of legal capital, so does it facilitate criminal enterprises. Just as ordinary international business transactions can be concluded at the speed of light, so can unethical and illegal ones. Just as local destinies often cannot be explained without taking into account global factors, local crime victimization may not be fully understood without reference to global forces. Just as social relations do not require a simultaneous 'presence' in a given place, no longer are all elements of serious crimes in one country or region. The social organization of crime is increasingly international and sophisticated rendering national control mechanisms obsolete. As the autonomy of nation states is reduced, even domestic crimes can neither be prevented nor sanctioned without cross-national collaboration.

In the past we have seen how organizations became a weapon for crime.[29] We have also seen how they served to distance the criminal hand from the criminal mind.[30] In the global age, this 'distance' is stretched even further as the organizations are more compartmentalized and spread throughout the world. In addition, both criminal hands and criminal minds may be absent, far away from the locus of the crime. In many instances, crimes are so well camouflaged that only specialists can detect them and realize the risks involved. Many offences are recognized only when the problems become so big that they cannot be swept under the rug (for example, when there is no more room between the rug and the ceiling).

Globalizing processes relate to all three types of criminogenic conditions. Illicit opportunities are produced by the fragmentation of enterprises and transactions over more than one country. For instance, lawyers, who form and represent a shell corporation in a secrecy jurisdiction on behalf of someone far away, may not even know who is the owner of the company and for whom they are working. Such shell corporations offer tax advantages and shelter against regulation and the detection of misconduct. They also help to hide criminals' assets that are being sought by victims and prosecutors in distant places. Lawyers will see no problem with participating in such affairs. Not knowing the identity of their client, they do not have to know whether he is a drug trafficker, a corrupt dictator or a devious corporate executive. Even if required to testify, lawyers cannot offer any significant assistance to investigating authorities. So, controls get much weaker.

Secrecy and anonymity hinder investigators by covering the tracks of the 'global offender'. Illegal financial transactions and losses that must be reported can be conducted and hidden through offshore entities of global enterprises. Secrecy jurisdictions serve as a 'black box' through which all manner of illegal activities can be shielded against prosecution and punishment.[31] In a sense, this sort of black box makes serious crimes disappear. Many crimes are so well organized and concealed that they are nowhere recorded. Few, if any, outsiders know that they have been committed.

The recent financial scandals of BCCI,[32] Barings, Daiwa and Sumitomo highlight the same systemic problems. They all operated internationally. Gross negligence and serious misconduct were known to, or could be detected by, only a few experts or those with privileged access to information. The agents we trust to prevent abuses of power did not live up to their responsibilities (for example, auditors, directors, high level executives, regulators). All cases involved misconduct that went on for too long before the whistle was blown. Victimization was not limited to one country. Victims suffered losses because of people they had never met who were located overseas. Each of these cases constituted global systemic risks that teams of people and organizations in various countries struggled to reduce.

Globalization also contributes to the conditions that nourish a new type of crime – 'crime without law violation'. We have seen how this is possible in the brief examination of the cross-border trade in toxic waste and of corrupt practices. Lawyers, accountants, former government or military officials who may act as consultants or private businessmen after they leave public office, can offer advice on how to engage in risky and harmful practices without breaking the laws of the countries where different operations take place. Transactions criminalized in many parts of the world may be concluded in countries that allow and welcome them. Expert professionals can assist in structuring transactions, so that no country's laws are broken although the final outcome is clearly unethical or 'criminal'. Corporate structures become complex and compartmentalized, so that firewalls are effectively raised, protecting both the company and its executives from knowledge of wrongdoing and liability. Financial transactions that are disallowed or must be reported, can be booked to offshore subsidiaries and branches. Research experiments, manufacturing and distribution of commodities or services that are outlawed or controlled in some countries can take place in countries with friendlier regulations.

The pharmaceutical industry is one example of how such opportunities are maintained and exploited by TNCs. The initial testing of drugs can be conducted in the developing world where safeguards are lower, civil lawsuits are unlikely and other forms of protest have slim chances of success. Countries with lax standards are used for first approval and manufacture, so that developing world markets can be entered, before final approval is made by more demanding developed world agencies. Components of dangerous and banned drugs can be made in places allowing their manufacture and then marketed in countries that have not banned them.[33] The developing world is not only used as a laboratory with guinea pigs, but also as dumping ground for dangerous products.[34] Drugs with serious side effects are exported to several countries, with the list of side effects getting shorter the farther to the south the drugs are going. Defective and harmful products, such as the Dalkon Shield intrauterine device (IUD), can be exported and sold around the world despite their ban in the home country.[35]

Other examples of crimes without law violations include the use of child labour in poor countries that condone it by companies that then export the manufactured goods to countries that criminalize the practice. Taxes may be evaded legally through the practice of price transfer, which allows the profits to be booked in countries with no income tax.[36] Dirty money can be laundered in countries requiring no reporting of even substantial amounts of cash deposits (for example, Panama) and then transferred to Western banks that may not know its criminal origin (and do not care to find out).[37] Globalization has enabled financial institutions to do overseas what they are disallowed to do at home. As the BCCI scandal has shown, it has become possible for a financial institution to not have a home at all.[38]

The problems relative both to the 'black box' and 'crimes without law violation' are systematically generated and reproduced through the processes of globalization. This is because, ultimately, globalization creates, perpetuates or activates criminogenic asymmetries.

GLOBALIZATION AND CRIMINOGENIC ASYMMETRIES

Globalization processes produce a number of asymmetries with complex criminogenic effects. In other words, asymmetries provide the catalyst for globalization to produce criminal opportunities, motives to take advantage of those opportunities and weaker controls. Asymmetries come in various forms and affect all sectors of commerce and finance. We can identify cultural, economic, political, technological, legal and other asymmetries. As we shall see, however, most of them are interlinked with or simultaneously constitute power asymmetries.

Globalization reinforces inequalities of power and wealth both within nation states and among them. It maintains and intensifies global hierarchies of privilege, wealth and control.[39] Power asymmetries can be discerned in most spheres of social and economic interactions in different forms. For instance, knowledge asymmetries and risk distribution asymmetries end up systematically attracting and linking the powerful with the powerless.[40] This is clearly demonstrated in the case of toxic waste (non-)regulation discussed above. Technological asymmetries are also increased in global markets, leading to underground markets for nuclear or other materiel that is embargoed or in short supply.[41] By reproducing and intensifying divisive social relations, globalization inevitably generates poles of resistance and opposition.[42]

The tendency towards universalization is countered by a resurgence of nationalism and emphasis on ethnic identities.[43] This contradictory dynamic combines with asymmetric power relations and politics in various parts of the world to give rise to fundamentalism. These, in turn, nurture all sorts of illegal markets as conflicts may translate into armed confrontations, which necessitate weapons, information and skills that are in short supply because of prohibitions and embargoes. Treaties aiming at the non-proliferation of particular weapons or dual-use technology may be proposed and promoted by nation states who already possess them. This adds fuel to the fire of geopolitical, religious or ethnic conflicts. More to the point for our purposes here, this series of power, ideological and demand-supply asymmetries creates illegal markets for technology, arms and other controlled goods and services. In addition, such illegal markets will be interconnected with drug trafficking, terrorism, corruption, money laundering, capital flight, etc. Plenty of arguments and justifications will enable numerous individuals, groups or organizations to participate in those markets. Some will be motivated by profit, others by religious or ideological convictions, and still others by the pursuit of the perceived national interest. In that context, blind eyes will be easy to secure and border controls will become porous.

The time–space compression activates the criminogenic potential of existing power and economic asymmetries too. Power asymmetries are again at work when TNCs employ global media to market their goods and services in places where substantial numbers of people cannot afford them. Disjunctions between goals and means may be very few in rigidly stratified societies that do not encourage high social mobility. In such societies, people may not feel that they are lacking something, even if they are 'objectively' deprived. As Durkheim and Merton have shown, societies in turmoil or characterized by structural and cultural contradictions can expect high rates of deviance. Whenever a culture promotes ambitions that the society cannot help fulfil, there are frustrations and strain towards crime. Globalization breaks societal barriers and encourages new needs, desires, fashions. In this way, it promotes the adoption of non-membership reference groups for comparisons that can be unfavourable and upsetting. Globalization systematically causes in other words relative deprivation, which may lead to deviance and crime.[44] It creates or dramatically broadens awareness of pre-existing economic asymmetries, whose criminogenic potential is now activated.

34

The criminogenic potential is activated through the cultivation of awareness of economic asymmetries and the widespread interpretation of them as unnecessary and changeable. 'Image Is Everything', 'Just Do It' urge advertisers and thereby furnish mottos for consumerism. Newly constructed needs, new ideals that are culturally promoted, legitimated and widely regarded as attainable, old and intensified economic asymmetries combine to increase discontent. Shortages of desired goods give rise to smuggling operations and black market networks, as illustrated by the illegal car trade between Eastern and Western Europe and the illegal trade in various commodities between China and Hong Kong.[45] People from deprived areas are strongly motivated to immigrate to the places where the 'goodies' are available.[46] Many become vulnerable to serious crime as they are prepared naively to trust fraudsters who guarantee them decent jobs in promised lands, only to end up in forced prostitution.[47] When quotas are imposed on new immigrants, then illegal alien markets develop that are very expensive, highly corrupt and exploitative for those who wish to emigrate.[48] Many criminogenic effects of political asymmetries, economic asymmetries and relative deprivation can be seen in the aftermath of the collapse of the USSR and disillusionment with Western democratic policies and capitalism.[49] In many cities of the former USSR drug addiction increases geometrically. An electronics engineer, for example, could not live on his US$3 per month and moonlighted as a taxi driver. When his taxi broke down, he turned to selling poppy straw, for which he was arrested.[50] Corruption is also widespread: a Russian policeman who refused a bribe was told after the defendant was acquitted: 'You know, you're really an ass ... You refused $25,000. The judge made $75,000'. Another officer in Tajikistan stated: 'we are not going to arrest our own people over opium. ... There is nothing to eat here. We have only opium and the stones from the mountains.'[51]

Relative deprivation has a revolutionary potential too.[52] Cross-border communications convey the inevitability of injustice and inequality, inspire change and foster rebellion. In the past, the ideals of the French Revolution generated violent upheavals in the Balkan peninsula against the autocratic Ottoman rule.[53] In the process of globalization now, events in one corner of the planet can affect feelings and encourage people located in another corner to rebel against aggression by a neighbouring state. East Timor is a case in point. The independence of the Baltic States and the UN response to Iraq's annexation of Kuwait 'have given rise to unequivocal statements about the unacceptability of aggression by a big power against its small neighbour and the sacrosanct nature of that right to self-determination of which the Timorese were so cynically deprived'.[54]

Globalization renders cultural asymmetries criminogenic and brings about another sort of more questionable and criminal type of disembeddedness. The increased contact between countries with an art-rich past and countries with an art-collecting present results in illicit transfers of national treasures from their original sites to artificial contexts. There is a huge global market of art items that are removed or stolen from primarily economically underdeveloped countries and channelled to Western private collections, museums or galleries. In the process of rooting paintings or frescoes out of their original context, many pieces of art are destroyed or damaged.[55]

The social organization of art theft is quite complex and includes public officials in the country of origin as well as the final destination. A combination of legal and cultural asymmetries leads to the cleansing of stolen art through countries with laws that conveniently legitimate the ultimate possessors, in a way reminiscent of money laundering.[56] In addition, there is a market in counterfeit art, as supply is insufficient to satisfy the thirst of international art collectors. Again, the profits in these markets are substantial and the risks of punishment low. Economic problems in some developing world countries motivate counterfeiters to sell fake art to rich foreigners. This activity 'is looked on favourably as a source of income that can improve the standard of living in the villages where the counterfeiters work'.[57]

Going back to the financial sector, globalization renders frauds easier, faster and safer. The internationalization of business, the frequent travel and the familiarization of executives with diverse and conflicting rules, further facilitate misconduct. In such cases, globalization leads to a relativization of norms and easier law violations with clear conscience consistently with the more general 'compliance crisis' that Rosenau has noted.[58] The legal and regulatory asymmetries persist and multiply despite the emergence of transnational institutions that pave the ground and facilitate capital globalization. In fact, such institutions generate their own criminogenic effects. On the one hand, they intensify asymmetries in a number of ways and, on the other, they provide no adequate normative and regulatory framework.

The IMF and World Bank type of institutions offer certain assistance through loans and the financing of projects in less developed countries.

The terms of the loans, however, frequently involve austerity measures that recipient governments must impose on their citizens. If these governments wish to either refinance the loans or get new lines of credit, they must implement strict and 'liberal' economic policies. This process erodes autonomy and increases dependence on Western sources. It also creates domestic unease and discontent that may lead to regional or civil conflicts. The Permanent Peoples Tribunal in Rome has condemned IMF conditions and policies as illegal.[59] In this light, it is not surprising that some developing world governments sought to circumvent IMF conditions and turned to BCCI for assistance.[60] Projects funded by these institutions have sometimes assisted more Western corporations than the 'beneficiary' countries. Companies often got contracts to deliver works that were not really needed, for which there was no commitment on the part of the recipient country, and which were often left incomplete. Corrupt leaders of the countries involved (who pocketed 'commissions' and straightforward bribes) and the Western corporations were the main beneficiaries.

Other institutions facilitate the globalization of trade by promoting exports of domestic products. They do this, however, all too often through protectionist policies that produce a number of asymmetries. Protectionism generates incentives for the diversion of trade, adds inequalities, creates strains among traders from various countries and introduces disincentives for effective controls. The European Union's Common Agricultural Policy (CAP) and similar programmes, for example, create demand and supply asymmetries, maintain artificial price asymmetries for the same goods, perpetuate unequal economic exchanges (something-for-nothing transactions) and enhance global inequalities.[61] Differential pricing depending on the country of origin or final destination encourages smuggling activities, false declarations and 'phantom trade'. Subsidies and price supports foster surplus production of goods that occasionally have to be destroyed. Ironically, as people in many parts of the world die of starvation, people in other parts destroy food supplies in order to keep the prices high.

Developing world countries are then even more dependent on Western/Northern countries for their development. The aid they receive, however, is often 'imposed' or of debatable quality.[62] In addition, aid programmes themselves are criminogenic. They facilitate fraud against recipient countries, which are anxious to receive as much as possible and, therefore, unlikely to complain if a part of the aid is rotten or substandard. Not surprisingly, we have seen cases of powdered milk sent to drought areas or machines delivered without training staff and manuals. Moreover, much of what is officially recorded as aid comes in the form of military equipment and weapons, which fuels conflict and the associated illegal markets (Rwanda and the 'aid' from European countries preceding the genocidal events is a recent case in point).

Further, transnational institutions have failed to provide an international normative framework and enforcement mechanisms to ensure predictability in economic activity and the control of illegal transactions. The development of international law and treaties has lagged behind the realities of globalization. Attempts to establish a permanent international criminal court have not yet succeeded.[63] International law used to legitimate policies and practices of powerful nation states (for example, slavery). Now, its role is more ambiguous. International law can be used against powerful states. Although the ruling was never enforced, Nicaragua was successful in its case against the USA before the World Court for the support of the Contra activities and the illegal mining of ports.[64] In the past, international law used to regulate relations between states. Now, however, citizens can take government agencies to court (for example, to the EU Court of Justice). Finally, as the US–USSR bipolarity disappeared, the geopolitical context that supported international law for decades disappeared, leaving little to replace it.[65]

It is true that the UN, the World Trade Organization, the OECD, the European Union, the Council of Europe and other organizations have been assuming a growing number of responsibilities in either directly regulating international transactions or in influencing national regulation and promoting processes of legal harmonization.[66] These organizations' guidelines and suggestions, however, are only occasionally and inconsistently followed by national governments. Experience shows that even when some regimes, principles, laws or 'gentlemen's agreements' (for example, the Basle Concordat on banking practices) are in place, their implementation or enforcement is most of the time purely symbolic and selective at best (cf. the long list of unenforced UN resolutions with the rare determination to punish Iraq's invasion of Kuwait). Most cooperation has proved to be on an *ad hoc* basis, rather than long-term and grounded on commonly shared rules.

The BCCI case illustrates most vividly the international normative gap and near-complete inability to regulate and control risky and harmful transactions. BCCI was based in Luxembourg and Grand Cayman, headquartered in London and operated in 72 countries. No country's laws or agencies could stop the banking services offered to spies, tax cheats, terrorists and drug traffickers. There was no consolidated supervision of the bank's operations by any national authority. A 'College of Supervisors' that consisted of representatives of some central banks and attempted to oversee BCCI's activities proved a failure. The bank collapsed in 1991 with the liquidators reporting that up to US$9 billion was unaccounted for. The victims were spread throughout the world, with most money lost to developing world individuals and governments. The most powerful central banks, established accounting firms and an international roster of influential board directors could neither prevent the disaster nor limit its impact by closing the bank earlier. The Basle Concordat was amended to take into account the BCCI lesson, but even central bankers admit that it cannot prevent such failures in the future.[67]

In effect, both regulatory and criminal law enforcement functions are stubbornly in the hands of national bodies that pursue objectives and employ methods that are inconsistent with each other. The legal asymmetries activated by globalization also increase systemic risks in the interconnected financial markets. The contradiction of national oversight of global firms and markets raises grave concerns among regulators. As the chairman of the British Securities and Investments Board has noted, 'What we need is a realistic way of reconciling the mismatch between globally active groups and markets and nationally based supervision.'[68] Nation states do not merely act as catalysts for the processes of globalization to bring out criminogenic asymmetries. In many instances, they are also directly responsible for them.

NATION STATES, CRIMINOGENIC ASYMMETRIES AND GLOBAL DYSNOMIE

Although globalization undercuts the autonomy of some nation states more than others, even the most powerful of them have to make concessions and depend on foreign assistance. The use of 'black boxes' by wrongdoers hampers everyone's investigative efforts. The use of the Internet allows the penetration of any country for legal and illegal purposes alike. A 'virtual' bank may be set up on the World Wide Web, operate out of a Caribbean tax paradise and defraud tax-break hunters from the wealthiest countries. The commission of 'crimes without law violations' victimizes even the richest nation states, as the case of 'legal' tax evasion demonstrates. If fugitives take refuge overseas, their capture and punishment requires international collaboration, even if their crime is domestic. Arresting and imprisoning domestic drug sellers cannot begin to solve the problem of a multinational network of drug-related enterprises.

Ironically, despite the gradual loss of nation states' power to act and influence their own environment without external constraints, it is the exercise of state power that ultimately contributes to global crime opportunities and crime facilitation. Reduced national autonomy does not make states less responsible for crime causation. It is national policies and agencies, the exercise of asymmetric state powers, an obsession with sovereignty and nationalist resistance against international regulation that account for criminogenic asymmetries.

All asymmetries discussed above are the doing of national authorities. It is their economic policies that bear responsibility for relative and objective deprivation. It is their protectionism and subsidization of domestic industries, while they preach 'free markets' and 'liberalization of trade' to others, that impair the efforts of less developed countries to narrow the gaps. It is their monetary policies and control of international organizations that preserve asymmetric development and growth. It is authoritarian regimes that cause ethnic and political violence. It is their hegemonic policies and support for dictatorial regimes overseas that provoke international terrorism and fundamentalism. It is their selective control and promotion of domestic military industries that fuel armed conflicts – note that industries from the permanent members of the UN Security Council produce the overwhelming majority of weapons. It is their unwillingness to share knowledge, information and technology that breeds unease and inequalities. It is their prohibitions of commodities and services in demand that create illegal opportunities. It is their inability or unwillingness to reduce the demand for prohibited goods and services that perpetuates the illegal markets. It is their imposition of quotas for new immigrants that gives rise to the inhumane smuggling of illegal aliens. It is their resort to criminal justice methods to deal with the consequences of their policies that provide incentives for more sophisticated organization of crime and raise the price of corruption.

In many instances, it is conflicting foreign policies and covert activities of secret services that generate illegal markets and facilitate crime. Such policies may be legal or illegal by domestic standards, but they almost invariably violate international law and customs regarding non-interference in the internal affairs of other countries. The secret funding of Islamic fundamentalist rebels, for example, was authorized by the US Congress, because they were fighting the USSR-supported regime in Afghanistan. A good part of the substantial amount of money was reportedly transferred through BCCI and corrupt Pakistani military officials. Drug trafficking was tolerated, as it contributed to the cause of anti-communism by supplementing the US funds. When the covert operation stopped with the end of the Cold War, former allies were left to their own devices. They had plenty of arms, access to extensive drug lands and smuggling infrastructure, networks of corruption and, of course, feelings of vengeance toward those who abandoned them. In this context, no one should be surprised at the chaos and international crime problems that followed.[69]

Sometimes, there are conflicts between official and actual foreign policies of powerful states. The Iran-Contra and the arming of Iraq affairs show how criminal markets are created and supported by hypocritical or unlawful practices and how a wide range of legitimate professionals, companies and unsavoury characters inevitably get involved. In the process of conducting such policies, criminal conduct is facilitated in a number of ways. State actors justify it to themselves and others (when discovered) as 'following orders', serving the country, fighting communism, protecting national security or paving the ground for new markets after a country is 'democratized' and converted to a 'free market'. Illegal conduct of officials is covered up. Even the common criminals on whom state agents have to rely for certain transactions are effectively provided with general immunity on grounds of national security, in case the existence of a covert operation is revealed.[70]

Transnational corporations have also played a role in such enterprises. Even TNCs, the presumed antagonists of the nation state, are in a symbiotic relationship with at least some powerful Western countries. The expansion, lower costs and profitability of many TNCs owe a great deal to national administrations that reproduce the conditions that are most amenable to their continuing growth. States guarantee safe investment environments, create markets through foreign aid, promote trade through diplomatic missions, pass supportive regulation in trademarks, copyright, mergers and acquisitions, and purchase defence and communication equipment. In addition, TNCs depend to a large extent on public funding for their research and development.[71]

TNCs have often coopted national leaders, who then oppressed their own people and allowed TNCs to pollute the countryside, exploit local labour, disregard safety regulations, avoid taxes, etc. In other cases, TNCs benefited from direct action from their home government. The US has a rather long history of unorthodox interventions overseas. They range from the threat of trade sanctions if the target country does not allow a US-based tobacco company to freely advertise cigarettes to the overthrowing of legitimate governments and the undermining of democratic processes.[72] Marine Corps General Smedley Butler has made the point:

> I spent 33 years ... being a high-class muscleman for big business, for Wall Street and the bankers ... I helped purify Nicaragua for the international house of Brown Brothers in 1909–1912. I helped make Mexico and especially Tampico safe for American oil interests in 1916. I brought light to the Dominican Republic for American sugar interests in 1916. I helped make Haiti and Cuba a decent place for the National City Bank boys to collect revenue in. I helped in the rape of half a dozen Central American republics for the benefit of Wall Street.[73]

The effects of exploitation can have even longer-term consequences. As former imperial powers grant independence to their colonies, they often cut the subsidies that sustain the local government. This happens after natural resources have been depleted or contracted away. Other small states are used by hegemonic states as military bases in exchange for 'aid'. As local people work for the foreign bases or live on welfare, the prospects for self-sufficiency are effectively destroyed. Such states turn themselves into tax havens and secrecy jurisdictions, as a way of generating revenue. They may be aware that their jurisdictions are used to commit serious financial crime, but are not overly concerned about fraud victimization or tax evasion affecting rich countries and former colonial powers. Their sympathy toward defrauded white people who took advantage of them for decades or centuries is limited.[74]

The mounting problems in the control of costly economic crimes point up the clear need for an international solution. More than ever before, international law is a *conditio sine qua non* for the maintenance of world order and security. The problem with this proposition, however, is that it would require additional shifts of competence and power from nation states to transnational institutions. The more powerful a government is, the more it has to lose by contributing to such a pooling of sovereignty. Hence the tremendous resistance by countries of the rich North to the establishment of international norms and procedures. Power politics disallow these developments, unless they can be used as a legitimating tool for controversial or self-serving policies. Former President Bush's rhetoric about a 'new world order' and enthusiastic commitment to some international laws lost its momentum after the end of the Persian Gulf War. The promise of a more active UN proved to be illusory. After all, the UN has inherently limited independence and cannot be expected to act against the countries that finance it or have veto power.

Indeed, the USA and other prominent members of the coalition against Iraq have resisted the development of an international criminal code and permanent court. The same applies to specific international initiatives regarding, *inter alia*, aggression, genocide, the protection of the environment or the prevention of theft of natural and cultural property from countries in the South.[75] Cooperation occurs only when the diverse national interests converge, which appears to happen only rarely. National conflicts and partial commitments to international bodies and law perpetuate or enhance power, legal and cultural asymmetries. They also undermine the legitimacy of existing international norms and custom, thereby weakening overall allegiance to these norms and torpedoing predictability in cross-border conduct.

Regionalisms, nationalisms, fights over symbolic representations of sovereignty and the insistence on exclusive competence to enact and enforce laws within their territory bring about further asymmetries. This is because gaps generated by resistances to global control mechanisms are sought to be filled by national measures. At the same time, despite efforts to harmonize standards and approaches in some areas (for example, copyright, drugs), legal and cultural traditions remain extremely diverse and sometimes incompatible. This causes malfunctioning polynomie and renders the global legal environment dysnomic. The globalization of markets and enterprises, therefore, entails increasingly fragmented regulation. The more a company grows into new markets, the less amenable it becomes to control, accountability and consolidated supervision.

To the extent that transactions take place within one jurisdiction or within jurisdictions with similar legal traditions, the task environment is relatively easy to handle. Businesses are clear about the rules of the game, while supervisors can regulate more readily.[76] To the extent that transactions cross jurisdictions with differing legal traditions and cultures, both compliance and control become highly problematic. Legal cacophonies are accompanied by jurisdictional conflicts, nightmares in collaboration, cultural conflicts and power differentials among both actors and regulators.

The process of European integration and the regulation of European Union programmes, such as the Common Agricultural Policy (CAP), highlights the clash between centralizing forces of globalization and attempts at decentralization. The EU effectively represents a recognition of interdependence and the need for cooperation. Powers and competence to make decisions and policies affecting its 15 members are shifted to EU organs. Despite the important pooling of sovereignty, national authorities remain in charge – with the exception of the very contested powers of the EU Commission with respect to competition and anti-trust rules – of enforcing EU regulations and policing the borders. There is no EU power to enact or enforce criminal law. As a result, the EU funds, to which member states contribute unequally, are protected by national and local authorities, whose priorities lie elsewhere and may be reluctant to prosecute contributors to the regional economy. The national penal laws applicable to EU frauds vary substantially. EU regulations and fraud are hard to explain to juries, and boring and unintelligible to national judges and law enforcers.[77] Efforts to resolve jurisdictional issues for multinational cases started in the 1970s and are still ongoing. All this makes the control of EU frauds wanting.

EU member states are also responsible for fraud-inviting EU rules and programmes. Although the blame is usually placed on the EU Commission and the 'Eurocrats', it is national government ministers who make up the EU Council, the chief law-making EU institution. As ministers represent often contradictory national and regional interests, the rules and decisions they make reflect the political compromises that are made at the non-public negotiating table. The resulting regulations are often ambiguous and unintelligible even to national customs officials who are asked to apply them. In order to achieve the majority required on a particular issue, the objective and terms of EU regulations may be intentionally unclear. Traders regard such rules as unnecessary hassle and do not see any immorality in their violation.

EU regulations are not only imperfect but also too numerous for national controllers to keep abreast of them. The changing national moods and ruling parties in member states, shifting priorities and commitment to European integration, the enlargement of the EU and the need to remedy problems created by loopholes in previous regulations, make for constant amendments and rule proliferation.

The combined effect of the uneven process of European integration, piecemeal controls, regulatory inflation with intended ambiguities, is to render some EU programmes inherently dysnomic. The whole process leads to an over-legalization of certain areas, which requires increased reliance on legal and accounting experts. This in turn leads to reduced visibility, accountability and detectability of misconduct.[78]

If the problems are serious within the relatively developed and integrated EU, they are barely manageable in the global markets. The fragmentation of control creates massive opportunities to slip through the cracks of the parochial regulatory patchwork, as professional advisers can more easily point to abundant legal asymmetries.[79] It also provides incentives and motives for enterprises to use these opportunities. By operating in countries with conflicting standards not only do they have higher compliance costs, but they experience increased hardship to abide by the laws of all countries where they operate. Occasions arise when they may have to break the laws of one country, if they observe those of another. In such cases, globalization produces yet another type of crime – 'crime due to respect of domestic law'.

Several cases from the banking sector exemplify this dilemma. Many financial institutions operate both in the USA and in 'black box' jurisdictions in the Caribbean, the Pacific and Europe. As criminal clients use the offshore banking facilities for their transactions, US law enforcers ask the US branches of these institutions to produce the records that are indispensable for prosecution. Since the records are physically within secrecy jurisdictions, the banks cannot comply with US court orders. The governments in such secrecy jurisdictions regard these demands of US authorities as a violation of their sovereignty and take further measures to ensure that US attempts to obtain confidential records are frustrated. Caught in the middle are the banks, the non-party witnesses, who are required to either ignore a US court order and face contempt of court charges or to produce the records and violate banking and criminal laws of the country in which the records are located.[80] At stake is not only the question of sovereignty, but also strong financial interests. Tax havens and secrecy jurisdictions derive substantial revenues from the banking industry. It is tax advantages and confidentiality that draws legitimate and illegitimate businesses to offshore locations. Given the lack of universal tax and regulatory standards, globalization has unleashed a competitive struggle among nation states to attract as many investments and businesses as possible. Given the gigantic market for secrecy and tax advantages, countries have succumbed to the temptation to regulate more laxly than others.[81] In other words, at precisely the time when better regulation was needed, globalization has fostered 'competitive deregulation'.[82] In the end, attempts to regulate nationally and curb globalization are doomed to fail. In fact, they become a Sisyphean task given that 'much of the globalization today is the result of regulatory barriers, which drove borrowers and investors to find ways around national regulation'.[83] We finally come full circle. We started with processes whereby globalization undermines state autonomy and increases or activates asymmetries, including discrepancies in legal traditions and regulatory practices. We now see that it is also independent actions of states and asymmetric national regulations that make for globalization.

CONCLUSION

If globalization is inevitable, what can be done about the economic crime problems that accompany it? Globalization has brought into closer contact, interaction and interdependence, countries with unequal power and diverse cultures, legal traditions, and economic and political outlooks. The roots of the growing problem of economic crime have been located in the criminogenic asymmetries that offer illegal opportunities, create motives to use such opportunities and make it possible for offenders to get away scot-free. Asymmetries will continue to exist, some of them will even grow. It must be impressed that many asymmetries ought to remain, especially in the sphere of culture. Crime fighting cannot and should not seek the standardization of everything on a global level. The task is to diminish or eradicate undesirable asymmetries and to reduce the criminogenic effect of those we wish to preserve or cannot do much about. Despite the grim picture portrayed above, the foregoing analysis offers some clues for solutions. Since nation states play such an important role in criminogenesis, crime control is not beyond their reach. They certainly have the power to do something about it. The question is do they have the will to do so and what can be done to strengthen existing levels of commitment?

Public discourses in many Western countries show a serious concern about international crime (at the June 1997 meeting of the Summit of Eight, global crime threats were high on the agenda). An important objective, then, is to bring to the fore the links between their own actions and the crime risks they generate. If state policies create asymmetries, state actions can stop them from growing or eliminate them altogether. Some states have attempted to solve their international crime problems by enforcing domestic laws extraterritorially. While some of these attempts may be understandable, they are counter-productive and sometimes in violation of international law.[84] Such exercise of asymmetric powers causes unease with friendly countries and cooperative partners, undermines the legitimacy of international laws and undercuts efforts at a principled rather than *ad hoc* collaboration.

In some areas, such as the fight against drug trafficking, there is growing consensus and a process of coordination. Harmonization can be attempted even with respect to crimes that are hard to define, such as corruption. Countries may be invited to criminalize under their own legal systems a list of acts that effectively constitute abuses of official power. This approach is sensitive to issues of sovereignty and respect for different traditions.[85] Sanction gaps may be narrowed given a wide agreement on the necessity to limit bank secrecy, to disallow the political offence exception for extradition purposes, to take the profits away from corrupt officials through fines and to confiscate the illicit proceeds.

Beside domestic law changes, consistent international cooperation and conventions resolving jurisdictional conflicts, it is imperative to pursue a stronger international criminal law. In order to avoid selective enforcement or dead letter laws, principles and rules must be debated in international fora, such as the UN or the WTO.[86] (In that process, care must be taken to give a voice to all constituents, including less powerful developing countries. This is the best way to strengthen the legitimacy of international law and to promote future compliance and full cooperation in its enforcement. The risk in forging agreements under the influence of powerful states on the basis of some particular case of 'bad guys' is that future interpretations will vary reflecting the underlying and unaddressed cultural, legal, and other asymmetries.)

Although essential, criminal law and justice measures are no panacea. Technically, no criminal laws are broken when many of the crimes referred to above are committed. The collection of evidence and prosecution of many other crimes is such a costly nightmare that even the most conscientious law enforcers will find that the public interest will be better served by concentrating on more solvable offences. The main goal is not to put corporate managers behind bars, but to minimize the risks of organizational misbehaviour. That goal may be better served through regulatory harmonization, which can be beneficial also for the companies concerned. Fewer regulatory asymmetries will lower both criminogenesis and compliance costs. Corporations are more likely to comply with rules they accept than with rules they perceive as arbitrary and unwarranted.[87] It may be possible, thus, to collaborate with companies for better all-round results without resort to criminal law.[88] In the banking sector, there are serious efforts underway by think tanks, academics and financial institutions to develop international standards that the industry can live with and the regulators can enforce. The same process may be encouraged in other industries.

Powerful states and corporations will not always participate whole-heartedly in processes that ultimately involve power sharing. Cooperation, harmonization of rules and the emergence of international regimes require a degree of consensual knowledge, a shared understanding of common risks and problems to be solved.[89] A vital element of a strategy to fight global economic crime, therefore, is to contribute to consensual knowledge about its causes and consequences. Policy makers and the public must be made aware of the boomerang effects of their country's domestic and foreign policies and TNC practices.[90] The most powerful will need the most convincing about the 'own goals' they might score.

Adverse effects on developing countries have not always been seen as 'our concern' in the West and have not elicited the reactions that domestic social problems do. Yet, the transboundary consequences of harmful acts mean that offenders become victims at the same time. When a company exploits lax environmental regulation and few resources for enforcement south of the border, pollution spills back into the North. When banned pesticides are marketed to developing countries, but fruits are imported back home, we are the ultimate victims. Crimes against the environment abroad affect the climate at home causing unusual floods, hurricanes or other weather changes. Intervention in the internal affairs of other countries results in acts of terror against fellow civilians. Exploitation of children, women and others' labour, leads to loss of jobs and discontent at home. When a company is caught bribing officials overseas, its share prices fall in the domestic stock market. When a TNC is found to sell a harmful product in foreign markets, overseas victims may be able to bring legal action in the home country and gain substantial restitution, which again lowers the stock price. Such hidden costs of criminogenic asymmetries generated by state and TNC actions must be considered in cost and benefit analyses conducted in order to decide on the desirability of a policy.

In such cases, domestic voices and pressure may have a more significant impact on the official response to unlawful practices overseas. State agencies at home may be forced to take remedial action (for example, in the Barlow Clowes affair). More effective, however, are preventive measures. It is much better, for example, for legislators and policy makers to promote the highest possible standards of safety in all countries. From a moral point of view, products or work conditions found to be hazardous to the home population should not be regarded as less risky for other populations. Some countries persistently ask poorer countries to do something about the production of drugs affecting youths in the West. By the same token, developing countries can ask the home states of TNCs to agree to international standards and to assist in obtaining TNC compliance with them. There are no two ways about it; in a global market, only widely accepted and enforced international rules can curb the threat of economic crime. States have the power and a moral obligation to move in that direction both on self-interest and ethical grounds.

Politicians and policy makers will not take too many initiatives, however, without the support or demand of public opinion. Citizens must become more active and think globally too. They must put informed pressure on their representatives to act with global responsibility. Globalization offers new opportunities for information gathering and mobilizing public support and opinion. In addition to the above boomerang effects, there are further reminders of often unintended consequences of Western actions. We can see, read or hear about atrocities in remote lands in graphic detail. Non-profit organizations and non-governmental agencies are better equipped to gather information, video evidence of the results of TNC or our country's policies overseas and prepare documentaries for public education.

The concentration of power in TNCs, supranational institutions and powerful countries can be opposed by smaller nations, communities, political or environmental movements.[91] Successful leadership in reducing legal asymmetries can be provided even by tiny countries. Costa Rica, for example, set higher standards for pharmaceuticals than those in the rest of South America. Because production costs would be too high for companies to have different standards for Costa Rica and the other countries in the region, they applied the higher standards for all countries.[92] This highlights the potential for 'globalization from below',[93] which is growing with the ability to use the global means of communication to spread awareness and create bonds and solidarity on particular areas of concern. Consumer action and boycotts can affect giants like Shell and Nestlé, as well as their competitors who learn from the experience. Citizens can privately sue a company and achieve much more than the state can manage through criminal procedures because the burden of proof is not as tough. Ford, for example, was found not guilty of manslaughter for the manufacture and sale of Pinto cars that top executives knew were defective and would lead to serious injuries and death; yet, burn victims were successful in their civil suits against the company. Environmental groups in the USA have also been very successful with the strategy of suing polluters. As resources available in rich countries become more accessible to the rest of the world, citizens from different countries may join in class actions in the most favourable jurisdiction.

A parallel objective is to appeal to 'other selves' of corporate executives and public officials. It is wrong to assume that managers are one-dimensional and only think of their company's quarterly figures and bottom line.[94] They have multiple selves, they face value conflicts and dilemmas and they make decisions under strained conditions. We have seen how asymmetries allow rationalizations to clear people's conscience of any pangs about questionable activities. A public policy task is to reverse that process, to hinder the process of particularizing cases and creating acceptable exceptions to rules. Educational and citizen groups need to make clear how criminal and irresponsible are the final outcomes. Business ethics codes at the company, country, region or international level are an indispensable supplement to regulation and public pressure. (These are all measures in addition to other self-regulatory arrangements. Whistle-blowers must also be invited to report misconduct and effectively protected – rather than vilified and financially ruined when they testify against current or former employers.)

Accountability and transparency must be maximized in both government and economic activities. Processes of democratization in the post-Cold War era favour efforts in that direction. Democracy and active citizen participation can only function on the basis of valid information and education. It is again a state responsibility and duty to enhance educational standards and facilities for its population. It is a civic task to ensure that states meet this obligation.

When everything else fails, another goal for citizen groups and state authorities alike is to investigate, and reveal detected and unpunished misconduct to the wider public and international community. Scandal is an opportunity for reform and can have cathartic effects. It is well worth exposing neo-colonialist tendencies in the form of allowing exploitation of other countries' cultural or natural wealth through permissive laws favouring the Western possessors. It is well worth drawing attention to the hypocrisy of countries fighting money laundering and professing sound management of the global financial system, when they simultaneously encourage capital flight from the developing world. Shaming can have a reintegrative function.[95] The role of embarrassment should not be under-estimated as an attempt to partially redress power asymmetries.

All this, of course, requires strong citizen participation in common (that is, global) affairs. Local networks and groups must take advantage of the new global opportunities and link up with counterparts elsewhere. At the same time, care must be taken not to engage in overzealous 'extraterritorial' interventions of particular groups against the will and interests of other countries. There have been incidents, for example, of environmental groups from the North going to the South to disrupt deforestation or other environmental catastrophes. This is fine, so long as it is in accord with local desires and priorities. Just as IMF should not 'impose' aid and attach unrealistic conditions, citizens groups ought not to dictate environmental policy in other countries. The problem sometimes is that poorer countries see patronizing environmentalists getting involved in freezing their economic development and growth. It is of paramount importance to realize that developing countries cannot be the lungs for the rest of the world without costs. The rich West and North must make a commitment to finance this type of preservation of global treasures. For example, TNCs and wealthy countries must be persuaded to compensate adequately for the rights of research for new drugs and treatments, for the non-deforestation. They must also provide an alternative for the economic growth and self-sufficiency of the countries concerned.

In short, we must work toward the development of international law and control agencies enjoying legitimacy. The more nation states resist integration and pooling of sovereignty, the more they insist on national controls, the more numerous become the cracks in regulatory patchworks and the less effective control they have over crimes that victimize their own citizens. A safer, healthier, less asymmetric, more peaceful, global village ultimately serves the interests of powerful and weak alike. If states fail to learn the lessons of short-sightedness and play their leadership role, citizens will have to become much more active and assume more responsibilities. For the moment, it remains an open question as to whether we will collectively make use of the control opportunities furnished by globalization to counter its criminogenic effects. If we do not, the price may be very high.

NOTES

1. A different and shorter version of this paper has appeared in the *European Journal of Law Reform*.
2. R.J. Barnet and R.E. Muller, *Global Reach: The Power of the Multinational Corporations* (New York: Simon and Schuster, 1974); J. Braithwaite, *Corporate Crime in the Pharmaceutical Industry* (London: Routledge & Kegan Paul, 1984); W.J. Chambliss, *On the Take: From Petty Crooks to Presidents* (Bloomington: Indiana University Press, 1988); M.B. Clinard, *Corporate Corruption: The Abuse of Power* (New York: Praeger, 1990); R.J. Michalowski and R.C. Kramer, 'The Space Between Laws: The Problem of Corporate Crime in a Transnational Context', *Social Problems*, Vol.34, No.1 (1987), pp.34–53; N. Passas, 'European Integration, Protectionism and Criminogenesis: A Study on Farm Subsidy Frauds', *Mediterranean Quarterly*, Vol.5 No.4 (1994), pp.66–84; P. Shrivstava, *Bhopal: Anatomy of a Crisis* (Cambridge, MA.: Ballinger, 1987).
3. R. Godson and W.J. Olson, *International Organized Crime: Emerging Threat to US Security* (Washington, DC: National Strategy Information Center, 1993); R.T. Naylor, 'From Cold War to Crime War: The Search for a New "National Security" Threat', *Transnational Organized Crime*, Vol.1 No.4 (Winter 1995), pp.37–56; P. Williams, 'Transnational Criminal Organizations and International Security', *Survival*, Vol.36, No.1 (Jan.–Feb. 1994), pp.96–113.
4. N. Passas, 'Structural Sources of International Crime: Policy Lessons from the BCCI Affair', *Crime, Law and Social Change*, Vol.20, No.4 (1993), pp.293–305; N. Passas, 'The Mirror of Global Evils: A Review Essay on the BCCI Affair', *Justice Quarterly*, Vol.12, No.2 (1995), pp.801–29; A. Tickell, 'Making a Melodrama Out of a Crisis: Reinterpreting the Collapse of Barings Bank', *Environment and Planning D: Society and Space*, Vol.14 (1996), pp.5–33.
5. As Sutherland argued decades ago, there is no reason to leave the definition of crime, the subject matter of criminologists, to administrators or politicians.
6. M.C. Bassiouni, 'Enslavement as an International Crime', *International Law and Politics*, Vol.23 (1991), pp.445–517; Dwight C. Smith, 'Some Things that May Be More Important to Understand About Organized Crime than Cosa Nostra', in N. Passas, *Organized Crime* (Aldershot: Dartmouth, 1995).

7. A. Szasz, 'Corporations, Organized Crime, and the Disposal of Hazardous Waste: An Examination of the Making of a Criminogenic Regulatory Structure', in Passas, ibid.
8. U. Beck, *The Risk Society* (London: Sage, 1992); Center for Investigative Reporting and B. Moyers, *Global Dumping Ground: The International Traffic in Hazardous Waste* (Washington, DC: Seven Locks Press, 1990).
9. M.B. Clinard, *Corporate Corruption: The Abuse of Power* (New York: Praeger, 1990).
10. M. Critharis, 'Third World Nations are Down in the Dumps: The Exportation of Hazardous Waste', *Brooklyn Journal of International Law*, Vol.6, No.2 (1990), pp.311–39.
11. M. Johnston, 'Corruption, Inequality and Change', in P.M. Ward, *Corruption, Development and Inequality* (London and New York: Routledge, 1989), pp.13–37; R. Klitgaard, *Controlling Corruption* (Berkeley: University of California Press, 1988); N. Passas, *Regional Initiatives Against International Corruption* (Report to the United Nations, Crime Prevention and Criminal Justice Program, 1997a, Vienna, Austria. Published as Report of the Secretary-General, E/CN.15/1997/3).
12. R.T. Naylor, 'The Insurgent Economy: Black Market Operations of Guerilla Organizations', *Crime, Law and Social Change*, Vol.20 (1993), pp.13–51; and RT. Naylor, 'Loose Cannons: Covert Commerce and Underground Finance in the Modern Arms Black Market', *Crime, Law and Social Change*, Vol.22 (1995) pp.1–57; Observatoire Géopolitique des Drogues, *The Geopolitics of Drugs: 1996 Edition* (Boston: Northeastern University Press, 1996).
13. J. Kwitny, *The Crimes of Patriots: The True Tale of Dope, Dirty Money, and the CIA* (New York: Norton, 1987).
14. Passas, 'European Integration, Protectionism and Criminogenesis: A Study on Farm Subsidy Frauds', op. cit.
15. I. Wallerstein, *Historical Capitalism* (London: Verso, 1983).
16. J. Rosenau, *Turbulence in World Politics* (Brighton: Harvester Wheatsheaf, 1990).
17. R. Gilpin, *The Political Economy of International Relations* (Princeton: Princeton University Press, 1987).
18. A. Giddens, *The Consequences of Modernity* (Cambridge: Polity, 1990).
19. A.T. McGrew, 'A Global Society?', in S. Hall, D. Held and A.T. McGrew, *Modernity and its Futures* (Cambridge: Open University Press, 1992), pp.62–102; L. Sklair, *Sociology of the Global System* (New York and London: Prentice Hall and Harvester Wheatsheaf, 1995).
20. D. Harvey, *The Condition of Postmodernity* (Oxford: Basil Blackwell, 1989).
21. Ibid.
22. Ibid.; and A. Giddens, *Modernity and Self-Identity* (Cambridge: Polity, 1991).
23. Giddens, *The Consequences of Modernity*, op. cit.
24. R. Murray, 'The Internationalization of Capital and the Nation-State', *New Left Review*, Vol.67 (1971), pp.84–109.
25. S. Hall, 'The Question of Cultural Identity', in Hall, Held, and McGrew, *Modernity and its Futures*, op. cit., pp.273–316.
26. Z. Bauman, *Intimations of Postmodernity* (London: Routledge, 1992).
27. R.O. Keohane and S. Hoffman, 'Institutional Change in Europe in the 1980s', in idem, *The New European Community: Decisionmaking and Institutional Change* (Boulder: Westview, 1990), pp.1–39.
28. McGrew, 'A Global Society?', in Hall, Held and McGrew, op. cit., pp.62–102.
29. S. Wheeler and M.L. Rothman, 'The Organization as Weapon in White-Collar Crime', *Michigan Law Review*, Vol.80 (1982), pp.1403–27.
30. J. Braithwaite, 'Criminological Theory and Organizational Crime', *Justice Quarterly*, Vol.6 (March 1989), pp.333–58.
31. J. Blum and A. Block, 'Le blanchiment de l' argent dans les Antilles: Bahamas, Saint Maartin et Iles Caïmans', in A. Labrousse and A. Wallon, *La Planète des Drogues* (Paris, Seuil, 1993), pp.73–102.
32. N. Passas, 'The Genesis of the BCCI Scandal', *Journal of Law and Society*, Vol.23, No.1 (1996), pp.52–72; N. Passas, 'Accounting for Fraud: Auditors' Ethical and Legal Dilemmas in the BCCI Affair', in W.M. Hoffman, J. Kamm, R.E. Frederick and E. Petry, *The Ethics of Accounting and Finance* (Newport, CO: Quorum Books, 1996b), pp.85–99.

33. J. Braithwaite, *Corporate Crime in the Pharmaceutical Industry* (London: Routledge & Kegan Paul, 1984).
34. D.A. Bryan, 'Consumer Safety Abroad: Dumping of Dangerous American Products Overseas', *Texas Tech Law Review*, Vol.12 (1981), pp.435–58.
35. P. Cashman, 'The Dalkon Shield', in P. Grabosky and A. Sutton, *Stains on a White Collar* (Sydney: The Federation Press, 1989), pp.92–117; M.B. Clinard, *Corporate Corruption: The Abuse of Power* (New York: Praeger, 1990); Mintz, *At Any Cost: Corporate Greed, Women and the Dalkon Shield* (New York: Pantheon, 1985).
36. S. Picciotto, *International Business Taxation* (New York, Quorum Books, 1992).
37. M. Levi, 'Pecunia non Olet: Cleansing the Money-Launderers from the Temple', *Crime, Law and Social Change*, Vol.16 (1991), pp.217–302. Interestingly, recent arguments about the role and responsibility of Swiss banks relative to the Nazi gold during the Second World War could be made about the role and responsibility of big Western banks today. Just as the neutral Swiss could tell that the gold coming from Germany was forcibly taken from Jews, banks can at least suspect that the hundreds of billions of dollars coming from the developing world are proceeds from drug and arms trafficking, dictators' plunder, flight capital, corrupt payments, evaded taxes, etc.
38. Passas, 'The Mirror of Global Evils: A Review Essay on the BCCI Affair', op. cit.
39. R. Walker, *One World, Many Worlds* (New York: Lynne Rienner, 1988).
40. U. Beck, *The Risk Society* (London: Sage, 1992).
41. M.T. Klare, 'Secret Operatives, Clandestine Trade: The Thriving Black Market for Weapons', *Bulletin of Atomic Scientists*, Vol.44, No.3 (1988), pp.16–24; M. Klare, *Rogue States and Nuclear Outlaws: America's Search for a New Foreign Policy* (New York: Hill and Wang a division of Farrar, Straus and Giroux, 1995).
42. G. Modelski, *The Principles of World Politics* (New York: Free Press, 1972).
43. D. Harvey, *The Condition of Postmodernity*, op. cit.; Wallerstein, op. cit.
44. N. Passas, 'Anomie, Reference Groups, and Relative Deprivation', in N. Passas and R. Agnew, *The Future of the Anomie Tradition* (Boston: Northeastern University Press, 1997b), pp.62–94.
45. J. Vagg, 'The Borders of Crime', *British Journal of Criminology*, Vol.32, No.3 (1992), pp.310–28.
46. S. Hall, 'The Question of Cultural Identity', in Hall, Held and McGrew, op. cit. pp.273–316.
47. L. Shelley, 'Post-Soviet Organized Crime', *Demokratizatsiya*, Vol.2, No.3 (1994), pp.341–58.
48. W.H. Myers III, 'Orb Weavers – The Global Webs: The Structure and Activities of Transnational Ethnic Chinese Criminal Groups', *Transnational Organized Crime*, Vol.1, No.4 (Winter 1995), pp.1–36.
49. S. Handelman, 'The Russian Mafiya', *Foreign Affairs*, Vol.73, No.2 (1994), pp.83–96; Shelley, op. cit.
50. Observatoire Géopolitique des Drogues, *The Geopolitics of Drugs: 1996 Edition* (Boston, Northeastern University Press, 1996).
51. Ibid.
52. Ibid.
53. R.G. Hovannisian, 'Etiology and Sequelae of the Armenian Genocide', in G.J. Andreopoulos, *Genocide: Conceptual and Historical Dimensions* (Philadelphia: University of Pennsylvania Press, 1994), pp.111–40.
54. J. Dunn, 'East Timor: A Case of Cultural Genocide?', in ibid., pp.171–90.
55. P.L. Margules, 'International Art Theft and the Illegal Import and Export of Cultural Property: A Study of Relevant Values, Legislation, and Solutions', *Suffolk Transnational Law Journal*, Vol.15 (1992), pp.609–47.
56. J.E. Conklin, *Art Crime* (Westport, CT: Praeger, 1994).
57. J. Brooke, 'Faced with a Shrinking Supply of Authentic Art, African Dealers Peddle the Illusion', *New York Times*, 17 April 1988, H51.
58. J. Rosenau, *Turbulence in World Politics* (Brighton: Harvester Wheatsheaf, 1990).
59. R. Falk, 'Rethinking the Agenda of International Law', in Nordenstreng and Schiller, op. cit., pp. 418–31.

60. Passas, 'Structural Sources of International Crime: Policy Lessons from the BCCI Affair', op. cit.
61. Passas, 'European Integration, Protectionism and Criminogenesis: A Study on Farm Subsidy Frauds', op. cit.; M.J. Roarty, 'The Impact of the Common Agricultural Policy on Agricultural Trade and Development', *National Westminster Bank Quarterly Review* (February 1987), pp.18–28.
62. EU Court of Auditors, *Special Report No. 1/87 on the Quality of Food Aid*, (Brussels, OJ No. C 219/1, 1987); B.E. Harrell-Bond, *Imposing Aid: Emergency Assistance to Refugees* (Oxford: Oxford University Press, 1986); W. Shawcross, *The Quality of Mercy* (London: Fontana, 1985).
63. B. Ferencz, 'An International Criminal Code and Court: Where They Stand and Where They're Going', *Columbia Journal of Transnational Law*, Vol.30 (1992), pp.375–99.
64. A. Chayes, 'Nicaragua, the United States, and the World Court', in V. Blasi, *Law and Liberalism in the 1980s* (New York: Columbia University Press, 1991), pp.69–107.
65. R. Falk, 'Rethinking the Agenda of International Law', in Nordenstreng and Schiller, op. cit., pp.418–31.
66. R. Cox, *Power, Production and World Order* (New York: St. Martin's Press, 1987); Passas, 'European Integration, Protectionism and Criminogenesis: A Study on Farm Subsidy Frauds', op. cit.; Passas, *Regional Initiatives Against International Corruption*, op. cit.
67. Passas, 'Structural Sources of International Crime: Policy Lessons from the BCCI Affair', op. cit.; Passas, 'The Mirror of Global Evils: A Review Essay on the BCCI Affair', op. cit.
68. *Financial Times*, 6 June 1997, p.7.
69. Observatoire Géopolitique des Drogues, *The Geopolitics of Drugs: 1996 Edition*, op. cit.
70. Kwitny, op. cit.; P. Mantius, *Shell Game* (New York: St. Martin's Press, 1995); M. Phythian, *Arming Iraq: How the U.S. and Britain Secretly Built Saddam's War Machine* (Boston: Northeastern University Press, 1996); L.E. Walsh, *Iran-Contra: The Final Report* (New York: Times Books, 1994).
71. C.J. Hamelink, 'Globalism and National Sovereignty', in Nordenstreng and Schiller, op. cit., pp.371–93.
72. Clinard, op. cit.
73. Ibid.
74. L. Gurwin, 'Fantasy Islands: Ministaatjes als Speelterrein vor Internationale Fraudeurs', *Financieell Economisch Magazine*, Vol.25/26 (17 Dec. 1988), pp.73–82.
75. M. Critharis, 'Third World Nations are Down in the Dumps: The Exportation of Hazardous Waste', *Brooklyn Journal of International Law*, Vol.6, No.2 (1990), pp.311–39; R. Falk, 'Nuremberg: Past, Present, and Future', *Yale Law Journal*, Vol.80 (1971), pp.1501–28; Falk, 'Rethinking the Agenda of International Law', op. cit.; B. Ferencz, 'An International Criminal Code and Court: Where They Stand and Where They're Going', *Columbia Journal of Transnational Law*, Vol.30 (1992), pp.375–99; P.L. Margules, 'International Art Theft and the Illegal Import and Export of Cultural Property: A Study of Relevant Values, Legislation, and Solutions', *Suffolk Transnational Law Journal*, Vol.15 (1992), pp.609–47.
76. This is by no means to say that domestic controls are faultless. In fact, jurisdictional clashes, antagonisms and non-cooperation among national agencies are very common, especially in the USA. Domestic 'turf wars' add to the regulatory cacophony produced by globalization. In BCCI-type of cases, which involve both domestic and cross-border crime, the lack of coordination of local, federal and foreign agencies reaches its peak.
77. N. Passas, *Frauds Affecting the Budget of the European Community*, Report to the Commission of the European Communities, 1991; N. Passas and D. Nelken, 'The Fight Against Fraud in the European Community: Cacophony Rather Than Harmony', *Corruption and Reform*, Vol.6 (1991), pp.237–66.
78. Passas, 'European Integration, Protectionism and Criminogenesis: A Study on Farm Subsidy Frauds', op. cit.
79. R.J. Michalowski and R.C. Kramer, 'The Space Between Laws: The Problem of Corporate Crime in a Transnational Context', *Social Problems*, Vol.34, No.1 (1987), pp.34–53.
80. H. Harfield and R.E. Deming, 'Extraterritorial Imperatives' *Case Western Reserve Journal*

of International Law, Vol.20 (1988), pp.393–403; S.B. Piñera-Vasquez, 'Extraterritorial Jurisdiction and International Banking: A Conflict of Interests', *University of Miami Law Review*, Vol.43 (1988), pp. 449–91.

81. I. Walter, *Secret Money: The World of International Financial Secrecy* (London: George Allen & Unwin, 1985).

82. R. Dale, *The Regulation of International Banking* (Cambridge: Woodhead-Faulkner, 1984); J.W. Dean, 'Conservative Versus Liberal Regulation of International Banking', *Journal of World Trade*, 1 (February, 1989), pp.5–15.

83. D.A. Bryan, 'Consumer Safety Abroad: Dumping of Dangerous American Products Overseas', *Texas Tech Law Review*, Vol.12 (1981), pp.435–58.

84. A. Abramovsky, 'Extraterritorial Abductions: America's 'Catch and Snatch' Policy Run Amok', *Virginia Journal of International Law*, Vol.31 (1991), pp.151–210; A.F. Lowenfeld, 'Kidnapping by Government Order', *American Journal of International Law*, Vol.84, No.3 (1990), pp.712–16; Organization of American States, 'Legal Opinion on the Decision of the Supreme Court of the United States of America', *Criminal Law Forum*, Vol.4, No.1 (1992), pp.119–34; N. Passas and J. Blum, 'Intelligence Services and Undercover Operations: The Case of Euromac', in S. Field and C. Pelser, *Invading the Private? Accountability and the New Policing in Europe* (Aldershot: Dartmouth, in press); N. Passas and R.B. Groskin, 'International Undercover Operations', in G. Marx and C. Fijnaut, *Undercover: Police Surveillance in Comparative Perspective* (Amsterdam: Kluwer, 1995), pp.291–312.

85. Passas, *Regional Initiatives Against International Corruption*, op. cit.

86. Michalowski and Kramer, op. cit.

87. M.D. Ermann and J.R. Lundman, 'Deviant Acts by Complex Organizations: Deviance and Social Control at the Organizational Level of Analysis', *Sociological Quarterly*, Vol.19 (Winter 1978), pp.55–67.

88. B. Fisse and J. Braithwaite, *Corporations, Crime and Accountability* (Cambridge: Cambridge University Press, 1993).

89. E.B. Kapstein, 'Resolving the Regulator's Dilemma: International Coordination of Banking Regulations', *International Organization*, Vol.43, No.2 (1989), pp.323–47.

90. U. Beck, *The Risk Society* (London: Sage, 1992).

91. Rosenau, op. cit.; Wallerstein, op. cit.

92. J. Braithwaite, 'Transnational Regulation of the Pharmaceutical Industry', *Annals, AAPSS*, Vol.525 (1993), pp.12–30.

93. R. Falk, 'Rethinking the Agenda of International Law', in Nordenstreng and Schiller, op. cit.

94. Braithwaite, *Corporate Crime in the Pharmaceutical Industry*, op. cit.

95. J. Braithwaite, *Crime, Shame and Reintegration* (Cambridge: Cambridge University Press, 1989).

Organizing Transnational Crime:
Networks, Markets and Hierarchies

PHIL WILLIAMS

Transnational organized crime has become a major issue on the international agenda. In 1994, under the auspices of the United Nations, a World Ministerial Conference on the issue was held, rather symbolically, in Naples. Since then, with the support of member states, the United Nations has initiated the process of formulating a convention on transnational organized crime. It is also the topic of an increasing number of high-level meetings such as those of the P-8; there is a journal devoted exclusively to the subject; and it is a source of concern for governments in countries as diverse as South Africa, Mexico, Russia, Colombia and China. In some assessments, transnational organized crime is even characterized as a security problem rather than simply a challenge to law and order. In states in transition in particular, it is seen as a challenge to the process of democratization and the moves towards a market economy.

Yet, in one sense, there is nothing new about crossing borders in the pursuit of wealth through illicit means. Smuggling, for example, is one of the world's oldest professions and is based on differential opportunities for profit that result in rent-seeking behaviour by individuals or groups. In the eighteenth and nineteenth centuries, for example, there was a flourishing and well-organized contraband trade in which luxury goods such as liquor and fine silks were brought into England from France by well-organized groups. The smuggling groups were often organized by men of status within the local community in the counties of Kent and Cornwall; they developed fairly sophisticated methods of concealment to outsmart the customs and excise officers; and individual members had well defined roles and responsibilities.[1]

If smuggling of contraband has long been one of the staples of transnational crime, another has been trafficking in women. Ironically, the white slave trade of the nineteenth and early twentieth century generally involved the kidnapping and trafficking of European women who were taken to a variety of destinations in the Middle East and Asia. At the end of the twentieth century, the trafficking patterns tend to go from developing states and states in transition to the post-industrialized states. Nevertheless, the elements of degradation and exploitation remain the same – and the scale of trafficking in women has increased significantly.

Acknowledging the antecedents for contemporary transnational crime, however is not to ignore the very real increases in the phenomenon in the 1980s and the 1990s. What is new is not transnational crime as such but its scale and diversity: the range of activities pursued by criminal organizations has broadened significantly while the enterprises engaged in such activities have become more diverse. These developments have been accompanied by a marked expansion in both illicit markets and informal economies. With the revival of very familiar forms of crime, such as maritime piracy, and the development of relatively new forms of criminal enterprise, such as highly organized software piracy, transnational criminal enterprises have not only become more pervasive but have also grown in both power and wealth. Just as licit business has become transnational in character, so has much enterprise crime.

The transnational criminal of today tends to be active in several countries, going where the opportunities are high and the risks are low. Moreover, markets for illicit goods and services can encompass national, regional or even the global arena with illicit commodities trafficked across national borders as a matter of course. New opportunities have opened up and they have been grasped eagerly and effectively, leaving law enforcement making valiant but largely unsuccessful efforts to match the inventiveness, adaptability and resilience of the sophisticated criminal organizations they now have to contend with. Although law enforcement agencies have moved towards the internationalization of their activities they still have much to do to respond effectively to criminal organizations that routinely violate national borders and undermine national sovereignty. Cooperation among law enforcement bodies in different countries has improved, but is still hampered by traditional concepts of sovereignty that serve to constrict and constrain national law enforcement agencies. Criminals, in contrast, ignore or transcend borders in the pursuit of profit, while also using variations in national laws, in the effectiveness of criminal justice systems, and in the efficiency and effectiveness of law enforcement bodies to minimize the risk that they will be apprehended or punished. Moving beyond the reach of national law enforcement is a defensive measure that members of criminal organizations often use. In some cases, this brings with it remarkable new opportunities. For example in South Africa there has been considerable controversy over a reputed Mafia member who entered the country in the mid-1980s and seemed to have had the protection of top politicians and law enforcement officials in undercutting efforts to extradite him to Italy. Whether or not the person has been active on behalf of the Mafia is uncertain; it is clear though that he has been able to use South Africa as a safe haven.[2]

It is not an exaggeration, therefore, to suggest that most organized crime at the end of the twentieth and the beginning of the twenty-first century is transnational in scope, while government responses remain predominantly national. Analysts, with a few exceptions, have been even slower in coming to terms with the new realities. Indeed, many studies of organized crime, especially in the USA, have continued to treat it as essentially a domestic problem, often focusing on the local manifestations rather than recognizing that transnational activities have become central to the functioning of many criminal organizations. Some of the major organizations that have emerged have more in common with major transnational corporations than they do with the old style mob. Not all criminal entities have achieved this level of sophistication, of course, and some organized criminal activity still occurs exclusively at the local level. Nevertheless, even much of this activity can be understood as the local retail ends of what have become large transnational markets. 'Think global act local' is as much a part of transnational crime as it is of transnational business.

The starting point for this analysis, therefore, is that organized crime is not what it was. Indeed, the use of the term 'organized crime' is so evocative of the Prohibition era in the USA that it tends to obscure the magnitude of what has become a critical challenge to democratic governance, to transition and modernization processes, and to national security in many parts of the world.

Against this background, this paper seeks to elucidate the concept of transnational organized crime and to explore its major manifestations. It locates transnational organized crime within an environment characterized by interdependence, globalization and a weakening of state authority in many parts of the world. It also suggests, however, that in some illicit markets transnational criminal organizations are only one of several players. The next section attempts to elucidate the critical concepts and offer some clarification for the discussion. This is followed by an analysis of why criminals have gone transnational, with an attempt to discern the answer in both macro and micro levels of analysis. The following section looks at different perspectives on the way transnational crime is organized. It suggests that traditional models of criminal organizations that emphasize hierarchical or pyramidal structures are not particularly appropriate to transnational criminal organizations or transnational markets and argues that the key to understanding transnational criminal organizations and the markets they inhabit is through the concept of criminal networks, which are active in criminal markets that are actually populated by a myriad of other actors. This emerges very clearly in the section examining transnational markets in fauna and flora and in commercial sex. The final section of the paper considers some of the ways in which transnational organized crime might be examined in the future and the particular role that academics can play in helping both to understand and combat the phenomenon.

THE KEY CONCEPTS AND DEFINITIONS

What is Transnational?

The notion of transnational activities has its roots in the discipline of international relations. Much of the important conceptual work on transnational ideas and concepts was done by Robert Keohane, Joseph Nye and Samuel Huntington in the early 1970s. The standard definition was offered by Keohane and Nye. It delineates transnational activity in terms of the movements of information, money, physical objects, people or other tangible or intangible items across state boundaries, when at least one of the actors involved in this movement is non-governmental.[3] Understood in these terms it is hardly surprising that a good deal of organized criminal activity would become transnational. As Edward Morse has noted, virtually any tangible item involved in such processes is likely to have a significant economic dimension in that it can be treated as a commodity or service to which monetary value can be attached.[4] Since organized crime involves the provision of commodities and services that are illicit, then it is not surprising that we have seen the development of transnational criminal organizations that transfer commodities across national jurisdictions against the wishes of the governments involved.

Transnational Crime

The concept of transnational crime has gradually come to mean 'criminal activities extending into and violating the laws of several countries'.[5] This is different from both international crimes (that is, crimes recognized as such by international law, such as war crimes) and local crimes that can be influenced by factors beyond the boundaries of the affected jurisdiction but are, in effect, limited to one jurisdiction.[6] If there is sometimes uncertainty about the precise categorization of particular criminal activities, however, the most common and distinctive feature of transnational crime is that it involves the crossing of borders or national jurisdictions. Although this might seem a very simple notion, it is more complex than it initially appears since border crossing is effectively multi-dimensional. Indeed, there are five separate components or categories of border-crossing that help make crime transnational:

1. *Perpetrators* – the actual or potential perpetrators of crime who cross borders in the course of their activities (crossing borders in order to commit acts of violence, for example) or in efforts to evade law enforcement and seek a safe haven. Russian hit men who have engaged in contract killings in several West European countries fit this category.

2. *Products* – either illicit products such as drugs, or licit products that are stolen and smuggled out of the country (cars), or licit products that are taken out of the country in violation of export restrictions (art and antiquities), or licit products that are imported to another country in violation of import restrictions or international embargoes (arms to Yugoslavia). The list here is a long one and includes drugs, arms, nuclear materials, counterfeit goods, intellectual property theft, cars, fauna and flora, and arts and antiquities.

3. *People* – illegal aliens who enter countries (either clandestinely or using false documentation) in violation of immigration restrictions, and women and children who are trafficked across borders to fulfil demand in the global sex trade. In effect, the people in this category are treated as human commodities.

4. *Proceeds* – the profits derived from illicit activity. Criminal enterprises, whether transnational or domestic in scope, are

61

primarily about the pursuit of profit. In many jurisdictions, however, the money obtained through criminal activities such as drug trafficking is subject to seizure and forfeiture. Consequently, this money is often moved through a variety of foreign jurisdictions in order to obfuscate the trail. It often ends up in offshore financial centres or bank secrecy jurisdictions that are not readily amenable to efforts to seize the funds by national authorities in the country in which the initial crimes were committed.

5. *Digital signals* – the transmission of digital signals or what is, in effect, a 'virtual' as opposed to a physical border crossing. These signals can take the form of child pornography, malicious code that is designed to attack or destroy computer and information systems, or electronic bank robberies that move funds illegally from legitimate accounts to a location where they are available to the perpetrators. Because of the global nature of information space, much digital crime is inherently transnational in character.

Another complication stems from the fact that different national jurisdictions criminalize different activities. Nevertheless, a significant number of activities are dealt with in international conventions. These conventions – the most famous of which is probably the UN Convention of 1988 against Illicit Trafficking in Narcotics Drugs and Psychotropic Substances, which covers money laundering and precursor chemicals as well as drugs themselves – represent both a shared understanding among states that certain activities need to be regulated, prohibited or criminalized. As well as reflecting this common understanding, international conventions can also be understood as norms, aspirations and guidelines that all states should adhere to. In reality, of course, not all states are signatories to international conventions dealing with transnational crimes. Furthermore, even when they do formally adhere to a particular convention, implementation of its injunctions is not always as full and effective as might be desired. In connection with this analysis, however, the critical point is that conventions reveal or highlight areas where there is a convergence of view among states on certain criminal activities. The United Nations has also moved towards the adoption of a convention on transnational organized crime. This will help to bring a greater semblance of order to the notion of transnational crimes. At the same time, there are areas of transnational criminal activity where conventions – or even national laws – are not yet in place. The digital realm is perhaps the most important and is an area where many national jurisdictions are running to catch up with the explosion of both licit and illicit activities associated with the Internet and the World Wide Web.

Whatever the precise crime, however, it is clear that not all transnational crime is organized crime. Some transnational crimes are acts of individuals; others are illicit actions (for example, the dumping of toxic waste) engaged in by businesses that are otherwise engaged in legitimate commercial activities. Yet others, however, are committed by organizations (and these can take various forms and be of various sizes) that exist specifically for the pursuit of profit through illicit activity. The focus of attention here is on this last category.

Transnational Organizations and Transnational Criminal Organizations

In a seminal essay in the early 1970s, Samuel Huntington carefully delineated the major characteristics of transnational organizations. He suggested that such organizations carry out centrally directed operations in the territory of two or more nation states, mobilize resources and pursue optimizing strategies across national boundaries, are functionally specific, and seek not the acquisition of new territories but their penetration.[7] These characteristics apply equally well to transnational criminal organizations. Yet there are also crucial ways in which criminal enterprises differ from most other transnational organizations (apart from terrorists) that work within the legal framework imposed by national governments. Huntington, for example, noted that

> in most instances a transnational organization can conduct its operations only with the approval of the government claiming sovereignty over the territory in which it wishes to operate. Consequently, the transnational organization and the national government have to reach an access agreement defining the conditions under which the operations of the former will be permitted on the territory of the latter.[8]

Transnational criminal organizations do not accord neatly with these generalizations: access is achieved not through consent but through circumvention. Furthermore, criminal organizations usually function effectively not through bargaining about an access agreement but through systematic activities designed to evade government efforts to control or halt their illicit activities. In some cases, they take major initiatives to corrupt governments, trying to achieve a form of systemic or 'institutionalized corruption' that, in effect, allows them to operate on or through national territory with impunity. While this could be interpreted as striking an illicit or under-the-table bargain with the state authorities, it certainly does not fit the normal type of bargains or access agreements as understood by Huntington. Furthermore, in some instances, criminal organizations obviate the need for such bargains by dealing not with the licit power structure but with the illicit. Colombian drug trafficking organizations in the late 1980s and early 1990s forged a very effective alliance with Sicilian criminal organizations that was instrumental in opening up the European market for Colombian cocaine. It allowed the use of existing drug distribution routes in Europe, and was effectively a strategic alliance that allowed the Colombian trafficking organizations to diversify into a new market at a time when the US cocaine market had become saturated.

In yet other cases there is no need for transnational criminal organizations to reach agreement with state authorities as many states lack the capacity to interfere, to any significant degree, with criminal activities, whether their territory is being used as a source of supply of illicit commodities, for transhipment or for distribution to customers. This is particularly true for developing states, and states in transition, where law enforcement and criminal justice capabilities are poorly developed, border control is minimal to nonexistent, and weapons, drugs, stolen cars, arms, artefacts, and fauna and flora are trafficked and sold without hindrance.

It is clear from all this that transnational activity is as open to criminal groups as to any other group. Indeed, in some respects, the character of criminal organizations makes them particularly well placed to exploit the new opportunities for transnational activity. Since such groups tend to operate outside the rules, norms and laws of domestic jurisdictions, they are likely to have few qualms about crossing national jurisdictions. While some licit organizations also operate outside the rules – and BCCI provides a perfect example – these organizations are not usually created in order to do this. Indeed, BCCI started with noble motives as a bank for the developing world. It was not set up as a transnational criminal enterprise with an explicit agenda of obtaining profits through activities that involved the crossing of national borders. In this sense, and irrespective of whether the focus is on Italian Mafia groups trafficking in arms to the Middle East, Russian criminal groups laundering money through Gibraltar, Antwerp and London and trafficking women to Israel, Colombian drug traffickers seeking new markets in the former Soviet Union, Nigerian fraudsters seeking to entice foreign businessmen with their infamous 4-1-9 schemes, Chinese snakeheads bringing boatloads of illegal immigrants to the USA, or Dutch computer criminals hacking into US computer systems, transnational criminal organizations can be understood as transnational organizations par excellence.

They can also be understood as illicit counterparts to transnational corporations. Parallels between transnational corporations and transnational criminal organizations, of course, are imperfect or incomplete. Certainly transnational criminal organizations lack the formal structure of major transnational corporations Nevertheless, many criminal organizations – like transnational corporations – have a home base in one country and operate across national borders in one or more host states. The home base generally provides a low risk environment as the state is either weak, acquiescent, corrupt or collusive. Conducting operations from this safe home base, they seek to meet demands for one or more illicit products, smuggling goods to host states where there is a market for their products. Some groups provide a single product. Colombian criminal organizations, for example, restrict their commodities to drugs (although some have diversified into heroin as well as cocaine) whereas other criminal organizations traffic in a wide range of products. Whatever, the product range, however, organizations that move products from their home state to host or market states, often use one or more transhipment states, which are generally characterized by ease of transit and ready access to the final destination.[9]

From the perspective of criminal organizations, there is also a fourth category of states – those that offer assistance in moving, laundering and protecting the proceeds of criminal activities. Offshore financial centres and bank secrecy havens are important service states for criminal activities. While some of these jurisdictions will cooperate with foreign law enforcement, they generally place a high premium on secrecy and, in some cases, it is actually a criminal offence for a bank official to disclose any information about the bank's clients. Not only do these service states welcome money with little regard to its origins, but bank officials and accountants are often helpful in devising schemes that make it extremely difficult for investigators to catch the money even when they are successful in following the money trail. In some cases, they will set up 'walking accounts' in which any inquiries about an account immediately lead to the transfer of the money within the account to another jurisdiction.

WHY CRIMINAL ORGANIZATIONS BECOME TRANSNATIONAL

To understand why criminal enterprises move from operations at the domestic level to engaging in transnational activity, it is necessary to explore both the macro-level (where such developments can be seen in part as a response to interdependence and globalization), and the micro-level where it is necessary to identify the specific calculations that an individual criminal enterprise might make – intuitively or explicitly – before embarking on transnational ventures.

The Macro-Level: Globalization and the New Environment

There has been widespread discussion of the positive consequences of interdependence and globalization, and the emergence of transnational organizations that embody a new and very attractive form of 'global citizenship'. Just as globalization has facilitated the emergence of transnational forms of licit business, it has also facilitated the rise of illicit business and the criminal enterprises that engage in illicit activities. Transnational crime is the dark side of interdependence and globalization. Not all global citizens have a sense of citizenship, responsibility and obligation; some are ruthless, exploiting new opportunities to enrich themselves through any means available. In this connection, it should be noted in passing that the discipline of international relations has long witnessed a dispute about the importance of economic interdependence and the rise of non-state actors. Liberal institutionalists have long emphasized that economic linkages are very positive, and that transnational actors for the most part have a positive and integrative effect on international politics. The argument here is the opposite, suggesting that there is another side to globalization that needs to be considered. Criminal organizations represent a more malevolent kind of transnational actor, but one that is as deeply entrenched as any non-governmental organization. Where transnational criminal organizations accord with the interdependence and globalization theorists, however, is in the challenge they pose to the state. If sovereignty was at bay from transnational corporations, it is under siege from transnational criminal organizations. In this connection, James Rosenau has argued that although non-state actors lack the attributes of sovereignty this is often an advantage rather than a constraint – they are sovereignty free rather than sovereignty bound. They are important not because of 'their legal status, capabilities or sovereignty' but because of their 'capacity to initiate and sustain actions that are outside the bounds of state activity, and that challenge the traditional dominance of states'.[10] Many of these sovereignty free organizations have managed to 'obfuscate, even elude, the jurisdiction' either of a single state or of the state system as a whole.[11] This has become even easier as a result of globalization and the political, economic, social and technological developments that are often encapsulated under this rubric.

The vast increase in international trade in the second half of the twentieth century, the information and communications revolutions and the development of a truly global financial system have all provided conditions facilitating the growth of business, whether licit or illicit. The business sections in bookstores are full with titles emphasizing the new global imperative, the requirements for competing effectively in a global marketplace, the importance of strategic alliances as a way of neutralizing competitors and entering new markets, the utility of offshore financial centres for minimizing taxation responsibilities, the potential of investments in emerging markets. The injunctions are as relevant to illicit businesses as they are to licit and the opportunities as easily exploitable by those with dirty money as by those with legitimate capital. Indeed, as far as the facilitation of transnational organized crime is concerned, globalization is important for several reasons:

- The globalization of trade, technology, transportation, communications, information and financial systems provides new opportunities for criminal enterprises to operate across national borders. The free trade system has made it easy to embed illicit products in the vast amount of imports and exports that now characterizes international trade. Indeed, illicit trade often develops a parasitic relationship with licit trade, as is evident from the growing number of seizures of drugs (and more recently illegal aliens) being transported in inter-modal containers.
- One of the characteristics of globalization has been significant

population movements driven by a mix of push and pull factors that range from ethnic conflict and environmental degradation to the desire for economic betterment. The increase in migration and the growth of ethnic networks that transcend a whole range of national borders has proved valuable to the operations of criminal organizations. While it is clear that most immigrants are law-abiding citizens and are, in fact, more likely to be the victims rather than the perpetrators of crimes, it is also clear that Colombians in the USA, Turks and Kurds in Western Europe and Nigerians dispersed throughout Southeast Asia, Western Europe and the USA, have greatly facilitated the creation of network structures for the supply of illicit goods and other forms of organized crime. Ethnic communities can be understood as an important resource for transnational criminal enterprises. They provide recruitment opportunities, cover and support. Recruitment based on ethnic loyalties is particularly easy when the immigrant groups have not been fully integrated into their adopted society. As one analyst observed: 'Many immigrant groups have been totally marginalized in Europe, some live in cultural ghettos. They readily provide some of the personnel for international organized crime'.[12] The low status and poor conditions of many Turkish immigrants in Western Europe, for example, means that the rewards offered by Turkish criminal organizations for assistance in smuggling heroin from Southwest Asia into Western Europe, are very attractive. Even casual participation or involvement on the margins can yield greater rewards than can be obtained through the licit economy. At the same time, many immigrant communities, such as Chinese and Pakistanis, are not only very resourceful but also engage in a wide range of commercial and trading activities that can provide excellent cover for illicit activities. Such groups are also very difficult to penetrate. The barriers of language and culture provide integrated defence mechanisms that are strengthened by ties of kinship and inherent suspicion of authority. Just as transnational corporations have their local subsidiaries, transnational criminal organizations have their ethnically based criminal groups within immigrant communities.

- The global financial system is increasingly based on digital or 'megabyte money' that can be moved rapidly and anonymously and can be traded, exchanged and cleaned or legitimized via a whole array of financial instruments, such as derivatives and futures.[13] The global financial system has multiple points of access and, once in the system, money can be moved with speed and ease and with a minimum of interference from regulators. Following the money across multiple jurisdictions is a complex and costly task for law enforcement and, even if criminal money is identified, obtaining it from offshore financial centres and bank secrecy havens is a formidable task at best. In many respects, the contemporary global financial system has become a money launderer's dream and a nightmare for law enforcement. In one case in the Netherlands, the proceeds of criminal activity were laundered in 45 seconds while the subsequent investigation took 18 months.[14]

If the growth of transnational organized crime can be seen as a natural concomitant of a globalized and interdependent world, not all criminal organizations have a capacity or desire to exploit the new opportunities. Some, for whatever reason, remain localized in their operation. It is important, therefore, to look at why some criminal organizations decide to go transnational and thereby exploit the various opportunities provided by globalization.

The Micro-Level: Specific Incentives to go Transnational

While globalization provides opportunities for transnational criminal organizations, it does not explain why particular organizations move into certain product markets or are active in specific national jurisdictions beyond their home state. To understand this, it is essential to move to the micro-level and examine the situation as perceived by criminal organizations themselves. Among the factors they are likely to regard as important are the following:

- *Attractive markets or sources.* One reason why some criminal enterprises engage in transnational activities is that they are attracted to host countries where there is significant demand for the products and services they supply. In other instances, a host country might be a significant source of products that can be stolen and trafficked to meet a burgeoning market elsewhere. In the USA, for example, there are many criminal organizations involved in supplying illicit drugs to a large body of consumers. At the same time, American cars and sport utilities vehicles are stolen for markets elsewhere. In some instances, the same organizations that are involved in bringing drugs or illegal aliens into the country are also responsible for the theft and trafficking of cars to Latin America and other destinations. In other words, although some states more obviously provide more lucrative markets than do others, the flows of illicit products are not all in the same direction. Women from the Newly Independent States, for example, are trafficked to Western Europe where they are in high demand, while luxury cars stolen in West European countries are trafficked to the east where there is also a high demand.

- *Differential profits.* The most attractive markets, of course, are not only those in which there is large scale consumer demand but also those in which prices – and profit levels – are high. Differential profits in different national markets provide incentives for criminal organizations to penetrate these markets. Drugs are not unique in the mark-up or value added as they move through the chain from producer country to the consumers – what is distinctive is simply the extent of the mark-up. In some cases, of course, the problem is not illicit products, but licit products that have large variations in prices from one market to another – often because of taxation policies. In cases where there are significant variations in prices of products, such as cigarettes, and where there is a common and highly permeable border, then either new criminal enterprises will emerge to meet the demand for cross-border trafficking – as happened with Indian involvement with cigarette smuggling on the USA-Canada border – or existing criminal groups will diversify into this area.

- *Differential regulations and laws.* Elsewhere in this work, Nikos Passas uses the term 'criminogenic asymmetries' to describe differences among states that encourage transnational criminal activity.[15] One of these differences concerns national regulations. Where regulations are relatively lax or poorly implemented in critical sectors such as finance and banking, this is an invitation for criminal organizations to move into the state and exploit the lacuna.

- *Differential risks.* Another consideration is the differential abilities of states to impose risks. It bears emphasis that the distinctiveness of illicit business lies not in the profit side – all enterprises seek to maximize profits – but in the risks transnational criminal organizations face from law enforcement and government. Risks, of course, are pervasive in business. The way licit businesses guard against risk is through insurance arrangements. Historically insurance was developed to cover such traders as the Venetians, the

Dutch and the British when those traders were outside the jurisdiction of political authorities capable of providing both protection and arbitration in the event of disputes. Yet this highlights an important difference between licit and illicit business. For licit business it was the weakness or inadequacy of the state that led to the development of insurance; in contrast, if the state is weak or inadequate then this is generally beneficial to criminal organizations. Extending this further, transnational criminal organizations differ from most transnational corporations primarily in the particular kinds of risk they confront. All businesses have to deal with the risks posed by competition, by government interventions in the market, by changing consumer tastes and so on. The risks facing criminal organizations, however, are distinctive: they stem from the illicit nature of their activities, the fact that neither they nor their rivals are bound by rules, norms and regulations in the way that licit corporations are, and the fact that they operate within an industry in which violence is an integral means to resolve interorganizational disputes. Perhaps most important of all however, these risks result from the activities of governments that are attempting to put TCOs out of business. Whereas licit corporations have to deal with competitors and with government regulations, transnational criminal organizations have to deal with an enemy – law enforcement authorities – whose major purpose is to disrupt and ultimately destroy them. A large part of their criminal activities, therefore, can be understood as an attempt to neutralize or circumvent law enforcement, thereby reducing risks to the business. Indeed, there is a constant dialectic between illicit business and law enforcement that does much to shape the character of transnational criminal organizations and to determine in which specific jurisdictions they operate.[16] This is not to imply that transnational criminal groups will avoid high-risk states. If such states also provide attractive and lucrative markets, then they will also become host states. The criminal organizations will engage in illicit activities within them while trying to contain or minimize the risks by continuing to operate primarily from a low-risk jurisdiction.

To take advantage of global opportunities and criminogenic asymmetries, criminals have to organize their activities in ways that reduce transaction costs, prevent, contain or mitigate the risks they face from law enforcement, and ensure an effective supply of illicit products (or licit products acquired and moved across borders illegally). The next section of this paper looks at the issue of how transnational criminal organizations are structured to best achieve these goals.

THE STRUCTURE OF TRANSNATIONAL CRIMINAL ORGANIZATIONS

One of the key issues in the analysis of organized crime has long been the question of just how organized it really is. On this issue there are two contrasting paradigms. The first equates organized crime with the traditional Mafia model. The major components are a clear-cut hierarchy, well-defined role specialization within the hierarchy, the exercise of control, authority and initiative from the top downwards, the attempt to establish monopoly control over illicit markets, the use of violence and the use of corruption. This traditional paradigm of organized crime is most obviously associated with Donald Cressey.[17] At the opposite extreme is the market paradigm – perhaps best exemplified in the work of Peter Reuter and R. Thomas Naylor – which suggests that most organized crime is in fact disorganized and that illicit markets operate like any other market with a mixture of organizations supplying goods and services to the consumers.[18] A concomitant of this is that criminals are organized primarily for governance rather than for entrepreneurial activity. It has also been contended by Naylor that criminal entrepreneurs seek market share rather than monopoly control, and that notions of them as large powerful organizations that challenge governments and threaten national security are gross exaggerations.[19]

In the area of transnational crime, Naylor has been particularly critical of Claire Sterling and her allegations that there is a global conspiracy of crime, a 'Pax Mafiosi' composed of major criminal conglomerates increasingly working in alliance with one another.[20] It is hard to disagree with his critique. At the same time it should be emphasized that Sterling's approach – like that of Cressey at the national level – actually underestimates the challenge by over-simplifying it. If the problem of organized crime was simply a national or global conspiracy, it would actually be easier to deal with. The reality is not only more messy but also more unsettling and less susceptible to simple solutions. Large, fixed monolithic, strictly hierarchical, structures are relatively easy targets. They are vulnerable to decapitation and other forms of dismantling. In contrast, the multiplicity of organizations and the fact that many have looser, less formal network structures makes them highly resistant to decapitation efforts and actually more difficult to contain. The problem was neatly encapsulated by a British customs officer who commented that a smuggling organization is like a 'plate of spaghetti. Every piece seems to touch every other, but you are never sure where it all leads. Once in a while we arrest someone we are sure is important. Well he may have been up to that moment, but once we get him, he suddenly becomes no more than a tiny cog. Someone else important pops up in his place.'[21]

This suggests that there might be a third paradigm for understanding transnational organized crime – cantered around the networks that organize the supply of illicit goods and services, the theft and trafficking of licit goods, and the unrestricted trafficking of restricted commodities.[22] To argue this is not to dismiss the parallels between transnational criminal organizations and transnational corporations but to underline them. In fact, transnational corporations themselves have increasingly moved towards looser, more fluid network structures and away from the very centralized approaches that initially characterized their operations. Their structures have become more malleable and less hierarchical in response to the need to understand and exploit local conditions. If this has led to more dynamic management and greater flexibility and responsiveness, it is also an area where transnational criminal enterprises have been ahead of their licit counterparts. Illegality has compelled them to operate in covert fashion and to focus less on fixed structures and sunk costs than on flexible and adaptable organizational structures and on forms of functional cooperation among groups with complementary skills.

Unfortunately, there is still a tendency in law enforcement circles and among some academic analysts to treat centralized hierarchies as synonymous with organized crime and to treat networks as disorganized crime. This is a mistake. A network is, in fact, a highly sophisticated organizational form. David Ronfeldt of the RAND Corporation has argued that society has gone through a long evolutionary process that has been dominated successively by tribes, hierarchies and markets. In each case, the new form of organization did not replace the previous one but surpassed it in terms of effectiveness and efficiency. Ronfeldt argues that society is now in a fourth stage in which networks are emerging as the predominant organizational form and one that has significant advantages especially over more traditional bureaucratic hierarchies.[23]

A network can be understood very simply as a series of nodes that, in one way or another, are connected together. The nodes can be individuals, organizations, firms or even computers, but the critical point is that there are significant linkages among them. Networks vary in size, shape, membership, cohesion and purpose. Networks can be large or small, local or global, domestic or transnational, cohesive or diffuse, centrally directed or highly decentralized, purposeful or directionless. A specific network can be narrowly and tightly focused on one goal or broadly oriented towards many goals; and it can be either exclusive or encompassing in its membership. Networks are at once pervasive and intangible, ubiquitous and invisible, everywhere and nowhere. Less prosaically, they facilitate flows of information, knowledge and communication as well as more tangible commodities. They operate in the licit sectors of the economy and society as well as the illicit. This enormous variability makes the network concept an elusive one while, on a practical level, it also makes networks very difficult to combat.

Networks provide a means to achieve a variety of goals. In effect, they are neutral regarding the nature of the goals and can be used for positive or negative purposes. One of their strengths, however, is the capacity to flow around physical barriers and across legal or geographical boundaries. Networks, in effect, transcend borders and are the perfect means of conducting business in a globalizing world.

While not all network organizations are transnational in scope or ambition, there is a natural congruence between transnational or cross-border activities and network structures, irrespective of whether the networks operate exclusively in the legitimate sector or in supplying illicit (prohibited or stolen) goods and services. In this connection, the capacity of individual criminals or groups in one country to extend their network through linkages with their counterparts in other countries gives organized crime and drug trafficking a transnational character that makes it much more difficult to combat.

Criminal networks are very efficient and effective at forging cooperative links with one another. Indeed, there are occasional reports of summit meetings between organized crime bosses of various national groups. Such reports, however, suggest a formality to the linkages that is not warranted. They also suggest that national criminal organizations are far more monolithic than is really the case. In actuality, some leaders of some criminal organizations from some nations meet with other leaders of other criminal organizations from other nations. To dignify these meetings as summits is to over-inflate their importance. Arguing this, however, is not to deny the importance of linkages among various criminal networks. In one sense, these linkages or alliances are simply a means of overcoming limitations and coopting potential competitors. Marketing and distribution, for example, are much easier where local knowledge and experience are available. This explains, in part, why Colombian drug trafficking organizations established a cooperative alliance with the Sicilian Mafia. This facilitated the entry of major Colombian drug trafficking enterprises into the European drugs market – something that without such an alliance had been enormously difficult.[24] While this particular alliance seems to involve long-term patterns of cooperation – and can therefore be described as a strategic alliance (or even a joint venture) – other forms of cooperation and collaboration are less ambitious. They include tactical alliances or alliances of convenience that are essentially short-term, service or contract relationships (in which one criminal enterprise works on a contract basis fulfilling specific functions for another enterprise) and supplier relationships that encompass several transactions to one-off spot sales.[25] If one thinks of criminal networks as highly fluid, constantly moving entities, then the less ambitious arrangements fit the model very well.

Conversely, more ambitious cooperative relationships among criminal organizations can be difficult to sustain. In some cases, cooperation can have significant costs for one of the participants. Colombian drug trafficking organizations, for example, initiated a whole series of cooperative ventures with their Mexican counterparts to smuggle cocaine into the USA. Increasingly the Mexicans were paid in cocaine and used this to become the dominant force in the US cocaine market west of the Mississippi. Although the Colombians continue to cooperate with Mexican organizations, this proved a double-edged sword and one that lost them significant market share. In effect they created a competitor. Something similar happened in Europe where Turkish drug traffickers used Albanian networks to help transport heroin through the dangerous Balkans route, and then found that the Albanians were going into business for themselves and pushing the Turks out of certain markets. In the case of the Colombians, they have responded to the Mexican challenge in several ways. Colombian drug trafficking networks have focused once again on trafficking drugs through Florida and the Caribbean, rather than across the southwest border, and have also consolidated their connections with Dominican networks that do much of the trafficking in the eastern USA. In the final analysis, therefore, it is clear that networks can respond rapidly to opportunities and threats, to both the challenge of competition and the benefits of cooperation.

Networks also cross easily from the illicit sector to the licit sector. The connections between the underworld and members of the upper world provide important support for criminal enterprises involved in various illicit activities. Such enterprises extend their network to include lawyers, doctors, bankers and other financial professionals who help them both to conceal and to invest their profits. Criminal networks can readily extend their reach, coopting individuals and organizations in ways that facilitate, enhance or protect their activities. On occasion they will simply recruit individuals in powerful positions or with powerful connections. In other cases the organized crime–corruption networks are more institutional in character and the exchange relationships within them more formalized. A long-standing example of such a network was the linkage between the Mafia and the Christian Democratic Party in southern Italy. Here the benefits for the Party included Mafia assistance in mobilizing the vote while, for its part, the Mafia received political protection and support that made Italy a low-risk environment within which and from which to conduct a wide range of criminal activities.

Cooption can be achieved through corruption and bribery on the one hand, coercion and intimidation on the other, or indeed through some mixture of both. In this connection, an interesting feature of corruption networks is that they are dynamic rather than static and increase in importance and value over time. A network link between a low-level criminal and a junior official will become much more significant as the criminal becomes more powerful and the official becomes more senior. In these circumstances, the exchange relationship between them becomes much more substantial in terms of the favours done by the official and the payoffs provided by the criminal. The official is not part of the criminal enterprise *per se*, but he is a vital node in the criminal network As such, he provides important services to the network including critical and timely intelligence about government and law enforcement activities. Indeed, if enough people in important government positions are corrupted and coopted in this way then the network can almost certainly count on a high degree of protection against vigorous enforcement efforts.

Ironically, although both organized crime and corruption have been subject to extensive and systematic analysis, the link between the two phenomena and the importance of corruption networks in facilitating criminal activities have been given scant attention. Yet, in countries such as Mexico, Colombia, Nigeria and Russia the linkages between criminals and officials have become one of the most serious impediments to the achievement of democratic governance and the operation of a free market economy. Collusive links also exist at lower levels with law enforcement and customs officials accepting or imposing bribes in return for free passage of various kinds of contraband. Corruption networks, at both the political and the operational levels are as insidious as they are pervasive and make organized crime increasingly difficult to counter.

The contention that criminal enterprises can best be understood as network organizations is nowhere more evident than with Chinese organized crime. Although there is a formal structure embodied in the Triads, Chinese criminal activity is largely carried out through informal networks and specific transactions, rather than formal organizational structures. More often than not these networks are transnational in nature, based as they are on the larger self-reliant communities of overseas Chinese who rely heavily on support from friends, relatives and business associates to provide business capital. Several aspects of these communities serve to support Chinese criminal enterprises. These include *guanxi*, with its sense of reciprocal obligation, the hazy line between legitimate and illegitimate activities, the commingling of licit and illicit business, the Chinese penchant for gambling, and the isolation and self-reliance of Chinese communities that have resulted in the development of a sophisticated if informal system for moving money, known as *fie chien*. The enterprises are characterized by redundancy and resilience because of a very diversified portfolio of criminal activities.

To emphasize that much organized crime is network based, is not to suggest that it is undirected. The most effective criminal networks have a core that provides the steering mechanism, establishes the basic purpose of the network, puts together the major functional role specializations and sets up other key network components. Trust is critical to the functioning of the network and is based on or achieved through a variety of bonding mechanisms including ethnicity, family and kinship, common experiences (such as prison time) – or in the Chinese case discussed above, *guanxi*. At the same time, the networks have peripheries where trust, as such, is less important. The capacity to extend networks into the licit sector and coopt those who could otherwise inhibit the operation of illicit markets is critical to the functioning of these markets. Indeed, one way of understanding these markets is in terms of networks of intermediaries that link the supplier and the customer. This emerges even more clearly in the next section.

THE OPERATION AND STRUCTURE OF ILLICIT MARKETS

There are many black markets that are transnational in scope. Among the more important items that are trafficked across national borders are illicit drugs, nuclear materials, light armaments, fauna and flora, women and children for the global sex trade, and stolen art and antiquities. The analysis here, however, focuses on only two of these – fauna and flora and women.

In recent years the black market in fauna and flora has received considerable attention, largely because of widespread acknowledgement of the importance of bio-diversity and a concomitant recognition that certain species of animals and plants are in danger of extinction. These concerns are enshrined in the Convention on International Trade in Endangered Species of Wild Flora and Fauna (CITES). In spite of CITES, however, there are large and flourishing black markets in rare species ranging from Siberian tigers to Thai orchids. The demand side of this trade stems from collectors who want to own rare animals, breeders who want them for profit, those who want to use particular animal parts in herbal medicines or aphrodisiacs, and those who want to use parts such as skins or ivory tusks for various forms of ornamentation. As with many other illicit markets, it is the demand from these customers that provides much of the impetus for the illegal trade and that encourages suppliers into the market.

The scale of this trade is enormous. Interpol figures suggest that in the USA trafficking of animals is worth US$1.2 billion a year in some 90,000 unauthorized shipments, while the global trade is estimated to be worth around US$5 billion annually.[26] The supply chains for animals and animal products start with villagers and hunters, but also involve transnational criminal networks. It has been claimed that Asian criminal organizations are significant participants in trade in rhinoceros horns and tiger parts while in Europe the Neapolitan Camorra is deeply involved in trafficking of animals.[27] Not surprisingly the price paid for these products increases significantly as they near the consumer. The initial suppliers obtain very little of the profits. Among those involved in the illicit market are:

- Hunters, trappers or poachers who kill or capture the animals.
- Criminal organizations that are involved in the trafficking and are probably the most important single group of intermediaries in facilitating passage from the initial suppliers to the final consumers.
- Corrupt customs officers and officials who connive at the trade in return for payoffs.
- Retail Chinese medicinal outlets that sell products containing animal parts that are believed to have healing powers or to act as aphrodisiacs.
- Artisans who carve ivory for decorative jewellery or art objects.
- Unscrupulous pet stores or dealers who are willing to sell rare species of bird or animal to collectors or breeders.
- Customers who care only about possessing or consuming the final product and have no qualms about the source of supply or the impact of their purchases.

What emerges from even this very brief survey is that criminal organizations are an integral part of the illicit market, but that they are certainly not the only players and that other participants are also very important.[28] Much the same is true of trafficking in humans. Control of prostitution is perhaps the world's second oldest profession. It is also a profession that has expanded considerably and taken on new dimensions with the development of a wide range of trafficking networks that tend to bring women from east to west and south to north. Among the reasons for the growth in the trafficking of women have been the ease and speed of travel, the breakdown of barriers between east and west, a market that has become much more cosmopolitan and customers who are enticed by the exotic elements provided by foreign prostitutes.[29] Foreign women are also more vulnerable than their domestic counterparts and easier to control for the pimps and criminal organizations that profit from their activities. Against this background, a USA-based non-governmental organization, the Global Survival Network (GSN), used undercover tactics to investigate the women trafficking business. The GSN report concluded that criminal organizations both inside Russia and elsewhere play a critical role in the trafficking business and are either directly or indirectly involved in transporting the women. In some cases, trafficking organizations simply make pay-offs to organized crime groups; in others the criminal organizations are more directly involved.[30] The report also noted that corruption in government and law enforcement is important in facilitating trafficking, citing examples of where this has occurred. From this and other reports, it appears that the main participants in this illicit market are:

- Women who through force of economic or personal circumstances decide that travel abroad to work as a dancer, maid or, in some cases, a prostitute is better than living in current conditions. Some of these are trafficked voluntarily but are then coerced into prostitution.
- Women who are tricked into going abroad for work or romance and who then find themselves in a position of servitude and used for commercial sex.
- Women who are coerced and/or forced into travelling abroad for prostitution. Such cases are involuntary at every stage. In some cases the women go and stay because of threats to their families.
- Brokers and agencies who recruit the women, often using false promises.
- Criminal organizations that either engage in the trafficking directly or facilitate the trafficking for the agencies and entrepreneurs involved.
- Corrupt officials who assist in provision of passports, visas, work permits and any other documentation that is required.
- Brothel owners and criminal groups who pay the suppliers and initially put the women to work.
- 'Guards' who help to ensure that the women do not try to escape and inflict punishment in the event of an attempt. These can range from the men who provide muscle for organized crime to Nigerian 'mamas' who are often associated with forms of witchcraft and exercise psychological rather than physical control.
- Additional brothel owners to whom women are sold as part of a constant process of turnover.
- Corrupt policemen and officials who take payoffs for turning a blind eye to the sex trade in their jurisdiction.

In short, trafficking in women generally goes through a variety of stages and is facilitated not only by criminal networks and entrepreneurs who provide most of the organization, but also by the connivance, corruption and collusion of authorities in source and destination countries.

It is clear from both these examples that illicit markets tend to be populated by a complex mix of actors with transnational criminal organizations playing a large but not exclusive role. In the case of prostitution of both women and children, for example, criminal groups control a significant portion of the business and are instrumental in maintaining supply. Yet, supply would be more problematic were it not for the collusion of villagers willing to sell their children. Furthermore, the business would not be nearly so profitable without the connivance of segments of the tourist industry to provide sex tours to countries such as Thailand. Similar connivance can be found in the art and antiquities business, both with customers who care about particular acquisitions but not about their legality, and with dealers and auction houses that do not always exercise 'due diligence' about provenance. The essential point about these markets, however, is that criminal enterprises are at the core of the supplier networks. These networks are then extended along functional lines to include all the other components necessary to ensure that the trafficking process works smoothly.

Two other points about markets and networks are worth adding. The first is that many illicit markets are now global in scope. If most of them involve trafficking of illicit products from the developing world or states in transition to the developed world, there are exceptions to this. The most important of these exceptions are armaments and stolen cars. Luxury motor vehicles in particular go from the countries of Western Europe to states in transition in Eastern Europe and the former Soviet Union and to developing states in Africa, from the USA to Central and South America and the Middle East, and from South Africa to its northern neighbours. This is an interesting reversal of the direction of most illicit flows.

The second point is that once a trafficking infrastructure is in place, the product line is virtually irrelevant. In several cases of nuclear material trafficking through Turkey, for example, those involved included individuals who had previously been arrested for trafficking in antiquities.[31] This should not be surprising. Whatever the product, the problems of circumventing customs and law enforcement agencies are more or less the same. This is done through imaginative modes of concealment or circuitous routes that facilitate the avoidance of most checkpoints. But it can also be done through corruption, which is not only a major problem in its own right but also one of the most important concomitants of most trafficking activities. At the same time various trafficking activities have spawned lucrative cottage industries or service industries especially in forging of documents, end user certificates and the like. These have become indispensable to the functioning of illicit markets and have become critical parts of the networks that dominate these markets.

THE ROLE OF ACADEMIC ANALYSIS

It is not the intention here to provide a comprehensive analysis of what can be done to respond to the challenge posed by transnational organized crime. The following paragraphs are merely intended to offer a few observations on what academics can do to enhance understanding and to enrich the policy debate. In this connection, an unfortunate distinction is often made between practical approaches followed by law enforcement and theoretical analysis. A sharp dichotomy of this kind, however, is unwarranted. There are several things that theoretic approaches can bring to practical law enforcement efforts: detached and more comprehensive analysis that goes well beyond specific cases; a certain heuristic value; a strategic perspective that is often lacking in law enforcement; an assessment of future trends in the structure of criminal organizations, their location, strategies and activities; and insights from comparative analysis that highlight the significance of the cultural aspects of criminal organizations and activities. The discussion here, however, focuses on two main areas: the importance of strategic analysis in combating transnational crime and the role of academics in collecting and disseminating certain kinds of information.

Strategic Analysis and its Implications

If it is accepted, as argued above, that the key to understanding transnational organized crime is the role played by networks, there are several theoretical and practical implications. Perhaps the most important is the need to identify the vulnerability of criminal networks and to consider how their activities can best be disrupted. It might be possible, for example, to identify critical nodes in the network that, if removed, could seriously inhibit its functioning.[32] Such nodes might have particularly significant connections, while others might embody critical functions. The essential requirement for them to be deemed critical, however, is that they are not easily substituted or replaced. In a similar vein, one of the most important dimensions of criminal networks concern the points at which they connect with the licit world often through corruption.[33] At the practical level, therefore, law enforcement efforts could be directed towards the removal of these critical nodes and licit-illicit connections and away from the product seizures that currently still dominate much of the activity directed against transnational crime.

Another area where analysis could be important is in developing a strategic approach.[34] Transnational criminal networks are in adversarial relationships with governments such as that of the USA (even as they are colluding with other governments) and it is important to recognize that governments can influence their behaviour and their calculations. To do this, however, requires comprehensive strategies that encompass prevention control and mitigation measures. The US government has gradually, moved, towards this, as was evident in President Clinton's International Crime Control Strategy. Yet more could be done in this direction using insights from other areas such as business and military strategy. Target hardening, for example, is usually seen as a military concept, yet could be applied in very interesting ways to financial institutions and to industries that are vulnerable to infiltration by organized crime. Similarly, the kind of SWOT (strengths, weaknesses, opportunities, threats) analysis that is done in many businesses could be combined with a 'red-team' approach to understand rather better the way criminal enterprises view their environment. Understanding a complex set of adversaries is the key to influencing, disrupting, or destroying them. To fully achieve this level of understanding, however, it is necessary to use a multi-disciplinary approach combining insights from international relations, criminology, anthropology, economics and business, and political science.

In this connection it is also necessary to think through the implications of successful strategies against particular targets. Law enforcement successes range from the arrest and incarceration of key individuals to the disruption or dismantling of a major organization. For example, with a mixture of pressure and assistance from the USA the Colombian government succeeded in turning back the threat posed to democratic governance by powerful drug organizations that seemed to have become a law unto themselves and virtually a 'state within a state'. The Medellín and Cali drug trafficking organizations have been significantly weakened. Yet the cocaine industry continues to flourish. Moreover, although the industry in Colombia has been 'flattened', Mexican drug trafficking organizations have emerged as major players in their own right, both exploiting and exacerbating the extensive corruption and culture of *mordida* that have long been hallmarks of Mexican political and economic life. In other words, even successful measures against criminal organizations tend either to increase the rapidity of promotion within organizations or encourage a form of organizational succession. Short-term success can have adverse long-term consequences, leaving law enforcement facing a more diverse, less familiar and in some respects more intractable set of adversaries. A strategic perspective, therefore, needs to incorporate a long-term perspective that goes beyond the immediate target of law enforcement activities.

Data Collection, Monitoring and Early Warning

Academics are also well placed to expand efforts in the area of reliable and uniform data collection. More sophisticated methodologies need to be devised and greater use made of the information available in the private sector. Bodies such as the International Anti-Counterfeiting Coalition and the Software Publishers Association have been in the forefront of efforts to obtain data on the scale of the problem facing licit business from activities such as software piracy and counterfeiting of goods, while ECPAT (End Child Prostitution in Asian Tourism) and the Global Survival Network have helped to illuminate the scope of trafficking in women and children. At the same time, there should not be an overly rigid preoccupation with numbers. Transnational organized crime is not like domestic crime where trends in murder or burglary rates can be highly revealing. In the area of nuclear material smuggling, for example, the number of incidents matters far less than the quality of the material that is being trafficked and, in particular, whether or not it is weapons-grade or simply radioactive garbage.[35] Insofar as measurement is deemed necessary, the focus should be on estimates of commodity flows, albeit with a profound recognition that these are inherently imperfect. The more important endeavour should be to anticipate developments. Transnational crime and transnational organized crime are areas where an intelligence approach is far more appropriate than statistics. In this connection, a possible role for

84

academics is to establish monitoring and early warning systems based on open sources. These could focus on the kinds of organizations, markets and networks discussed above. Particular emphasis would need to be given to dynamic aspects of the criminal world such as the possible redistribution of criminal activity from one region to another (perhaps because the opportunities are greater and the risks are lower), the efforts by criminal networks to coopt political and economic elites, the development of new illicit market niches or the supply of new products and services, and the development of cooperative relationships among criminal organizations that provide multiplier benefits. In addition, attention should be given to identifying anomalies that might reveal new directions or developments and offer opportunities for proactive initiatives by governments.

Such a monitoring and early warning system based on open sources would be an ambitious undertaking, but is feasible given increasingly effective search technology, smart search agents and the growing amount of information available in digital databases. It is also something that is perhaps better done outside than inside government as there are fewer restrictions on the focus, fewer vested interests and more opportunities to identify anomalies or trends that are inconsistent with government expectations. The results of this could also be disseminated. The monitoring and early warning center could act as a clearing house to disseminate information to academics, professionals and law enforcement analysts – who, in turn, could be encouraged to provide items to the monitoring database. The result would be a gradual emergence of an analytical network of scholars and law enforcement professionals that would help to illuminate the future development of criminal networks and thereby provide a better basis from which to attack transnational organized crime.

NOTES

1. See David Phillipson, *Smuggling: A History 1700-1970* (Newton Abbot: David and Charles, 1973).
2. De Wet Potgieter, *Contraband: South Africa and the International Trade in Ivory and Rhino Horn* (Cape Town: Queillerie, 1995), p.160.
3. Robert O. Keohane and Joseph S. Nye Jr (eds.), *Transnational Relations and World Politics.* (Cambridge, MA, Harvard University Press, 1972).
4. Edward Morse, in ibid.
5. Quoted in Gerhard O.W. Mueller, 'Transnational Crime; An Experience in Uncertainties', in S. Einstein and M. Amir, *Organized Crime: Uncertainties and Dilemmas* (Chicago: Office of Criminal Justice International, University of Illinois at Chicago,

1999) pp.3–18, quote on p.3.

6. Ibid.

7. See Samuel Huntington, 'Transnational Organizations in World Politics', *World Politics*, Vol.25, No.3 (April 1973), pp.333–68.

8. Ibid., p.355.

9. See Richard Friman, 'Just Passing Through: Transit States and the Dynamics of Illicit Transshipment', *Transnational Organized Crime*, Vol.1, No.1 (Spring 1995), pp.65–83; Shona Morrison, 'The Dynamics of Illicit Drugs Shipments and Potential Transit Points for Australia', *Transnational Organized Crime*, Vol.3, No.1 (Spring 1997), pp.1–22.

10. James Rosenau, *Turbulence in World Politics* (Princeton, NJ: Princeton University Press, 1989), p.253.

11. Ibid., p.251.

12. Frank Bovenkerk, 'Crime and the Multi-ethnic Society: A View from Europe', *Crime, Law and Social Change*, Vol.19 (1993), pp.271–80, at p.279.

13. This is a major theme in Joel Kurtzman, *The Death of Money* (New York: Simon and Schuster, 1993).

14. This is based on an interview with a Dutch law enforcement officer.

15. For example, in his presentation at the International American Society of Criminology. Panel at the American Society of Criminology 49th Annual Meeting, San Diego, 19–22 November 1997.

16. The author is grateful to Ernesto Savona for his insights on the importance of risk for criminal organizations.

17. Donald Cressey, *Theft of the Nation* (New York: Harper and Row, 1969).

18. Peter Reuter, *The Organization of Illegal Markets: An Economic Analysis* (Washington DC: National Institute of Justice, 1985); and R. Thomas Naylor, 'From Cold War to Crime War: The Search for a New National Security Threat', *Transnational Organized Crime*, Vol.1, No.4 (Winter 1995), pp.37–56.

19. See Naylor, ibid.

20. See ibid. for the critique. For Claire Sterling's argument see *Thieves' World* (New York: Simon and Schuster, 1994).

21. Timothy Green, *The Smugglers* (New York: Walker, 1969), p.9.

22. For a fuller analysis see Phil Williams, 'The Nature of Drug Trafficking Networks', *Current History* (April 1998), pp.154–59. The analysis here draws on this article.

23. David Ronfeldt, *Tribes, Institutions, Markets, Networks: A Framework About Societal Evolution* (Santa Monica, CA: RAND P-7967, 1996).

24. For an excellent analysis see Patrick Clawson and Rensselaer Lee, *The Andean Cocaine Industry* (New York: St. Martin's Press, 1996), Chapter 3.

25. The analysis here builds on my earlier analysis, 'Transnational Criminal Organizations: Strategic Alliances', in Brad Roberts (ed.), *Order and Disorder after the Cold War* (Cambridge, MA: MIT Press, 1995), pp.235–50.

26. Inter Press Service, 21 July 1995.

27. Deutsche Presse-Agentur, 17 November 1994.

28. For an important glimpse into aspects of this market see De Wet Potgieter, op. cit., and Christopher Dishman, 'ATrafficking in Fauna and Flora', *Transnational Organized Crime* (forthcoming).

29. The argument here draws heavily on the author's introduction and the subsequent selections in 'Special Focus: Trafficking in Women and Children', *Trends in Organized Crime*, Vol.3, No.4 (Summer 1998), pp.3–66.

30. See Gillian Caldwell, Steven Galster and Nadia Steinzor, *Crime and Servitude: an Exposé of the Traffic in Women for Prostitution from the Newly Independent States* (Washington DC: Global Survival Network, 1997) excerpts from which can be found in ibid.

31. See Phil Williams and Paul Woessner, 'Nuclear Material Trafficking: An Interim Assessment', *Transnational Organized Crime*, Vol.1, No.2 (Summer 1995), pp.206–39 at p.220.

32. For a stimulating and helpful discussion of networks and the associated conceptual and theoretical issues see M.K. Sparrow, 'The Application of Network Analysis to Criminal Intelligence: An Assessment of the Prospects', *Social Networks*, Vol.13, No.3 (Fall 1991), pp.251–74; and M.K. Sparrow, 'Network Vulnerabilities and Strategic Intelligence in Law Enforcement', *International Journal of Intelligence and Counterintelligence*, Vol.5, No.3 (Fall, 1991).
33. There is surprisingly little work specifically linking organized crime and corruption. For an important exception to this see Margaret E. Beare, 'Corruption and Organized Crime: Lessons from History', *Crime, Law and Social Change*, Vol.28 (1997), pp.155–72.
34. This is discussed more fully by Roy Godson and Phil Williams elsewhere in this work.
35. For an excellent analysis of this problem see Rensselaer W. Lee III, *Smuggling Armageddon* (New York: St Martin's Press, 1998).

Criminal Fraternities or Criminal Enterprises?

LETIZIA PAOLI

This paper focuses on those lasting large-scale criminal organizations, such as the Italian Cosa Nostra and 'Ndrangheta, the American La Cosa Nostra, the Chinese Triads and the Japanese Yakuza, that are usually presented as the archetypes of organized crime. Indeed, though many scholars have long denied their existence,[1] most non-experts think of these organizations when they hear the term 'organized crime'.

This mental operation, the paper argues, is justified if the term 'organized crime' is used to refer to a set of criminal organizations.[2] In much of the current scientific and political debate, however, organized crime is nowadays equated with the provision of illegal goods and services. According to Block and Chambliss, for example, 'organized crime [should] be defined as (or perhaps better limited to) those illegal activities involving the management and coordination of racketeering and vice'.[3] Organized crime has thus become a synonym of illegal enterprise. According to a review of definitions carried out by Frank Hagan in the early 1980s, a consensus now exists among American criminologists that organized crime involves a continuing enterprise operating in a rational fashion and focused toward obtaining profits through illegal activities.[4]

If this second definition of organized crime is accepted, the above entities, which may be collectively termed as 'mafia associations', are no longer adequate as a model.[5] As the following sections show, the associations that are thought to be prototypical of organized crime are neither exclusively involved in illegal market activities, nor is their development and internal configuration the result of illegal market dynamics.

NEITHER FIRMS ...

Although their members are heavily involved in illegal businesses today,

88

neither the development nor the internal organization of mafia associations are the product of illegal markets dynamics. Indeed, all of the above-mentioned associations arose before the consolidation of modern illegal markets. With the exception of the American La Cosa Nostra, which grew out its Sicilian counterpart at the beginning of the twentieth century, all the above-mentioned associations are more than 100 years old. The Sicilian and Calabrian mafia sodalities date back to the middle of the nineteenth century.[6] The Heaven and Earth Society (*Tiandihui*), the Chinese 'secret society' out of which modern Triads[7] derive, was founded around 1760.[8] Finally, the ancestors of the modern Yakuza groups – that is, the itinerant bands of Japanese roadside gamblers (known as *bakuto*) and peddlers (*tekiya*) – are known to have been active since the early eighteenth century.[9]

Furthermore, throughout their existence, all the above-mentioned associations have carried out a plurality of functions, most of which are not related to the provision of illegal goods and services. Although the enhancement of the members' interests through mutual aid seems to have been the major 'official goal' of mafia-type associations ever since their founding, this general aim has been interpreted and applied by the affiliates in many different ways over the decades; that is, it has been translated into a plurality of 'operative goals'.[10]

The ends have been so different and often in open contradiction with one another that it is very difficult to select a single, typifying one. Sometimes mafia associations' members have responded to the effective needs of their communities, but more frequently they have denied them, imposing their dominion against the people's will. They have occasionally provided 'protection' to somebody requesting their services, but they have also established at times a veritable extortion regime, protecting 'clients' from their own mafia threats. Often they have fostered the interests of the higher social classes, gathering votes for their representatives; from time to time, however, they have defended the interests of the poorer people. They have usually supported the *status quo*, but sometimes they – most notably the Chinese Triads – have also fought for revolutionary aims.[11] They have been involved in a variety of economic activities. Although monopolizing practices have been carried out by most of these groups since their founding, the resources targeted have changed according to the stages of economic development in society at large. Even as far as illegal markets are concerned, the type of commodities and the extent of their involvement have undergone sudden and consistent changes, depending on the trends of the international illegal economy and the groups' capability to position themselves on the new routes.

The flexibility and ability of mafia organizations to adapt to changing economic and political conditions can be fully taken into account only by considering mafia consortia as functionally diffused organizations. They are the result of a centuries-old process of social construction during which they have been used by their members to achieve a plurality of goals and to accomplish a variety of functions. As Dian Murray puts it, the members of the first Chinese secret societies 'originally organized for one purpose sometimes found themselves mobilized for different ends, and simultaneously involved in activities where the distinctions between "legal" and "illegal", "protection" and "predation", or "orthodox" and "heterodox" blurred'.[12] Only by sacrificing empirical evidence is it possible to single out an encompassing function or goal that can characterize criminal organizations of a mafia type throughout their life.

Among them, even more than economic activities, political functions have always had a key relevance and it is to Diego Gambetta's merit that he brought attention to this dimension that had long been neglected in the scientific discourse on the mafia and organized crime. According to Gambetta, in fact, the Sicilian mafia is 'a specific economic enterprise, an industry that produces, promotes and sells private protection'.[13] The provision of protection is one of the most important functions historically played by mafia groups, a quintessential one, we could say, since it derives from their exercise of violence in areas of settlement. Gambetta's analysis is rather to be criticized for his one-sided emphasis on protection and his denial of the polyvalence of mafia groups. It is, furthermore, regrettable that for polemical reasons Gambetta overshadows the analogies between the mafia, as he defines it, and the state.[14] Such a similarity was instead outlined by Charles Tilly: 'if protection rackets represent organized crime at its smoothest, then war making and state making – quintessential protection rackets with the advantage of legitimacy – qualify as our largest examples of organized crime'.[15]

Although not employed on every occasion, ultimately violence constitutes the backbone of mafia power. Violence is used foremost by all the consortia under examination to secure the obedience of their own adherents and to punish those who have betrayed or not respected the group's authority. It is also routinely employed as a means to threaten, render inoffensive or even physically eliminate whoever endangers the power positions and the business activities of the group. Through the menace or the effective use of violence, mafia associations have also been trying – enjoying for a long time a fairly high degree of success – to impose their rules on society at large in their territory of influence. To employ Weberian terminology, we can say that, although they arise as a 'voluntary association (*Verein*)', – that is, an organization that claims authority only over voluntary members – they also frequently act as a 'compulsory organization (*Anstalt*)' – that is, a social group whose legal order is imposed with relative success on the outside.[16]

As such, criminal organizations of mafia type can be defined as political organizations in the Weberian meaning, that is, organizations that guarantee the subsistence and the validity of their own legal order within a given territorial area through the threat and the use of physical force.[17] Each *cosca* associated with either Cosa Nostra or the 'Ndrangheta, for example, claims sovereignty over a well-defined territory that usually corresponds to a village or to the district of a city. As the Sicilian mafia turncoat Leonardo Messina explained to the Italian Parliamentary Commission on Mafia Phenomenon:

> You must keep in mind that the families have their own businesses and that these concern everything related to the territory of the families themselves. For example, if in the community of Rome there were a family, everything that belongs to the community would interest it, whether politics, public works, extortions, drug traffickings, et cetera. In practice, the family is sovereign, it controls everything that happens on that territory.[18]

In every town and village of Western Sicily and Southern Calabria, almost all companies and firms regularly pay a 'protection' tax or *una tantum* – in money or in kind – to mafia families.[19] Although the amount of information available is much more scarce, a variety of sources indicate that even in Chinese communities, in Europe as well as in Asia and the USA, large parts of the population are victims of extortive mechanisms run by members of the Triads and other local criminal groups.[20]

Today we are used to thinking that government and business have always existed as separate organizations. Nonetheless, until after the beginning of the modern period neither governments nor business enterprises had the forms familiar to us. As Joseph Schumpeter pointed out, our terms 'state' and 'private' enterprise can hardly be applied to the institutions of feudalism without eliciting a distorted view of those institutions.[21] Under feudalism, in fact, the state was in a certain sense the private property of a prince, just as the fief was the private property of a vassal. While fulfilling political functions, such as the provision of internal order and protection against external enemies and the administration of justice, the feudal vassals were also expected to raise a profit from the management of the fief as a reward for defending the contract and returning the services provided by the feudal contract. As the historian Frederick Lane puts it,

> In a modern context, it may be shocking to consider government as a profit-seeking enterprise. But in the feudal system a fief holder was expected to manage his fief with an eye to profit. The successful baron might disdain bourgeois haggling over merchandise, but he was an expert in using military and governmental means of making money.[22]

The separation of force-using enterprises from the profit-seeking enterprises that we now call business firms took place at different times in different areas of Europe and in the rest of the world. In the case of mafia-type organizations, such a process of differentiation has even nowadays taken place only to a minimal extent. The latter, in fact, emerged in contexts where this separation had not yet been fully achieved and where the use of violent means was almost an unavoidable pre-condition of social ascent and have been impeded by state institutions from taking part in the wider process of differentiation because of their criminalization.

Not only the use of violence distinguishes mafia associations from modern firms, but also their internal organization and *modus operandi* are completely different. Mafia organizations are not specialized in any specific set of products to which a brand name can be attached. Second, none of the associations discussed here usually take part in illegal markets as a single collective unit. Every unit composing the Cosa Nostra, the 'Ndrangheta or the Yakuza, in fact, enjoys full autonomy in planning and carrying out economic ventures.

Even the affiliates of the single families usually enjoy a wide degree of autonomy and are free to undertake whatever type of economic enterprise they deem profitable in cooperation with other members as well as non-members.[23] The lower ranking members of Yakuza groups, for example, are expected to earn their living themselves and run autonomous economic enterprises exploiting the 'face', that is, the prestige of their *gumi* (family). Even though they must always be ready to provide their workforce in whatever economic or non-economic ventures the *oyabun* – the bosses – may decide to set up, their primary task is to earn money on their own and pass their bosses a quota of their profits.[24]

Likewise, in Hong Kong and other Chinese communities, members of local Triads are usually free to organize economic ventures, both on the legal and illegal side of the law and to enter into cooperative agreements with both members of other Triads as well as non-members as long as they provide a percentage of their earnings to their society of affiliation.[25] Finally, considerable entrepreneurial autonomy is also granted to the affiliates of the Sicilian and Calabrian mafia associations.[26]

... NOR BUREAUCRACIES

Despite the high degree of autonomy granted to members in the economic sphere, it still makes sense to consider the Cosa Nostra and the other groups as unitary organizations. Contrary to Donald Cressey's hypotheses, however, in none of the above-mentioned organizations does a single, all-encompassing bureaucracy exist. In fact, although they are usually portrayed by the media as centralized organizations, all of the associations discussed here are nothing more than consortia. The Calabrian 'Ndrangheta, for example, is actually made up of about 90 mafia families. An analogous number of groups make up the Sicilian Cosa Nostra, whereas the number of American Cosa Nostra families is usually considered to be 24.[27] The number of Yakuza groups exceeds 3,000 and, although no precise numbers are known, several different Triads are known to be active in Asia, America and Australia.

These consortia constitute segmentary societies. This is an organizational model often employed by anthropologists who, since the times of Henry Maine, have been confronted with the existence of a wide range of organizations that not only lacked stable leadership, but also official leaders. In segmentary societies lacking central political organs, societal boundaries coincide with the maximum range of structurally homologous units and it is upon their articulation that the social order depends.[28] Likewise, in mafia consortia each unit retains full autonomy and societal boundaries are drawn merely by the common cultural heritage and structural organization. They are founded on what Emile Durkheim called 'mechanical solidarity', that is, a solidarity 'derived from likeness, since the society is formed of similar segments and these in their turn enclose only homogenous elements'.[29]

In several cases, a process of centralization has been built upon these segmented structures. Among the families associated with the American and Sicilian Cosa Nostra and, more recently, among those belonging to the Calabrian 'Ndrangheta, this process of centralization has led to the institutionalization of superordinate bodies of coordination.[30] In Japan, three syndicates – the Yamaguchi-gumi, Sumiyoshi-rengo and Inagawa-kai – have succeeded in incorporating two-thirds of the 3,490 Yakuza groups recorded by the police.[31] The trend, however, is not univocal. There are no signs of a centralization process going on in the heterogeneous universe of Chinese organized crime. Furthermore, even when superordinate bodies of coordination exist, their competencies are rather limited. Usually their rationale lies in the need to minimize the visibility of criminal associations through the regulation of the internal use of violence. In fact, by prohibiting affiliates and single groups from indiscriminately using violence to settle conflicts within the mafia universe, the secrecy and safety of the whole coalition is protected. The control exercised by these superordinate bodies over economic activities is usually very low and a large degree of autonomy is left to the single corporate units.[32]

RITUAL KINSHIP TIES

Far from resembling a modern business firm, all the above-mentioned associations are founded on relations of ritual kinship, which means that they do not bind their members to the respect of a mere purposive contract – as a 'modern' firm or bureaucracy would normally do – but are founded on what Max Weber called 'status contracts'. As opposed to the purposive contracts, the latter 'involve a change in what may be called the total legal situation (the universal position) and the social status of the persons involved';[33] that is, with the entrance into the mafia group, the novice is required to assume a new identity permanently and to subordinate all his previous allegiances to the mafia membership. It is a life-long pact. As Judge Giovanni Falcone pointed out, the admission to Cosa Nostra 'commits a man for all his life. Becoming a member of the mafia is equivalent to being converted to a religion. You never stop being a priest; nor being a *mafioso*.'[34] In the Japanese Yakuza and, to a lesser extent, even in the Calabrian 'Ndrangheta and the Chinese Triads, such a life-long commitment is expressed with tattoos.[35] The affiliates to the Yakuza, in particular, often have their whole torso and thighs tattooed through a slow and painful process that might take a year to complete.[36]

Like most status contracts, the contract used by mafia organizations is also a contract of fraternization, by which novices are bound to become brothers of the other group members and to share a regime of 'generalized reciprocity' with them. The latter presupposes an altruistic attitude and behaviour without expecting any short-term reward.[37] The members of a mafia family have the obligation of helping each other materially and financially when requested or in case of need and unfailingly to stick to principles of sincerity and correctness in their mutual interaction, while the expectation of reciprocity, though asserted, is left undefined. As the *Procuratore del Re* Lestingi observed more than 100 years ago, the 'essential character of the mafia' lies in 'its aid without limits and without measure, and even in crimes'.[38]

The kin-like relation is established through ritual. The entrance into all the associations considered, in fact, takes place with a ceremony of affiliation, which constitutes a true 'rite of passage'. The ritual marks the change of position of those who undergo them and their assumption of the new status of member of a brotherhood. The main steps of the ceremony of initiation staged by the Cosa Nostra are, for example, the following: the candidate or, more usually, the candidates are presented in front of the entire family by the 'men of honour' responsible for their training and for assessing their criminal reliability. After the head of the family has explained the main rules of the Cosa Nostra to them, each novice is asked to choose a godfather among those present who then makes a small cut on the index finger of the novice's right hand so that some blood drops on the image of a saint. Finally, the neophyte swears an oath of faithfulness to the mafia organization with this picture burning in his hands.[39] Much more complex is, instead, the initiation rituals staged by the Triads from the nineteenth century onwards: during the initiation ceremony, the new members complete a mystical journey, recreating the passion of the five founder-members of the fraternity, swear 36 oaths and then drink a mixture of wine and blood.[40]

Interestingly, some elements of high symbolic relevance are employed by all associations. All of them, for example, make extensive reference to the iconography and terminology of the religion dominant in their context. In the ceremony staged by the Chinese *hui*, religious symbols are in evidence, whether Taoist or Buddhist.[41] In the 'Ndrangheta, the ceremony itself is called 'baptism',[42] while in both Southern Italian associations the crucial moment of the ritual – that is, the swearing of the oath – takes place with the burning image of a saint in one's hands. In all contexts, furthermore, blood is used. The symbolic meaning of these elements is evident: religious references aim to give a sacral valence to the ritual and, thus, reinforce its imperativeness, while blood presents a strong multivocality. In fact, blood refers to a process of rebirth to which the candidate is called, implies a sort of 'natural' kinship to which all the members belong and points to the ultimate punishment that may be granted in case of betrayal. 'One goes in and comes out of the Cosa Nostra with blood', the Mafia informant Antonino Calderone was told at the moment of his affiliation. '... You will see for yourselves, in a little while, how one enters with blood. And if you leave, you'll leave with blood because you'll be killed.'[43]

The kin-like relations created with the rite of initiation are then further reinforced with symbols and codes drawn from the kinship language. The basic units of the Sicilian and American Cosa Nostra are thus called families. Although mafia groups clearly distinguish themselves from the blood families of their associates to the point that no women are allowed, the term evokes and, at the same time, prescribes the cohesion and solidarity of blood ties.[44] In Japan the relationship between a Yakuza chief (*oyabun*) and his novice (*kobun*), which is the pillar of the whole association, is portrayed as the relationship between a father and a son.[45]

Relying on fictive kinship ties, mafia organizations enjoy a flexibility that has no parallel among contemporary business firms whose employment contracts are usually close to the ideal type of purposive contract. Founded on status contracts, mafia groups can be exploited in the pursuit of any short-term gain decided upon by their leaders. The subordinates, in a regime of generalized reciprocity, are not given a choice on whether or not to execute superiors' orders. Unlike purposive contracts, in fact, the contract binding them to a sodality of mafia type is long-term and non-specific. It does not contain a detailed list of services, beyond which the underwriter has no obligation. Indeed the contract is so comprehensive that the members are expected not only to deny family and friendship bonds but even to sacrifice their own life if the group requests it. Thus, even today, the reliance on status contracts strengthens the multi-purpose nature of mafia associations described above.

In exchange, individual members benefit from the collective action and the reputation of the group. The prestige of the associations is foremost exploited by affiliates in the pursuit of their licit and illicit businesses. Furthermore, when the management of some types of illicit activities (frequently racketeering and, sometimes, drug smuggling) is centralized, the proceeds are divided by the head of the family among the associates. In most 'Ndrangheta families, as well as in some Sicilian mafia groups, this practice is fully institutionalized to the extent that, each month, the heads of the families pay regular salaries to all the members of the *cosca*. All associations, furthermore, have a common account that is used to cope with exceptional financial needs of the affiliates, to meet their legal expenses in case of trial, to support the families of the imprisoned or dead members and, occasionally, to integrate the monthly salaries.

Thus, as is true of other pre-modern 'ritualized relationships',[46] the mafia appears to be characterized by 'a peculiar and distinct type of combination of instrumental and solidarity relationship, in which the solidarity provides the basic framework, yet within this framework various instrumental considerations, albeit very diffusely defined, are of paramount importance'.[47] In other words, mafia organizations represent a combination of specific exchange with what is termed in anthropological literature as 'generalized exchange'. This last expression, coined by Marcel Mauss in his essay 'Sur le don' and later elaborated by Claude Levi-Strauss, is nowadays employed to distinguish the non-utilitarian and unconditional relationships necessary to establish conditions of basic trust and solidarity in society and to uphold what Emile Durkheim called the 'pre-contractual elements of social life'.[48]

Membership in a mafia group is, hence, typified by a crisscrossing of instrumentality and solidarity, of personal selfishness and unconditional involvement. Whoever fails to take into account both sides of this relationship also fails to understand its deeper meaning as well as its strength.

KINSHIP, SECRECY, AND VIOLENCE: THE CLAN

The reliance on ritual kinship should not be regarded as an oddity of the associations under consideration. Indeed, although fraternalism has so far been a rather neglected theme of sociological reflection, it was one of the most widely available and persistently used forms of social organization in European, American and Asiatic history, at least from the Middle Ages onwards.[49] As Clawson points out, 'in societies where kinship remained the primary basis of solidary relations, fraternal association was effective because it used quasi-kin relations to extend bonds of loyalty and obligation beyond the family, to incorporate people into kin networks, or to create new relations having some of the force of kinship'.[50] Guilds, journeymen's societies, religious confraternities and village youth brotherhoods were founded on the social metaphor of brotherhood. Fictive kin relations, such as god-parenthood, also played a central role in late medieval and early modern Europe.

Fraternalism is not a peculiarity of the Western world. The relationship at the core of the Yakuza groups – the *oyabun–kobun* system – has been a pillar of the Japanese society at least since the eighteenth century, and only the modernization process undergone by Japan in the last 50 years has somehow reduced the relevance of this institution.[51] Likewise, several scholars of Chinese history have stressed a continuum linking secret societies to brotherhoods and the practice of blood oaths that have been widespread in Chinese society since the seventeenth century. Indeed, the Tiandihui[52] is only the most successful and longest lasting of a large number of fraternal associations (*hui* in Chinese), which had to resort to secrecy following the Qing state's decision in the early eighteenth century to outlaw and severely punish a wide variety of organizational practices associated with brotherhoods.

In mafia-type associations, ties of ritual kinship are reinforced by secrecy. The empirical degree with which each association has shielded itself from public view depends, in each historical context, on the attitude of the local state authorities and surrounding community. In Japan, for example, the overall level of secrecy enforced by Yakuza groups was rather low up until few years ago. Before 1991, when a law finally banned the *boryokudan* (the violent ones), most of the 3,500 Yakuza groups known to police forces were officially recorded organizations. They were listed in the phone book and had formal seats, whose entrances were usually decorated with their emblem and a signboard with their name.[53] Chinese Triads and Southern Italian mafia associations, instead, had been obliged to resort to secrecy much earlier in order to escape repressive measures from state authorities.[54]

A minimum pledge to secrecy, however, seems to have characterized all the associations discussed here throughout their history. All of them at least call on their affiliates to keep the rituals and the oaths they undergo secret and not to reveal the affairs of the group to non-members. The reason for such a pledge is that secrecy is a powerful bond to strengthen group cohesion. By defining its external boundaries through secrecy, in fact, the group poses itself as a 'living totality', a whole, enclosed, self-sufficient world in opposition to the larger one that contains it. Complete independence from external control is postulated: the group puts itself forward as a total and totalitarian institution.[55] The claim that the secret group exercises upon its members also becomes total.

Through contracts of fraternization reinforced by secrecy, each group associated with a mafia-type consortium aims to represent what Durkheim called a clan: that is, an organization that has 'a mixed nature, at once familial and political. It is a family in the sense that all the members who compose it are considered as kin of one another':[56] although many bonds are consanguineous, however, it also includes non-kin. The clan is, at the same time, 'the fundamental political unity: the heads of clan are the only social authorities'. As in simple societies, mafia groups claim to be the only world for their members and their chiefs demand to exercise absolute authority on the affiliates and on all the matters of their lives. The absoluteness of such a claim was clearly seen by the Prosecutors of the Procura della Repubblica di Palermo:

> From the moment of his 'combinazione' [that is, the ritual affiliation], the man of honor progressively becomes aware of having lost a meaningful part of his autonomy and individuality; he no longer 'belongs to himself', because he now belongs to Cosa Nostra, he is an integrating part of a system that organizes his life.[57]

THE ADVANTAGES FOR ILLEGAL MARKETS

The clannish structure of mafia organizations has turned out to be a major advantage when they enter illegal markets. Owing to the lack of a public power, in fact, the latter have no 'systemic trust'.[58] This type of trust, in fact, depends on the existence of laws and a public apparatus capable of enforcing them, the creation of which is closely linked to the development of national states. In the illegal arena, instead, as much as in traditional societies, trust necessarily has only a personal basis. For these reasons, long-term relationships between illegal entrepreneurs as well as stable criminal partnerships prove to be easier to establish and to maintain among people already bound by blood ties, by membership to a brotherhood or by a common ethnic, religious or political background.

By imposing, in an authoritative manner, a new identity on the affiliates, the ceremony of initiation and the apparatus of legitimation developed by all the associations involved strongly reduce the chances of betrayals and double-crossings. The relationships of trust and solidarity, created by ritual kinship ties, favour the pooling of material and human resources for the achievement of common aims, as well as the development of economic transactions even among members who do not know each other personally. Moreover, when socialization processes fail, the ruling bodies developed by each group belonging to these confederations sanction members' violations and are able quickly to mobilize a military apparatus to defend the group and its interests from external threats. Finally, in an environment where the flow of information is heavily constrained, the group's reputation for violence and reliability turns out to be a strategic asset for each single member in the pursuit of his own licit and illicit entrepreneurial activities.

This list of advantages does not imply that mafia associations necessarily retain a monopolistic or oligopolistic position on national and international illegal markets. Granted, in the communities where they are based, the Cosa Nostra and the other criminal fraternities discussed here often directly control a considerable portion of illegal market activities and/or extract protection taxes from the majority of smaller, independent operators. As we have seen, claiming to exercise a territorial sovereignty on those areas, they are frequently able to impose an extensive protection racket on legal enterprises as well.

Outside their own communities, however, the mafia-type associations and their members have no pre-constituted advantage and, as other illegal markets operators, are subject to the rules and trends of economics. Hence, for example, the role of the American La Cosa Nostra families in illegal markets in the USA has been sharply reduced by the rise of a myriad of more risk-prone, inventive entrepreneurs, with better contacts either in the communities of the final consumers or (in the case of drugs) with wholesale distributors.[59] Likewise, as a result of a worldwide concentration process of heroin refining in source countries and the change of world heroin trade routes, the Sicilian Cosa

Nostra families have been increasingly expelled from the profitable stages of heroin refining and import in the USA since the mid-1980s.[60] Even the wholesale positions retained by Cosa Nostra and 'Ndrangheta affiliates in the Italian narcotics markets are currently threatened by the competition of several new criminal entrepreneurs – primarily Turks, Albanians, North Africans and Nigerians – with better contacts in production centres and a higher propensity to use violence.[61] Likewise, at least in the USA, the Triads are today excluded by many profitable businesses, most notably smuggling in drugs and human beings, that are instead run by more flexible, aggressive entrepreneurs.[62]

THE DISADVANTAGES OF KINSHIP

Although particularly effective for coping with the peculiarities of a stateless, illegal environment, the reliance on non-economic ties entails a high price in term of economic efficiency. First, all criminal groups intensively relying on fictive and blood kinship ties face rigid restrictions in recruiting personnel. Notwithstanding a high prolificacy rate, the extension that a blood family can reach is limited. In turn, contracts of fraternization are effective only among people who already share a common background.

As a result, mafia organizations are often unable to internalize the specialized competencies necessary to become involved in the most profitable ventures of the informal and legal sectors of the world economy. Sometimes they are also prevented from entering illegal markets, if the latter constitute only a small appendix of the legal one. For these reasons, Sicilian and Calabrian mafia families were not able to enter the wholesale segments of the international trade in arms and money for many years. Long unable to launder the proceeds of drug trade themselves, in the 1970s and 1980s these groups relied on the services of characters belonging to the sphere of financial crime and in some of these deals – most notably, those with Michele Sindona and Roberto Calvi, ended up losing considerable sums of money.[63] Analogous restrictions are still faced by most mafia associations as far as the markets in information, gold and precious stones are concerned.[64]

Additionally, mafia organizations are also plagued by many internal drawbacks. As mentioned above, they owe much of their strength and flexibility to the moral strength of the community bonds that create these conditions of trust and solidarity on the basis of which it becomes

101

possible to promote the personal interests of the affiliates through mutual support. At the same time, it is precisely in the necessity of maintaining a balance between these two different 'registers', of preventing the prevalence of selfish calculation over group morality, that an element of potential fragility and disorder for mafia consortia lurks. As Eisenstadt and Roniger pointed out, synthesizing the literature on ritualized personal and patron/client relationships, a tension between the emphasis on purely solidary relationships and concrete – power and instrumental – obligations seems to characterize all these types of personal relations.[65] Relationships among the affiliates of a mafia group are also constantly shaken by such tension.

In the daily life of all criminal associations of a mafia type, the prescription of group fraternity and solidarity is weakened if not completely betrayed by the conflicts in interests, the rivalries and the personal ambitions of the members who attempt to exploit the strength of the group's unconditional relationships for the achievement of specific – personal or factious – goals. The precarious equilibrium between generalized and specific exchange is also constantly threatened by the process of institutionalization that necessarily entails the structuring of instrumental and power relations, betraying the values of fraternity and equality that are prescriptively put at the core of mafia relationships.

To these 'permanent' factors of tension, two further ones must be added that have emerged in the last 40 years. First, the growing involvement in economic activities during the post-war period has produced a weakening of the in-group morale in many mafia consortia, stimulating illicit entrepreneurial alliances with non-members and increasing economic deals among the mafia comrades. Moreover, another important factor of disequilibrium springs from the fact that most mafia associations have undergone a process of delegitimation within their own local communities and have lost most of the 'positive' functions they used to carry out. As the language of fraternalism loses its grip on the larger society, mafia associations have had growing problems to make their recruits internalize the fiction – the necessary fiction – implied by the fraternization contract, while the need to increase secrecy within and around the associations leads to the neglect of rituals and the shortening of new members' socialization processes. Among the families associated with the Sicilian Cosa Nostra, such a trend has already had devastating effects, as the exponential growth of mafia turncoats in the early 1990s proves: as of 30 June 1996, more than

430 Justice collaborators came from the ranks of the Sicilian mafia.[66] Even though they have been around for many years, criminal organizations of the mafia type seem to have growing problems in maintaining the fragile equilibrium between the specific and generalized exchange that their success in illegal markets and their very survival depend upon.

CONCLUDING REMARKS

The main conclusions that can be drawn from the analysis of the development and organization of mafia associations can be synthesized in the following statements. Although far from being decisive in the illegal market competition, ritual kinship ties are necessary to build large-scale illegal organizations. To be effective, the ritual brotherhood that is created must, moreover, be ready to use violence to implement its own rules *vis-à-vis* its members and occasionally non-members; that is, it must be perceived as a clan by its members, as a familial and political institution to which all other allegiances are subordinated.

This organizational formula – a mix between ritual kinship and violence – seems to be essential for the survival of large collectivities 'on the wrong side of the law', because all major illegal organizations resort to it. In addition to the mafia organizations that we have just reviewed, in fact, the clannish model of organization is employed by terrorist groups and juvenile gangs.

These collectivities are seldom included in the standard definitions of organized crime because their primary goal is perceived as not being economic. Nonetheless, their internal organization has many similarities with that of mafia associations. Although some juvenile gangs are little more than an informal clique, the longest lasting ones are usually set up on the model of brotherhood, employ ceremonies of initiation that create contracts of fraternization similar to those of mafia groups, and commit their members to mutual aid even in crime.[67] Granted, terrorist groups do not usually express relations among members with the language of kinship. As much as the Cosa Nostra and the other above-mentioned consortia, however, they also require an absolute commitment from their members and complete subordination to the collective interests and goals. Moreover, all these entities set themselves up as juridical and political communities, with their own system of rules and mechanisms, including the use of violence, to enforce them.

Furthermore, although they are founded with ideological or expressive aims, both juvenile gangs and terrorist groups frequently end up being heavily involved in illegal businesses. As Albert Cohen pointed out, 'boys' gangs produce a lot of crime, but crime is typically far from being their *raison d'être*. The central concern of gangs has to do with relational problems and relational reward: status, warmth, security, cohesiveness and the like'.[68] Likewise, terrorist groups frequently commit robberies, impose extortion regimes in their areas of influence and participate in illegal transactions to finance their political struggle.[69]

Numerous examples of this can be given, ranging from the Hell's Angels and the white supremacists groups of North America and northern Europe,[70] which have become increasingly involved in drug trafficking in the last two decades, to the Kurdish Communist Party and the Burmese and Colombian insurgents groups. The *Fuerzas Armadas Revolucionarias de Colombia* (FARC), for example, the largest Colombian guerrilla group, imposes a ten per cent protection tax on most coca producers.[71] The numerous insurgent groups in Northern Burma, on the other hand, have been directly managing poppy cultivation and opium refining since the mid-1960s in order to finance the fight against their political enemies.[72] Because they rely on strong non-economic ties, these collective actors are able to operate in illegal markets in a more organized way than the average illegal enterprises, which cannot rely on such resources.

Although usually overlooked, the similarities between mafia organizations and terrorist groups and juvenile gangs are so many and so deep that they deserve to be systematically investigated. If we define organized crime as a set of criminal organizations, it makes no sense to draw arbitrary lines between those allegedly involved in profit-oriented activities and those that are not. Criminal organizations certainly differ from one another depending on their aims and the emphasis they give them. But, as we have seen in the case of mafia consortia, defining a collectivity only according to their aims can be tricky, because goals change. Although the group's official goal may remain unchanged, new aims usually appear with time. Furthermore, all collective entities are subject to the phenomenon of the 'displacement of goals'. As time goes by, the interest in the survival of the group, irrespective of the content of its activities, tends to exceed the achievement of the group's official aims.[73] Different aims should thus not be regarded as an impediment to comparative analysis, nor can they serve as an excuse to postpone a much-needed systematic reflection on the requirements that collectivities 'on the wrong side of the law' must meet in order to consolidate and last.

NOTES

1. J.L. Albini, *The American Mafia. Genesis of a Legend* (New York: Appleton Century Crofts, 1971); D.C. Smith Jr, *The Mafia Mystique* (New York: Basic Books [1975] 1990); H. Hess, *Mafia and Mafiosi. The Structure of Power* (Westmead: Saxon House [1970] 1973); P. Arlacchi, *Mafia Business. The Mafia Ethic and the Spirit of Capitalism* (Oxford: Oxford University Press [1983, 1986, 1988]).
2. According to Peter Reuter, for instance, 'organized crime consists of organizations that have durability, hierarchy and involvement in a multiplicity of criminal activities ... The Mafia provides the most enduring and significant form of organized crime.' See P. Reuter, *Disorganized Crime. The Economics of the Visible Hand* (Cambridge: MIT Press, 1983), p.175.
3. A. Block, and W.J. Chambliss, *Organizing Crime* (New York and Oxford: Elsevier, 1981), p.13.
4. F. Hagan, 'The Organized Crime Continuum: a Further Specification of a New Conceptual Model', *Criminal Justice Review*, Vol.8 (Spring, 1983) pp.52-7.
5. See L. Paoli, 'The paradoxes of organized crime', unpublished manuscript, and 'Il crimine organizzato in Italia e in Germania', in V. Militello, L. Paoli and J. Arnold (eds.), *Il crimine organizzato come fenomeno internazionale: manifestazioni empiriche, prevenzione e repressione in Italia, Germania e Spagna* (Freiburg: edition iuscrim, 2000).
6. L. Paoli, 'The pledge to secrecy: culture, structure and action of mafia associations', Ph.D. dissertation, European University Institute, Firenze (1997); and *Fratelli di mafia. Cosa Nostra e 'Ndrangheta* (Bologna: Il Mulino, 2000); P. Pezzino, *Una certa reciprocità di favori. Mafia e modernizzazione violenta nella Sicilia postunitaria* (Milan: Angeli, 1990) and ed. 1995, P. Pezzino (ed.) *Mafia: industria della violenza. Scritti e documenti inediti sulla mafia dalle origini ai giorni nostri* (Firenze: La Nuova Italia, 1995); S. Lupo, '"Il tenebroso sodalizio". Un rapporto sulla mafia palermitana di fine Ottocento', *Studi storici*, anno 29, No.2, pp.463-89; and *Storia della mafia dalle origini ai giorni nostri* (Rome: Donzelli, 1993).
7. The term 'Triad' was created by the Britons to represent a symbol employed by *Tiandihui* members to refer to the three main forces of the universe: heaven, earth and man.
8. D. Murray, in cooperation with Q. Baoqi, *The Origins of the Tiandihui. The Chinese Triads in Legend and History* (Stanford: Stanford University Press, 1994).
9. D.E. Kaplan and A. Dubro, *Yakuza: The Explosive Account of Japan's Criminal Underworld* (London: Futura, 1987); and D.H. Stark, 'The Yakuza: Japanese crime incorporated', unpublished Ph.D. dissertation, University of Michigan (1981).
10. C. Perrow, 'The analysis of goals in complex organizations', *American Sociological Review*, Vol.26 (1961), pp.854-66.
11. J. Chesneaux, *Secret Societies in China in the 19th and 20th Century* (London: Heinemann, 1971).
12. Murray, op. cit., p.2.
13. D. Gambetta, *The Sicilian Mafia. The Business of Private Protection* (Cambridge, MA and London: Harvard University Press, 1993), p.1. Gambetta's aim is, in fact, to mark the distance and to criticize sharply what he calls the 'relativist ideology', which is traced back to the theories of the Sicilian jurist Santi Romano. According to Gambetta, such an approach, which claims the possibility of more than one legal system within a society, 'has enjoyed popularity with all kinds of antiliberal circles right, left, and center' and has provided the intellectual justification for the 'peculiar mixture of cynicism and Catholicism which represents the quintessence of Italy's political structure'. See

Gambetta, op. cit., p. 6; and S. Romano, *L'ordinamento giuridico* (Firenze: Sansoni, 1918, 1977).
15. C. Tilly, 'War making and state making as organized crime', in P.B. Evans, D. Rueschemeyer and T. Skocpol (eds.), *Bringing the State Back In* (Cambridge: Cambridge University Press, 1985), pp.169–91, at p.169.
16. M. Weber, G. Roth and C. Wittich (eds.) *Economy and Society* (Berkeley and Los Angeles: University of California Press, [1922] 1978), p.52.
17. Ibid., p.54.
18. Commissione Parlamentare d'inchiesta sul fenomeno della mafia e sulle altre associazioni similari, *Audizione del collaboratore di giustizia Leonardo Messina* (Rome: Camera dei Deputati, XI legislatura, 4 dicembre 1992), p.516.
19. Tribunale di Reggio Calabria, Ufficio del Giudice per le Indagini Preliminari, *Ordinanza di custodia cautelare in carcere nei confronti di Labate Pietro + 17* (7 gennaio 1994).
20. K.-L. Chin, *Chinatown Gangs. Extortion, Enterprise, and Ethnicity* (New York: Oxford University Press, 1996).
21. J.A. Schumpeter, *Capitalism, Socialism and Democracy* (London: Allen & Unwin, 1981), pp.169; 201.
22. F.C. Lane, *Venice and Its History, The Collected Papers of F. C. Lane* (Baltimore: The John Hopkins Press, 1966), p.418; see also G. Poggi, *Lo Stato. Natura, sviluppo e prospettive* (Bologna: Il Mulino [1991] 1992).
23. Only few economic ventures may be prohibited by the organization's normative code, usually on the grounds that they would stain the collective reputation of the group. For example, the Sicilian and American Cosa Nostra and, with less emphasis, the Calabrian 'Ndrangheta strongly forbid their affiliates from organizing prostitution and present this clause as a sign of distinction between them and non-*mafiosi*; See Paoli, *Fratelli di mafia*, op. cit., and *The Pledge to Secrecy*, op. cit., *passim*.
24. D. Seymour, *Yakuza Diary* (New York: Atlantic Press, 1996).
25. US Senate, Permanent Subcommittee on Investigations of the Committee on Governmental Affairs, *Trade in Conventional Weapons: the International Arms Bazaar*, Hearing, 102nd Congress, 1st Session (Washington DC: Government Printing Office, 1991), pp.90, 101; K.-L. Chin, 'Chinese organized crime', unpublished; J. McKenna, 'Organized crime in Hong Kong', *Journal of Contemporary Criminal Justice*, Vol.12, No.4 (1996), pp.316–28.
26. Paoli, *Fratelli di mafia*, op. cit., pp.203–9; and *The Pledge to Secrecy*, op. cit., *passim*.
27. Paoli, *Fratelli di mafia*, op. cit.; and *The Pledge to Secrecy*. op. cit., *passim*; President's Commission on Organized Crime, *The Impact: Organized Crime Today*. Report to the President and the Attorney General (April 1986).
28. M.G. Smith, *Corporations and Society* (London: Duckworth, 1974), p.98.
29. E. Durkheim, *The Division of Labor in Society* (New York: The Free Press, [1893, 1902, 1933] 1964), pp.176–7.
30. D. Cressey, *Theft of the Nation* (New York: Harper and Row, 1969); Tribunale di Palermo, Ufficio Istruzione Processi Penali, *Ordinanza-sentenza di rinvio a giudizio nei confronti di Abbate Giovanni + 706* (novembre 1986); Procura della Repubblica di Reggio Calabria, Direzione Distrettuale Antimafia, *Richiesta di ordini di custodia cautelare in carcere e di contestuale rinvio a giudizio nel procedimento contro Condello Pasquale + 477* (luglio 1995); Paoli, *Fratelli di mafia*, op. cit., pp.62–82; and *The Pledge to Secrecy*, op. cit., *passim*.
31. National Police Agency, *White Paper on Police: Organized Crime Control Today and Its Future Task*, excerpt (Tokyo: National Police Agency, 1989); Japan Embassy in Rome, 'Data provided to the Italian Ministry of the Interior', unpublished typescript (Rome, 1993).
32. Paoli, *Fratelli di mafia*, op. cit., p.62 ff.; and *The Pledge to Secrecy*, op. cit., *passim*.
33. Weber, op. cit., p.672.
34. G. Falcone, in cooperation with Marcelle Padovani, *Cose di Cosa Nostra* (Milan: Rizzoli, 1991), p.97.
35. Paoli, *Fratelli di mafia*, op. cit., p. 98; and *The Pledge to Secrecy*, op. cit., and E. Ciconte, *'Ndrangheta dall'Unità ad oggi* (Bari: Laterza, 1992), pp. 40–2.

36. Seymour, op. cit., pp.25-6.
37. M.D. Sahlins, *Stone Age Economics* (Chicago and New York: Aldine Atherton, 1972), pp.193-200.
38. F. Lestingi, 'L'associazione della Fratellanza nella provincia di Girgenti', *Archivio di Psichiatria, Antropologia Criminale e Scienze Penali*, V (1884), pp. 452-63.
39. Tribunale di Palermo, Ufficio Istruzione Processi Penali, *Ordinanza-sentenza di rinvio a giudizio nei confronti di Abbate Giovanni + 706* (novembre 1986); Falcone, op. cit., pp.91-7.
40. Chesneaux, op. cit.; W.P. Morgan, *Triad Societies in Hong Kong* (Hong Kong: 1960).
41. Chesneaux, op. cit.
42. Tribunale di Milano, Ufficio del Giudice per le Indagini Preliminari, *Ordinanza di custodia cautelare in carcere nei confronti di Abys Adriano + 394* (6 giugno 1994), pp.815, 874; Ciconte, op. cit., pp.32-5.
43. P. Arlacchi, *Men of Dishonor. Inside the Sicilian mafia: An Account of Antonino Calderone* (New York: William Morrow [1992] 1993), p.68.
44. Paoli, *Fratelli di mafia*, op. cit.; and *The Pledge to Secrecy*, op. cit.
45. D.E. Kaplan and A. Dubro, *Yakuza: The Explosive Account of Japan's Criminal Underworld* (London: Futura, 1987); Seymour, op. cit.
46. S.N. Eisenstadt, 'Ritualized personal relations. Blood brotherhood, compadre, etc.: some comparative hypotheses and suggestions', *Man*, Vol.96 (1956), pp.90-5; see also S.N. Eisenstadt and L. Roniger, *Patrons, Clients and Friends. Interpersonal Relations and the Structure of Trust in Society* (Cambridge and London: Cambridge University Press, 1984).
47. Eisenstadt, op. cit., p.91.
48. Eisenstadt and Roniger, op. cit.
49. M.A. Clawson, *Constructing Brotherhood. Class, Gender and Fraternalism* (Princeton: Princeton University Press, 1989); D. Ownby, *Brotherhoods and Secret Societies in Early and Mid-Qing China. The Formation of a Tradition* (Stanford: Stanford University Press, 1996); H. Tegnaeus, *Blood-Brothers. An Ethno-Sociological Study of Blood-Brotherhood with Special Reference to Africa* (New York: Philosophical Library, 1952).
50. Clawson, op. cit., p.15.
51. I. Ishino, 'The Oyabun-Kobun: a Japanese ritual kinship institution', *American Anthropologist*, Vol.55 (1953), pp.695-707.
52. 'Tiandihui' is the original, Chinese name of the association that was later called 'Triad'.
53. Kaplan and Dubro, op. cit.; Seymour, op. cit.
54. Paoli, *Fratelli di mafia*, op. cit.; and L. Paoli, 'The *Pentiti*'s contribution to the conceptualization of the mafia phenomenon', in V. Ruggiero, N. South and I. Taylor (eds.), *The New European Criminology, Crime and Social Order in Europe* (London: Routledge, 1998), pp.264-85; Murray, op. cit.; Ownby, op. cit.
55. E. Goffman, *Asylums* (New York: Anchor Doubleday, 1961).
56. Durkheim, op. cit., p.175.
57. Procura della Repubblica di Palermo, Direzione Distrettuale Antimafia, *Richiesta di applicazione di misure cautelari nei confronti di Abbate Luigi + 87* (23 dicembre 1993), p.189.
58. N. Luhmann, *Trust and Power* (Chichester: Wiley, 1979), pp.68-9.
59. P. Reuter, 'The Decline of the American mafia', *Public Interest* (Summer, 1995), Vol.120, pp.89-99.
60. Paoli, *Fratelli di mafia*, op. cit.; and L. Paoli, 'Droga-Traffici', in Cliomedia (ed.), *Mafia, Enciclopedia elettronica* (Torino: Cliomedia, 1998).
61. L. Paoli, 'The future of Sicilian and Calabrian organized crime', in S. Einstein and M. Amir (eds), *Organized Crime: Uncertainties and Dilemmas* (Chicago: University of Illinois Press, 1999), pp.155-86; and L. Paoli, 'Illegal drug markets in Milan', Report to the European Monitoring Centre on Drugs and Drug Addiction (Freibug 2000).
62. K.-L. Chin, *Chinese Subculture and Criminality* (Westport: Greenwood, 1990).
63. L. Paoli, 'The Banco Ambrosiano case: an investigation into the underestimation of the relations between organized crime and economic crime', *Crime Law and Social Change*, Vol.XXIII, No.4 (1995), pp.345-65.

64. T. Naylor, 'The Underworld of Gold', *Crime, Law and Social Change*, Vol.25 (1996), pp.191–241.
65. Eisenstadt and Roniger, op. cit.
66. Ministero dell'Interno, *Relazione sui programmi di protezione, sulla loro efficacia e sulle modalità generali di applicazione per coloro che collaborano alla giustizia – I semestre 1996* (Rome: Senato della Repubblica, doc. XCI, n. 1, XIII legislatura, 1996).
67. M. Sánchez-Jankowski, *Islands in the Street. Gangs and American Urban Society* (Berkeley: University of California Press, 1991); R.C. Huff (ed.), *Gangs in America* (Newbury Park: Sage, 1990).
68. A. Cohen, 'The concept of criminal organisation', *British Journal of Criminology*, Vol.17, No.2 (1977), pp.97–111.
69. R.T. Naylor, 'The insurgent economy: black market operations of guerrilla organizations', *Crime, Law and Social Change*, Vol.20 (1993), pp.13–51; K. Maguire, 'Fraud, extortion and racketeering. The black economy in Northern Ireland', *Crime, Law and Social Change*, Vol.20 (1993), pp.273–92.
70. K. Cornils and V. Greve, *Rechtliche Initiativen gegen organisierte Kriminalität in Dänemark* (Copenhagen: Univ., Det retsvidenskabelige Institut, 1990s).
71. F.E. Thoumi, *Political Economy and Illegal Drugs in Colombia* (Boulder: Lynne Rienner, 1995).
72. A.W. McCoy, *The Politics of Heroin: CIA Complicity in the Drug Trade* (Brooklyn: Lawrence Hill Books, 1991).
73. R. Michels, *Political Parties. A Sociological Study of the Oligarchical Tendencies of Modern Democracies* (New York: The Free Press, [1915] 1962).

Organized Crime and Ethnic Minorities: Is There a Link?

FRANK BOVENKERK

Every time new signs of organized crime are discovered in modern, urban societies, with striking frequency some ethnic minority – either recent or still unassimilated immigrants or some indigenous minority such as Native Americans in the USA or gypsies in Europe – is singled out as the source of the trouble. In the 1980s, the construction business in French-speaking Belgium was infiltrated by Italian job contractors, and murders committed there were attributed to the Camorra of Naples. In 1996 the trade in black-market cigarettes in Berlin was in the hands of Vietnamese gangsters whose conflicts with each other led to outright gang warfare. In the UK, prostitution for a long time was in the hands of a small group of Maltese. A description of the groups engaged in the Western world's drug trade reads like a list of foreign and local ethnic minorities.[1] They include Colombian and Mexican cartels, the Cuba Connection, Chinese Tongs and Triads, Japanese Yakuza, Vietnamese gangs, Jamaican Posses, as well as Indian and Iranian groups. Ever since the drug trade was criminalized at the start of the century, its history has largely involved cosmopolitan minorities from the Balkans, the Middle East, Egypt and a few large cities in the Far East.[2]

If we take certain groups of emigrants as our point of departure, in any number of countries we repeatedly come up against the same organized crime groups. Nigerians specialize in credit card fraud and drug courier services, Russians go in for oil swindles, trafficking in women and extortion, and Turks and Kurds not only run the heroin trade in Europe but also smuggle illegal aliens.

The connection with minorities is also evident in recent official reports. This certainly holds true for the USA, although one might rightfully say that, by definition, organized crime is a minority matter there since everyone but the Native American is an immigrant. But, in countries that have been in existence for more than two or three centuries, some people are more immigrants than others. At any rate, it is striking how the borderlines of organized crime coincide with ethnic boundaries. In the USA official committees, such as the one headed by Senator Kefauver in the early 1950s, have long viewed organized crime as being run by minorities, specifically by Italians. In the 1980s, the Kaufman Committee also referred to criminal organizations with a different ethnic background. In Canada, the Organized Crime Committee Report drawn up by the Canadian Intelligence Service refers to ethnic criminal groups, meaning Asian ones.[3] In Australia the steering committee chaired by Bill Coad published a report giving the impression that the bulk of organized crime is committed by immigrants from overseas.[4] In 1993, the British National Criminal Intelligence Service published a preliminary survey showing that organized crime is almost exclusively the province of ethnic minorities.[5] Finally, a Dutch Parliamentary Inquiry report devoted much of its attention to immigrant and foreign criminal groups.[6] There are thus abundant empirical grounds for at least wondering whether there might be some link between organized crime and ethnic minorities.

ACCEPTABILITY OF THE QUESTION

Is the question socially relevant and is it ethically acceptable to pose it? To most academic criminologists, the involvement of ethnic minorities in any sort of crime is a rather delicate matter. In twentieth-century history, drawing a link between criminality and ethnic or national descent or the status of a minority has led to any number of theoretical and political miscalculations and misconceptions. The presumed inferiority and high crime rates of minorities have been used as arguments to stigmatize and victimize them.[7] The discussion on possible connections between 'race', intelligence and criminality is taboo in the field of criminology.[8] Many criminologists have reacted by refuting even the possibility of any such connection or any assumption that organized crime might involve an 'alien conspiracy'.[9]

Taboos, however, are unacceptable in any science, and in this specific case there are certain reasons *not* to avoid posing the question. First, the first victims of organized crime are often people from the very same minority. Did not the Italian Mafia that Americans are so apprehensive about start in New Orleans with the extortion of Italian shopkeepers by *La Mano Nera*, the Black Hand?[10] Chinese laundry and restaurant owners have experienced their share of extortion, as have today's

110

Russian emigrant businessmen. Second, the mere association with organized crime can have disastrous effects on the status of the entire national or ethnic group the criminal organizations are from. In the case of Russian emigration, Rosner has argued that the stereotype of the mafia even preceded their entrance to the USA.[11]

Third, in some cases, immigrants who engage in organized crime are manipulated into carrying out criminal projects devised and planned by a coalition of politicians, bureaucrats and crime bosses in their native country. The Turkish immigrant communities in Western Europe and their commercial infrastructure are being used in this way and smugglers justify their actions by alluding to their patriotism, particularly in the battle against the enemies of the Turkish nation.[12] The old saying goes that the criminals are also the victims.

Fourth, the rise of organized crime can be a sign of some other problem that needs to be addressed. In the functionalist discourse of their day, Sutherland and Cressey wrote: 'Just as pain is a notification to an organism that something is wrong, so crime is a notification of a social maladjustment ... a symptom of social disorganization'.[13] Organized crime by minorities can be a sign of social deprivation, the formation of an underclass or discrimination. Minorities have a right to be protected by the government and to be helped in surmounting whatever disadvantages they are faced with. For these reasons, the question of a possible link between minorities and crime is a very legitimate one indeed.

THEORETICAL RELEVANCE

Is it theoretically relevant to pose this question? The idea of a link has been discredited by a stereotyped treatment of policymakers and enforcers who have focused on the exotic aspects of ethnicity or subculture. History has been turned into legends and traditions were supposed to explain rigid group structures and initiation ceremonies. According to Mahan, investigators fell into 'the ethnicity trap' by analysing organized crime as a self-contained cultural environment.[14] Instead, the sociologically relevant question should be whether ethnicity and organized crime overlap and if it is ethnicity that explains anything. Perhaps such a link is only spurious because (a) the term ethnic minority is inherently problematic and the product of a racially biased social construction, or (b) the term organized crime is questionable and its definition inevitably leads to the stipulation of minorities as the culprits, or (c) organized crime as an economic phenomenon merely follows the logic of the market regardless of the ethnic descent of the people engaging in it.

Possibility One

Let us start with the first possibility. Being a member of a minority automatically means that being branded a criminal is more likely. Is not the notion of crime, at any rate the kind of crime that is detected by the police and prosecuted by the courts, one-sidedly focused on norm violations in the lowest segments of society, particularly on the part of young men and the categories that represent a high crime risk such as the unemployed? Ethnic minorities are over-represented in the lowest segments of society, and the number of young people is usually proportionally high among recent immigrants. In addition, there is the selective effect of racial prejudice against groups that are visibly different from the rest of the population. It is so easy for minorities to become the victims of moral panic as soon as the police and others claim they present an acute problem.[15] Virtually the only media attention minorities get focuses on crime and social problems. Successful minorities have no news value. Overseas Americans, Germans or any other emigrants from rich nations have not been implicated in organized crime. In general, one might wonder whether the whole notion of ethnic minorities does not constitute a target for reification because it allows qualities such as criminality to be treated as the property of particular groups.[16]

This bias is clearest in cases where organized crime is committed by people who are not members of any minority at all. Take the example so often cited in criminology textbooks, the rise of organized crime during Prohibition in the USA from 1920 to 1933. We all know it mainly entailed smugglers who were Italian, Irish or Jewish. In Chicago and other large cities, mostly in the East of the country, this was certainly the case, and Johnnie Torrio, Al Capone, Legs Diamond and Dutch Schulz were all notorious hoodlums. Thirsty people must also have lived outside these cities; but who was distilling and selling bootleg liquor in the American South and in the rural areas where there were few if any recent immigrants? In a recent criminography on a region in Kentucky, Potter and Gaines note that 'redneck crime groups' and a veritable 'Dixie Mafia' emerged in the days of Prohibition.[17] It is clear that these groups were continuations of the hillbilly liquor tradition, but they were not included in the annals of organized Prohibition crime. Were their activities not recognized as organized crime because they lacked the right ethnic background and, therefore, the alien quality to be taken seriously as such?

In today's world of drugs, there is the same kind of distortion. The large drug trade organizations work with the ethnic minorities from the drug production or transit countries in the developing world. But in the Netherlands, the up and coming market of chemical drugs, ecodrugs such as hallucinatory mushrooms, and part of the world trade in cannabis is in the hands of 100 per cent Dutch dealers and their companies and networks. Some of the wealthiest drug dealers in the world are ethnic Dutchmen.[18]

So this much is clear – it is easy to focus on minorities and this is due, in part, to the methods the police use. But the question is now whether this selectivity also applies to the consensual acts that organized crime often consists of. To what extent does proactive policing discriminate against minorities? There is also a great deal to be said for a diametrically opposed assumption. In dealing with minorities, the police come up against an obstinate stance fed by bad memories of the police in the old country or more recent unpleasant experiences with them in the new one. Unwillingness to cooperate might also stem from solidarity or it might be the direct result of intimidation within the group. Anyway it is difficult for the police to recruit reliable informants. The languages minorities speak can present a problem, and for some of the dialects it is difficult to find interpreters to work at police interrogations or to translate tapped telephone conversations. Nor is there much hope of getting the police in the suspects' native country to help conduct international investigations, particularly if some of the authorities there are themselves active in transnational criminal organizations. Finally, the police and the judiciary may not want to be reproached for discriminating against minorities, which is another reason why they tend to leave them alone.

Possibility Two

Now for the second possibility: the link is a spurious one and is the result of a discriminatory interpretation of the term 'organized crime'. Modern-day criminology textbooks draw a clear distinction between organizational crime and organized crime. The chapters about organizational crime often have terms such as 'corporate crime' in the title. Organized crime is described in separate chapters as such or as syndicated crime. Very different theories have been formulated about these two basic categories of crime. The theories on organizational crime try to explain how and why organizations that start out being legal can gradually turn to crime, whereas the theories on organized crime concentrate on how the members of the underworld are organized to earn money by way of criminal methods.

In the early days of criminology, this distinction was not drawn. Under President Hoover, the first American committee to investigate organized crime was headed by George Wickersham from 1929 to 1931. The committee was interested in gangsters, but it was also interested in businessmen gone wrong, and it put them both in one and the same category of organized crime.[19] The distinction between the two was first drawn in a famous lecture by Edwin Sutherland, who introduced the term 'white-collar crime' in 1939. The problem with this term is that it specifies the social status of the perpetrators, since white-collar crime is committed in the course of a respectable occupation by persons of respectability.[20] It was from this conception that the terms 'occupational crime', 'organizational crime' and 'corporate crime' later emerged. The theories have since diverged, thus producing two separate fields of science and quotation communities, as it were.

Since the 1980s, however, there have been increasing doubts as to the usefulness of this distinction. After all, organizational and organized crime both pursue dishonest profits, both of them violate the law and, in actual practice, the borderlines are unclear between these two forms of crime. Furthermore, is classifying gangsters solely according to their social class not an expression of precisely the kind of class prejudice Sutherland had highlighted?[21] After all, they both use violence, one to get even for unpaid debts and the other by exposing the public and company employees to the hazards of their more profitable production methods.[22] In keeping with this line of reasoning, it is no wonder we mainly come across ethnic minorities in organized crime, and not in corporate crime or organizational crime. After all, their low socio-economic position is even an explicit feature of many of the definitions of minorities.

Up to now, this criminological paradox that was introduced with Sutherland's point of view has never been satisfactorily settled. In practice, in his own personal line of reasoning, each author more or less opts for his own standpoint and definition. In the Netherlands, Fijnaut *et al.* have formulated a definition that distinguishes a separate category that primarily pertains to the more traditional forms of crime: 'organized crime involves groups primarily focused on illegal profits that systematically commit crimes with serious repercussions for society and are capable of shielding these crimes relatively effectively, in particular by way of their willingness to use physical violence or eliminate individuals by means of corruption'.[23] The advantage of a definition that covers the traditional forms of organized crime – smuggling, extortion rackets, the commercial exploitation of vice – is that the crime type as described has a low entrance threshold and is thus relatively open to minorities on the periphery of society. This version of organized crime entails acts based in part upon the use of violence or the threat of it, and it can thus be noted that organized crime relies on *personal* violence, and not on the impersonal forms of violence that go with organizational crime. It is true: one consequence of choosing this definition is indeed that there is more of a chance of coming across minorities.

Possibility Three

The third explicit refutation of the ethnicity thesis is formulated by authors who take the functioning of the economy as a point of departure for their analysis of organized crime. According to Potter and other authors, organized crime is solely based upon an extension of the principles of legitimate business into illicit areas, which does not have any implications at all as to the ethnic background of the people who engage in it.[24] Alan Block has repeatedly demonstrated that it is the political system and the market in America, which was mainly locally oriented in the 1920s and 1930s and is now far more international, that determine the nature and dimensions of criminal activity. He rejects the idea of a centrally led criminal organization that is run from some distant country and therefore represents a specific ethnic group.[25] In fact it is hard to conceive of the American underworld without the typically American political structure – machine politics in the cities and so forth – and the very specific history of labour unions there. Peter Reuter is perhaps the clearest protagonist of this point of view when he demonstrates that activities such as bookmaking, gambling on the numbers and loan sharking in the New York area are carried out by small and ephemeral enterprises and are not run by a central Mafia organization on the basis of subcultural values.[26]

The fact remains though that in their empirical historical studies, these same authors keep coming across Jewish, Italian, German, Chinese and other minority entrepreneurs. Organized crime is perpetrated within the market segment of the small enterprise and in city politics, and minorities are typically over-represented there. This might also explain why some minorities are less involved – if at all – than others in the rackets. The extent to which minorities in the USA have opted for small independent enterprises or careers in politics on the road to upward social mobility and assimilation does say something about the extent to which they are involved in crime. In the words of Mark Haller, who conducted research into the Chicago underworld in the first half of the century: 'In important respects, each ethnic group was characterized by different patterns of adjustment, and the patterns of involvement in the organized underworld often reflected the broader patterns by which each ethnic group struggled to find a niche within the larger society.'[27]

On the grounds of these considerations and the thrust of the preceding analysis, it is clear that the connection between organized crime and minorities is theoretically relevant and calls for further research. As long as the terms minority and organized crime are clearly defined, the extent to which certain ethnic groups or the entrepreneurs and politicians from these groups play a role in organized crime is a question of empirical evidence. The question is now what specific factors other than the general factors of social class formation and economic activity can help explain this connection.

EXPLAINING THE ETHNIC CONNECTION

The analysis now focuses on three groups of factors: political and geographical causes, a sociological explanation, and the extent to which ethnic organized crime is culture-related.

Political and Geographical Causes

Let us start from the political and geographical perspective. Organized crime is strong in countries that are weak and in regions where the government has not succeeded in effectuating a monopoly on violence. Border areas, less accessible regions and economically depressed districts have traditionally been the site of lawlessness, rebelliousness, banditry and piracy. If these regions are the territory or sanctuary for certain peoples, tribes or family clans, it puts a clear ethnic stamp on the problem of crime. Wherever national borders traverse settlement regions of this kind, the conditions are perfect for smuggling. Local leaders (feudal lords, war lords etc.) have developed smuggling traditions by exploiting their power relations with formal authorities. This is clearly explained in Alfred McCoy's masterly account of the history of the heroin trade.[28] The Golden Triangle is precisely such a border region, since the Shan States in Burma, the Hmong tribes of Laos and the ethnic rebel armies (Kuomintang) in the ill-defined highland zones of Thailand fit this description perfectly. This also holds true of the remote province of Yunnan in China and the border region between Afghanistan and Pakistan where the Pushtun tribe is effectively in power. The same rule about politically and socially marginal border regions pertains to the ones in southern Italy and Galicia in the Iberian peninsula, around the Mediterranean in the Rif Mountains of Morocco and Algeria, Corsica and so forth, and the border region of Turkey, Iraq and Iran inhabited by Kurds. The globalization of the world economy, however, may have driven local lords to the capitals of their countries to organize smuggling on a higher level, as has happened in Mexico, Baluchistan (Pakistan) and other regions of the world.

Sometimes the ethnic and regional diversity in a larger political unit leads to specializations in organized crime, as in the case of the former Soviet Union. As a Russian sociologist notes:

> The Solntsevo gang runs the gambling business, the Kazan gang is in charge of loans, the Chechens handle exports of petroleum, petroleum products and metals, banking operations, and the trade in stolen cars, Azerbaijani groups are into the drug business, the gambling business and trade, Armenian gangs deal in car theft, swindling and bribery, the Georgians are partial to burglary, robbery and hostage-taking, the Ingush's areas are gold mining, trade in precious metals and weapons deals, and the Dagestanis are involved in rape and theft.[29]

One observer has explained in detail how these specializations are exported from these regions to the West via emigration.[30]

Minorities embroiled in political conflicts with the central government or with neighbouring countries are particularly apt to be open to the organized crime option since they can use the profits it provides to further their cause. Central governments, in turn, use

117

minority henchmen to manipulate organized crime for their own purposes. As the history of the heroin trade demonstrates, minorities can be extremely useful as allies in global conflicts such as the Cold War.

Today's urbanized and industrialized world has been host to immigrants from precisely these regions, some of whom come in as migratory workers and political refugees – in practice it is often difficult to distinguish between the two – and, in part, organized crime has come in with them. This does not necessarily mean ethnic conflicts and the battles that accompany them back home are reproduced; there is an underworld tendency to join forces to evade the repressive apparatus of the state. However, political problems in the countries to which organized crime is connected can well be exported. In this sense, there is some truth to the alien conspiracy thesis so many eminent American criminologists have refuted in an effort to disprove the myth of the Mafia. Transnational criminal organizations may not have moved to the wealthy West for the purpose of undermining international security, but they did do so to earn large sums of money with illegal transactions for reasons that in some cases at least are linked to political objectives as well as personal greed.

The next specific political constellation can be found in strong nations with indigenous minorities living on their own territory where they have their own rules and do not have to adhere to the laws of the land. This is the case with Native Americans who run casinos in the USA. In Spain, gypsies are largely in charge of the retail trade in drugs and the authorities generally let them be. Margaret Beare gives an example of how legally operating entrepreneurs can make use of minorities. Up until the first half of the 1990s, Canadian tobacco manufacturers exported far more cigarettes to the USA than the market there could absorb. They were then smuggled back to Canada and sold far below the official price, which was forced up by taxes. There is no doubt the tobacco industry deliberately allowed this to happen. The smugglers were Indians whose reservations were situated along the lengthy border between Canada and the USA that is so difficult to patrol.[31]

The last politically and geographically influenced variant of organized crime can be observed among trading minorities or middlemen minorities.[32] People from a certain ethnic group, clan or region who are dispersed all across the globe set up trade and international payment transaction networks. Overseas Chinese, Lebanese, Indian, Parsis, Pakistanis and Arab emigrants are all good examples. They have followed the historical examples of Jews, Armenians and Greeks. The ethnic communities they found are at global trade intersections. The ports with well-known underworld traditions such as Marseilles, Hamburg, Odessa, Alexandria, Shanghai, Sydney and New York all house a cosmopolitan melting pot of these groups. Now that air traffic has mushroomed, the same can be expected in the vicinity of commercially important airports. These minorities are structurally in an excellent position to use their knowledge of world trade and finances to take advantage of the possibilities offered by organized crime. These groups have been reported to be active in usury, pawnbroking, the liquor fraud. Chinatowns in the USA have often contained vice districts.[33] In times of economic and political turbulence, however, they can periodically become the target of local hostility, as the Chinese recently experienced in Indonesia, with the standard allusions being made to their criminal tendencies. Since it is so clearly a case of scapegoating, it is not easy to determine to what extent middlemen minorities really do play a role in international organized crime.

The Sociological Explanation

The most well known sociological theory about organized crime up to now and the one with the widest explanatory range is undoubtedly Robert K. Merton's anomie theory, which is known in criminology as the strain theory. The American Dream makes everyone yearn for economic success, but there are not equal opportunities for one and all to attain this goal. The result of this strain is a social and moral climate where people devise alternative and, if necessary, illegal ways to reach this goal after all. Whenever American authors apply this theory to empirical research, it always pertains to immigrants who attain the 'American way of life' via crime. This, then, is how this perspective has led to the theory of social mobility or ethnic succession.[34] However, the original version of the strain theory did not make any assumption about ethnic descent. The strain is most marked where there is the greatest distance between the promise of material success and the limitations of actual reality keeping people from attaining it. In itself, this does not say anything about the ethnic background of the people concerned. But the strain can be expected to be greatest for the poor segments of society, and thus for the minorities who are disproportionately represented among the poor.

The strain theory and all its ramifications work from the assumption that crime is organized along ethnic lines. Ethnic affiliations seem to be taken for granted, no matter how many examples there are in the underworld of cooperation between different ethnic groups or prominent members of them. O'Kane describes the fixed sequence of stages that new immigrants pass through as they climb the 'crooked ladder of social mobility'. It begins with individual criminality, which leads to the formation of teenage groups, prison friendships and so forth. The second stage consists of intra-ethnic rivalry, leading to the emergence of new leaders. Then there is inter-ethnic rivalry, with various ethnic organizations turning against each other. At stage four they accommodate the conflict and cease engaging in pointless violence. After a certain amount of time, the new ethnic gang gains supremacy. In stage six, the decline of the ethnic gangs as a result of assimilation into American society, the gang is succeeded by the next wave of immigrants who are now the 'barbarians'.[35]

It is not clear though why some ethnic groups follow this pattern whereas others do not, or only to a far smaller degree. On the basis of recent experiences with immigration and the rise of organized crime in Europe as well as North America, a few comments can nonetheless be made about the possible material background of these ethnic affiliations. Supporters of the strain theory and ethnic succession assumed that immigration was an irreversible process that took place in a limited period of time for each group, and that organized crime was a matter of American criminality. Any number of immigration waves are now in full swing and internationalization fuelled by rapid and cheap transportation is now spreading all across the globe. Unlike the case a century ago, this has enabled immigrants to remain materially, culturally and politically connected to their home country. If they import organized crime, it is often by exploiting their home country's resources. Some immigrants from Colombia, Mexico, Turkey, China, Pakistan and so forth bring in drugs from their old country and take advantage of the large-scale transport of passengers and freight to the new one to move contraband without it being noticed. Smuggling illegal aliens, human parts, children for adoption and endangered species are all ethnic enterprises directly connected to the home country.[36] The same holds true in the other direction for smuggling arms or selling stolen cars. In addition, opportunities for safely channelling the proceeds of criminal activities to the home country are a comparative advantage that should not be underestimated. Covertly or quite openly, developing world governments encourage their subjects to send criminal capital

120

home to provide the country with foreign currency. What is more, internal revenue services fail to work effectively, and legal instruments to enforce illegal asset forfeiture procedures either do not exist at all, or are rarely put into practice. These aspects are outside the scope of the strain theory. The capital is traditionally invested in the following generation, especially in the USA where giving children a good education is an expensive matter, but one that gives the family a boost on its way up the social ladder. Nowadays, the proceeds of ethnic organized crime are largely invested in the home country.

There is also a second reason why certain minorities turn to organized crime. It has to do with the marginal social position some minorities occupy in addition to their low socio-economic status. Groups that are not assimilated yet or have been forced into the periphery by their long-term structural social disadvantages have very few ties to the conventional world. This can eliminate the moral precepts that keep groups who have invested in the conventional world from turning to organized crime and its promise of quick profits. During Prohibition, what moral objection could there be for Italians – from a real 'wine country' – to distilling or importing alcoholic beverages? Similarly Jews tended to view Prohibition as an internal problem of a Protestant world that did not have anything to do with them. In the Netherlands, in their research on the Turkish and Kurdish wholesale trade in drugs, Bovenkerk and Yesilgöz came across a similar set of shared techniques of neutralization.[37] There is a Turkish proverb: 'If the faucet is open, why not go fetch a bucket?'; it is not surprising then that very few members of this minority can see what objection there could be to engaging in the drug trade in the Netherlands, where the government is lenient as regards the *use* of drugs, which, in fact, is allowed. For a group such as the Turks, who are not yet well integrated into Dutch society, there is still not enough social control as regards the kind of conduct disapproved of by conventional society to keep the members from engaging in the drug trade.

The simple model of the opportunity theory in criminology, as formulated by Cohen and Felson, might help to explain which ethnic minorities run the greatest risk of getting involved in organized crime.[38] The risk is greatest, they state, if criminals are available, if there is an objective opportunity for crime and if social control does not work. Viewed from the strain perspective, in principle minorities in a low socio-economic position are open to the temptations of organized crime. The preservation of ties with the home country can give a minority group that is able to take advantage of the resources there an objective opportunity to earn an ample illegal living. If these two conditions are met and there is not enough social control to keep people on the straight and narrow path, then a minority is a greater organized crime risk.

The Cultural Perspective

Finally, there is the cultural perspective. To what extent do cultural elements make it easier for the members of certain minorities to turn to organized crime? This question can be approached on the grounds of the political, social and economic requirements for success in organized crime. Reasoning in a functionalist fashion, Albert K. Cohen summed up the problems every criminal organization has to solve in order to function.[39] These organizations have to be able to exert control over information, in other words the product has to be visible to the client, but acts that are punishable by law have to be concealed. Law enforcement has to be neutralized. Essential services such as capital, insurance, banking and legal assistance, have to be provided. The market has to be regulated and there have to be conflict resolution procedures to make it possible. The illegitimacy of the illicit acts has to be neutralized – what objections can there be to drinking or gambling?

The first two problems can be solved by loyalty within the criminal organization and within the seclusion of the ethnic community where the criminal activities are devised. The social functions of the ethnic group's primordial connection are solidarity and trust. The 'family' serves as its symbol, but these often constitute networks of relationships within one ethnic group such as *guanxi* among Chinese.[40] This point of view is expressed by Homer.[41] These conditions are in evidence if the ethnic community is hostile to the government, if there is a strong social norm of keeping matters secret from outsiders, if being loyal to each other is an important value and if social relations are based upon reciprocity. Of course, not everyone in the ethnic community plays an active role in organized crime, but there is still a closed front to the outside world. The Italian law-abiding father of Sammy Gravano told his children about the racketeers they were growing up among in Philadelphia: 'They are bad people, but they are our bad people.'[42] If anyone threatens to violate the code, there is the option of intimidating him, or of threatening to take hostage his relatives in the home country. A close ethnic community facilitates the control of criminal activity from the first stage of production through the final stage of street selling.[43] Ethnic minorities who live abroad can also provide a safe shelter for people from the mother organization who want to go into hiding. According to Bundeskriminalat sources, Italian communities in some German cities have sheltered murderers and other members of the Mafia.

The third problem is harder to solve if minorities are not a local power factor to the extent that they can influence the political and appointment policies of the local authorities or successfully engage in corruption. In the history of minorities in the large cities of Canada as well as the USA, this was indeed the case. But in many cases, this is a serious stumbling block for minority criminal organizations. Virtually by definition, minorities do not have a lot of power.

The fourth requirement is easier to meet. Since the underworld cannot turn to the authorities to enforce order, they have to do it themselves, and they do so by using violence or the threat of violence. 'Contemporary criminal organizations for the use of violence in the service of order would provide us with a living museum of forms that, in other sections of society, are extinct, archaic or vestigial.'[44] This use of violence can be observed among local minorities or immigrants from the Third World, though most other people are unfamiliar with it. In their research on the Turkish Mafia, Bovenkerk and Yesilgöz note that a strikingly large number of the crime bosses have a background of blood feuds in Turkey.[45] The last problem, the one pertaining to legitimacy, has already been dealt with in the section on techniques of neutralization.

In connection with all this, Homer has rightly observed that saying a specific cultural feature is in keeping with a criminal organization is not the same as saying a specific minority group is inclined towards organized crime.[46] After all, there are so many elements that are not at all functional. In the USA, Italians have attracted an inordinate amount of police attention with ostentatious funerals for Italian gangsters. A high level of violence is not functional because it forces the authorities to intervene. A low profile would be far more logical. The integration of immigrants also produces an unsuspected paradox. On the one hand minorities would do well in corruption and gaining political influence. But on the other they should not be too integrated as they would lose the advantage of their cultural bonds and conceptions.

123

CONCLUSION

Let me try to summarize the arguments presented in the preceding analysis. First, empirical reality gives us ample reason to pose the question of whether organized crime is widespread among minorities, and there are no real ethical or social objections to research into this link. Second, although it is a touchy subject and there are any number of pitfalls to be avoided in the methodology and reasoning techniques, it is feasible to conduct research into this question on the basis of explicit definitions of the terms 'minorities' and 'organized crime'. Third, there are three good theoretical grounds for assuming there really is such a link: there are political and geographical factors that make such a linkage probable; following the logic of strain theory, it is clear that under certain conditions, some minorities run a heightened risk; and finally, illegal organizations can sometimes thrive within the seclusion of ethnic minority communities. The implication of all this is that the topic deserves to be on the research agenda.

NOTES

1. See Michael D. Lyman and Gary W. Potter, *Drugs in Society; Causes, Concepts and Control* (Cincinnati: Anderson Publishing, 1996); and Vincenzo Ruggiero and Nigel South, *Eurodrugs; Drug use, Markets and Trafficking in Europe* (London: UCL Press, 1995).
2. Observatoire Géopolitique des Drogues, *Atlas Mondial des Drogues* (Paris: Presses Universitaires de France, 1996), Part III.
3. Margaret E. Beare, *Criminal Conspiracies. Organized Crime in Canada* (Toronto: Nelson Canada, 1996).
4. *Coad Report on the Review of Commonwealth Law Enforcement Arrangements* (Canberra: Australian Government Printing Service, 1994).
5. National Criminal Intelligence Service, *An Outline Assessment of the Threat and Impact by Organized/Enterprise Crime upon United Kingdom Interests* (London: HMSO, 1993).
6. Cyrille Fijnaut *et al.*, *Organized Crime in the Netherlands* (The Hague: Kluwer Law International, 1998).
7. Ronald B. Flowers, *Minorities and Criminality* (New York: Greenwood Press, 1988).
8. Andrew Karmen, 'Race, Inferiority, Crime, and Research Taboos', in Edward Sagarin (ed.), *Taboos in Criminology* (Beverly Hills and London: Sage, 1980), pp.81–114.
9. For a fuller discussion see Joseph L. Albini, *The American Mafia: Genesis of a Legend* (New York: Irvington, 1971). How the appreciation of ethnic involvement in crime may change, however, is demonstrated by post-Second World War authors who have discovered that contrary to the history of Jews who were defenceless victims of the Holocaust in Europe, there has been a strong Jewish element in the US underworld and these Jewish gangsters fought back! This comes out in Rich Cohen, *Tough Jews. Fathers, Sons and Gangster Dreams* (London: Jonathan Cape, 1998).
10. Thomas M. Pitkin and Francesco Cordasco, *The Black Hand. A Chapter in Ethnic Crime* (Totowa, NJ: Littlefield, Adams, 1977).
11. Lydia Rosner, *The Soviet Way of Crime: Beating the System in the Soviet Union and the USA* (South Hadley, MA: Bergin & Garvey, 1986).
12. For a fuller discussion see Frank Bovenkerk and Yücel Yesilgöz, *De Maffia van Turkije* (Amsterdam: Meulenhoff, 1998).

13. Edwin H. Sutherland and Donald R. Cressey, *Principles of Criminology* (Chicago: J.B. Lippincott, 1960), 6th ed., p.23.
14. Sue Mahan (ed.), *Beyond the Mafia – Organized Crime in the Americas* (Thousand Oaks, CA: Sage, 1998) p.52.
15. William J. Chambliss, 'Crime Control and Ethnic Minorities', in Darnell F. Hawkins (ed.), *Ethnicity, Race and Crime: Perspectives Across Time and Space* (New York: State University of New York Press, 1995).
16. Marian FitzGerald, 'Minorities, Crime, and Criminal Justice in Britain', in Ineke Haen Marshall (ed.), *Minorities, Migrants, and Crime. Diversity and Similarity Across Europe and the United States* (Thousand Oaks, CA: Sage, 1997), pp.36–61.
17. Gary Potter and Larry Gaines, 'Organized Crime in Copperhead County: An Ethnographic Look at Rural Crime Networks', in Jay Albanese (ed.), *Contemporary Issues in Organized Crime* (Monsey, NY: Criminal Justice Press, 1995), pp.61–85.
18. See Fijnaut *et al.*, op. cit.
19. Dwight C. Smith, Jr., 'Wickersham to Sutherland to Katzenbach: Evolving an "Official" Definition for Organized Crime', *Crime, Law and Social Change*, Vol.16, No.2 (1991), pp.135–54.
20. Edwin H. Sutherland, 'White Collar Criminality', *American Sociological Review* Vol.5 (1940), pp.1–12.
21. See Jay S. Albanese, 'What Lockheed and La Cosa Nostra have in Common', *Crime and Delinquency* (1982), p.232 and Kitty Calavita and Henry N. Pontell, 'Savings and Loan Fraud as Organized Crime: Toward a Conceptual Typology of Corporate Illegality', *Criminology*, Vol.31, No.4 (1993), pp.519–48.
22. Maurice Punch, *Dirty Business* (London: Sage Publications, 1996).
23. Fijnaut *et al.*, op. cit.
24. Gary W. Potter, *Criminal Organizations. Vice, Racketeering, and Politics in an American City* (Prospect Heights, IL: Waveland Press, 1994).
25. See Alan A. Block, *East Side–West Side. Organizing Crime in New York 1930–1950* (New Brunswick: Transaction Books, 1985) and Alan A. Block, 'The Serious Crime Community in Oil and Banking', *Journal of Financial Crime* (1998).
26. Peter Reuter, *Disorganized Crime: The Economics of the Visible Hand* (Cambridge, MA: MIT Press, 1983).
27. Mark H. Haller, 'Ethnic Crime: The Organized Underworld of Early 20th-Century Chicago', in Melvin G. Holli and Peter d'A. James (eds.), *Ethnic Chicago: A Multicultural Portrait* (Chicago: William B. Eerdmans, 1995), Chapter 19.
28. Alfred W. McCoy, *The Politics of Heroin. CIA Complicity in the Global Trade* (New York: Lawrence Hill Books, 1991).
29. Quoted in Phil Williams (ed.), *Russian Organized Crime. The New Threat?* (London and Portland, OR: Frank Cass, 1997) p.7.
30. Guy Dunn, 'Major Mafia Gangs in Russia', in ibid., pp.63–87.
31. Margaret E. Beare, 'Corruption and Organized Crime: Lessons from History', *Crime, Law & Social Change*, Vol.28, No.2 (1997), pp.155–72.
32. Edna Bonacich and John Modell, *The Economic Basis of Ethnic Solidarity. Small Business in the Japanese American Community* (Berkeley: University of California Press, 1980).
33. Ivan H. Light, 'The Ethnic Vice District: 1890-1944', *American Sociological Review*, Vol.42 (1977), pp.164–79.
34. See Daniel Bell, 'Crime as an American Way of Life', in M.E. Wolgang, L. Savitz and N. Johnston (eds.), *The Sociology of Crime and Delinquency* (New York: Wiley, 1953) and Francis A.J. Ianni, *Black Mafia: Ethnic Succession in Organized Crime* (New York: Simon and Schuster, 1974).
35. James M. O'Kane, *The Crooked Ladder. Gangsters, Ethnicity, and the American Dream* (New Brunswick and London: Transaction, 1993).
36. Alex P. Schmid (ed.), *Migration and Crime: Proceedings of an Ancillary Meeting held on May 3, 1995, in Cairo, Egypt on the occasion of the United Nations Ninth Congress on the Prevention of Crime and the Treatment of Offenders* (Milan: ISPAC, 1995).
37. For the theoretical perspective on this see Gresham M. Sykes and David Matza, 'Techniques of Neutralization: A Theory of Delinquency', *American Sociological Review*, Vol.59 (1957), pp.34–41.

38. Lawrence E. Cohen and Marcus Felson, 'Social Change and Crime Rate Trends: A Routine Activity Approach', *American Sociological Review*, Vol.44 (1979), pp.588-608.
39. Albert K. Cohen, 'The Concept of Criminal Organization', *The British Journal of Criminology*, Vol.17, No.2 (1977), pp.97-111.
40. Michael Agelasto, 'Cellularism, Guanxiwang, and Corruption: A Microcosmic View from Within a Chinese Educational Danwei', *Crime, Law & Social Change*, Vol.25, No. 3 (1996), pp.265-88.
41. Frederic D. Homer, *Guns and Garlic. Myths and Realities of Organized Crime* (West Lafayette, IN: Purdue University Press, 1974).
42. Peter Maas, *The Underboss, Sammy the Bull Gravano's Story of Life in the Mafia* (New York: Harper, 1997), p.1.
43. Beare, *Criminal Conspiracies. Organized Crime in Canada*, op. cit., p.76.
44. Cohen, op. cit., p.108.
45. Bovenkerk and Yesilgöz, op. cit.
46. Homer, op. cit.

Transnational Chinese Organized Crime Activities: Patterns and Emerging Trends

KO-LIN CHIN, SHELDON ZHANG and ROBERT J. KELLY

Chinese crime syndicates[1] have risen to such prominence in the past two decades that they have become a subject of great concern to law enforcement and government officials in the USA, Canada, Australia and Europe.[2] US law enforcement authorities now consider Chinese crime groups to be the second most serious organized crime problem in America. Furthermore, it is speculated that Chinese criminal groups may surpass Italian organized crime groups in importance in the near future.[3] Despite the widely reported increase of Chinese crime groups in heroin and human trafficking activities, in recent years only a handful of serious research studies have been conducted.

In this analysis, we first clarify the various Chinese crime groups that are often considered to make up the 'Chinese Mafia', and then examine in detail their two major transnational criminal activities – heroin trafficking and human smuggling. We propose an enterprise model for analysing transnational Chinese organized crime activities because of the extensive involvement of Chinese businesses in different parts of the world and their shared profit-seeking orientation. The demarcation lines between legitimate and illegitimate business transactions are often blurred.

Between 1984 and 1998, we conducted a series of studies on Chinese organized crime groups covering four main areas: (1) a descriptive analysis of various Chinese crime groups in the USA and Asia; (2) problems of extortion in New York City's Chinese community; (3) the structure and activity of Chinese gangs; and (4) Chinese alien smuggling.

THE 'CHINESE MAFIA'

Many adolescent and adult Chinese groups are involved in transnational criminal activities.[4] These groups – which include triads, tongs, street gangs, drug trafficking groups and human smuggling rings – are diverse in their structures and criminal activities. To the law enforcement community and even the mass media, however, they are often viewed as part of a common 'Chinese Mafia'. The use of this generic term, 'Chinese Mafia', obscures the varied historical, cultural, social and economic conditions that gave rise to these different types of Chinese crime groups.

Hong Kong-Based Triads

Triad societies in Hong Kong are alleged to be the largest, most dangerous and best organized crime groups in the world.[5] They stemmed from patriotic secret societies formed three centuries ago to fight against the oppressive and corrupt Qing dynasty. The word 'triad' means the unity of three essential elements of existence – heaven, earth and humanity. When the Qing dynasty (1644–1911) collapsed in 1911 and the Republic of China was established, some of these societies began to be involved in criminal activities.[6] According to one source, today there are roughly 160,000 triad members in Hong Kong, belonging to more than 50 factions.[7]

Triads in Hong Kong appear to be in control of not only most illegitimate enterprises (such as gambling and prostitution) but also many legitimate businesses.[8] Street violence in Hong Kong, sometimes involving hundreds of armed gangsters, is believed to be mostly triad-related.[9] Some societies are believed to be well organized, their members highly disciplined and their leaders the most influential figures in Hong Kong.[10]

Triad activities are not limited to Hong Kong and its adjacent regions such as Macao. Law enforcement agencies in China, North America, Europe and Southeast Asia have reported that, in their jurisdictions, triad activities such as extortion, gambling, heroin trafficking and immigrant smuggling, are on the rise.[11]

Taiwan-Based Organized Gangs

According to Willard Myers, the 'Taiwanese are the most powerful and important ethnic group in transnational Chinese organized crime'.[12] The emergence of criminal organizations in Taiwan can be traced back to the 1950s, the period following China's recovery of Taiwan from Japan.

Crime groups in Taiwan were once mainly involved in activities such as operating or protecting illegal gambling dens and brothels, collecting debts, extorting protection money from business owners and street violence.[13] However, since the mid-1980s it has been alleged that these crime groups have become active in drug trafficking,[14] people smuggling,[15] arms trafficking, collusive bidding for government projects, and other more sophisticated crimes.[16]

Much of the business community in Taiwan believes that organized crime has penetrated legitimate businesses. Members of organized crime groups are reported to be owners of restaurants, coffee shops, nightclubs, movie companies, cable television companies, magazine companies and construction companies.[17] Moreover, some gang members are actively involved in futures trading, the stock market and other commercial activities.[18]

In the early 1980s, gangsters in Taiwan were reported to be heavily involved in manipulating the outcomes of local elections. Through intimidation and vote buying, Taiwanese gang members assured the election of political candidates they worked for.[19] In the late 1980s, to protect themselves from frequent crackdowns on organized crime by the authorities, gang members themselves often ran for public offices.[20] According to a former Minister of Justice of Taiwan, many legislators, assemblymen and local representatives are believed to be active or former members or associates of organized crime groups.[21] This has led people in Taiwan to wonder whether Taiwan is actually ruled by these gangsters.[22]

China-Based Criminal Organizations

In the late 1970s, China opened its door to the West and began to reform its economy. As China started to move from a planned economy to a market-driven economy, crime rates began to rise. Not only were more individual offenders arrested for committing crimes but also more were charged with involvement in organized crime activities. Although Chinese government officials have been reluctant to acknowledge that there is an organized crime problem in the country, they are nevertheless forced to admit that there are many 'organized crime-like' organizations existing in China that threaten law and order in the country.[23]

Over the past 10 years, under the influence of – and with financial support from – organized crime members from Hong Kong, Macau and

Taiwan, many indigenous organized gangs have flourished in the provinces of Guangdong, Fujian, Zhejiang and Yunnan. These crime groups are alleged to be heavily involved in trafficking drugs from the Golden Triangle to Hong Kong and markets in China via Kunming; smuggling Chinese to Hong Kong, Taiwan, Japan, Australia and the West; smuggling cigarettes and stolen cars into China from Hong Kong; operating gambling and prostitution houses; extorting and exploiting legitimate businesses; in addition to a wide range of other crimes such as robbery and murder.[24]

USA-Based Tongs

The word 'tong' simply means 'hall' or 'gathering place'. Tongs in the USA were first established in San Francisco in the 1850s following the first wave of Chinese immigration. Prior to the emergence of tongs, Chinese communities in the USA were controlled by the dominant family or district associations. Immigrants whose last names were shared by few or who came from a small village were not accepted by the established associations. To fend for themselves, they banded together and established the tongs. Because there were no special qualifications for recruitment by the tongs, they expanded rapidly. Rival tongs were soon drawn into street battles known as the 'tong wars'.[25] More than 30 tongs were formed in the USA.

The tongs, like the family and district associations, provided many necessary services to immigrants who could not otherwise obtain the help they needed. The tongs also acted as power-brokers, mediating individual and group conflicts within the community. Most tong members are gainfully employed or have their own businesses. They pay dues to the tong and visit them occasionally to meet people or to gamble, and attend the association's banquets and picnics a few times a year. However, leaders of the tongs make decisions and control the groups' daily affairs. These leaders are more likely to affiliate with street gangs and to be involved in illegal activities.

Historically, tongs have been active in operating or providing protection for opium use and dealing, gambling and brothels.[26] Over the past three decades, however, some tong members have been arrested for narcotics trafficking or immigrant smuggling. Although a tong, as an organization, has never been indicted for its involvement in transnational crime, US authorities usually view tongs as organized crime groups that are heavily involved in transnational crime.[27]

USA-Based Street Gangs

There are more Chinese street gangs in New York City than in any other American city. Hence, New York is considered the centre of Chinese organized crime in the USA. The first Chinese street gang, the Continentals, was formed in 1961 by native-born Chinese high-school students; their primary objective was self-protection. Subsequently, new gangs such as the White Eagles, Black Eagles, Ghost Shadows and Flying Dragons, began to emerge. During their emergent stage, Chinese gangs were, in essence, martial arts clubs headed by Kung Fu masters who were tong members.

During the late 1960s and early 1970s, the gangs transformed themselves completely from self-help groups to predatory groups. They terrorized the community by demanding food and money from businesses and robbed illegal gambling establishments. When the youth gangs began to 'shake down' merchants and gamblers who were themselves tong members, the tongs decided to hire the gangs as their street soldiers to protect themselves from robbery and extortion, and to solidify their position within the community.

In the 1980s, new gangs such as the Fuk Ching, White Tigers, Tung On, Green Dragons, Golden Star and Born-to-Kill emerged in the peripheries of New York's Chinatown and in the outer boroughs of Queens and Brooklyn, following the emigration patterns of Chinese businesses and residents. Beyond the major Chinese urban communities in New York, San Francisco and Los Angeles, where Chinese gangs were first established, forms of Chinese gangs also became active in Oakland, Dallas, Houston, Falls Church, Arlington, Philadelphia, Chicago and Boston.

Heroin Trafficking Groups

Several facts are known about drug trafficking among the Chinese. Chinese heroin traffickers are not involved in retailing the drug. They normally bulk-sell it to Italian, African-American or Hispanic dealers. They also tend to be closely associated with Dominican Republic crime groups. These heroin traffickers are mostly independent entrepreneurs whose small businesses (restaurants, trading companies or retail stores) serve as 'fronts' for the heroin trade. Most of them enter the drug trade with short-range objectives, but the immense profits become intoxicating and make it difficult to quit. Among the drug traffickers, low-level couriers tend to be heavy gamblers and illegal immigrants who are in debt. When apprehended, Chinese traffickers are usually cooperative with law enforcement officials and do not resist arrest. They accept arrest as part of their fate. They do not condemn themselves as immoral criminals; instead, they view themselves as drug-dealing entrepreneurs whose primary goal is to make money.

Since 1986, Chinese with diverse backgrounds have been involved in large-scale heroin trafficking. Those arrested have included illegal immigrants from China, Hong Kong, Taiwan, Thailand and other Asian countries, US permanent residents and American citizens, including community leaders, business people, restaurant owners, workers and the unemployed.

Not only are Chinese drug traffickers difficult to characterize by their backgrounds, they are also not necessarily members of triads, tongs or gangs. Drug Enforcement Administration agents in New York have stated that there is insufficient evidence to suggest that triads, tongs and gangs dominate the heroin trade. These agents describe the trafficking groups as ranging from loose confederations of businessmen and smugglers who collaborate on a single deal to complex organized crime operations.

Snakeheads or Human Smuggling Groups

Human smugglers are called 'snakeheads' both in China and among the communities of overseas Chinese. Our series of studies on Chinese alien smuggling has found that human traffickers are divided into big snakeheads and little snakeheads. In general, a big snakehead is a person who invests money in a smuggling operation and oversees the operation. This person, often an overseas Chinese, is usually not known by the person being smuggled. A little snakehead, or recruiter, is a person who works as a middleman between a big snakehead and the human clients. He or she usually resides in China and is mainly responsible for recruiting clients and collecting down-payments.

Big snakeheads tend to be perceived as capable business people with power, wealth, formidable reputations and connections. Most big snakeheads are from areas adjacent to Fuzhou, the capital city of Fujian Province in southern China, but live in the USA, Hong Kong or Thailand. In our studies over the past few years, our research subjects repeatedly mentioned that Taiwanese in Taiwan, Brazil, Panama and Bolivia were also active in human smuggling. In addition, we have found that a small number of high-ranking or retired Chinese officials were involved in human smuggling. Little snakeheads, on the other hand, are local Chinese residents rather than overseas Chinese. People of all walks of life – including low-level government employees, close friends or relatives of big snakeheads, as well as the unemployed and even housewives – can become little snakeheads.

It is not clear how many Chinese immigrant smuggling organizations or networks exist. Estimates have varied widely, from only seven or eight to as many as 20 to 25. Most smugglers themselves do not have any clue as to how many Chinese smuggling groups exist worldwide. Some put the figure at around 50. There is a close working relationship among the leaders and others in the smuggling network, especially among snakeheads in the USA and their counterparts in China. More often than not, all those in the smuggling ring belong to a family or an extended family, or are close friends.

HEROIN TRAFFICKING

Chinese crime groups are alleged to be involved in many transnational organized crimes, such as credit-card fraud, money laundering, copyright piracy, illegal goods and stolen car smuggling. In this analysis, the two crimes considered as the primary Chinese international organized crime activities (that is, drug trafficking and human smuggling) are used to illustrate how these activities are carried out by various Chinese criminal organizations.

Chinese immigrants have historically been thought to be heavily involved in opium use and trafficking. In US Senate hearings of 1877 on Chinese immigration, government officials and police officers testified that San Francisco's Chinatown was beleaguered with then-legal opium dens. Little is known about the role Chinese dealers played in the American drug trade between 1914 and 1965. It is alleged, however, that, after the liberalization of the immigration laws in 1965, Chinese criminals, many of them sailors, brought heroin into the USA.[28] The seamen turned the heroin over to drug dealers in Chinatown, who in turn sold it to drug dealers of other ethnic groups.

The Emergence of Chinese in Drug Trafficking

After 1983, the amount of heroin imported into the USA from Southeast Asia increased dramatically.[29] In 1984, law enforcement officials claimed that Chinese drug traffickers were responsible for about 20 per cent of the heroin imported into this country. They also alleged that 40 per cent of the heroin in New York City was of Southeast Asian origin.[30]

In 1986, the number of heroin cases involving Chinese offenders began to rise dramatically. Drug enforcement and customs officers took notice of the increase in the number of Chinese heroin couriers arriving in American airports from Hong Kong and Bangkok. Each courier concealed 10–15 pounds of high-quality Southeast Asian heroin in luggage, picture frames and other items, in an attempt to bypass customs checkpoints.

In 1987, there was a dramatic change in the importation methods employed by the Chinese.[31] Instead of using drug couriers, Chinese heroin traffickers began to make use of their expertise in international trade. Large quantities of heroin (from 50 to 100 pounds or more) began to arrive in the seaports of Newark and Elizabeth, New Jersey, and in Chicago, hidden in cargo containers shipped from Asia. The drugs were carefully stuffed in furniture, frozen seafood and nylon sport bags, to evade customs officials.[32]

In addition, Chinese drug traffickers began to stack 10–15 pounds of heroin in parcel boxes containing commodities that could conceal the odour of the drug.[33] The boxes were sent from either Thailand or Hong Kong, and arrived in New York City via Oakland, California. Chinese drug traffickers also began to utilize air cargo to smuggle a large amount of heroin into the USA.

In 1987, law enforcement authorities solved more than 20 heroin-trafficking cases involving Chinese importers and seized a record 200 kg of 95 per cent pure Southeast Asian heroin, as well as millions in drug money.[34] Drug enforcement authorities suggested that of all the heroin seized in New York City in 1987, 70 per cent was of Southeast Asian origin, compared with 40 per cent in 1984.[35] The purity of the heroin in the streets of New York City rose from 5 per cent in the early 1980s to 40 per cent in 1987. In short, the American drug enforcement community was overwhelmed with the sudden surge in heroin importation among the Chinese.[36]

Despite law enforcement efforts, Chinese involvement in narcotics trafficking continued to increase in 1988.[37] In Chicago, drug enforcement authorities seized 160 pounds of heroin hidden in religious statues arriving from Bangkok. Top-level Chinese smugglers were arrested in New York City for importing several hundred pounds of heroin into the USA. In Boston, 180 pounds of heroin were found inside a bean sprout washing machine shipped from Hong Kong. In the meantime, law enforcement authorities in Asia, especially in Thailand and Hong Kong, were stunned by the amount of heroin the Chinese were trying to send to the USA. Thai authorities confiscated 2,800 pounds of heroin destined for New York City, and Hong Kong authorities seized a record 861 kg of heroin bound for the USA.[38]

The arrests of major Chinese drug traffickers continued unabated in 1989. In February, as the result of a worldwide drug enforcement operation known as Operation 'White Mare', the Organized Crime Drug Enforcement Task Force seized approximately 800 pounds of heroin and US$3 million cash in Queens, and arrested 38 defendants in the USA, Hong Kong, Canada and Singapore. The drugs were imported into the USA via Hong Kong, hidden in hundreds of rubber tyres for lawn mowers. A Chinatown community leader was indicted for his role as middleman for the foreign-based sellers and the American buyers.[39] Throughout 1989, other Chinese heroin trafficking groups were apprehended by drug enforcement agencies in the USA, Canada, Hong Kong and Australia.[40]

By 1990, it was estimated that 45 per cent of the heroin smuggled into the USA, and 80 per cent of the heroin imported into New York City, was Southeast Asian.[41] By that time, law enforcement authorities in the USA, Canada, Australia, the Netherlands and Britain claimed that the Chinese dominated the heroin trade in their respective jurisdictions.[42]

In June 1991, drug enforcement authorities found 1,200 pounds of heroin in a warehouse in Hayward, California.[43] The drugs were imported into the USA in a container from Bangkok via Kaoshiung, Taiwan. Four Taiwanese merchants residing in California and a Hong Kong citizen were arrested for the crime. So far, it is the largest heroin seizure in the USA.[44] (See Table 1 for a list of the major heroin arrests involving Chinese drug traffickers.)

In 1992 and 1993, many high-level heroin traffickers in New York City's Chinatown were convicted by the US government, thus effectively putting many Chinese drug trafficking groups out of business. However, based on the number of arrests made and the huge amount of heroin seized over the past decade, it is fair to say that Chinese traffickers are still one of the most active groups in international heroin trafficking. Recently, Chinese have been arrested

TABLE 1
A LIST OF MAJOR HEROIN ARRESTS IN THE USA INVOLVING CHINESE
OFFENDERS (1986-1992)*

Date	Heroin amount	Transship point	Arriving point	Concealed in	Offenders' country of origin	Methods
09/86	33 lb	Bangkok	Newark Seaport	Furniture	Taiwan	Sea cargo
11/86	10.5 kg	Hong Kong	JFK Airport	Jingsen Tea	China	Courier
01/87	15 kg	Bangkok	Elizabeth Seaport	Furniture	Taiwan	Sea cargo
02/87	57 lb	Bangkok	Newark Seaport	Furniture	China	Sea cargo
12/87	34 lb	Hong Kong	Long Beach	Boat	Hong Kong	Courier
12/87	165 lb	Unknown	Unknown	Nylon bags	Hong Kong	Sea cargo
02/88	160 lb	Bangkok	Chicago Seaport	Statues	Thailand	Sea cargo
02/88	2821 lb	Bangkok	New York City	Rubber bales	Unknown	Sea cargo
03/88	100 lb	Hong Kong	New York City	Parcel boxes	Hong Kong	US Post
03/88	1000 lb	Bangkok	Seattle, New York	Ice buckets	China	Sea cargo
03/88	7 lb	Shanghai	San Francisco	Gold fishes	China	Air cargo
03/88	32 kg	Hong Kong	New York City	Tea	Hong Kong	Air cargo
03/88	46 kg	Hong Kong	New York City	Unknown	Hong Kong	Air cargo
04/88	130 lb	Hong Kong	San Francisco etc.	Unknown	Hong Kong	Sea cargo
06/88	77 lb	Hong Kong	LA Airport	Can opener	Taiwan	Air cargo
09/88	183 lb	Hong Kong	Boston Airport	Machine	Hong Kong	Air cargo
02/89	800 lb	Hong Kong	New York City	Rubber tyres	Hong Kong	Sea cargo
05/89	40 kg	Guangzhou	New York City	Umbrella	China	Sea cargo
10/89	45 kg	Unknown	Chicago Airport	Unknown	China	Air cargo
01/90	18 lb	Unknown	Norfolk, CT	Toys	Unknown	Air cargo
01/90	65 kg	Hong Kong	Los Angeles	Lychee cans	Vietnam	Sea cargo
02/90	92 lb	Hong Kong	Elizabeth	Soy sauce	Unknown	Sea cargo
06/91	1285 lb	Taiwan	Oakland	Plastic bags	Taiwan	Sea cargo
03/92	77 lb	Singapore	Newark Seaport	Tiles	Singapore	Sea cargo

*Source: Official reports and media accounts.

not only for importing heroin but also for acting as middlemen (selling a few pounds to dealers of other ethnic groups). Indeed, there is evidence that Chinese drug dealers work closely with Hispanic dealers and distributors in New York City.[45]

Chinese Gangs and the Heroin Trade

As soon as Chinese were found to be active in importing heroin into the USA, law enforcement authorities began to allege that Chinese gangs were behind the dramatic upsurge in narcotics trafficking.[46] Authorities charged that gang members, along with tong and triad members, were the main culprits in promoting the heroin trade.[47] The media simply accepted the official position and blamed Chinese gangs and tongs for the upsurge in the heroin trade.[48] A careful review of the heroin cases reported in the media involving Chinese offenders, however, suggests that only a small number of Chinese gang leaders are involved in the trade.[49] Between 1983 and 1993, only three Chinese gang leaders were convicted for heroin trafficking. Ordinary gang members were rarely arrested for drug trafficking. Although dozens of co-defendants were implicated in these gang-leader-related cases few, if any, of the co-defendants were found to be connected with gangs.

Based on our research, we have found that only gang leaders and a small proportion of ordinary gang members were involved in the heroin trade. Of the 62 subjects we interviewed in New York, only 10 (17 per cent) admitted they had participated in the drug business. Furthermore their involvement in the drug trade was not a concerted or organized activity of their respective gangs. Most of our respondents were not associated with the use or the sale of drugs.

In summary, the role of Chinese gangs in heroin trafficking is rather similar to that of other ethnic gangs in cocaine or crack trades.[50] A report on gangs and drugs in Los Angeles also concluded that gangs are rarely involved in drug dealing on a collective level.[51] From our own research and the extensive literature review, it is fair to conclude that some Chinese gang members (particularly a few gang leaders) participate in heroin trafficking – but on their own. We have not found any convincing evidence that their respective gangs as collective entities are also involved in the drug trade.

The Connection between Chinese Organized Crime and Heroin

There is sufficient evidence that Chinese play a role in the heroin trade, but the precise connection between heroin trafficking and organized Chinese crime groups is as unclear as the role of Chinese street gangs in the drug trade. Several questions need to be addressed to clarify this connection. First, how reliable are the law enforcement estimates of the proportion of Southeast Asian heroin among all heroin available in the USA? Some observers question the techniques authorities employ in these estimates. Second, what percentage of the Southeast Asian heroin being smuggled into the USA is actually imported by Chinese traffickers? Since Italians, Nigerians, Pakistanis, Israelis and members of other ethnic groups are also involved in importing heroin from Southeast Asia to America, the increase in the amount of Southeast Asian heroin in the USA should not be interpreted automatically as the work of Chinese traffickers. Recently, a US Department of State report indicated that Nigerians are responsible for the bulk of the Southeast Asian heroin imported into the USA.[52] Third, one must ask, of the Southeast Asian heroin brought into the USA by Chinese traffickers, what proportion is actually imported by members of the gangs, tongs and triads? Is it possible that most Chinese heroin dealers do not belong to any of these types of criminal organizations?

Answers to these questions are not easy to find. To date, no gang, as an organization, has been indicted for narcotics trafficking. However, individual gang members have been arrested for heroin trafficking. The same is true with regard to the tongs and the triads. Thus, as one researcher puts it, the connection between drug trafficking and Chinese organized crime (gangs, tongs or triads) is weak at best.[53] A senior DEA officer also reached the conclusion that most Chinese heroin importers are not members of the Chinese underworld.[54]

HUMAN SMUGGLING

In 1978, the USA established diplomatic relations with the People's Republic of China. This boosted the legal immigration from China to the USA.[55] Because of limited immigration quotas, however, only a small number of Chinese whose relatives live in the USA as citizens have the opportunity to come to America legally. Consequently, some Chinese turn to 'snakeheads' or professional smugglers for help. Since the 1980s, transnational human smuggling has emerged as a service industry that rivals many multinational conglomerates in both its revenue and scope of operations. Immigration officials in the USA,

Taiwan, Hong Kong, Macau, Japan, Australia, Hungary, Italy, the Netherlands and Canada have been alarmed by the dramatic increase in the number of undocumented Chinese residing in their countries.[56]

There are several ways an illegal Chinese immigrant can enter the USA. One technique is to travel to Mexico or Canada from China and then enter the USA by illegally crossing the border.[57] The second method involves air travel. Many unauthorized Chinese fly into major American cities via any number of transit points, which can be any city around the world.[58] Some arrive in Florida from South America by small airplane. Between August 1991 and July 1993, a third means of entry to the USA became popular; a large number of Chinese were smuggled into the country aboard fishing trawlers. In June 1993, a ship called the *Golden Venture*, with more than 260 men and women aboard, became stranded on a New York City beach. Ten passengers drowned while attempting to swim ashore.[59] In all, between 1991 and 1998, 40 ships, with more than 6,000 Chinese on board, were found in the waters off Japan, Taiwan, Indonesia, Australia, Singapore, Haiti, Guatemala, El Salvador, Honduras and the USA (see Table 2).

Unlike Mexican illegal immigrants, who enter the USA at little financial cost, each illegal Chinese immigrant must pay a smuggler about US$30,000 for services (as discussed later). By 1998, the charge had been increased to approximately US$45,000 per person. Since thousands of Chinese are smuggled out of their country each year, people trafficking is a very lucrative business. A senior immigration official has estimated that Chinese organized crime groups make more than US$3 billion a year from human smuggling operations.

Owing to the lack of specific data, we can only describe in general how our subjects came into contact with their little snakeheads, what types of arrangements had to be made before they were transported out of China and the cost of the smuggling.

Contacting and Screening Clients

Of the 300 illegal immigrants we interviewed in New York, only 11 said they were initially approached by little snakeheads. The majority (74 per cent) initiated contact with little snakeheads themselves, mainly through friends or relatives in China. Some subjects (12 per cent) found their snakeheads through relatives and friends living abroad. The data suggest that smugglers have been moving their recruiting activities to mainland China by hiring their resident friends and relatives to recruit clients. This

TABLE 2
VESSELS CAUGHT SMUGGLING CHINESE TO THE USA (1991-1998)·

Date	Place where it was discovered	Vessel name	Flag	Number of passengers
Aug. 1991	Los Angeles	I-Mao	Taiwan	131
Jan. 1992	Guatemala	Lo Sing	Taiwan	216
Jan. 1992	Guatemala	Chen Fong	Taiwan	150
Feb. 1992	Honolulu	Yun Fong Seong	Taiwan	96
Feb. 1992	Honolulu	Discoverer	Taiwan	51
Feb. 1992	Los Angeles	San Tai	Taiwan	85
June 1992	Honolulu	Lucky	Belize	119
July 1992	Guatemala	Jinn Yin	Unknown	Unknown
Sept. 1992	Morehead City, NC	Chin Wing	Honduras	150
Sept. 1992	Los Angeles	Hong Sang	Taiwan	158
Sept. 1992	Honolulu	Eing Dong Ming	Taiwan	137
Sept. 1992	New Bedford, MA	Unknown	Unknown	200
Oct. 1992	Yokohama, Japan	Dai Yuen	Taiwan	142
Dec. 1992	San Francisco	Manyoshi Maru	Honduras	180
Dec. 1992	Baja California	Sea Star	Honduras	300
Dec. 1992	Guatemala	Shann Der	Unknown	Unknown
Jan. 1993	Singapore	Solas	Jamaica	128
Feb. 1993	Marshall Islands	East Wood	Panama	528
Apr. 1993	Baja California	Jenn Yang	Taiwan	306
May 1993	Jacksonville, FL	Mermaid	Honduras	237
May 1993	San Diego	Chin Lung Hsiang	Honduras	199
May 1993	San Francisco	Pai Sheng	Honduras	250
June 1993	San Francisco	Pelican	USA	120
June 1993	San Francisco	Angel	USA	184
June 1993	New York	Golden Venture	Honduras	293
June 1993	Indonesia	Ever Rise	Honduras	156
July 1993	Baja California	To Ching	Taiwan	254
July 1993	Baja California	Long Sen	Taiwan	170
July 1993	Baja California	Sing Li	Taiwan	236
July 1993	Guatemala	An Shien	Taiwan	55
Apr. 1994	San Diego	Jin Yinn	Taiwa	113
June 1994	Norfolk, VA	Captain Denny	USA	126
July 1994	Bahamas	Unknown	Dominican Rep.	36
Mar. 1995	San Diego	Fang Ming	Taiwan	106
Apr. 1995	San Diego	Xin Ji Li	South Korea	200
May 1995	Zhejiang	Wen Ji	Unknown	44
July 1995	Honolulu	Jung Sheng	Panama	139
Oct. 1996	Bermuda	Xing Da	China	109
Aug. 1997	San Diego	Lapas No. 3	Mexico or China	69
June 1998	Bay Head, NJ	Oops II	USA	22
Total	40 ships			6,195 passengers

·Source: US Immigration and Naturalization Service and media accounts.

change seemingly occurred sometime in the early 1990s. According to various accounts, big snakeheads normally pay recruiters or little snakeheads somewhere between US$500 and US$1,000 per recruit.[60]

As mentioned above, little snakeheads are usually family members, relatives or good friends of big snakeheads. If little snakeheads are unable to recruit clients themselves, they turn to members of their extended families and friends to act as a second tier of little snakeheads. This is especially true in the case of sea smuggling, where hundreds of recruits need to be lined up in a short period of time. Occasionally, according to our subjects, former clients who were now living in the USA were asked by snakeheads to recruit from among their friends and relatives in China.

Preparing to Leave

The US media has reported that, since 1989 when modern smuggling by sea began, smugglers have allowed many of their customers to board smuggling ships without the need of a guarantor or a down payment.[61] Our data do not support this assertion. Only 28 (nine per cent) of our New York subjects were allowed by their smugglers to leave China without a guarantor or a down payment. Most needed either to make a down payment or to provide the name and address of a guarantor, or both. Yet, it appears that from 1989 to 1993, there was an increase in the number of subjects who came to the USA without a down payment or a guarantor. Our data also show that the need to have a guarantor was not as critical in 1993 as it was in the 1980s. Instead, smugglers required their clients to make a down payment, especially if they were to be smuggled by ship.

The average cost of a down payment for a person to be smuggled into the USA was US$3,069, but the mode was US$1,000. After the down payment has been made and/or the name and address of a guarantor has been provided, the smuggler and the customer may sign a contract. Many rules are stipulated in these contracts but it is not clear how closely the signing parties follow these rules. One chilling aspect of these contracts is the understanding by both parties that the smugglers can hold their clients as hostages if the clients, upon arrival in the USA, do not come up with the smuggling fee.

After a contract is signed, the customers wait for the smugglers to inform them of the departure time. About one in five of our subjects needed to wait only a week or less, and more than half waited for a month or less. Only about 15 per cent had to wait for more than three months. The length of the waiting period did not change from 1988 to 1993, remaining at about two months. However, the amount of time smugglers needed to move their customers out of China differed significantly by smuggling method. The average waiting period was 29 days for subjects who left China by ship, 46 days for those entering the USA by land, and 73 days for those who left China by air.

Smuggling Fee

Our respondents paid an average of US$27,745 for their illegal passage, ranging from a minimum of US$9,000 to a maximum of US$35,000. The average smuggling fee in 1988 was US$22,956, and it increased about US$2,000 each year after that, with the exception of 1991 and 1992. The average smuggling fee in 1993 was US$29,688.

Of the three routes, the air route appeared to be the most expensive (US$29,070), followed by the sea route (US$27,560). The least expensive was the land route (US$26,276). Between 1988 and 1993, the smuggling charge for the air route increased the most (from US$23,500 in 1988 or before to US$31,230 in 1993).

Patterns of Air Smuggling

Of the 143 respondents in our New York study who flew to the USA, 138 (96 per cent) either flew out of China or left their country overland through either Hong Kong or Myanmar. Of those who left China by air, only seven flew directly to the USA. Most of those who went through Hong Kong subsequently went to Bangkok, the capital of Thailand. All those who crossed the China-Myanmar border also travelled to Bangkok. It was in Bangkok that most of our subjects were congregated after leaving China, and Bangkok-based snakeheads obtained travel documents for their clients to go either directly to the USA or to another transit point.

If smugglees did not fly to the USA from Bangkok, then they usually went to another transit point, mostly likely a city in Asia. From there, most took a direct flight to the USA. A few travelled through as many as nine transit points. However, most of the respondents went through only two or three transit points, mostly in Asia. Table 3 shows the patterns of air routes utilized by the respondents.

TABLE 3
AIR ROUTES USED BY RESPONDENTS (*N* = 143)

Direct flight (N = 7)

One transit point (N = 20)
Hong Kong (7)
Japan (5)
Singapore (3)
Thailand (2)
Russia (2)
Bolivia (1)

Two transit points (N = 32)
Hong Kong, Thailand (12)
Hong Kong, Bolivia (3)
Hong Kong, Brazil (3)
Hong Kong, Peru (2)
Hong Kong, the Netherlands (1)
Hong Kong, Colombia (1)
Hong Kong, UK (1)
Hong Kong, Dominican Republic (1)
Hong Kong, Russia (1)
Myanmar, Thailand (3)
Singapore, Pakistan (1)
Singapore, Belgium (1)
Japan, Saipan (1)
Russia, the Netherlands (1)

Three transit points (N = 35)
Hong Kong, Thailand, Indonesia (2)
Hong Kong, Thailand, Egypt (1)
Hong Kong, Thailand, Spain (1)
Hong Kong, Thailand, Dominican Republic (1)
Hong Kong, Thailand, Guyana (1)
Hong Kong, Thailand, Austria (1)
Hong Kong, Thailand, Malaysia (1)
Hong Kong, Thailand, Germany (1)
Hong Kong, Thailand, Pakistan (1)
Hong Kong, Thailand, France (1)
Hong Kong, Thailand, Bolivia (1)
Hong Kong, Thailand, Taiwan (1)
Hong Kong, Thailand, Singapore (1)
Hong Kong, Singapore, Thailand (2)
Hong Kong, Singapore, Russia (1)
Hong Kong, Singapore, Japan (2)
Hong Kong, Taiwan, Indonesia (1)
Hong Kong, Taiwan, Argentina (1)
Hong Kong, Taiwan, South Korea (1)
Hong Kong, Ecuador, Colombia (1)
Hong Kong, Bolivia, Argentina (1)
Hong Kong, Japan, South America (country unknown) (1)
Hong Kong, Indonesia, Malaysia (1)
Myanmar, Thailand, Czech Republic (2)
Myanmar, Thailand, Philippines (1)

TABLE 3 (CONTINUED)
AIR ROUTES USED BY RESPONDENTS (*N* = 143)

Myanmar, Thailand, Japan (1)
Myanmar, Thailand, Japan (1)
Myanmar, Thailand, Singapore (1)
Singapore, Thailand, France (1)
Japan, Brazil, Bolivia (1)
Pakistan, Austria, Romania (1)

Four transit points (N = 19)
Hong Kong, Thailand, Hong Kong, Taiwan (1)
Hong Kong, Thailand, Sri Lanka, Thailand (1)
Hong Kong, Thailand, Singapore, Turkey (1)
Hong Kong, Thailand, France, Brazil (1)
Hong Kong, Thailand, Sri Lanka, Germany (1)
Hong Kong, Thailand, Fiji, Saint Tan Island (1)
Hong Kong, Singapore, Thailand, Spain (1)
Hong Kong, Singapore, Bolivia, Peru (1)
Hong Kong, Singapore, Denmark, Norway (1)
Hong Kong, France, Bolivia, Peru (1)
Hong Kong, Bolivia, Peru, Bolivia (1)
Singapore, Thailand, Singapore, Germany (1)
Singapore, Thailand, Bolivia, Ecuador (1)
Thailand, Singapore, Indonesia, Taiwan (1)
Myanmar, Thailand, Singapore, Indonesia (1)
Myanmar, Thailand, Czech Republic, Germany (2)
Myanmar, Thailand, Singapore, Malaysia (1)
Bolivia, Peru, Panama, Costa Rica (1)

Five transit points (N = 13)
Hong Kong, Thailand, Malaysia, Singapore, Taiwan (1)
Hong Kong, Thailand, Nepal, Thailand, Singapore (1)
Hong Kong, Thailand, Singapore, Czech Republic, Germany (1)
Hong Kong, Thailand, Vietnam, Singapore, Sweden (1)
Hong Kong, Thailand, Cambodia, Singapore, Australia (1)
Hong Kong, Thailand, Bangladesh, Germany, Norway (1)
Hong Kong, Panama, Austria, Panama, Colombia (1)
Hong Kong, Senegal, UK, Uruguay, Saint Lucia (1)
Myanmar, Thailand, Singapore, Malaysia, Japan (1)
Myanmar, Thailand, Indonesia, Singapore, Taiwan (1)
Myanmar, Thailand, Yugoslavia, Czech Republic, Russia (1)
Myanmar, Thailand, Yugoslavia, Czech Republic, West Germany (1)
Myanmar, Thailand, Nepal, India, Germany (1)

Six transit points (N = 8)
Hong Kong, Thailand, France, Brazil, Argentina, Chile (1)
Hong Kong, Thailand, Russia, Austria, Spain, UK (1)
Hong Kong, Thailand, Morocco, Algeria, Morocco, Spain (1)
Hong Kong, Nepal, India, Saudi Arabia, Africa, Portugal (1)
Hong Kong, Nepal, India, Saudi Arabia, Ethiopia, Portugal (1)
Hong Kong, Singapore, Thailand, Singapore, Malaysia, Japan (1)
Hong Kong, Germany, Venezuela, Thailand, Singapore, Germany (1)
Vietnam, Laos, Thailand, Singapore, New Zealand, Tonga (1)

Seven transit points (N = 4)

TABLE 3 (CONTINUED)
AIR ROUTES USED BY RESPONDENTS (N = 143)

Hong Kong, Thailand, Cambodia, Russia, France, Spain, Italy (1)
Hong Kong, Thailand, Sri Lanka, Thailand, Singapore, Korea, Japan (1)
Hong Kong, Indonesia, Hong Kong, the Netherlands, Russia, Holland, Germany (1)
Myanmar, Thailand, Laos, Vietnam, Russia, Germany, France (1)

Eight transit points (N = 1)
Myanmar, Thailand, Singapore, Thailand, Russia, Austria, Spain, UK (1)

Nine Transit Points (N = 1)
Hong Kong, India, UK, Barbados, Guyana, Cuba, Barbados, Venezuela, Brazil (1)

Table 4 illustrates the seven countries most likely to be passed through by the respondents who flew to the USA. Almost two out of three went through Hong Kong, more than half through Thailand and about one out of four went to Singapore before arriving in the USA.

TABLE 4
TOP SEVEN TRANSIT COUNTRIES FOR AIR SMUGGLING (N = 143)

Number of respondents who travelled through		Per cent of the air sample
1. Hong Kong	91	64
2. Thailand	83	58
3. Singapore	37	26
4. Myanmar (Burma)	22	15
5. Japan	13	9
6. Russia	13	9
7. Bolivia	11	8

For those who entered the USA by air, not only the number of transit points varied but also the length of stay in transit points. Most spent about seven days in their first transit point, and about a month in their second transit point. Some respondents stayed from two to twelve months in their second transit point, perhaps because of difficulties in obtaining travel documents or because they were 'sold' by their original snakeheads in China to snakeheads in the second transit point. After spending a substantial amount of time in the second transit point to obtain travel documents, most respondents spent only a few days in the remaining, if any, transit points. It took an average of 106 days for the 143 respondents to arrive in the USA. Ten respondents spent a year or more in various transit points before they landed in the USA.

Most of those who flew to the USA travelled in small groups of three to four immigrants, unaccompanied by a guide or a snakehead. If a group was guided, the guide was mostly likely to be a Chinese who spoke English and either Mandarin or the Fuzhou dialect.

It is difficult to pinpoint which city has been the most likely final transit point for Chinese immigrants who flew into the USA. This is because the immigrants in this study flew to the USA from 44 cities. With the exception of Bangkok (20), Tokyo (11) and Germany (10, city unknown), none of the other 41 cities figured prominently on the list of final transit points. Nevertheless, it is clear that New York City was the most likely entry point for our subjects who came by air. Of those who flew to America, 95 (66 per cent) entered the USA through John F. Kennedy (JFK) airport in New York City. Another 36 (25 per cent) flew into Los Angeles International Airport. Other arrival cities included Miami (5), Honolulu (4), San Francisco (2) and Chicago (1).

Most air travellers (58 per cent) arrived in the USA with travel documents, either genuine or fake. The 83 respondents who arrived with passports mentioned altogether 15 types of passport. Passports issued by Taiwan (24), Singapore (15) and the People's Republic of China (14) were the most likely passports used. The majority of those who entered the USA with a passport were also in possession of a tourist visa, most likely counterfeit. Those arriving with genuine Chinese passports often possessed bona-fide business visas issued by US consulates in China. Two respondents said they entered the USA with contrived green cards or advanced parole certificates.

Players in a Smuggling Group

Once a human smuggler characterized a Chinese smuggling network as a dragon and noted that '… although it's a lengthy creature, various organic parts [of the body] are tightly linked'. Besides big and little snakeheads, a smuggling organization includes many specialized roles:

- *Transporters.* If an immigrant leaves China by land or by ship, a China-based transporter helps him or her get to the border or to the smuggling ship. Transporters based in the USA are responsible for taking smuggled immigrants from airports or seaports to safe houses.
- *Corrupt public officials.* Chinese government officials accept bribes in return for Chinese passports. Law enforcement authorities in many transit countries are also paid to aid the illegal Chinese immigrants entering and exiting their countries.
- *Guides and crew members.* A guide is a person responsible for moving

illegal immigrants from one transit point to another, or for aiding immigrants in entering the USA by land or by air. Crew members are people employed by snakeheads to charter smuggling ships or to work on them.

- *Enforcers.* The enforcers, themselves mostly illegal immigrants, are hired by big snakeheads to work on the smuggling ships. They are responsible for maintaining order and for distributing food and drinking water.
- *Support personnel.* Support personnel are local people at the transit points who provide food and lodging to illegal immigrants.
- *Debt collectors.* A US-based debt collector is responsible for locking up illegal immigrants in safe houses until their debt is paid, and also for collecting smuggling fees. There are also China-based debt collectors.

CONCLUSION

There are many similarities between heroin trafficking and human smuggling: both are transnational crimes involving many countries; both are very lucrative; both involve gang members in the USA as service providers; both appear to be dominated by a unique group of people who are well travelled, possess international links and are familiar with the Golden Triangle (that is, the main source of heroin and the major exit point for many undocumented Chinese); and both are considered victimless crimes, at least by the Chinese offenders, and consequently little social stigma is attached to engaging in these illicit activities. Smugglers view both crimes simply as lucrative business activities. Therefore, it is defensible to examine heroin and human smuggling as economic activities. These enterprises depend on flexible international networks, entrenched in the infrastructure of the opium growing and sending communities and in many transit countries; networks in which individuals and groups contribute their time, energy, expertise and capital to generate lucrative profits (see Table 5).

Organizationally, we have made the following observations. First, these groups tend to be small and their formations are mostly haphazard through coincidental social meetings or informal referrals, rather than systematic. The small size makes them highly adaptable to market constraints. The smugglers are parts of networks that have little bureaucratic structure (limited vertical hierarchy), even though their operations may involve working with partners in diverse countries.

TABLE 5
THE ROLE AND FUNCTION OF VARIOUS CHINESE CRIME GROUPS IN
HEROIN TRAFFICKING AND HUMAN SMUGGLING

	Heroin trafficking	Human smuggling
Hong Kong-based triad societies	Trafficking heroin from the GoldenTriangle to Hong Kong via China or Thailand and exporting to Australia and Europe	Smuggling Chinese to Hong Kong
Taiwan-based crime groups	Trafficking heroin from the Golden Triangle to Taiwan via Thailand or China	Providing ships and passports to US- and China-based snakeheads or acting as transit point snakeheads, also involving in smuggling Chinese to Taiwan
China-based crime groups	Working together with Hong Kong- and Taiwan-based crime groups in trafficking heroin from the Golden Triangle to China and exporting to Hong Kong or Taiwan	Acting as little snakeheads for foreign-based big snakeheads
US-based tongs	Some tong members, working together with heroin traffickers, triad members or gang leaders involved in importing heroin into the US	Some tong members, especially members of Fujianese organizations, are involved in smuggling Chinese to the US
US-based gangs	Some gang leaders, working together with heroin traffickers, triad members or tong members, involved in importing heroin into the US	Mainly helping the big snakeheads collecting the smuggling fee
Heroin traffickers	Mostly Chinese entrepreneurs in Hong Kong, Taiwan, China, Southeast Asia, Australia and Europe Some heroin traffickers are also involved in it	
Snakeheads or human smugglers	Some snakeheads are former heroin traffickers Mostly US- or Thailand-based Fujianese with friends and relatives in China and major transit points, involved in smuggling Chinese to the USA, Japan and Europe	

Although sharing a common ancestry, the same dialect or the same hometown origins may increase the shared understanding and expectations of the smuggling activities, smugglers need not possess these prerequisites to take part in the smuggling operations. The alliance is merely a business arrangement involving only those who have valuable resources to contribute. Few are found to have absolute control over an entire smuggling operation.

Second, although there is little hierarchical differentiation, the division of labour is highly developed among traffickers and smugglers. Each member operates to fulfil specific functions, with minimum redundancies. For instance, in human smuggling, overseas smugglers dominate in arranging the international transportation and developing a global network of rendezvous points. The Fujianese entrepreneurs, on the other hand, recruit clients and provide payment guarantee.

Third, most contacts among smugglers and traffickers are dyadic, and most of those involved appear to honour their contracts, though we found a few cases of payment problems. For instance, most human smuggling cases caught by law enforcement agencies result from unanticipated disruptions encountered by the smugglers or the illegal immigrants, such as failure to pass Immigration and Naturalization Service (INS) interrogations at the port of entry. However, anonymity can also result in unnecessary delays and even disasters when one fails to deliver promised 'cargo' on time. The loss of a key player in the transnational operations can severely weaken the effectiveness of the smuggling organization.

Fourth, there is a lack of connections between these small entrepreneurs and the traditional Chinese organized crime organizations – the tongs and triads. This observation does not deny the involvement of Chinese gangs in drug trafficking and human smuggling. We merely argue that heroin trafficking and alien smuggling are vastly different from the traditional choice of racketeering activities in the Chinese community such as extortion, gambling and prostitution. Heroin trafficking and human smuggling do not appear to be monopolized by any crime syndicates.

It seems to be the case that a new generation of non-triad (that is, having no connections with triad societies, tongs and street gangs) Chinese criminals are emerging on the global crime scene. These non-triad criminals are responsible for the bulk of the heroin imported into the USA and for the smuggling of Chinese to the USA and many other countries, and they are more likely than people of the triad subculture to infiltrate the larger society through drug trafficking, human smuggling, money laundering and other types of transnational crime. They are wealthier, more sophisticated and better connected than the former Chinatown tong members. They are not committed to the rigid triad subcultural norms and values, thus enabling them to assemble quickly when the criminal opportunity arises and to dissolve after the criminal conspiracy is carried out.

Thus, we are observing the development of a different criminal subculture, be it for the sale of drugs or the smuggling of human or other illicit commodities, among the Chinese in the USA, Hong Kong, Canada, Australia, Europe and other parts of the world. Members of this subculture include import-export businessmen, community leaders, restaurant owners, workers, gamblers, housewives and the unemployed. It is extremely difficult to penetrate this subculture because members have no prior criminal records, no identifiable organization and no rigid structure, or clearly defined deviant norms and values. They can conceal their criminal activities through their involvement in lawful business activities. Their participation in criminal activities is sporadic rather than continuous. In other words, they may participate or invest in one heroin deal, collect the illegal gains and put the money in real estate or other legal businesses such as restaurants. They may not be involved in any illegal activities for a prolonged period of time until another opportunity arises. Since their illegal activities are non-predatory, they can thrive without the assistance of members of the triad subculture.

Chinese alien smugglers and heroin traffickers have been able to evade most law enforcement efforts thus far. Although there have been few successes in federal prosecutions and little impact on alien smuggling activities, most law enforcement strategies are still built on the assumption that large crime organizations (such as the Triads) are behind the smuggling operations.[62] The lack of success of US anti-trafficking and smuggling efforts has been due in part to insufficient guidance from empirical research and in part to a deep-rooted institutional tradition that focuses on fighting a clear and distinct enemy. To policy makers and law enforcement administrators, it is disconcerting to fight the masses of entrepreneurs who somehow find each other to form a temporary alliance to carry out a transnational operation.

If law enforcement authorities focus only on the triads, tongs and Chinese gangs, and view them as the only crime groups responsible for transnational Chinese organized crime activities, or mistakenly label those non-triad criminals as part of the triad subculture and attempt to fight them as such, this will have far-reaching and unfortunate consequences. Clearly, there is a serious lack of knowledge of the organizational characteristics and patterns of operations of these heroin traffickers and human smuggling rings, upon which effective law enforcement strategies can be built. For instance, a hierarchically structured criminal organization can be best dealt with by the removal of the leadership (that is, the strategy of going after the big fish), while small entrepreneurial groups are most sensitive to disruption of resources (that is, removal of any business contacts). What we need to do is to focus our attention on the development of both the triad subculture and the Chinese smuggling subculture simultaneously and to prevent the coalition of these two equally destructive forces.

NOTES

1. Support for this paper was provided in part by Grant 89-IJ-CX-0021 and 89-IJ-CX-0021 (S1) from the National Institute of Justice and SBR 93-11114 from the National Science Foundation. The opinions expressed are those of the authors and do not reflect the policies or views of the US Department of Justice and the National Science Foundation. An earlier version of this paper was presented at the Second International Conference for Criminal Intelligence Analysts in London, in March 1999. The authors would like to acknowledge the comments from Therese Baker and the reviewers of this paper.
2. Ko-lin Chin, *Chinatown Gangs: Extortion, Enterprise, and Ethnicity* (New York: Oxford University Press, 1996).
3. US Senate, *Asian Organized Crime. Hearing before the Permanent Subcommittee on Investigations of the Committee on Governmental Affairs*, 3 October, 5–6 November 1991 (Washington, DC: US Government Printing Office, 1991).
4. Ko-lin Chin, *Chinese Subculture and Criminality: Non-traditional Crime Groups in America* (Westport, CT: Greenwood Press, 1990).
5. Martin Booth, *The Triads* (New York: St Martin's Press, 1991).
6. W.P. Morgan, *Triad Societies in Hong Kong* (Hong Kong: Government Press, 1960).
7. Mung-yuen Chang, 'Facts about Hong Kong Triad Societies', *Wide Angle Magazine* (in Chinese) (May 1991) pp. 30–9.
8. Fight Crime Committee, *A Discussion Document on Options for Changes in the Law and in the Administration of the Law to Counter the Triad Problem* (Hong Kong: Fight Crime Committee, Security Branch, 1986).
9. Sheng Zhang, *The Activities of Hong Kong Organized Crime Groups* (in Chinese) (Hong Kong: Tien Ti, 1984).
10. Chang, op. cit.
11. James Dubro, *Dragons of Crime: Inside the Asian Underworld* (Markham, ONT: Octopus Publishing Group, 1992).
12. Willard Myers, 'The Emerging Threat of Transnational Organized Crime from the East', *Crime, Law & Social Change*, Vol.24 (1994), p.195.
13. Jin-chen Ng, *My Life in the Black Society* (in Chinese) (Taipei: Five Thousand Years, 1986).
14. Gerald Posner, *Warlords of Crimes* (New York: McGraw-Hill, 1988).

15. Ko-lin Chin, *Illegal Chinese Immigrants in America* (Philadelphia: Temple University, 1999).
16. Chung-hsin Cheng, *On the Problem of Hoodlums, Underworld Gangs and the Organized Crimes in the Republic of China: A Current Survey and Counter Measures* (Taipei: Ministry of Justice, Investigation Bureau, 1993).
17. Zong-xian Chi, *Gangs, Election, and Violence* (in Chinese) (Taipei: Jiao Dian Publishing Co., 1985).
18. Chang-fung Chen, *The Emergence and Decline of the Bamboo United Gang* (in Chinese) (Taipei: Shing Ho Publications, 1986).
19. Zong-xian Chi, op. cit.
20. Yi-hung Liu, 'It's Time to Discuss the Legality of the Anti-Hooligan Law', *China Times* (in Chinese), (21 July 1995), p.23.
21. 'Ministry of Justice Reveals the Number of Politicians with Organized Crime Background'(in Chinese), *World Journal* (19 November 1996), p. 53.
22. Julian Baum, 'Hard Guys Get Hit: Public Outrage Spurs Crackdown on Gangs', *Far Eastern Economic Review* (19 February 1996), pp.18–20.
23. Ping Ho and Jao-jun Wang, *Mainland China Organized Crime* (in Chinese) (Taipei: China Times Publishing, 1993).
24. Ping-hsiung Wei, Tao Auyang and Sahun-an Wang, *Crime and Public Policy under Market-Oriented Economic Conditions* (in Chinese) (Beijing: Public Press, 1995).
25. Richard Dillon, *The Hatchet Men: The Story of the Tong Wars in San Francisco's Chinatown* (New York: Coward-McCann, 1962).
26. US Senate, *Report of the Joint Special Committee to Investigate Chinese Immigration* (New York: Arno Press, 1978).
27. Ko-lin Chin, *Illegal Chinese Immigrants in America*, op. cit.
28. Ker-ting Chou, *Ghosts and Spirits in New York City's Chinatown* (in Chinese) (New York: People and Events, 1993).
29. Robert Bryant, 'Chinese Organized Crime Making Major Inroads in Smuggling Heroin to US', *Organized Crime Digest*, Vol.11, No.17 (1990), pp.1–6.
30. President's Commission on Organized Crime, *Organized Crime of Asian Origin, record of hearing III – 23–25 October 1984, New York, N.Y.* (Washington, DC: Government Printing Office, 1984).
31. Anthony DeStefano, 'The Asian Connection: A New Main Line to U.S.', *New York Newsday* (14 Feb. 1988), p.5.
32. US Senate, *Report of the Joint Special Committee to Investigate Chinese Immigration*, op cit.
33. Richard Lay and Chris Dobson, 'Rise and Fall of Machine Gun Johnny', *South China Morning Post Spectrum* (14 March 1993), p.4.
34. Yuan-ling Huang, 'The Number of Chinese Heroin Cases Increased Dramatically in 1987', *World Journal* (6 January 1988), p.36.
35. Ronald Koziol, 'Multimillionaire Charged in Heroin Case', *San Francisco Examiner* (27 April 1988), p.A7.
36. Robert Stutman, 'Emerging Criminal Groups in Heroin Trafficking', *Statement made before the Select Committee on Narcotics Abuse and Control, US House of Representatives* 10 July 1987.
37. Steven Erlanger, 'Southeast Asia is Now No. 1 Source of U.S. Heroin', *New York Times*, (11 February 1990), p.A26.
38. Richard Esposito and Sheryl McCarthy, 'Record Heroin Bust Sends Agent Searching in NY', *New York Newsday* (14 February 1988), p.5.
39. Michael Marriott, 'Heroin Seizure at 3 Queens Sites is Called Biggest U.S. Drug Raid', *New York Times* (22 February 1989), p.B5.
40. Gwen Kinkead, *Chinatown: A Portrait of a Closed Society* (New York: HarperCollins, 1992).

41. US Senate, *Report of the Joint Special Committee to Investigate Chinese Immigration*, op cit.
42. Robert Bryant, 'Chinese Organized Crime Making Major Inroads in Smuggling Heroin to U.S.', *Organized Crime Digest*, Vol.11, No.17 (1990), pp.1–6; Dubro, op. cit.; Ian Dobinson, 'Pinning a Tail on the Dragon: The Chinese and the International Heroin Trade', *Crime and Delinquency*, Vol.39, No.3 (1993), pp.373–84; Toon Schalks, *Chinese Organized Crime in the Netherlands* (The Hague: National Criminal Intelligence Service, NCB Interpol, 1991); David Black, *Triad Takeover: A Terrifying Account of the Spread of Triad Crime in the West* (London: Sidgwick & Jackson, 1992).
43. Dan Morain and Philip Hager, 'Officials Call Heroin Seizure a Major Victory', *Los Angeles Times* (22 June 1991), p.A24.
44. Joseph Treaster, 'U.S. Officials Seize Huge Heroin Cache', *New York Times* (22 June 1991), p.10.
45. US House of Representatives, *Public Hearings on Emerging Ethnic Crime Group Involvement in Heroin Trafficking*. New York, Select Committee on Narcotics Abuse and Control. (Washington, DC: Government Printing Office, 1987).
46. President's Commission on Organized Crime, op. cit.
47. Michael Powell, 'Tong Influence in Chinatown Turns to Drugs', *New York Newsday* (27 February 1989), p.7.
48. Jerry Seper, 'Chinese Gangs and Heroin Cast Lawless Shadow', *Washington Times*, (28 January 1986), p.A1; Stanley Penn, 'Asian Connection: Chinese Gangsters Fill a Narcotics Gap Left by U.S. Drive on Mafia', *Wall Street Journal* (22 March 1990), p.A1.
49. Leonard Buder, 'Top U.S. Target in Heroin Trade Seized at Hotel', *New York Times*, (15 March 1988), p.B5; Richard Esposito and Sheryl McCarthy, 'Record Heroin Bust Sends Agent Searching in NY', *New York Newsday* (14 February 1988), p.5; Michael Marriott, 'Heroin Seizure at 3 Queens Sites is Called Biggest U.S. Drug Raid', *New York Times* (22 February 1989), p.B5; Joseph Treaster, 'U.S. Officials Seize Huge Heroin Cache', *New York Times* (22 June 1991), p.10.
50. Malcolm Klein, *The American Street Gang* (New York: Oxford University, 1995).
51. Los Angeles County District Attorney's Office 1992.
52. US Department of State, *International Narcotics Control Strategy Report* (Washington, DC: Government Printing Office, 1994).
53. Dobinson, op. cit.
54. Robert Stutman, 'Emerging Criminal Groups in Heroin Trafficking', Statement made before the Select Committee on Narcotics Abuse and Control, US House of Representatives, 10 July 1987.
55. Min Zhou, *Chinatown: The Socioeconomic Potential of an Urban Enclave* (Philadelphia: Temple University, 1992).
56. William Glaberson, '6 Seized in Smuggling Asians into New York', *New York Times* (5 May 1989), p.B3; Alan Boyd and William Barnes, 'Thailand an Open Door for Illegal Passages', *South China Morning Post* (22 June 1992), p.6; Dubro, op. cit.; Marita Eager, 'Patten in Tough Stand against Illegals', *South China Morning Post* (18 July 1992), p.3; Bonny Tam, '198 Illegals Arrested in Tin Shui Wai', *South China Morning Post* (8 September 1992), p.2; Jeffrey Stalk, 'Dutch Focus on Smuggling of Chinese', *International Herald Tribune* (7 May 1993), p.1; Adam Lee, 'Macau Drive Against Illegals', *South China Morning Post* (2 September 1992), p.7.
57. Glaberson, ibid.
58. Donatella Lorch, 'A Flood of Illegal Aliens Enters U.S. via Kennedy: Requesting Political Asylum is Usual Ploy', *New York Times* (18 March 1992), p.B2; Prasong Charasdamrong and Subin Kheunkaew, 'Smuggling Human Being: A Lucrative Racket that Poses a Threat to National Security', *Bangkok Post* (19 July 1992), p.10.
59. Jane Fritsch, 'One Failed Voyage Illustrates Flow of Chinese Immigration', *New York Times* (7 June 1993), p.A1.

60. Pamela Burdman, 'Huge Boom in Human Smuggling – Inside Story of Flight from China', *San Francisco Chronicle* (27 April 1993), p.A1.
61. Ying Chan, 'China Ships' Unholy Cargo', *New York Daily News* (18 May 1993), p.7.
62. See 'Fact Sheet: Alien Smuggling Policy', US Department of State Dispatch (Fact sheet released by the White House, Office of the Press Secretary, Washington, DC, on 18 June 1993).

PART 2
CRIMINAL ACTIVITIES AND MARKETS

Maritime Fraud and Piracy

JAYANT ABHYANKAR

In December 1979, the ship M.V. *Salem* set sail from Kuwait with a cargo of crude oil worth US$56 million, intended for Italy. The oil, however, never reached Italy; instead the vessel diverted to South Africa and secretly discharged her cargo in defiance of existing sanctions. She continued up the coast of Africa until she was scuttled by her crew off Senegal. At this point, meticulous planning and execution began to degenerate into farce. The *Salem* sank in view of another vessel and left no significant oil slick. Her crew, rescued from lifeboats, claimed they had spent hours fighting an engine room fire, but were clean and neatly dressed. They were all carrying passports and suitcases, but not the ship's log.

Nine separate investigations of the *Salem* case around the world led to criminal proceedings in Britain, the USA, Greece and the Netherlands. The legal consequences of the affair were probably played out only in 1987 when a Dutch court dropped charges against a Dutch businessman, alleged to have been one of the ringleaders. The lack of evidence in that case resulted, at least partly, from the, unsurprising, reluctance of the South African authorities to co-operate.

The *Salem* is probably the most celebrated and extravagant example to date of a maritime fraud. But it is symptomatic of a problem to which the transportation industry is particularly vulnerable. International trade brings together people of different traditions, laws and institutions Relationships are based on trust. In the event of this trust being misplaced, or of something else going wrong, cultural difficulties between trading partners will be compounded by jurisdictional problems and by the fact that, once a ship has left port, it is not easy to know what she is doing.

TYPES OF FRAUD

The range of maritime fraud is startlingly wide and, as with other types

157

of crime, is constantly being expanded in line with the ingenuity and imagination of the people who practice it. Indeed, today's maritime fraud can be defined as a combination of various criminal acts such as forgery, barratry, piracy, theft, arson, etc., where one or more parties end up losing money, goods or even the vessel. Maritime crime and frauds can be classified into the following types: documentary; charter party; insurance; container crime, deviation phantom ships; and piracy.

DOCUMENTARY FRAUDS

Many maritime frauds are really documentary frauds that, of course, involve false or forged documents used to deceive. In the maritime context these documents are usually bills of lading and commercial invoices - or sometimes nothing more elaborate than a telex message.

Buyers and sellers are often separated by political legal and geographical bathers. Sellers have a natural reluctance to part with goods until the purchase price is paid. Conversely, buyers prefer to pay on delivery of goods. The gap between payment and delivery of goods is bridged by the documentary credit system (UCP 500). The mechanism of this system is well known. The buyer instructs his bank (the issuing bank) to open a letter of credit in favour of the seller. The issuing bank instructs the paying bank in the seller's country to hand over the purchase price when the seller tenders documents confirming shipment of the goods. In a collection arrangement, for example, a payment against documents (DP) transaction, the payment takes place in the buyer's country. The seller instructs a bank in the buyer's country to hand over the documents of title to the goods to the buyer upon receipt of payment. Both the documentary credit and the collection arrangements rely on the honesty of the trading partners and can be easily abused. A fraudulent seller can cash the letter of credit by presenting bogus documents for a non-existent cargo. Alternatively, the cargo can be of lesser quality or quantity. Sometimes the same cargo is sold to two or more buyers, and the purchase price collected from each. This was attempted several times in the 1990s with Nigerian oil. Finally, a fraudulent buyer can present forged bills of lading in a DP transaction and collect the cargo without paying for it.

A classic documentary fraud concerned the vessel *Helga Weir*. An Egyptian buyer agreed to purchase a number of second-hand vehicles from a Belgian exporter, whom he had known for some time. A few months later, the Belgian, with a German associate, travelled to the Cairo offices of the buyer. He explained that he was unable to provide the second-hand vehicles, but that his colleague from Germany could. A proforma invoice was produced and indicated that the potential supplier company was registered in Liechtenstein. The buyer thought that he was getting an extremely good bargain and agreed to proceed.

The following day, the Egyptian buyer went to his bank and arranged for a letter of credit for 350,000 Deutschmarks to be opened in favour of the Liechtenstein company, which had an account at a Swiss Bank. Only two documents were called for under the letter of credit – a clean bill of lading and the beneficiary's invoice. The German exporter, on receipt of notice that a letter of credit had been opened in favour of the Liechtenstein company, obtained a bill of lading on which a company called Red Med Lines appeared as the carrier. This company had, in truth, gone into liquidation some nine months previously. The German exporter, who had no intention of making any shipment, completed the bill of lading to show that five Mercedes Tipper Trucks had been shipped on the *Helga Weir* at Hamburg. In reality, the *Helga Weir* was discharging cargo at Lisbon on that date. The bill of lading, together with an invoice that showed the seller as Vias Establishment of Vaduz, were duly presented to the Swiss Bank in Zurich, where payment was made to the beneficiary.

When his vehicles failed to arrive, the Egyptian buyer made attempts to contact the German exporter. When he proved untraceable, the buyer turned to the Belgian exporter for assistance. The Belgian, however, claimed that he had only acted as an introducer of the business and was reluctant to become involved in any attempts to resolve the matter. Similarly, although a criminal offence took place in Zurich as a result of the issuing of a forged bill of lading to obtain the money, the Swiss Bank refused to become involved in any criminal complaint as it had suffered no loss, having been reimbursed from Cairo. For its part, the Liechtenstein company was controlled, as many companies are in that country, by a lawyer who was prevented by law from disclosing its true owner.

One thing which emerges from this case is that one can be deceived even when dealing with known and trusted people – the Egyptian importer thought he could rely on the Belgian exporter.

It is worth, in this connection, considering a another case. An English company wished to buy 300 tons of antimony, a special mineral ore, imported from the People's Republic of China (PRC). A Hong Kong company, Wang Shun, offered to provide this antimony, but proposed that it should be conveyed by a feeder vessel to Taiwan and from there on the M.V. *Fluvius* to Rotterdam. The reason given was that if the government of the PRC thought the product was going to Taiwan, it would treat the matter as a domestic sale and offer a lower price. This was a lie and, in retrospect, it seemed hardly convincing. The PRC would have been more likely to impose an embargo on Taiwan than to offer a discount. Further, it was a peculiar route – it would be more logical to sail from Taiwan, to Hong Kong, to Europe than the other way round.

In any case, the English company accepted these terms. But Wang Shun shipped nine containers of scrap — not antimony — on the feeder vessel. The master issued nine bills of lading for scrap, which was what he had loaded. Wang Shun substituted these bills by false documents procured from a shipping company, Cosmopolitan Lines. Like Red Med Lines in the *Helga Weir* case, Cosmopolitan Lines was in liquidation. These false bills were presented together with a certificate of origin, which Wang Shun had no difficulty in forging, to the negotiating bank, which made payment for the antimony. Wang Shun simply went into liquidation before the fraud was discovered and the offenders have never been traced.

International trading will always involve some risk, for the reasons elaborated above. However, this risk can be minimized by taking certain preventive measures. Most important, since everything depends on trust, traders should, as far as possible, restrict their dealings to established companies that they know something about – even if, as seen from the case of the *Helga Weir*, this is not foolproof. This ideal may further be rendered problematic by the absence of well-known carriers on certain routes and the effective anonymity of some charterers and owners. Nevertheless, there are several organizations (including the International Maritime Bureau) in a position to provide topical information on potential trading partners if requested. A requirement to seek and assess this type of information is indeed formalized in the Institute Cargo Clauses.

Second, traders should consider how the documentary credit system could best be used to their advantage. Payment against documents, as defined above, is certainly safer for the buyer – but it is not so satisfactory for the seller, since the buyer can default. Sellers should give careful consideration to the backing documents they require for a letter of credit and insist on a performance bond in appropriate cases.

Cargo owners can insist on a pre-loading inspection of the goods, or the vessel – although this, of course, adds to costs. Further, insurers can insert classification clauses, insisting that vessels used meet certain standards or, as is rarely done in practice, they can require that the names of proposed vessels be notified to them. On a more basic level it is easy and elementary, to check that a proposed vessel does, in fact, exist, does have the necessary capacity to carry the cargo and was where she was supposed to have been when the bills of lading were issued.

Cargo owners should also be aware of clauses in bills of lading that give them greater (or less) protection. For example, freight collect terms, under which the freight is payable — when the cargo is discharged, are clearly more favourable to cargo owners than freight pre-paid terms. In general, cargo owners should be cautious of bills of lading, which are subject to charter parties, unless they themselves are the charterers. The effect will be that they are being bound by a contract to which they were not a party (only the ship owner and the charterer are parties to a charter party), and which they have probably never seen.

Masters should ensure that cargo signed for on bills of lading is actually on board, and, where practicable, should themselves sign the bill of lading. Cargoes should only be released against a duly endorsed bill of lading.

At least, in the case of valuable cargoes, masters should be instructed to radio their position at certain times during the voyage. There is also the possibility of appointing a supervisor to travel on the ship to ensure the security of the cargo, although this can clearly be expensive.

Finally, there are six clear warning signs that should put traders on their guard:

- The goods might be in strong demand or not readily available.
- Low prices might be quoted or the source of supply might be unusual.
- The method of payment might be unusual, or it might be required to be made to a third party, or to an intermediary.
- The names used by companies involved might resemble those of well-known business houses.
- There might be pressure for fast acceptance or fast issuance of documentary credits.

- It might be proposed that a bill of lading be acceptable even though the goods are inconsistent with it – this is, in fact, granting an indemnity for an incorrect document and is illegal in many jurisdictions.

CHARTER PARTY FRAUDS

Many sea voyages are made under the terms of a charter party. The success of this type of voyage depends on all parties, the ship owner, the charterer and the cargo owner fulfilling their obligations. When one or more of the parties fails to do so, the resulting contractual mess usually requires a great deal of investigation and negotiation if anything is to be salvaged. Failures occur for two reasons, which often become blurred in practice: fraud and business failure. A typical fraud will concern a time charter party, under which a vessel is hired on a per diem basis and hire is usually paid in fortnightly instalments in advance. The time charterer pays the first hire and the vessel proceeds to the loading port where the cargoes are loaded. The shipowner authorizes the release of freight pre-paid bills of lading to the charterers who pass them on to the cargo owner in exchange for freight (that is to say, the transportation charges). In other words, the shipowner is releasing a document acknowledging the cargo owner's title to the goods on board his ship and that can be negotiated as representing these goods. He does this in recognition of the fact that his freight has been paid, although in fact all that he has received is the first two weeks hire.

What happens next is that the ship sails from the loading port to her destination and the charterers abscond with the entire freight, which they have collected from the cargo owner. The shipowner is contractually bound to deliver the cargo under the bills of lading, which he has issued. But since he is no longer receiving his freight he might not have the financial resources to do so.

The cargo interests almost always lose when a charter party fails. If the seller has not been paid under the letter of credit, he is faced, at best, with a long wait, possibly aggravated by penalties for late delivery. As soon as something appears to go wrong the buyer may fly to stop payment under letters of credit by, for example, finding technical deficiencies in the documents. The cargo owner will sometimes also find himself helpless against a shipowner who, in a variation of charter party fraud, claims an exorbitant amount to repair 'engine damage' after a voyage has started. Further, the crew of a stranded ship might be tempted to start selling the cargo, sometimes with the consent of the shipowner and, sometimes in certain jurisdictions, 'legally' with the help of unscrupulous local lawyers who are prepared to take advantage of the fact that the genuine cargo owner is far away in another jurisdiction.

On the scale of vulnerability, the shipowner is in an intermediate position. When a default occurs he can take the time to examine his options, knowing that his vessel is safe from arrest by the cargo owner on grounds of delay – as long as he acts reasonably. The charterer, especially when his company is registered in a country of convenience, and the beneficial ownership is difficult to trace, has least to lose. If there are any problems he can often just walk away and disappear.

The frequency of chartering failures and the absence of real sanctions, create a climate favourable to the fraudsters. Like many fraudsters in other fields, the charter party fraudster can protect himself by saying that he failed through a series of bad business decisions rather than criminal intent.

INSURANCE FRAUDS

One way to make a vessel disappear is to sink (or 'scuttle') the vessel, and pretend that the cargo was on her before she sank. This, of course, was attempted in the *Salem*. There is also scuttling 'for its own sake' - whether to make a false insurance claim or to get rid of a useless vessel. This is known as hull fraud. It is more common, as one would expect, in a depressed market.

A vessel loaded a cargo of steel in Italy, worth US$300,000, for the UK. Ten days later the vessel was reported sunk north of Morocco. The crew, picked up from lifeboats by a Spanish ferry, claimed that a leak had developed in the engine room. It did not take a great deal of imagination to deduce that there was something suspicious about this event. The vessel sank in calm seas, in the early hours of the morning when there was no other ship in sight, but among busy shipping lanes where 'survivors' were certain to be picked up. Further, Moroccan industrialists had made several approaches to the Italians to obtain information on the type of steel that the vessel was carrying. Lastly, it appeared that the master was a part owner of the vessel.

The crew was landed by the ferry in Bilbao and they dispersed. However, they were later traced to a French prison, having been convicted of smuggling drugs in a different vessel. The captain insisted that the first vessel had sunk accidentally. However, one of the other crew members admitted that she had been scuttled, and that the cargo had been discharged earlier in Morocco. The vessel had also been used regularly for drug smuggling, but was getting old and had outlived its usefulness. There was, therefore, an element of hull fraud in this deception. This indicates that analytical categories of fraud, although they are useful, often overlap.

CONTAINER CRIME

Back in the mid-1970s, in the early euphoric days of containerization on a large scale, a Canadian representative at an Interpol conference on port crime said 'the container has made no difference to cargo crime except that the goods are now gift wrapped'. This was true then and has become still truer with the passage of time. More to the point, the prognosis is not all that good. The container has eliminated the petty pilferer to a great extent but, in terms of percentage value, he was always more of a nuisance than a problem. Instead, various types of criminal have infiltrated the system. We have the theft of the total container, either by force or by a manipulation of the system; we have theft of the contents, either by the opportunist or by organized crime; and we have fraud.

The theft of the whole container is sometimes accomplished by the comparatively simple means of hijacking, although this method has always been restricted to certain countries and still further restricted to urban areas. There have also been some spectacular thefts of complete containers from overnight parking areas. But, although these can be called container thefts they are, in principle and technique, no different from the whole-load theft that used to be commonplace in the days of conventional cargo – containerization did not produce the phenomenon.

It is now becoming increasingly common for the theft of a whole container to be accomplished by altering paperwork or, in this high-tech age, the manipulation of a computer entry. The benefit to the criminal of this type of theft is that there are no witnesses and sometimes a great deal of time can elapse between the time of the theft and the time that the investigators manage to identify the method. This time lapse often means that the trail of evidence has grown cold.

As opposed to the theft of the whole container, theft of part of the contents is far more common both in individual instances and in overall value. This is because it is possible to steal from a container and so disguise the manner of entry that the fact of loss does not become apparent until the container reaches its destination - which might well be both months later and many thousands of miles away. The difficulty is then one of identifying the venue of the crime and, as important, the appropriate law enforcement agency to conduct any enquiry. Even if the venue is identified, the time lapse often militates against effective investigation. This type of crime is increasing whereas, a few years ago, criminals might take a few cases or cartons from a container, now the trend seems to be that 50 per cent or more of the contents will disappear. Indeed, in one case of a three-container shipment to an African port, the loss rate was 80 per cent of the contents of each of the three containers. In another instance, involving a consignment from a Spanish port to Lebanon, the loss was 96 per cent of the contents of a container loaded with leather garments.

The uninitiated will ask how this can happen or how can it be tolerated. It can happen because the container system was not designed with sufficient foresight given to questions of security of contents, and it is tolerated because insurance provides a buffer against negative commercial consequences. In the early days a system of sealing was introduced, but this system suffered from three fundamental errors:

1. First, the criminal fraternity quickly found that many of the early seals could be compromised in that they could be opened and then closed again without any identifiable trace. Although seals have improved in design, this can still happen with some that are on the market.
2. It was then found that the locking mechanism of the container itself could be opened and closed again without trace and without ever touching the seal. There has been little improvement in design and this can still happen.
3. Finally, the system of examining and recording seals was quickly eroded by the technicalities of the container handling system.

The initial handling system had a requirement that seals should be examined during the transit of the container. This was considered an essential part of the system because the sanctity of the seal was the only replacement for the repeated tally process that existed in the days of conventional cargo. Unfortunately, increasingly sophisticated handling systems, combined with speed of throughput, meant that it was physically impossible to examine seals. This, together with the fact that examination of seals on a busy terminal brought with it a safety risk, has produced a 'system by default' in which seals are not always examined when they should be and sometimes never at all. In some areas of operation it is a deliberate management policy not to examine seals because any identified discrepancy could possibly impose on the facility a liability for loss, which it is not obliged to accept. In the words of one through-transit operator 'we receive a box, we handle a box, we deliver a box, we are not responsible for quantity or condition of content'. These commercial attitudes have spawned the well-known clauses 'shipper's load and count' and 'said to contain'. This should not be taken to imply criticism of these commercial positions, rather to identity and highlight the incompatibility of good security practices with commercial expedience.

The last type of crime to enter the container field is that of fraud. This is particularly interesting not only because the crimes are often extremely well accomplished but also because of the unique circumstances in dealing with such cases.

It is a basic principle of insurance that if a cargo does not exist then it cannot be insured and, therefore, there cannot be any insurer liability. This means that when cargo arrives at a destination either totally absent or different in specification to the insured cargo, then an insurer may discount all liability. The importer or exporter, depending on the terms of shipment, is left not only with the actual financial loss but also with the problem of trying to prove that the cargo existed and was stolen and, therefore, trying to establish the liability of the insurer. For example, it is not unusual for an insurer, when faced with the apparent circumstances of a shortage of goods in a container that was sealed at point of origin and was apparently still sealed at point of receipt, to say that the goods must have been short-loaded and that the apparent loss is not an insured risk. Whilst this is both understandable and convenient for the insurer, it does not, of course, acknowledge that seals can be opened and closed again without trace and that a container can be opened and closed without trace or even touching the seal. This state of affairs will automatically leave the importer at odds with his supplier, both blaming the other, and has led to more than one instance in which there is a doubt as to whether the container has been short-loaded at point of origin, or the out-turn under-declared at point of receipt at destination. In short, is there a theft, a fraudulent consignor or a dishonest consignee?

The same situation will apply when there has been a substitution of contents, that is 'scrap for new' or just the replacement of weight with rubbish. Again, the insurer may well take the position that the substitution could not have taken place in transit and so the loss is not an insurable risk.

Probably the most spectacular theft/fraud circumstances occurred towards the end of 1988 when 30, 20-foot containers were supposedly each loaded with 996 cartons of canned mushrooms at an inland depot in mainland Hong Kong. These containers were then shipped on two different deep-sea vessels to Rotterdam, in the Netherlands. From there they were shipped by four different feeder vessels to five different consignees in Scandinavia, with delivery taking place over a period of about three weeks. Each one of the 30 containers was empty. The problem was then a dual one that not only was it desirable to find the mushrooms but also to decide who was responsible for looking for them. The insurers took the understandable view that such a widespread total loss could not have been theft and that the only alternative, fraud on the part of the consignor in Hong Kong made this a non-insurable shortage. The various aggrieved consignees were left in the position where they had to take individual action to recoup their individual losses from Hong Kong.

At the beginning of this section, it was suggested that the prognosis is not all that good. Whilst the treatment of the subject has not been in very great depth, it is obvious that, before improvement can be expected, many different factors must come together.

- There would need to be a standardization of seals to minimize the possibility of interference. There would need to be a complete re-design of the container-locking mechanism to ensure that the sealing device and the locking system were separate from one another.
- There would need to be a complete reappraisal of operations to ensure that the procedure for examining seals, so essential in the early days, was re-introduced to ensure that interference did not go undetected.

- Perhaps the most important factor of all would be to re-introduce a system of automatic liability of a terminal or carrier for the contents of what he handles or carries and to limit the 'catch-all' of insurance. Quite obviously, these factors are not going to come to pass and, while commerce finds that it can live with the level of crime as it presently exists, there is no catalyst to produce an alternative. In short, if the commercial climate does not exist for alteration, things will stay as they are.

DEVIATION FRAUDS

In August 1979, a Cypriot vessel named M.V. *Betty* loaded 3,500 tonnes of reinforced steel and 5,000 cubic metres of timber at Rijeka for Jeddah in Saudi Arabia. Instead of heading for the Suez Canal, the vessel deviated to Lebanon and illegally discharged her cargo in the port of Jounieh. The Saudi merchants were infuriated by this episode. The Saudi authorities promptly imposed a ban on all ships calling at Saudi ports that had earlier passed through Lebanon.

In a strange way, the culprits in the *Betty* deviation were instrumental in highlighting the problem of maritime crime at an international level. The *Betty* affair hit the headlines and, on 29 October 1979 the Lebanese government requested the Intergovernmental Maritime Consultative Organization (IMCO; now known as International Maritime Organization, IMO) to examine the question of criminal barratry and the unlawful seizure of ships and their cargoes. This event was also the catalyst for the formation of the International Maritime Bureau in 1981.

What is Deviation?

In a contract of carriage or for the purpose of marine insurance, deviation means departing from the contract route or the usual route. The permissible reasons include saving life, aiding a vessel in distress or obtaining medical aid. The vessel resumes her normal course after the cause resulting in the deviation ceases to operate. Where maritime crime is concerned, however, the word 'deviation' is associated with the theft or mis-appropriation of the cargo by the shipowner. Instead of proceeding to the agreed destination, the vessel deviates en route to another destination where the cargo is sold illegally. The vessel is then deliberately sunk, is reported to be sunk or simply vanishes by changing its identity and reappearing under another name. Though the end result is usually the loss of cargo, there are different causes for vessels to deviate.

Frustration of the Charter Party

During the early 1970s the price of crude oil quadrupled and, as a result, there were newly rich oil-producing states in the Middle East and West Africa. With this newfound wealth these states began importing vast quantities of capital goods, such as cement and steel. At that stage no one realized that the existing ports could not possibly cope with the increased throughput. As a result, acute congestion of up to six months built up in ports such as Lagos. Usually enterprising charterers who did not foresee such a long delay in the voyages chartered these vessels. Many charterers could not meet the hire/demurrage payments. As a result, the shipowners were in a difficult position. Their ships were loaded with cargoes and, in most cases, they were contractually bound to deliver the goods whether or not they were paid under the charter party. Some shipowners offloaded and warehoused the cargo in other ports under a lien for outstanding hire/demurrage. The less honest shipowners realized that instead of warehousing the cargo, huge profits could be made by simply selling it. The political instability in Lebanon meant that a vessel could deviate there and easily sell the cargo in one of the illegal ports. Alternatively, certain ports in West Africa, such as Conakry in Guinea Bissau, were willing to receive these stolen cargoes.

Financial Difficulties of the Shipowners

These cases involve shipowners who are not dishonest but operate on a tight shoestring budget. It only requires a small problem such as delay in the voyage owing to monsoons to cause a cash-flow problem. If the owner has no back-up funds he may be induced into committing a crime, deviating and selling the cargo.

Reasons Beyond Shipowner's Control

It is said, 'strange things happen at sea'. At times, even innocent ship owners get into an unforeseen situation where the voyage becomes frustrated and ends up in an illegal activity. A classic example is the unfortunate final voyage of M.V. *Caspar*. She loaded general cargo from Bombay for Jeddah. The voyage up to Jeddah was uneventful. When she

169

arrived off Jeddah, the port authorities refused her permission to enter the port. The reason given by was that in the past she had traded with Israel and consequently was blacklisted by the Arab Boycott Authority. The shipowner was left in a difficult position. The vessel had traded with Israel but that was under her previous ownership. However, the Arab Boycott Authority in Damascus was not willing to accept this fact. The vessel was running out of fuel and provisions and the crew was getting restless. Having exhausted all legitimate channels and not being able to satisfy the authorities, the ship owner ordered the vessel to deviate to Djibouti. By this time, some two months had passed since the vessel had entered the Red Sea. The owner was running out of funds and he considered various options including scuttling the vessel. Fortunately, the crew refused to become involved. Ultimately, after almost one year, the vessel proceeded to Egypt where the cargo was transhipped and the vessel was sold for a mere 30,000 Egyptian pounds.

Shipowner Intends to Defraud from the Outset

Unlike the above three types in this category, the deviation here is premeditated and well planned and should be termed as proper 'illegal deviation'. The vessel changes her name, deviates and illegally discharges her cargo. In most cases of deviations, the vessels are not sunk but re-appear under another identity. This type of deviation is prevalent in areas where the ports are not under close supervision because of civil war or civil disorder, or in cases where the authorities turn a blind eye because of trade sanctions. One country, which was the favourite for deviation frauds, was Lebanon. Illegal deviation first achieved real prominence with the exploitation of the problems of Lebanon where, from the late 1970s to the early 1990s, law and order, as commonly understood, did not exist. With a hungry, ready market for goods of almost any kind, it was not surprising that the marine criminal arose ready, as always, to meet a need. This peculiar crime was rampant but then an alteration in the power structure in the Lebanon caused it to decline. However, there is a lesson to be learned by closely examining the Lebanese deviations, for they could recur in any region facing political instability and civil war.

Lebanese Deviations

The Eastern Mediterranean has a reputation for being a problem area for the shipping industry, so much so that at certain times, shipowners could negotiate cheaper insurance for their vessels if they avoided the Eastern Mediterranean. After the Bermuda Triangle and the Golden Triangle, we now have the Levant Triangle to plague us, covering the area between Greece, Port Said and Tripoli (Lebanon). If reports of so-called 'sinkings' were believed, this triangle was a graveyard.

In Eastern Mediterranean countries there were many small shipowners in intense competition. Consequently, their profits were marginal. Adding to the problem was the general shipping slump. Further, hijacking was rife. In the late 1980s, there was a marked increase in cargo losses, as more and more ships diverted to and unloaded in Lebanese ports. Vessels reported sunk were 'found' unloading in Lebanon.

The following case illustrates a typical deviation. In November 1990, M.V. *Chariot I* loaded 4,000 tonnes of aluminium ingots worth US$8 million at Brat in Romania for Trieste in Italy. En route she changed her name to M.V. *Ra Ra* and deviated to the port of Ras Salaata. Acting upon information that a vessel was discharging aluminium in Ras Salaata, the IMB made contact with the Lebanese Prime Minister's office. The Prime Minister at the time, Dr Selim Hoss, acted positively and ordered the police to seize the vessel. When the police arrived in Ras Salaata they found that all cargo except 200 tonnes had been carted away by the criminals. The master and the crew had run away after removing the steering wheel. The police towed the vessel to the nearby port of Tripoli using a spanner to steer the vessel!

The IMB investigators immediately proceeded to Tripoli and along with the police began searching for the cargo. They recovered over 2,000 tonnes, which were scattered and secretly stowed all over northern Lebanon. Some of the cargo was found hidden in the gardens of residential estates and covered with canvas. The recovered cargo was subsequently re-shipped and returned to the rightful owners in February 1991. When the IMB investigators boarded the *Ra Ra,* for the first time the identity of the vessel was discovered. The fraudsters had purchased her in 1988 and named her the *Santa Maria I.* Thereafter, the vessel began her criminal career and over the next two years went through the following name changes: *Santa Maria I, Senator, Sea Wind, Phoenix, Nasos I, Asco I, Peggy, Peggwa, Chariot I,* and *Ra Ra.* During these two years the vessel was used to deviate and steal cargoes of PVC, steel, tomato paste and aluminium. The total value of the stolen cargo was US$14.8 million.

The claims against underwriters had continued to mount and action rather than words was called for. As a result the Eastern Mediterranean

Investigation Team (EMIT) was set up with the aim of providing sufficient information to enable interested parties to evaluate and take appropriate action to reduce their own losses. This research was commissioned jointly by the Salvage Association and the International Maritime Bureau, and received the support of a number of insurance organizations. The findings of EMIT were as follows,

- Beirut and its fifth basin had been the most popular destination for deviating vessels, followed by Ras Salaata.
- Of the crew involved in these deviations, Lebanese accounted for the major group (35 per cent), with Ghanaians (12 per cent), Greeks (10 per cent) and Egyptians (6 per cent) making up the other leading groups.
- Nine nations' flags were used by the deviating and associated vessels. The main flags used being those of Lebanon (39.4 per cent), Cyprus (23.5 per cent) and Panama (14.7 per cent).
- Vessel size was predictable with the majority being between 1,001 and 3,000 gross tons (52.9 per cent). Another 26.4 per cent were in the 3,001 to 5,000 bracket, and 14.7 per cent were over 5,000 tons. Two vessels (5.8 per cent) were under 1,000 tons, the smallest being the *Smeen* at 494 gross tons.
- As for the vessels' ages, none was under 15 years old. Ten vessels were under 20 years, but the majority were over 20 years with three vessels exceeding 30 years.
- There was no evidence of a single 'godfather' or Mafia-type organization having control over all of the illicit trade. However, several well-defined groups, some involved in vessel ownership and others involved in distribution emerged.

The EMIT findings were published and for the first time the magnitude of the problem became clear. Many cargo owners and insurers became more cautious and the frequency of deviations slowed. This effort proved that when the industry takes pro-active measures, positive results can be obtained. The success in the recovery of cargo aboard *Chariot I* demonstrated to the criminals that the industry and the authorities were not going to allow them to continue with these thefts. This deterrent, and the gradual return of political stability in Lebanon, resulted in the end of these frauds. No deviation into Lebanon has taken place since this event and at long last the problem of 'Lebanese deviations' was resolved.

Other Deviations

Deviations have continued in different shapes and forms in other parts of the world, however. The following case is a classic example of a deviation in the guise of alleged salvage and general average. On 3 September 1994, M.V. *Al Fath* (grt 12,896, built 1970) sailed from Paranagua (Brazil) for Madras loaded with 14,000 tonnes of bagged sugar. Instead of sailing around South Africa, she chose the longer route via the Mediterranean, which added 2,100 miles to the voyage; that is, extra sailing of about nine days plus the cost of Suez Canal transit. On 5 October 1994, Lloyd's casualty section reported that on 4 October the vessel had stopped in position 32°36'N 27°43'E owing to engine problems and shortage of diesel oil. Salvage assistance was in hand. It was subsequently discovered that salvor vessels M.V. *Ibrahim* and M.V. *Al Fath* were, in fact, 'sister ships' beneficially owned by El Path Company for International Trade S.A.E. The alleged salvage operation was completed when *Ibrahim* towed *Al Fath* into Alexandria. The owners declared that the two masters had agreed on a private salvage agreement and declared general average. Cargo interests were asked to pay US$2.8 million as their contribution.

On 18 October 1994, *Al Fath* changed her name to *Cape Vincent* under a six-month provisional registry from Malta. She remained in Alexandria over the next five months. Owners continued to demand US$2.8 million as a contribution from the cargo interests. The cargo interests refused to give in to this unprecedented demand towards salvage. Protracted negotiations, however, resulted in a commercial settlement between the cargo interests and El Path Company, the beneficial owners of *Al Fath* and *Ibrahim*. On 17 March 1995, the cargo interests were forced to sell the cargo to a third party and suffered a loss of around US$1.5 million.

The inquiries conducted by the IMB indicated that there was no justifiable reason for the vessel to deviate. The so-called 'salvage' appeared to be more of a towage situation. The vessel's managers, International Maritime Services Company, gave various explanations for deviation, which seemed unreasonable. It was also discovered that the vessel had no hull insurance and the P&I cover was withdrawn soon after sailing from Brazil.

The salvage agreement between the masters of *Al Fath* and *Ibrahim*, undoubtedly prepared after the alleged salvage, is said to be a masterpiece of legal drafting. In practice it would have been extremely difficult to convince a local judge of the invalidity or unfairness of this agreement.

Under an Egyptian law of 1990 concerning salvage awards, private agreements are valid. Although this law was designed to protect the innocent, the above case illustrates that it can be used to make unprecedented and unilateral demands from the innocent cargo interests.

Prevention of Deviations

In most crime, from the start there is a direct conflict between the perpetrator and the victim. The perpetrator is endeavouring to commit an act against the will of the victim. In the crime of fraud, however, things are often very different as the fraudster deliberately goes to great lengths to please the victim. The fraudster will offer goods or services at a price the victim cannot refuse. So it is with deviation fraud, in which the shipowner disregarding his own costs is prepared to offer the hire of his vessel or to carry cargo at a rate that seems extremely attractive to the shipper or charterer. He can afford to do this for he has no intention of going to the expense of sailing his vessel to its legal destination. In most cases, the vessel will make a much shorter voyage to a port convenient for hijacking the cargo. The shipowner is paid with the freight, which will cover all or most of the cost for the shorter journey but then, when he sells the cargo, the sale is almost all profit, even though – because they are stolen – he will be obliged to accept less than the market value for the goods.

On top of this scenario, there is the ease with which vessels can sail around the world, visiting ports with little control or hindrance. Much has been written of flags of convenience, but because of lax registration procedure they still offer an excellent facility for the deviation fraudster. When the ship enters a port, the authorities will require production of the vessel's certificate, of registry and sometimes the classification certificates, but on sighting these documents are never verified with the issuing authority. So long as the master can produce a reasonable set of documents (although they might be false) a vessel will be allowed port facilities without hindrance. If deviation frauds are to be combated, therefore, port authorities and vessel agents must take a more active interest in the ships and owners they service. Having said this, the prevention of deviations must first start with the buyer.

Buying goods on cost and freight (C&F) or cost, insurance and freight (CIF) terms puts the risk for the sea voyage upon the buyer, yet delegates the responsibility for arranging carriage to the seller. Unless conditions of carriage were placed by the buyer (difficult within these terms) the seller will naturally go for the cheapest vessel he can find. If deviations are to be prevented, the buyer must take an active role in the carriage arrangements. He will then be in a position to evaluate the risks and act accordingly. In considering carriage, the buyer should consider the following requirements: deal with a reputable shipper or supplier; use well-established charter brokers and shipping lines; beware of offers of cheap freight rates; steer clear of single vessel companies of which nothing is known and which have no apparent assets; investigate the age and condition of the vessel, since experience has shown that vessels involved in deviation fraud tend to be at the end of their useful working life. If the buyer does this, the prospects for deviation will be reduced.

PHANTOM SHIPS

In the late 1970s an alarming number of frauds involving hull and cargo insurance was suspected in and around the South China Sea. This prompted marine insurers in Hong Kong, Singapore and Malaysia, and the London insurance market to set up the Far East Regional Investigation Team (FERIT) to enquire into these losses. FERIT concluded its investigations in September 1979. Its report stated that 27 of the 48 losses were highly suspicious. Of those, 16 vessels were probably scuttled and involved in fraud. The FERIT report was never made public, but maritime fraud of this nature reduced considerably following the release of the report to the insurers. Perhaps the investigation itself made the industry more aware, vigilant, and therefore less likely to fall prey to such fraud. Very few criminal prosecutions, however, resulted from FERIT's investigation. This meant that many fraudsters escaped and were potentially active.

Since the mid-1980s systematic thefts of entire shiploads of cargo have been reported in the same region. Investigations into these crimes strongly suggest the return of syndicates similar to those described by FERIT, albeit committing more sophisticated crimes of a documentary nature called 'phantom ship frauds'.

What is a Phantom Ship?

A phantom ship is a vessel with a phantom identity. The vessel is registered on the basis of false information provided to the registering authorities about the vessel's previous names, tonnages and dimensions, as well as the owner's identity. Consequently, on investigation after the crime, no trace can be found of the ship, its owner or, in most cases, the crew.

The vessels involved are often small bulk carriers or twin deckers under Honduran, Panamanian, Belize or St Vincent flags. Most vessels are 15–20 years old and poorly maintained. In addition, they do not have hull and machinery insurance or a P&I cover.

The creation of a phantom ship is facilitated by officials in ship registries who are prepared to register vessels according to details provided, without making any effort to verify the information. This occurs either because the system in that particular registry is not efficient, or in some cases, because of a high degree of corruption in the registration office.

The owners of the phantom ships are companies that exist only on paper. They are set up only a few days prior to the operation and use temporary offices. Names of the directors given to the company registry often turn out to be fictitious.

The crews employed for phantom ship operation are mostly Burmese, Thai or Filipinos. They are hired after paying US$300–500 or more as placement money to the agents. During the deviation, the crew members are paid twice or three times their normal salaries. In most cases, the details given in the passport or seaman book including the names — in the crew lists, are false. The certificates of competency of the officers are forgeries. Some crew members have been identified and traced by the IMB. Surprisingly, their families usually know little of their whereabouts. This, in itself, is highly suspicious and indicates that the crew is aware that the owners and officers are doing something wrong.

The agents selected by the owners of phantom ships in different countries are often small operators. Their main task is to book cargoes and collect freight for the owners. In order to attract more cargo, the freight charged is often lower than the market rate. The agents are introduced to the owners of phantom ships through a middleman and do not necessarily have direct contact with the owners. Therefore, when questioned, the agents are in no position to identify the shipowner.

The brokers involved in fixing the phantom vessels fail to carry out any checks on the shipowner. This may be because the commissions offered by the ship owner are more than is usual. In one instance, the commission earned by the broking chain was 12.5 per cent of the freight!

The cargoes targeted have included frozen prawns, timber, plywood, palm oil, textiles, resin, rubber, steel and copper concentrates. The cargoes involved are generally of high value, in great demand and can be easily disposed of. In some cases, these cargoes have been on order for some time by consignees who are awaiting shipment. In these scenarios the phantom ships step in, pick up the cargo and disappear. A typical incident case of a phantom ship operation is described below.

In July 1994, M.V. *Spica* loaded a cargo of 3024 tonnes of SIR 20 (Standard Indonesian Rubber) at Padang, Java. The consignment was destined for the port of Fangcheng, in Guangxi province of China. The *Spica* had an estimated transit time of 12 days, which meant an estimated time of arrival (ETA) in Fangcheng of around 10 August 1994. The vessel, however, never arrived. The owners of *Spica* were Spica Marine Investment Corporation, a company based at the same address as the managers, King Ocean Shipping Co. Ltd., in Mean Towers in Singapore. Both these companies had been set up by an Indonesian known as Sofian Alwi, in temporarily leased office facilities. Predictably, as soon as all the cargo was loaded and the documents issued, the offices were abandoned and Mr Alwi could no longer be found. Neither of these companies was a registered entity in Singapore. The freight for this shipment was paid to another company based in Jakarta, called P.T. King Ocean Shipping Co., which also did not exist and the addresses provided actually belonged to a local printing business.

When the *Spica* left Padang on 29 July 1994, she changed her name back to her original identity of *Lady Crystal*. The *Lady Crystal* was owned by a company called M.G.H. Marine S.A., Panama, which was under the management and control of another company called Egga Shipping Pte. Ltd. This company was owned by a Singaporean named Mr Goh who promptly disappeared and all his companies closed down. He is now wanted for questioning by the Singapore authorities for this incident.

The *Lady Crystal* proceeded to Hong Kong where the cargo was discharged to the order of a Hong Kong registered company called Best

Ocean Trading Company. The cargo was then re-shipped into Fangcheng aboard legitimate feeder vessels in two separate shipments: an initial shipment of 1002 tonnes, which arrived in late August 1994 and a second shipment of just over 1500 tonnes, which arrived in early October 1994. Both of these consignments were sold to a Chinese state-owned company based in Tiaqjin and both cargoes were detained by the police and the local courts owing to dispute over ownership. A little under 500 tonnes of cargo are still missing and enquiries continue to try to locate this batch. The *Lady Crystal* was subsequently arrested in Hong Kong by the mortgagee owing to default in payment by the owners and is now under judicial sale.

The above case clearly highlights two major factors in a typical phantom ship operation, that is, a ship-owning company that exists on paper and a temporary ship registration. The cargo is loaded, or purported to be loaded, into a vessel with a phantom identity. This prevents any subsequent investigation from establishing who the real owners are, what the true identity of the vessel is, where the cargo was illegally discharged and to whom, and who the crew really were. If no immediate purchaser is available, the stolen cargo is discharged into barges in international waters. These barges then take the cargo ashore where it is stored in warehouses until it is sold.

Associated Crimes–Hijacking of Ships in the Philippines

The owners of phantom ships have three means of acquiring vessels for their operations: to purchase them in the open market (owing to the rise in second-hand prices of vessels, this has become an expensive option), to create on paper new ownership for vessels already owned by the syndicates, or hijack or steal vessels to order. The first ship to vanish in what was a ten-year spate of hijackings, was the M.V. *Comicon* on 15 February 1980. Neither the ship nor her 25 crew members have ever been found. Other incidents included the following:

- In 1986, the M.V. *Antoinette* disappeared in Manila Bay while she was under arrest for non-payment of port charges.
- In 1987, a further three ships vanished in the Philippines: M.V. *Cresat 1* and M.V. *Mayon* disappeared while laid up in Manila Bay, and the M.V. *Irene* disappeared after running aground off the Cavite coast.
- On 26 May 1988, the bulk carrier *Negotiator* disappeared together with her six crew members from an anchorage at Subic Bay, Manila.

- On 13 September 1988, the Liberian motor ship *Silver Med* was hijacked by eight heavily armed men in Manila Bay.
- On 25 June 1989, the M.V. *Isla Luzon* with her 4,500 tonnes of steel cargo was hijacked off Iligan in Philippines.
- On 14 March 1990, three men posing as Customs Inspection Service officers boarded the 6,182 grt *Eastern Galaxy* while she was loading US$98 million worth of copper cathodes at the Philippine Associated Smelting and Refinery Corporation pier in Isabel, Leyte. A member of the crew spotted them moving about suspiciously. When challenged the three men held the crew at gunpoint and escaped down the ship's ladder to a waiting motorboat. They left behind a .38in revolver, 20 rounds of ammunition, plotting equipment and ship's documents for a phantom registered vessel called *Jimbo*.

Although there was some suggestion that these vessels were hijacked to be scrapped illicitly in the Far East, evidence showed that they were meant to be used in the phantom ship operations. Examples include the M.V. *Silver Med*, renamed *Sea Rex*, which disappeared in October 1988 with a cargo of rattan for Taiwan, and the M.V. *Isla Luzon*, renamed *Nigel*, which traded between Taiwan, China, Korea and Japan after being hijacked in June 1989.

According to information received by the IMB, ships can be hijacked to order in the Philippines for about US$300,000 and delivered within three days. In some cases, hijacking or stealing is arranged between the syndicates and dishonest ship owners to defraud hull insurers.

The arrest of Captain Emilio Chenko in 1992 by the Filipino authorities put an end to the hijackings in that country. Captain Chenko was instrumental in several hijackings, including that of M.V. *Tabango*, a tanker owned by the Philippine National Ocean Corporation. Captain Chenko was subsequently reported to have been shot dead while attempting to escape from a high-security prison in Manila.

False Registration of Vessels

A major difficulty encountered in the phantom ships investigations are temporary registrations issued indiscriminately by officials of some ship registries. The officials of the Panamanian, Honduran, Belize and St Vincent consulates prominently feature in issuing phantom registrations in the cases seen so far. Applications for registration are submitted to these officials by so-called Shipping Bureaux, Shipping Assistance, or Marine Companies based in the region. The cost of registering a phantom ship is several times higher than the normal fee. Documents bearing false information are submitted to the officials at the time of registration. As a result, the information, such as ship particulars and ownership details, stated in the Certificate of Provisional Registry or Patente Provisional de Navegacion is wrong. This means that a ship can be registered under several names with different particulars. In turn, this makes the task of tracing a phantom ship very difficult. Registration can even be obtained prior to a phantom shipowner physically taking control of a vessel. This method was used in the attempted hijacking of the M.V. *Eastern Galaxy.* Among the bill of lading forms and an outward foreign manifest was found a certificate of registration under the name of *Jimbo* with the same specifications as the *Eastern Galaxy.* This phantom identity provides the owners of phantom ships with an essential tool to commit theft and also offers them protection during any legal proceedings that might subsequently take place. Hence, arresting a phantom ship becomes extremely difficult for the injured party.

Disposing of Stolen Cargoes

Syndicates exist that specialize in disposing of stolen cargoes quickly and, if possible, 'legally'. IMB's investigations showed that a number of cargoes discharged from the phantom ships were discharged outside Singapore, in international waters, either into another vessel or a barge.

The stolen cargoes are sold directly by one of the paper companies or are stowed in a warehouse until a suitable buyer is found. In most cases, the stolen cargoes were sold to companies in China; occasionally they were sold to companies based in the Philippines. The syndicates find stowage places that are usually difficult to access. The cargo of timber stolen from M.V. *Harpers* was stowed in an army camp in the Guangxi province of China and guarded by armed soldiers until its disposal by the criminals. Another favourite location is the Zamboanga region in the Philippines where even the government agencies are reluctant to investigate.

Criminal Syndicates Behind Phantom Ships

The syndicate theory was first raised in the FERIT report. The report concluded that though no one particular syndicate was behind the numerous losses, there were sufficient links already evident between hull and cargo interests to justify the supposition that a number of independent small syndicates operated, and that there had been an exchange of the latest 'techniques' between them. The phantom ships investigations, so far, have also revealed the connection with syndicates. Indeed, some members of the syndicates operating phantom ships had featured in the FERIT report. They are now operating under different companies or addresses. Undoubtedly, they have a large number of contacts and a thorough knowledge of these illegal dealings from their previous employment.

The information obtained by the IMB shows that different groups of criminals are responsible for the phantom ship frauds. Most of the people involved are either Chinese, or of Chinese origin. They are involved in shipping, trading, banking or insurance and they either run their own business, or are employed by well-established institutions. (The exceptions to the 'Chinese connection' were observed in the thefts of cargoes aboard M.V. *Iskander* and M.V. *Efenora 8*, both of which revealed strong connections with syndicates from India.) The Chinese dialect determines the composition of the groups. The groups so far identified belong to the Cantonese, Shanghai or Fukien gangs. These are controlled by a small number of highly experienced businessmen, operating out of Hong Kong, Indonesia, the Philippines and Thailand. Operators and brokers spread all over the region, including China, Hong Kong, Taiwan, Singapore, Thailand, Malaysia, Philippines, Indonesia and South Korea, and gather intelligence and execute plans as directed by the ring leaders. This network provides the syndicates with information from many sources. Thus they are well informed about all activities in the market such as contracts, cargoes, ships and buyers. They are also well aware of any action taken by the industry or the authorities.

The criminal syndicates involved in the phantom ship operations are also believed to be involved in drug trafficking and movement of illegal immigrants from the region into North America. Some syndicate members hold passports of several countries. The IMB understands that these passports can be obtained from unofficial sources, but they are not necessarily forgeries.

Some members of the syndicates are known to the authorities in the region, but cannot be prosecuted owing to lack of evidence for their involvement in criminal dealings. The syndicates are closely associated

181

with and have access to members of governments and possibly to one of the royal families in the region. The syndicates exchange intelligence among themselves and avoid getting in each other's way. They are capable of resorting to any means, including violence, to satisfy their greed. Undoubtedly, they are extremely dangerous criminals and should not be treated lightly.

The Victims of Phantom Ships

The majority of the losses in phantom ship frauds have been borne by the cargo underwriters. On a few occasions, however, the consignees and banks had to pick up the entire loss. For example, in the case of M.V. *Nan*, the bank issuing the letter of credit in Indonesia was not paid by the consignee because discrepancies were found in the documents after the disappearance of the vessel with her cargo. In the loss of timber aboard M.V. *Harpers*, the cargo underwriters repudiated the claim as the policy was issued under the Institute Cargo Clauses 'C' and the theft by the carrier was not an insured risk. In this case the entire loss of US$4.5 million fell on the consignees. The underwriters in China hold the view that these losses are due to fraud and should not be covered by insurance. No compensation was paid to the assured for the loss of cargo from *Bona Vista 1* by the Chinese underwriters.

The Problems of Recovery

Thus far, the number of successful recoveries of cargoes stolen is low. First, it is not easy to locate the cargoes without accurate and speedy information. Second, it is very difficult to regain title to the cargoes once they are sold to another buyer. Third, the problems in seizing the phantom ship to recoup losses are even greater. To do so, the injured parties have to locate, identify, and prove to the court absolute links between the existing shipowner and the owner who was responsible for the crime.

Legal systems vary from country to country. For example, it is easier to arrest a vessel in Singapore than in Thailand. Legal proceedings in jurisdictions such as the Philippines could face greater uncertainty. Owing to the high costs that may be incurred and the low chance of success, legal action is not always financially viable. Even if a phantom ship is seized and sold by the court, the proceeds may not be sufficient after other priority claims are settled. As a result, several phantom ships that have been identified by the IMB are still free in the region. Indeed, the problems of investigating and prosecuting these type of crimes should not be underestimated. They can be dangerous and difficult, particularly in a county such as the Philippines.

The progression from simple cargo thefts to the phantom ship crimes, hijacking of vessels and carriage of illegal immigrants, suggests that the criminals are becoming increasingly confident and are ready to expand their territories. Consequently, shippers need to be made aware of measures to prevent them from failing prey to phantom ship frauds. An analysis of the past incidents indicates that phantom ships usually have the following profile:

- Panama, Honduras, Belize or St Vincent registration.
- 15 to 20 years old.
- Possible irregularity in registration details.
- Delay in arriving at load port.
- Shipowner/operator is invariably a 'one man show'.
- Crew are often Burmese.
- Crew do not go ashore and receive no personal mail in the load port.
- Level of commissions paid to brokers is high.
- Shipowner asks for the freight to be paid for into a personal bank account.

PIRACY

Piracy has always been romanticized by writers and filmmakers and many people harbour visions of bearded renegades sailing seas of endless blue, something akin to a maritime Robin Hood. The truth is that modern day piracy, of whatever form, is a violent, bloody, ruthless practice and is made more fearsome by the knowledge on the part of the victims that they are alone and absolutely defenceless and that no help is waiting just round the corner.

What is making the situation worse is that so many countries, instead of being positive about the difficulties, tend to be recessive and put forward copious arguments claiming either there is not a problem or explaining why they cannot do anything about it. Consequently, the practice flourishes and, unless some positive action is taken, we are on course for a dramatic increase. Already the previous two decades have seen six specific types of piracy, varying very much according to the region in which the practice was found.

First, there has always been what could be called 'Asian' piracy where ships would be boarded and, with the minimum of force if any at all, cash would be taken from the ship's safe. These attacks are not on the high seas as all the waters in the area are the territorial waters of one or the other of the two countries. A well-known target area is the Philip Channel between Indonesia and Singapore. The attacks take the form of intruders coming alongside a vessel underway, usually during the night, boarding it and then taking possession of whatever cash and negotiable valuables come easily to hand. The notable features of this type of attack are the degree of skill that is used to board the vessel, coupled with the fact that violence is not normally used unless resistance is offered. It is this comparatively 'non-violent' approach that, oddly enough, makes the problem difficult to combat.

During 1997, there were five officially reported attacks in the 'Asian' region. In statistical terms, therefore, the probability of a vessel being boarded when passing through the region is relatively small and, as the consequence is limited to loss of money or money's worth, then basic risk management conclusions will come into operation and the cost of prevention must not exceed the cost of the problem. There are, in the area, security organizations offering all types of guarding and escort systems which, although possibly effective, would be completely uneconomic.

Ideally, the question of the principle of the attack ought to be addressed by the two sovereign states concerned, although the political sensitivities that could be upset by the incursions of forces of the one into the territorial waters of the other, cause the problem to be given a low degree of priority by the authorities in the area.

In October 1992, the IMB set up the Piracy Reporting Centre in Kuala Lumpur. This is a 24-hour information centre to warn and assist vessels against pirate attacks. At the same time, some countries in the region had a 'clean up' operation against pirates. The net result of this was that the problem has become manageable, as seen in the annual number of piracy incidents in the Far East and South East Asia: 1991, 107 attacks; 1992, 83 attacks; 1993, 83 attacks; 1994, 71 attacks; 1995, 103 attacks; 1996, 141 attacks; and 1997, 110 attacks.

Second, we have 'West African' and 'South American' piracy where ships, mainly at anchor, are attacked by armed gangs that are much more disposed to be violent than their Asian counterparts. Here, the targets are cash, cargo, personal effects, ship's equipment, in fact anything that can be moved. These attacks have several unique characteristics:

- A high degree of violence demonstrated by the criminals boarding a vessel.
- The target items aboard the vessel are not only money and negotiable goods but also items of cargo and ship's equipment.
- The total value per attack tends to be higher than in the Philip Channel.
- There is a demonstrated lack of competence on the part of law enforcement.
- Some of the target vessels are at anchor.

The only similarity between the 'Asian' incidents and these pirates is that they come alongside in small craft and mount high-sided vessels with remarkable agility. From that point on, the similarity no longer exists as the attackers often offer gratuitous violence and will steal everything that is not well secured. One result, particularly if a ship's equipment is stolen, is that the safety of the vessel might be imperilled.

Prevention of this type of attack is a problem for several reasons. Despite improvement in available security equipment, there is no great response from the forces of law and order ashore. The response may vary marginally from county to county but, in general, there is no great enthusiasm on the part of law enforcement agencies to confront quite large groups of armed men with a proven predisposition towards violence. By the same token, those pundits who suggest a positive physical response by the crews of the vessels under attack must ask themselves if the advice they give is really in the best long-term interests of the vessel and the crew. It can be argued that any effort to repulse an attack, if successful, will save property. But, be assured that the vessel will be 'black-listed' and, when it eventually comes into port or returns on a later voyage, old scores will be settled – and what appeared to be a victory will soon be shown to be nothing but an expensive gain of the moment. With this type of attack, therefore, the response on the vessel should be passive – after alerting the shore authorities, the crew should forget bravery and retreat into a secure area of the vessel to 'ride out the criminal storm'. At the very worst, the consequences can be a financial loss but, when set against the alternative of death or injury that might result from the confrontation, there can really be no argument.

Third, we have seen the particularly odious form of piracy practised on the Vietnamese boat people where they would be robbed of what little they had, murdered apparently for no reason other than the sheer 'fun' of it and, as often as not, the women would be abducted or raped. The attackers in these cases are usually fishermen-turned-bandits because they find the spoils of their attacks on the refugees exceed what they can make by legitimate fishing. This fact, coupled with, perhaps, some resentment at the fact that the refugees are leaving, resulted in attacks of unbelievable ferocity.

In this area, control is difficult because of the same principle as holds ashore. On land, the peasant of one moment is the partisan fighter of the next and, in parallel on the sea, the fisherman of this moment is the pirate of the next, only to revert to type immediately after an attack. In this type of on-going battle where the opposition does not always wear his colours, it is difficult to mount effective restraint. Perverse though the logic might seem to some, it may well be that the British government's policy of non-voluntary repatriation of the Vietnamese refugees from Hong Kong saved the lives of those who did not even try to make a crossing in which some would undoubtedly have lost their lives.

Fourth, there is an extension into a different type of violence towards ships and their crews. Since the late 1980s, the Far East has seen several instances where ships were stolen. Whether these attacks should be called piracy or hijacking, as mentioned in the section on phantom ships, is purely academic. The result is the same for the victims. These attacks on vessels were not so much for what they contained - as often as not they were empty - rather the objective was to use the vessel itself by giving her a false new identity and turning her into a phantom ship. These phantom ships were then used to commit cargo frauds throughout the Far Eastern region. When they were stolen, if the existing crew was found to be 'surplus to requirements' its members were set adrift in boats and in one case at least, just thrown overboard. One such case was that of the *Isla Luzon,* which was seized off the southern Philippines. Some of the pirates were caught, tried and sentenced to up to 18 years imprisonment.

The fifth type of maritime attack to be considered are those with a military or political dimension. Notable among these was the attack on the *Achille Lauro* followed some time later by the totally different type of attack on the *City of Poros.* By contrast with the attack for purely monetary gain, the response both on the part of the potential target and by the forces of law and order has been to the highest degree. It is arguable whether the response has been effective in ensuring that there has been no repetition or whether the attacks were such as to be 'one-off' incidents. In either event, the world has been largely spared scenarios that, by any standards, were unacceptable.

Since 1991, there has been an increasing number of attacks on merchant vessels off Somalia in the Red Sea, and in one case a vessel was seized by one of the warring factions of a nearby state. These are expected consequences in an area where war and violence have become commonplace.

Finally, another violent form of piracy has recently emerged, breeding on the easy pickings to be made and the virtual certainty that no one on shore can, or will, respond. One early example, in August 1990, involved the Cypriot flag vessel *Marta*. On a voyage from Bangkok to Busan, while off the Thai-Cambodian border, *Marta* was boarded at night by heavily armed pirates. They obviously knew exactly where she would be and also had details concerning her cargo of tin plate worth US$2 million. The four attackers quickly overpowered the nine crew members of the vessel. Then followed a bizarre voyage during which the funnel was repainted by the pirates and the name of the vessel was changed to *V Tai* using ready-made stencils they had brought with them for the purpose. They also hoisted a Honduran flag, but oddly made no attempt to alter the port of registry displayed on the stern of the vessel. The vessel was forced to sail southwards for two days during which the crew remained handcuffed and blindfolded below. At the end of that time, the vessel dropped anchor and, during the night, the pirates began discharging the cargo of 2000 tonnes of tin plate into a barge that had come alongside with shore labour and forklifts to assist. The vessel then lay at anchor for another two days before making her way northwards. After yet another two days, while off the northeastern Malaysian coast, the pirates left in one of the ship's lifeboats taking the master as a hostage. The rest of the crew was released, badly shaken, with no radio and only parts of the ship's charts to find their way back to Bangkok as best they could.

A more recent example is the hijacking of the M.V. *Anna Sierra*. This incident also demonstrated the brutality of pirates who showed no regard for human life. What makes this case important is that it was the first time that a pirated ship and its cargo were found intact, with the pirates still on board. On 12 September 1995, the M.V. *Anna Sierra*;

flying the flag of Cyprus, sailed from Ko Si Chang, 50 miles south of Bangkok in Thailand, loaded with 12,000 tonnes of bagged sugar, with a value of US$5 million. She was bound for Manila in the Philippines, with a crew of 23 from Greece, Yugoslavia, Sri Lanka and Egypt. On 13 September 1995, at about 00:30 hours, the *Anna Sierra* was in a position 11°15′N, 102°00′E in the Gulf of Thailand when 30 armed pirates carrying submachine guns boarded. The pirates approached in a fast motorboat and boarded the ship, which was proceeding at full speed, then forced their way into the accommodation. The doors to the accommodation were machine-gunned in order to force the crew out of their cabins. The crew members, now under the control of the pirates, were handcuffed in pairs and forced into two small cabins. They remained locked in the cabins for two days.

In the early hours of 15 September 1995, in position 08°20′N, 107°14′E, 60 miles off the coast of Vietnam, eight of the crew were taken on deck where they were threatened with death. They were then forced overboard into a small raft in rough seas, without food, water or navigation equipment. Several hours later, the remaining 15 crew members were forced overboard into a life raft. The *Anna Sierra* then sailed away. The eight crew members were picked up 3 hours 20 minutes later by two Vietnamese fishing boats, who took them to Condao Island. The remaining 15 crew members were also rescued by Vietnamese fishermen and taken to Vung Tat. On 16 September 1995, the master telephoned the ship's owners from Vung Tau, who alerted the Cypriot authorities. The Cypriot authorities in turn contacted Interpol and the local US regional search and rescue authorities in Honolulu and the US Air Force, who alerted AMVER (American Mutual Vessel Search and Rescue).

On 18 September 1995, the shipowner contacted the IMB. The IMB launched an extensive search for the ship. A description of the ship and a photograph were circulated to harbour masters and shipping agencies in the region. A substantial reward was offered, on behalf of hull underwriters, for information leading to the location of the ship. On 5 October 1995, information was received by the IMB that the ship was in Bei Hai, southern China. IMB investigators went to Bei Hai to verify this information. On 8 October 1995, IMB investigators visited the port and found a ship *Arctic Sea* berthed at quay number four. They positively identified this ship as the *Anna Sierra*. The original name of the ship *Diagara* was still welded on the bows and the stern and the outline of the letters *Anna Sierra* was still visible.

The ship had arrived at Bei Hai anchorage at 10:00 hours on 20 September 1995, without prior notification. Documents presented by the master in the name of *Arctic Sea* were found to be false. Among the forged documents were bills of lading, representing the cargo as being of Thai origin but loaded in Brazil. It was also found that the perpetrators had illegally sold the cargo of sugar to a trader in Bei Hai in early September 1995, prior to the pirate attack. In the meantime, the Chinese Frontier Defence Authority (Banfong) detained the ship. Two armed guards were put on board. The passports of the 'crew' together with the ship's documents were seized. Of the 'crew' of 14, 12 had Indonesian passports and two Malaysian passports. These passports showed that the 14 'crew' members had entered Thailand at Bangkok Airport on 7 August 1995 by a Thai Airways' flight from Singapore. The passports did not bear exit immigration stamps from Thailand.

The master of *Arctic Sea* was a person calling himself Captain Bekas. He stated that his 13 crew members and he had joined a ship called *Polaris* at Bangkok and sailed to Manila. At Manila anchorage they were transferred to the *Arctic Sea* that had no crew. Thereafter, on 16 September 1995, they sailed the ship from Manila to Bei Hai arriving there on 20 September 1995. An examination of the charts for the area proved that the *Arctic Sea* could not have made this voyage in four days. Bekas then claimed that he had sailed to Bei Hai through the Straits of Hainan. This is impossible as these Straits are controlled by the Chinese military and no ship can sail through them without special permission. Similarly, the *Anna Sierra's* last position was known to be off Vietnam on the morning of 15 September 1995, when her crew was cast adrift by the pirates. The distance between this position and Manila is over 800 nautical miles. Thus, she would have needed a speed of 33 knots to complete a passage to Manila. The top speed of *Anna Sierra* was only 11 knots. Therefore she could not possibly have covered this distance in a day as claimed by Bekas. In addition, checks with Bangkok port showed that they had no record of a ship called *Polaris*. Manila port authorities also confirmed that no ship called *Polaris* or *Arctic Sea* had called there in September 1995.

Investigations by the Cypriot authorities showed that the 14 men had entered Bangkok on 7 August 1995, and waited there for the next five weeks until the departure of *Anna Sierra*. They then boarded the ship as a part of the gang on 13 September. At some stage, a part of the gang disembarked via the motorboat that had brought them to the ship.

These pirates took with them the ship's cash and personal effects of the crew. After dumping the crew overboard on 15 September 1995, the *Anna Sierra* sailed to Bel Hai. During the passage her name was changed to *Arctic Sea*. She arrived there on 20 September 1995. The distance between the last known position of the *Anna Sierra* and Bei Hai is 900 miles. Thus, the ship could only have proceeded directly to Bei Hai after dumping her crew overboard off Vietnam.

The Cypriot authorities immediately dispatched to Beijing a senior official of the Department of Merchant Shipping. Through diplomatic channels they requested the assistance of the People's Republic of China for intervention, referring to the relevant provisions on piracy in the International Convention of the High Seas of 1958 and the United Nations Convention on the Law of the Seas of 1982. On 24 October 1995, the Honduras Registry of Shipping confirmed to the IMB and the Cyprus authorities that *Arctic Sea* was not registered in Honduras.

IMB investigators submitted documents to the Chinese authorities providing irrefutable evidence of title to the cargo by the Indian buyers. Inquiries by the IMB also confirmed that the Honduran registry number shown in the *Arctic Sea* documents related to previous ships that were involved in the theft of shiploads of cargoes. In December 1995, the Chinese Public Security Bureau (PSB) officially declared that the ship calling herself *Arctic Sea* was in fact the *Anna Sierra*. The authorities, however, refused to hand over the ship to the shipowner stating that their inquiries were continuing. They did not disclose the nature of these inquiries. None of the pirate crew was formally interviewed. It is felt that in reality the Chinese authorities did nothing about the problem.

In February 1996, the shipowner was invited to take over the ship on the condition that an amount of US$400,000 was paid to the PSB for its costs and expenses. This condition was extraordinary in that no law enforcement agency makes a charge for its services. In July 1996, the 14 pirates were taken off the ship and placed in a guesthouse belonging to the PSB in Bei Hai. By the end of 1996, ten pirates were repatriated to their home countries.

Since the arrival of *Anna Sierra* in Bei Hai, the pirate crew had done nothing about maintenance on board. The ship's condition and her expensive cargo were slowly deteriorating. After July 1996, the ship was unmanned. On 1 January 1997, the PSB noticed that the ship's engine room and holds were partially flooded with seawater. In a desperate bid to salvage the situation the PSB started discharging the cargo. The Indian cargo owners became aware of the discharge and sent their representatives to Bei Hai. The PSB, however, denied them access to the ship or the cargo without giving any reason. Some 6,000 tons of cargo were discharged and taken to a warehouse in Hepu County, 30 km from Bei Hai.

By 31 January 1997, the ship's holds had taken in more seawater and she had developed a ten-degree starboard list. The port authorities refused to allow the ship to stay alongside and towed her to a position on the beach nearby where she still lies beached on soft sand.

In February 1997, the remaining four pirates were sent home. It is unbelievable that the 14 persons who had committed a serious offence of hijacking a ship were simply allowed to leave without being questioned. It is understood that the PSB claimed that it had no jurisdiction over the matter because these 14 persons had not committed an offence in China. This was in blatant disregard of various international conventions. In particular, the Rome Convention of 1988 on suppression of unlawful acts against the safety of maritime navigation specifically provides procedures whereby China, which is a signatory, could and should have exercised jurisdiction.

On 14 March 1997, the IMB learned through sources that the PSB had decided to sell the cargo locally. This extraordinary step was planned without any reference to the Indian cargo owner. It was further learned that local PSB officials were planning to sell the cargo at a price well below the market value to a *friendly local buyer*. Representatives of the Indian cargo owners again rushed to Bel Hai to stop this illegal sale. With intense diplomatic pressure from the Indian Embassy in Beijing and the IMB, this attempt to sell the cargo was aborted at that time. However, in early August 1997, the PSB finally auctioned the cargo without consulting the Indian cargo owners.

The losses suffered by the shipowner and cargo interests have run into millions of dollars. The criminal gang that organized the hijack of the *Anna Sierra* in September 1995, struck again in August 1996, by persuading a shipowner to accept a new crew, which then diverted a ship named *Samudra Samrat* to Fengcheng in southern China with the intention to illegally discharge her cargo. Her name was changed to *Celtic Ranger*. Despite IMB locating the ship as she sailed into port and presenting evidence of her false name and papers, the local authorities in Fengcheng refused to treat the diversion as a criminal matter. They refused to allow the judge from the maritime court in Guangzhou to arrest the ship and the following day she sailed out of port leaving behind all her papers and the passports of the 23 Indonesian crew. The cargo worth US$2.5 million destined for Vietnam has disappeared with the ship.

A third case involves *official* hijacking. The owner of *Hye Mieko* reported on 23 June 1995 that she was hijacked off Cambodia by a boat resembling a Chinese customs launch and forced to sail over 1,000 miles to Shanwei in Guandong Province, China. After her escorted arrival there, the authorities charged the ship with the intention of smuggling her cargo of cigarettes into China. Accordingly, she was arrested and the cargo seized. No ship went to the aid of the *Hye Mieko*, despite its plight and route being broadcast worldwide. The Chinese government denied the launch was one of its own on any official mission, and although officers of the Royal Navy in Hong Kong bypassed their political masters in a desperate plea to Whitehall, they were not allowed to intercept the ship.

IMPLICATIONS

The hijacking of the *Marta* and *Anna Sierra* display a high degree of organization. Further, a measure of the impunity with which subversion can be carried out can be judged from the fact that one of the pirates on the *Marta* said that this was the sixth such successful attack they had made in the preceding 18 months. To give proof to this claim, since the *Marta* incident there have been eight further incidents reported in the region and one could be excused for asking both 'why? and 'what will happen now?'.

The answer to the first question is simple – the pirates have all the advantages. They have the knowledge of what is being carried by specific vessels and, perhaps the most relevant point, they have all the sea room in which to operate. This and the fact that modern radar enables them to watch to see if they themselves are being followed means that they can wait and commit their crime with impunity, knowing that they will have time to escape at the first suggestion that any intervention force is on its way.

The difficulties of combating piracy are enormous. They stem not only from the sheer size of the sea areas to be covered, but also the strained financial circumstances of some governments. To create a response capability able to catch and match the pirates would require the expenditure of considerable resources and some countries just do not have that amount of money. When one adds to these difficulties the political problems that arise when pirates act in waters belonging to two neighbouring states and move quickly from one jurisdiction to another, it is little wonder that so much remains to be done. Consequently, governments have done little, although the humanitarian outcry in respect of the Vietnamese situation resulted in apparent action by the Thai government, albeit with international aid, to set up an anti-piracy unit in 1980. It is alleged that in the first eight years of operation and having spent some US$13 million, the unit did not catch a single pirate!

The answer to the second question is not so simple. Following in the wake of the *Achille Lauro* incident in fall 1985, the IMO responded with recommendations for 'the implementation of measures to prevent unlawful acts against passengers and crews on board ships'. The IMO both retained the initiative and maintained the impetus for this by conducting regional seminars on ship security matters in Puerto Rico, Greece and Japan, as well as discussing the issue in its Maritime Safety Committee. IMO's 1988 Rome convention on 'Suppression of unlawful acts against safety of maritime navigation' is meant to ensure that states take appropriate action against any person committing offences, such as seizure of ships by force, acts of violence against persons on board ships and the placing of devices on board a ship that are likely to destroy or damage it. The unique feature of this convention is that apart from extending the jurisdiction for the above offences, it encourages the states to consider extradition even where no extradition treaty exists.

While any initiative is welcome, in reality it is doubtful if the hardened criminals described above will be affected by such measures because the main problem is the lack of capacity to catch the pirates, not 'what to do with them once caught'. It has already been suggested that some coastal states lack the resources to react at sea and this is not only understood but also has to be accepted. What is lacking, though, is any form of co-ordinated response on-shore. Pirates operate at sea only for the purposes of committing their crime. At the end of the day they must come ashore somewhere to dispose of their gains — and this is where they would be vulnerable and law enforcement more efficient. This can only come about, however, if there is collective action by national law enforcement. At present, piracy does not loom too large on the law enforcement horizon of individual countries as it does not affect the local population. Literally, it is a problem of 'those that pass in the night'. It is hoped that during the twenty-first century, this parochial attitude will alter and countries co-operate to rid their seas of this menace.

Crime in Cyberspace

P.N. GRABOSKY

It has almost become trite to suggest that we are entering an age as significant and profound in its impact as was the Industrial Revolution. The convergence of computing and communications has already affected most if not all of the major institutions of society. It has created unprecedented opportunities for education, health services, recreation and commerce. Unfortunately, it has also created unprecedented opportunities for crime. Identifying these vulnerabilities, and mobilizing appropriate countermeasures, will be one of the great challenges of the twenty-first century. As discussed below, the challenge is so great that it defies the capacity of law enforcement alone to control. Consequently, new forms of policing, involving the harnessing of non-government resources, will become essential.[1] Given the fact that cyberspace knows no boundaries, and that computer crime often transcends national frontiers, effective countermeasures will also require a degree of international cooperation that is without precedent.

VARIETIES OF COMPUTER CRIME

The variety of criminal activity that can be committed with or against information systems is surprisingly diverse. Some of these activities are not really new in substance, only the medium is new. Others represent new forms of illegality altogether. The following generic forms of illegality, involving information systems as instruments and/or as targets of crime, are the subject of this paper and of a book on which it is based.[2] These forms of crime are not necessarily mutually exclusive, nor is the following list complete.

Theft of Information Services

Ever since the original 'phreakers' of a quarter-century ago attacked telephone systems out of curiosity, telecommunications services have been vulnerable to theft. From those whose motives were confined to simple mischief-making, to those who have made theft of services a way

195

of life and a major criminal industry, those who steal services pose a significant challenge to carriers, service providers and to the general public, who often bear the financial burden of fraud.

The market for stolen communications services is large. There are those who simply seek to avoid payment for or to obtain a discount on the cost of a telephone call. There are others, such as illegal immigrants, who are unable to acquire legitimate information services without disclosing their identity and their status. There are others still who need appropriate information services to conduct other illicit business with less risk of detection.

The means of stealing telecommunications services are diverse and include the 'cloning' of cellular phones, counterfeiting of telephone cards and unauthorized access to an organization's telephone switchboard.[3] In one case, hackers were reported to have obtained unauthorized access to the telephone facilities of Scotland Yard, and made US$1 million in phone calls.

Communications in Furtherance of Criminal Conspiracies

Modern information systems clearly provide an effective means by which offenders can communicate in order to plan and execute their activities. There is evidence of information systems being used to facilitate organized drug trafficking, gambling, prostitution, money laundering, child pornography and trade in weapons (in those jurisdictions where such activities are illegal). Although the use of information facilities does not cause such illegal conduct to occur, it certainly enhances the speed and ease with which individuals may act together to plan and to execute criminal activity.

Emerging technologies of encryption and high-speed data transfer can greatly enhance the capacity of sophisticated criminal organizations, and place their communications outside the reach of police. Increasingly, police are encountering encrypted communications and, as cryptography becomes more widely accessible, its use to conceal criminal communications is likely to increase markedly.[4]

Information Piracy/Counterfeiting/Forgery

Each year, it has been estimated that losses of between US$15 billion and US$17 billion are sustained by industry as a result of copyright infringement.[5] Arguably, the speed and accuracy with which copies of works may now be made has been dramatically enhanced by such modern technology as on-line information networks. Copyright infringement may occur quickly and without difficulty, and may be carried out by anyone capable of using the Internet. The Software Publishers Association has estimated that US$7.4 billion worth of software was lost to piracy in 1993 with US$2 billion of that being stolen from the Internet. By 1998 the losses were estimated at almost US$11 billion.[6]

As broadband services continue to become available with text, graphics, sound and video information being freely accessible via cable modems, the potential for copyright infringement involving such works will be enhanced enormously. Already in the USA it is possible to download compact disks and feature films from the Internet.

Dissemination of Offensive Materials

Content considered by some to be objectionable exists in abundance in cyberspace. This includes, among much else, sexually explicit materials, racist propaganda and instructions for the fabrication of incendiary and explosive devices. Information systems can also be used for harassing, threatening or intrusive communications, from the traditional obscene telephone call to its contemporary manifestation in 'cyber-stalking', in which persistent messages are sent to an unwilling recipient. In one recent case, a student composed a sadistic fantasy and sent it out over the Internet. He used the name of a fellow student as the story's victim, and was initially charged with communicating a threat, although this was later withdrawn.[7]

The rich diversity in thresholds of tolerance around the world, combined with the global reach of information, make this a particularly difficult regulatory challenge. What is offensive to authorities in the People's Republic of China might be welcome in overseas Tibetan communities. Materials offensive to religious leaders in Iran may fail to raise an eyebrow elsewhere.

Electronic Money Laundering

For some time now, electronic funds transfers have assisted in concealing and in moving the proceeds of crime. Emerging technologies will greatly assist in concealing the origin of ill-gotten gains. Large financial institutions will no longer be the only ones with the ability to achieve electronic funds transfers transiting numerous jurisdictions at the speed of light. The development of informal banking institutions and parallel banking systems may permit central bank supervision to be bypassed, but can also facilitate the evasion of cash transaction reporting requirements in those nations that have them. Traditional underground banks, which have flourished in Asian countries for centuries, will enjoy even greater capacity through the use of information technology.

With the emergence and proliferation of various technologies of electronic commerce, one can easily envisage how traditional countermeasures against money laundering may soon be of limited value. A criminal may soon be able to sell a quantity of heroin in return for an untraceable transfer of stored value to his 'smart-card', which he then downloads anonymously to his account in a financial institution situated in an overseas jurisdiction that protects the privacy of banking clients. He can discreetly draw upon these funds as and when he requires, downloading them back to his stored value card.[8]

Electronic Vandalism and Terrorism

As never before, Western industrial society is dependent upon complex data processing and information systems. Damage to, or interference with, any of these systems can lead to catastrophic consequences. A 1996 US government study estimated that some 250,000 separate attempts to penetrate US defence installations had occurred during the previous year.[9] Not all of these are attributable to harmless curiosity. Defence planners around the world are investing substantially in information warfare means of disrupting the information technology infrastructure of defence systems. Whether motivated by curiosity, vindictiveness or greed, electronic intruders cause inconvenience at best and have the potential for inflicting massive harm.

Sales and Investment Fraud

The use of the telephone for fraudulent sales pitches, deceptive charitable solicitations or bogus investment overtures is a billion-dollar-a-year industry in the USA. The intensification of commercial activity in the USA and globally, combined with emerging communications technologies, would seem to heighten the risk of sales fraud. Already evidence is emerging of fraudulent sales and investment offers having been communicated over computer networks and bulletin boards. Further developments in electronic marketing will provide new opportunities for the unscrupulous and new risks for the unwitting.[10]

Illegal Interception of Information

Developments in information provide new opportunities for electronic eavesdropping. From activities as time-honoured as surveillance of an unfaithful spouse, to the newest forms of political and industrial espionage, information interception has increasing applications. Here again, technological developments create new vulnerabilities. In New York, for example, two individuals used a sophisticated scanning device to pick up some 80,000 cellular telephone numbers from motorists who drove past their Brooklyn apartment. Had the two not been arrested, they could have used the information to create cloned mobile telephones that could have resulted in up to US$100 million in illegal calls being made.[11] The electromagnetic signals emitted by a computer might themselves be intercepted. Cables may act as broadcast antennas. Existing law does not prevent the remote monitoring of computer radiation.

Electronic Funds Transfer Fraud

The proliferation of electronic funds transfer systems will enhance the risk that such transactions may be intercepted and diverted. Existing systems such as Automated Teller Machines and Electronic Funds Transfer at Point of Sale technologies have already been the targets of fraudulent activity, and the development of stored value cards or smart cards, super smart cards and optical memory cards will no doubt invite some individuals to apply their talents to the challenge of electronic counterfeiting and overcoming security access systems. Just as the simple telephone card can be reprogrammed, smart cards are vulnerable to re-engineering. Credit card details can be captured and used by unauthorized persons. The transfer of funds from home between accounts and in payment of transactions will also create vulnerabilities in terms of theft and fraud and the widescale development of electronic money for use on the Internet will lead to further opportunities for crime. What for the past quarter-century has been loosely described as 'computer fraud' will have numerous new manifestations.[12]

The above forms of illegality are not necessarily mutually exclusive and need not occur in isolation. Just as an armed robber might steal an automobile to facilitate a quick getaway, so too can one steal information services and use them for purposes of vandalism, fraud or in furtherance of a criminal conspiracy.

Communication of some forms of prohibited material (such as that relating to the manufacture of drugs or explosive devices) may itself entail criminal conspiracy. Even legitimate telemarketing may be regarded as intrusive and offensive to some recipients. Intrusions and interceptions for purposes of industrial espionage may also be accompanied by theft of intellectual property.

In addition, a number of themes run through each of the forms of illegality described above. Foremost of these are the technologies for concealing the content of communications. Technologies of encryption can limit access by law enforcement agents to communications carried out in furtherance of a conspiracy, or to the dissemination of objectionable materials between consenting parties.

Also important are technologies for concealing a communicator's identity. Electronic impersonation, colloquially termed 'spoofing', can be used in furtherance of a variety of criminal activities, including fraud, criminal conspiracy, harassment and vandalism. Technologies of anonymity further complicate the task of identifying suspects.

THE TRANSNATIONAL IMPLICATIONS OF CRIME IN CYBERSPACE

International crime of a more conventional nature has proved to be a very difficult challenge for law enforcement. Computer- and telecommunications-related crime poses even greater challenges. There might be a lack of agreement between authorities in different jurisdictions about whether or not the activity in question is criminal at all, who has committed it, whether in fact it has been committed, who has been victimized because of it, who should investigate it and who should adjudicate and punish it. If an on-line financial newsletter originating in the Bahamas contains fraudulent speculation about the prospects of a company whose shares are traded on the Australian Stock Exchange, where has the offence occurred?

Other issues that might complicate investigation entail the logistics of search and seizure during real time, the sheer volume of material within which incriminating evidence can be contained and the encryption of information, which can render it entirely inaccessible or accessible only after a massive application of decryption technology.

COUNTERMEASURES

It has long been recognized that the criminal justice system is a very imperfect means of social control, and that effective crime prevention requires the contribution of families, schools and many other institutions of civil society. This is no less the case with crime in cyberspace than it is with crime in the streets.

It will be immediately apparent that the detection, investigation and prosecution of all of the above forms of criminality pose formidable challenges. Crime in the digital age can be committed by an individual in one jurisdiction against a victim or victims on the other side of the globe. The control of cyber-crime lies beyond the capacity of any one agency. What principles can we articulate to assist us in controlling computer crime?

Emphasize Prevention

It is a great deal more difficult to pursue an on-line offender to the ends of the Earth than to prevent the offence in the first place. The trite homily that prevention is better than cure is nowhere more appropriate than in cyberspace.[13] It applies no less to high-technology crime than it does to residential burglary. Just as one would be most unwise to leave one's house unlocked when heading off to work in the morning, so too is it foolish to leave one's information systems accessible to unauthorized persons.

Self-Defence should be the First Line of Defence

The first step in the prevention of on-line crime is to raise awareness on the part of prospective victims to the risks they face. Individuals and institutions should be made aware of the potential consequences of an attack on their information assets, and of the basic precautionary measures they should take. Those businesses that stand to gain the most from electronic commerce have the greatest interest in developing secure payments systems. Technologies of computer security, discussed below, can provide significant protection against various forms of computer crime. But there are other, 'low technology' measures that should not be overlooked. Perhaps foremost among these is staff selection. Surveys of businesses reveal that one's own staff often poses a greater threat to one's information assets than do so-called 'outsiders'. Disgruntled employees and former employees constitute a significant risk. Suffice it to say that great care should be taken when engaging and disengaging staff.

Non-Governmental Resources should be Harnessed Whenever Possible

Given the resource constraints that most governments face, it is desirable to enlist the assistance of private-sector and community interests in the prevention and detection of computer-related crime.[14]

Market forces will generate powerful influences in furtherance of electronic crime control. Given the immense fortunes that stand to be made by those who develop secure processes for electronic commerce, they hardly need any prompting from government. In some sectors, there are ample commercial incentives that can operate in furtherance of cyber-crime prevention. Information security promises to become one of the growth industries of the twenty-first century. Some of the new developments in information security that have begun to emerge include technologies of authentication. The simple password for access to a computer system, vulnerable to theft or determination by other means, is being complemented or succeeded altogether by biometric authentication methods, such as retinal imaging and voice or finger printing.

Detection of unauthorized access to or use of computer systems can be facilitated by such technologies as artificial intelligence and neural networking, which can identify anomalous patterns of use according to time of day and keystroke patterns.

Issues of objectionable content can be addressed at the individual level by blocking and filtering software, by which parents or teachers can prevent children's access to certain types of sites. Selective consumption of Internet content can be further assisted by classification schemes such as the Platform for Internet Content Selection.

The energies of private individuals can also be enlisted in furtherance of security and prosperity in cyberspace. A wide range of websites, under governmental or non-governmental auspices, invite private citizens to report suspected illegal conduct on the Internet to the authorities. Some, such as the Cyber Angels, invite disclosures of all kinds, while others tend to specialize in particular areas, such as fraud or child pornography. What might be described as an 'Electronic Neighbourhood Watch' enhances the capacity to detect some forms of electronic illegality.

There are other areas in which the state might arguably take a subordinate role to the individual. Consider violations of copyright or theft of intellectual property. In situations where civil remedies might be available to the victim, it is arguably more appropriate for the individual to secure his own rights than to rely upon the state to act on one's behalf. One could, of course, envisage circumstances where a wider state role may be justified – for example when the perpetrator in question is engaged in other criminal activity or when the theft in question has wider economic ramifications. But conferring rights upon the individual and providing the individual with the means of enforcing these rights may be appropriate in some circumstances.

In extreme cases, some would take the law into their own hands. The metaphor of cyberspace as a frontier is not entirely inapposite. There are vigilantes in cyberspace. In some instances, self-help by victims of telecommunications-related crime may itself entail illegality. 'Counter-hacking' by private citizens or by government agencies, has been suggested as one way of responding to illegal intrusions. A group calling itself Ethical Hackers Against Paedophilia (http://www.ehap.org/) has threatened to disable the computers of those whom they find dealing in digital child pornography.

A radical response to the problem of software piracy is to make use of so-called logic bombs, which are installed into programs. When activated through an act of unauthorized copying, the malicious code would destroy the copied data and even damage other software or hardware belonging to the offender. The potential for such practices to result in liability for criminal damage, however, makes their use problematic.

Enhancing the Capacity of Law Enforcement

The continuing uptake of digital technology around the world means that law enforcement agencies will be required to keep abreast of rapidly developing technologies. This will entail training in new investigative techniques. As new technologies are exploited by criminals, it becomes even more important for law enforcement not to be left behind. This is a significant challenge, given the emerging trend for skilled investigators to be 'poached' by the private sector. The collaboration of law enforcement with specialized expertise residing in the private sector will be a common feature in years to come.

One might also expect to see the use of fairly aggressive investigative methods in cyberspace. Even the domestic policing of tele-communications-related illegality will require measures that go beyond traditional law enforcement tactics. The technologies of encryption and anonymity noted above are invoked to justify aggressive investigative methods such as covert facilitation, more commonly referred to as 'stings'. In mid-1995, for example, the FBI charged an adult male who had arranged over the Internet to meet what he thought was a 14-year-old girl at a motel. The Internet contact was, in fact, an FBI agent. The accused was targeted because of his history of sex offences involving minors. Similar tactics have been directed at those who traffic in pornographic material, as well as perpetrators of telemarketing fraud. Law enforcement officers can easily pose on-line as prospective consumers of pornography. Laws will vary across jurisdictions with regard to the defence of entrapment, and the extent to which an offence was encouraged or suggested by police.

The Imperative of International Cooperation

The global nature of cyberspace necessitates the development of new strategies to combat criminal activity that can originate from the other side of the world. At present, if an Australian citizen were to be gullible enough to fall victim to a fraudulent investment scheme originating in Albania, he could count on very little help from authorities in either jurisdiction. But transnational electronic crime seems destined only to increase.

The basic approach to overcoming the transnational issues of crime in cyberspace lies in developing cooperation between nations. This is more easily said than done, given the significant differences in legal systems, values and priorities around the world.

Enlisting the assistance of overseas authorities is not an automatic process, and often requires pre-existing agreements relating to formal mutual assistance in criminal matters.[15] Nevertheless, there are numerous examples of successful measures.

Unilateral Action

Some governments may take unilateral action against their citizens or residents who commit criminal offences on foreign soil. Two of the most familiar examples in Australia are prosecutions for engaging in sexual activity with children,[16] and for war crimes alleged to have been committed in World War II. But, in many cases, this will still require the cooperation of a foreign government in obtaining evidence and possibly in extraditing the offender.

Bilateral Agreements

The mobility of criminal offenders in a shrinking world has increased the need for arrangements to facilitate the apprehension and repatriation of those who seek to evade the law by fleeing to another jurisdiction. The most common mechanism for this is extradition, which is done pursuant to a treaty or other formal arrangement between two nations.[17] Australia was the originator of 33 and the recipient of 37 extradition requests pending at 30 June 1997.

Since 1985, Australia has adopted a 'no evidence' approach as the preferred basis for international extraditions. The earlier approach required the production of a *prima facie* brief against the person sought, which effectively required foreign jurisdictions to produce evidence that accorded with Australia's technical rules of admissibility. This was particularly difficult for civil law countries. The new approach is reflected in most of Australia's modern extradition treaties and has generally facilitated cooperation between Australia and other jurisdictions.

Some jurisdictions seek to prosecute offences committed abroad by foreign nationals against their own citizens. The USA, for example, can seek extradition of alleged terrorists who have offended against citizens of the USA while abroad. Extradition is by no means an automatic matter, as the recent experience of Australian fugitive Christopher Skase illustrates. Moreover, other impediments exist. Some nations will not extradite their own citizens under any circumstances. Australia, as a matter of policy, will not extradite a fugitive who would face execution in the jurisdiction seeking his or her return. Those jurisdictions that do practice capital punishment may waive the death penalty in order to obtain the extradition of a fugitive.

There are circumstances in which, as an alternative to extradition, a nation may prosecute a citizen for offences committed in, and against the laws of, a foreign jurisdiction. Australia, for example, may prosecute Australian citizens for offences committed on foreign soil, provided the relevant conduct would have been an offence under Australian law had it occurred within Australia. This process is only available within Australia in circumstances where extradition has been refused on the sole ground that the person was an Australian citizen at the time of the offence, and only if the Commonwealth Attorney-General is satisfied that the requesting state would have refused extradition of its nationals in corresponding circumstances. There are no recorded cases of such prosecutions within Australia.

In addition to extradition, a variety of arrangements may be put in place to facilitate cooperation between nations in the location and collection of evidence in furtherance of criminal investigation. Mutual assistance treaties, as they are called, provide a legal basis for authorities in country 'A' to obtain evidence for criminal investigations at the request of authorities from country 'B'. Instruments of this kind cover a range of assistance including:

- the identification and location of persons;
- the service of documents;
- the obtaining of evidence, articles and documents;
- the execution of search and seizure requests; and
- assistance in relation to proceeds of crime.

Australia was the originator of 162 mutual assistance requests, and the recipient of 130 requests by other nations, which were pending at 30 June 1997.

The Mutual Assistance in Criminal Matters Act 1987 was amended in March 1997 to provide for 'passive' application of the Act to all foreign countries, rather than requiring the Act to be specifically applied to particular countries by regulation. This enables assistance to be provided and requested much more expeditiously than was previously the case.

In addition, the posting of law enforcement personnel overseas can facilitate the development of informal networks that can help expedite response to the various requests that may arise from time to time. Formal agreements are essential, but there is often no substitute for interpersonal contact. The Australian Federal Police (AFP) has 29 liaison officers stationed in 13 nations around the world. In addition to serving Australia's needs, the AFP and Australian consular staff are able to help overseas governmental authorities check on the probity of prospective investors from Australia. AFP liaison officers may also assist their hosts in the training of law enforcement personnel and in the exchange of intelligence.

Steps taken following the G-8 Birmingham meeting in May 1998 for nations to designate liaison offices that will be on call on a 24-hour basis illustrates the need for prompt concerted response to the problem of transnational digital crime.

CONCLUSION

It has become trite to suggest that the world is a shrinking place. On the one hand, this shrinking is highly beneficial. People around the world now enjoy economic, cultural and recreational opportunities that were previously not accessible. On the other hand, the rapid mobility of people, money, information, ideas and commodities generally, has provided new opportunities for crime, and new challenges for law enforcement agencies. Linkages between events and institutions at home and abroad are inevitable and will inevitably proliferate. This will require unprecedented cooperation between nations, and will inevitably generate tensions arising from differences in national values. Even within nations, tensions between such values as privacy and the imperatives of law enforcement will be high on the public agenda. New organizational forms will emerge to combat new manifestations of criminality. The twenty-first century will be nothing if not interesting.

NOTES

1. Peter Grabosky, 'The Future of Crime Control'. *Trends and Issues in Crime and Criminal Justice*, No.63 (Canberra: Australian Institute of Criminology, 1996).
2. P.N. Grabosky and Russell G. Smith, *Crime in the Digital Age: Controlling Telecommunications and Cyberspace Illegalities* (Sydney, NSW: The Federation Press, and New Brunswick, NJ: Transaction Publishers, 1998).
3. Russell G. Smith 'Stealing Telecommunications Services', *Trends and Issues in Crime and Criminal Justice*, No.54. (Canberra: Australian Institute of Criminology, 1996).
4. Dorothy Denning and William Baugh, *Encryption and Evolving Technologies as Tools of Organized Crime and Terrorism* (Washington DC: National Strategy Information Center, 1997).
5. US Information Infrastructure Task Force, *Intellectual Property and the National Information Infrastructure: Report of the Working Group on Intellectual Property Rights* (Washington DC: US Patent and Trademark Office, 1995).
6. See details provided by the annual report of the Business Software Alliance and the Software Publishers Association (SPA). On 1 January 1999 the SPA became the Software & Information Industry Association (SIIA). For the report see http://www.siia.net/piracy/news/ipr98.htm
7. Charles Platt, *Anarchy Online* (New York: Harper Prism, 1996).
8. Glenn Wahlert, 'Implications for Law Enforcement of the Move to a Cashless Society', In A. Graycar and P. Grabosky (eds.), *Money Laundering in the 21st Century: Risks and Countermeasures* (Canberra: Australian Institute of Criminology, 1996), pp.22–28.
9. United States, General Accounting Office, *Information Security: Computer Attacks at Department of Defense Pose Increasing Risks*. GAO/AIMD-96-84. (Washington DC: US Government Printing Office, 1996).
10. Tim Phillips, 'On-Line Business Crime', Paper Presented to the Australian Institute of Criminology Conference on Internet Crime, Melbourne, 16 Feb. 1998. http://www.aic.gov.au/conferences/internet/index.html#16
11. Tad Cook, 'Feds Arrest Two in Cell Phone Scam', *Telecom Digest*, vol.16, No.325, http://massis.lcs.mit.edu/telecomarchives/TELECOM_DIGEST_Online/
12. Russell G. Smith, 'Plastic Card Fraud', *Trends and Issues in Crime and Criminal Justice*, No.76 (Canberra: Australian Institute of Criminology, 1996).
13. Russell G. Smith, 'Best Practice in Fraud Prevention', *Trends and Issues in Crime and Criminal Justice*, No.101 (Canberra: Australian Institute of Criminology, 1999).
14. Grabosky, op. cit.
15. Following recent amendments to the Mutual Assistance in Criminal Matters Act 1987, Australia may now grant assistance in criminal matters to any country. Bilateral mutual assistance treaties are currently in force with 18 nations. A further four treaties have been signed, but are not yet in force.

16. Crimes (Child Sex Tourism) Amendment Act 1994.
17. By the end of 1997, Australia had signed bilateral extradition treaties with 32 countries. Of these, 29 were in force. A further 64 jurisdictions were covered by the London Extradition Scheme, which provides for the rendition of fugitive offenders among members of the Commonwealth of Nations. A special extradition relationship exists with New Zealand. Australian extradition laws have been applied to seven additional countries without a treaty. Australia has succeeded to extradition treaties entered by the UK with 21 countries in the late nineteenth and early twentieth centuries.

The Rise of the Modern Arms Black Market and the Fall of Supply-Side Control

R.T. NAYLOR

Four decades after the Second World War, a world divided between antagonistic nuclear superpowers seemed largely at peace.[1&2] To be sure, there were flare-ups – civil wars, insurrections and border clashes – some of them highly destructive of life and property. But each one seemed exceptional in cause, remarkable in effect and, in the minds of the citizens of the major powers, relegated to faraway places.

Today, by contrast, the entire globe, from Albania to former Zaire, from South Africa to North Ossetia, from Eastern Slavonia to the West Bank, seems wracked by political violence. These conflicts cannot be written off as merely 'internal' feuds and therefore the business, apart from outside 'humanitarian' hand wringing, of only the people directly involved. Their number and scale affect the world at large and each apparently intrastate conflict, by calling into question the position of ethno-sectarian minorities, has the potential to precipitate interstate clashes as well.

BEHIND THE BLOODBATH

In retrospect much of the peace of earlier decades was precarious, with the underlying tensions held in check by a number of constraints. One, to be sure, was the very Cold War alliance system that not only set limits to the autonomy of those under its thrall, therefore limiting interstate conflict, but also provided many states with a reason for existence, helping to reduce the potential for civil strife.[3]

That was reinforced by an ideological factor. Both sides preached their own version of universal humanism, creeds that at least on the surface transcended race and colour. At the same time, 'developing' countries could offer to their multi-ethnic populations the prospect that

209

the state could be an agent above tribe, clan or sect, to promote economic progress and integrate them equally into civil society.

Added to this was the illusion of the boundlessness of nature, once harnessed by productive capital and human ingenuity, and therefore of the seemingly limitless possibilities for economic growth. As long as everyone's living standard was rising it mattered little if a favoured few, within and between countries, saw theirs rising very much faster.

All that is now gone or rapidly disappearing. Stripped of Cold War rationale, many states have also lost whatever legitimacy they once possessed. Meantime, without Cold War restraints, their arsenals have become both a prize and a means of social strife. Nowhere was this more graphically illustrated than in the former Yugoslavia, propped up by both sides as a buffer and an ideological way station, and essentially abandoned to its own fratricidal devices once its usefulness was at an end.

Now the ideologies, too, are quite different. Racism seems rampant in much of the West. Emerging countries attempt to unify populations and paper over serious problems by focusing on ethno-religious solidarity. And in all too many 'developing countries', as the old colonially imposed borders cease to be accorded whatever limited legitimacy they once had, the notion of civil society is being rapidly replaced by a more primordial form of group identification. As a result, in country after country, minorities are being targeted for harassment, expulsion or extermination, particularly if they happen to be squatting on territory, physical or metaphysical, which another clan, sect or tribe happens to regard as its birthright.

There is much more at stake in this process of ethno-sectarian consolidation than merely determining who will control the resting sites of ancestral bones. And its causes lie much deeper than simply the perversity of human nature. It is true that some of these conflicts have been festering on their own for generations, with their origins lost to all but archaeologists. Others are the belated reaction to the territorial and social carve-ups imposed by the European colonial powers. Yet others were created or greatly exacerbated by the protagonists in the Cold War as a means of making trouble for allies of the other side. But many are largely attributable to contemporary conditions.

The most important of these conditions is the fact that with an ever increasing pressure on physical resources that are not merely limited, but in many cases rapidly depleting, with an ever worsening distribution of material wealth and ecological capital, ethnic and sectarian feuds are often surrogates for disputes over land and water, fish and forests, minerals and energy.[4]

It is true that contests over control of natural wealth have an ancient pedigree. Before the birth of modern agriculture in the eighteenth century, much of human history could be written around a cycle of one society slashing down forests, draining the water supply, depleting the most accessible minerals and exhausting the soil to such an extent that it had to pick up and colonize or conquer another area.[5] What is different today is that the process is virtually global in scope; the rate is accelerating, and it is occurring in societies where both numbers and expectations are unsustainably high. And that exacerbates the third major change that has taken place.

Once it was generally accepted that economic growth made social justice financially possible and morally essential. But today, economic performance and distributive justice have little in common. In many of the rich countries, as stock markets soar to dizzy heights, unemployment rates seem permanently stuck at double-digit levels while the social safety net is being torn full of holes. It has become less a matter of creating new wealth than of conniving and quarrelling over what does exist.

While certainly present before the end of the Cold War, the apparent triumph of 'free-market' liberalism made these trends all the stronger. Traditional forms of protectionism, economic and social, have disappeared from many sectors in the face of freer international movement of commodities, services and ideas, while fiscal restraints have made it all the more difficult to mitigate the effects. With populations robbed of social and economic security of the type the state was supposed to (though too often did not) provide, tribe, sect, clan and extended family are called upon to perform more and more of the functions previously assigned to the civic order. Inevitably loyalties get transferred, and those social units can all the more easily become the medium through which to express political frustrations in violent form. Furthermore, lacking the more limited ideological and political objectives of the Cold War era, armed clashes, by virtue of being more protracted, tend to take on a special, self-sustaining dynamic of their own. Once conflict has lasted for a sufficient length of time to wreck the civil economy, through physical destruction, collapse of domestic purchasing power and capital flight, it sets the stage for its own perpetuation, not least by the creation of a generation whose only skills, at what should be their peak productive years, are military and who therefore turn easily to criminal activity for survival. Thus, the distinction between crime and politics across great swathes of territory becomes murky. Warlords replenish their treasuries by theft, extortion and contraband traffic; while criminals carve out political fiefdoms on the rationalization, not necessarily incorrect, that in an increasingly stingy environment they can provide for their own at least as well, if not better, than the corrupt or incompetent leaders of the previous regime.[6]

This volatile combination of a breakdown in the old oligopoly of power, the resurrection of ethno-religious identification in place of membership in a civil society, and the triumph of savage capitalism with its increasing disparities in the distribution of income, wealth and ecological capital goes far to explain the present-day epidemic of political violence. Yet it does not go quite far enough. There is another reason for much of the current carnage, namely the triumph of a 'free market' in the instruments for effecting political and social change by violent means.

This, too, represents a dramatic change. For, in the past, conflicts were self-limiting, not just because they took place within a better-defined geo-strategic context with much clearer ideological and political objectives, but also because the major powers could adjust the temperature more or less at will through access to the tools of the trade. Historically the control mechanisms were of two sorts. On the supply-side of the arms market, there was the ability of the major powers to influence, even sometimes control, the movement of weapons, ammunition and spare parts around the world. On the demand-side, the ability of non-state actors to get even those weapons that escaped such political control was limited by their capacity to obtain the means of payment. Today, neither of those constraints seems operational. Weapons are easily available to all who have the ability to pay, and the global explosion of illicit activity has put the means of payment within the grasp of a remarkably diverse set of insurgent groups, paramilitary forces, militant religious sects and unabashed bandit gangs.

THE DISINTEGRATION OF SUPPLY-SIDE CONTROL

This was not always so. Typically in the past, after each major war, arms production fell sharply as those firms that could do so, reverted or converted to civilian production. Thus, the flow of new weapons was drastically diminished, and eventually the stock of second-hand material wore down. The irony today is that for the first time in history there exists fairly extensive international agreement on methods to control arms transfers. Yet never before has (conventional) arms proliferation been such a threat.

Until well into this century, arms were like any other commodity, freely traded except during wars, when one side would attempt to limit supplies to the other. Then, in the wake of the First World War, there emerged a popular consensus that the main responsibility for the carnage lay with the 'merchants of death', a cabal of arms manufacturers in league with weapons salesmen who secretly contrived crises and instigated conflicts to sell their merchandise.[7] That kind of thinking led to the first effort to impose visibility on arms transfers, a League of Nations-run international registry, as well as to national initiatives in the form of supply-side restrictions. In 1933 Belgium took the lead in imposing on its arms industry the requirement of a state-issued export license. It was an example virtually all countries would follow in decades to come.[8]

In the years following the Second World War there actually seemed some chance that arms transfers could be sharply limited, if not totally controlled. Over time countries came to agree that the business of arms manufacturing, where not already state-owned, would be state-regulated, and that they (China remains the one big exception) would issue no export licenses unless the would-be purchaser produced an 'end-user certificate' – essentially a pledge by relevant officials in the purchasing country that the arms were intended solely for the use of that country's military forces and would not be transferred to third-parties without permission of the country of origin. At the same time the world weapons trade was dominated by the USA and the Soviet Union who produced top-of-the-line equipment for their own forces and for their immediate allies, and gave away or transferred on the basis of soft credits, second-hand material to their Third World satellites. Even when the two superpowers came to face serious competition, it was initially from producers in Europe over whom the USA and Soviet Union could exercise a restraining hand.

The result was that, for several decades after the war, there was little evidence that a freewheeling world arms market could complicate the search for a lasting peace. While it was generally accepted that transfers of light weapons were going to be difficult to really restrict, the sector

213

dealing with major weapons systems, which were viewed as the really lethal stuff, was subject to a double political control – by the NATO-Warsaw Pact alliance system and by the virtual universalization of the end-user certificate. To be sure, there were problems that came to the fore during the Nigerian Civil War, the first one in history in which Africans fought each other with modern weapons. During that conflict gunrunners learned or honed many of the tricks that would subsequently become standard. They used third country diversions, false and misleading end-user certificates, multiple layers of intermediation and the trick of purchasing demilitarized planes that could be quickly and cheaply recommissioned. During that war, too, it became clear that governments were prepared to accommodate these tricks when it served their interests. Portugal, to weaken the moral position of the liberation movements in its colonies, hosted the main rebel buying mission, and permitted gun-running planes with obviously false registrations to refuel in Lisbon and the African colonies. Meantime France, to undermine Britain's position in West Africa, connected the insurgents with French intelligence-approved arms salesmen.[9]

However, even if such covert dealings in heavy equipment, such as aircraft, warships, major artillery pieces, tanks and the like, existed from time to time, they were assumed to be minor in scale, infrequent and susceptible of being stopped by tighter domestic enforcement and better international cooperation. Furthermore, it appeared there was little cause for concern even with regards to that sector of the arms market where formal controls seemed impossible to enforce, the part dealing with 'light' weapons. Certainly at the end of World War II there were masses of firearms, light machine-guns, hand-held rocket launchers and similar material in the territories of the former belligerent powers and scattered across war zones. However, not only were these weapons not taken very seriously, there actually were controls of a more informal nature that seemed, initially at least, quite effective.

During the 1950s the USA supported the efforts of a former Central Intelligence Agency (CIA) officer, Sam Cummings, to stockpile as much of the world's surplus as possible – so much so that at peak he could boast that he could equip 40 infantry divisions out of his warehouses. Backed by ample bank credit, Cummings could move quickly to take material off the open market and prevent it from falling into unwanted hands. He could act as a cut-out whenever the USA (or Britain) decided secretly to violate an international arms embargo to which they nominally adhered.

And, not least, he had built up an inventory of 'sterile' weapons of all types and makes, including ample amounts of East Bloc equipment that the CIA could call on when required to equip guerrilla or insurgent forces fighting against regimes backed by the Soviet Union. What made the arrangements especially useful was that Cummings never supplied a belligerent force without a nod from Washington.[10]

In the 1960s numerous wars of decolonization in Africa had brought freelances into the arms supply trade. Still, none yet could challenge Sam Cummings. Most of them were brokers rather than merchants, and therefore could not guarantee customer satisfaction with the same degree of reliability. They were hobbled by the traditional limitations of the black market, which could not assure regularity of supply. Moreover, given the expenses associated with smuggling goods, laundering money and paying off officials, prices on the black market tended to be higher.

This happy combination of a duopoly (and later an oligopoly) in the production of heavy weapons and a controlled 'black market' in light arms worked well for a time. With world production accelerating in the 1970s, it began to disintegrate, especially in the light weapons business. Then, in the 1980s, it collapsed completely – because of changes on both sides of the market equation.

On the supply-side, three factors were at work. The first was the fact that the old pattern of supplier states winding down arms production after each major conflict had been abandoned after World War II. The USA and the Soviet Union, followed by most other major industrial countries, in addition to not a few minor ones, made a commitment to keeping arms production at wartime levels.[11] Indeed, even the end of the Cold War has done remarkably little to reverse that trend.

There are many reasons for a country to maintain, or to build, its own arms industry. One is geo-strategic: a domestic arms-producing capacity might be seen to be essential to assure independence and/or influence in international relations. Another could be technological: weapons manufacturing was viewed as the leading edge in a process of learning-by-doing with spin-offs into the civilian sector, something especially important for developing countries intent on modernization. Yet another is economic: the arms industry might be considered an important and irreplaceable source of jobs and economic growth, precisely the belief that led to the entrenchment of the Permanent War Economy in the USA.[12]

This enormous expansion of productive capacity meant that the output of arms was far more than could be absorbed in the arsenals of the producing countries' own armed forces. The result was that the old pattern of controlled gifts or soft-credit sales by the major powers was replaced by an international sales drive. Producing countries of all shapes, sizes and ideological predilections were motivated by the desire to promote arms exports as a means of earning foreign exchange. In addition, it was frequently argued that exports and domestic military preparedness had to go together – exports permitted countries to acquire their own arsenals at a lower unit cost.[13] That new propensity to seek export markets was enhanced by the fact that as each new generation of weapons appears, it calls for the disposal of the previous one. Particularly in times of budgetary crisis, the obvious way to dispose of them is by sales abroad.

As time went on, the geo-strategic reasons for maintaining a domestic arms-producing capacity became less and less important in comparison with strictly financial ones, with the result that, today, the arms business has been almost completely commercialized just at the point in history when it is capable of doing the greatest damage.[14] This is a change of the utmost significance. With the manufacture of weapons being seen as so important to the economic well-being of so many countries, the rule has become not to employ economic resources to make what is necessary for military requirements, something that has logistical limits. Rather it is the reverse – military production, and foreign sales, take place all too often to meet the profit needs of the producers, and the employment and foreign exchange needs of the host country, things for which a country's demand is virtually unlimited. Under these circumstances, an exporting country will almost inevitably subject its customer list to considerably less scrutiny than was the case when the main purpose of arms transfers was to enhance the producing country's international power and prestige.

By the 1980s the system of export licensing based on end-user certificates had become a farce. These certificates could almost be assigned stars, much like restaurants in the *Guide Michelin*. A one-star certificate might be a pale imitation of a Bolivian or Nigerian one, obtained from a shady office in Brussels or Geneva – it would cost very little, though it might present serious risks of detection. A two-star certificate might be real, issued by a corrupted military attaché of an embassy – since it was better, the price was accordingly higher. A three-star certificate might bear the name of a high-level official in the country of issue, in return for a hefty sum deposited in an offshore bank account. At the top of the scale, rating four stars, might be a genuine certificate obtained from the top political authorities of a country that had quietly agreed to provide transit facilities – it would be issued not in return for a personal payoff but for a percentage of the contract value to be paid to the treasury of the country of nominal destination.[15]

In short, the end-user certificate ceased to be a technique of control so much as a tool for the personal enrichment of corrupt officials in the purchasing country, and a means by which selling countries could establish an alibi (the weapons were supposed to go elsewhere) whenever news of a sale to some embargoed or illegal destination leaked out. Even worse, by the end of the 1980s, the end-user certificate system had not only been hopelessly compromised by deceit and corruption, but another development had rendered it almost irrelevant.

The second factor at work to undermine traditional supply-side controls derived from the simple fact that arms are by nature durable, capable of being recycled from conflict to conflict. Thus, one 20-mm Lahti cannon built in Finland during the Second World War was, in the late 1940s, bartered to a European arms dealer for light machine-guns, then sold to an Italian dealer who resold it to the irregular Haganah forces in Palestine. In 1950 the Israeli army sold it back to the first merchant who subsequently unloaded it on Costa Rica. In 1955 that country peddled it to yet another arms dealer who had a customer, the Algerian Front de Libération Nationale, waiting. Five years later the weapon turned up in Panama, apparently in unusable condition. It was then shipped to the USA classified as a deactivated war trophy. By magic it acquired a new barrel and was passed on, first to anti-Castro activists and later to Haitian exiles plotting against the Duvalier regime, before it was finally impounded by the US government.[16] There are innumerable such stories in the arms business.

In the past such recycling was not a serious cause for concern. After each war, production of new material went into remission and the ravages of time and nature and minor conflicts eventually took care of the old stock. But now, with new material churned out on a more or less permanent basis by a host of producing countries, there is little chance of the stockpile actually falling. As long as the rate of production of new weapons exceeds the rate of physical deterioration or loss in battle of old ones, the world's available stock of weapons must inevitably grow. Moreover, each time a formal army decides to upgrade its arsenal, there is budgetary pressure to ease the financial burden by dumping the old ones on the second-hand market. This problem becomes considerably greater in an era of rapid model changes, when the rate of strategic obsolescence is far higher than the rate of technical depreciation.

Therefore, although the recycling of weapons from war to war is an old story, what is novel today is the sheer mass of second-hand equipment, the strong pressure to cut legal and moral corners in unloading it, and the downward trend in prices resulting from the glut. An AK-47 that used to cost about US$125 factory-fresh in the Soviet Union can now be picked up for US$30–$40 on the Russian flea market. In Uganda its price is about the same as that of a chicken, while in Angola and Mozambique it will exchange for the equivalent of a bag of maize. On the Cambodian black market it may go for as little as US$8.00, about the same price as that of a pair of fake designer jeans.[17] For the first time in history, it is the accumulated stock rather than the annual new flow that determines behaviour and sets the prices in the world market. It is exactly those accumulated stocks that have historically been least amenable to control. And that leads to the third reason that supply-side controls no longer work.

In the past, states supplied weapons in three distinct ways. They sold them legally and openly to other states, following the proper procedures of accepting and verifying end-user certificates before issuing export licenses. They sold them illegally and covertly to other states by diverting weapons through third parties or accepting false end-user certificates. And they secretly supplied non-state actors, working through cut-outs and intermediaries in the arms black market to hide the trail. All those things still occur. But today there is a new factor at work. Much of the clandestine portion of international arms transfers is the result of decisions not by states, acting directly or indirectly, but by autonomous actors, either corrupted military or political officials acting on their own account or, startlingly, by the actual users of the weapons. Guerrilla and insurgent groups, and the logistical apparatus that supports them, which traditionally appeared in the black market exclusively as buyers, are today functioning as suppliers as well. And that development derives from the emergence in zones of conflict of regional arms supermarkets stocked with seemingly unlimited supplies of second-hand weaponry.

The importance of such conflict zones for black market distribution comes not simply from the volumes of military supplies poured into them, but also from the fact that once arms are there, all trace is effectively lost, and they therefore can move out again with virtual impunity. A conflict zone is for weapons what an offshore banking centre with strict secrecy laws is for money – with the added advantage that anyone attempting to probe the secrets of the zone's arms business risks considerably more than the mere indignity of deportation. Indeed, so effective is the process that it has been known for intelligence agencies to deliberately ship more weapons than required for their purposes to a particular conflict area, just in order to be free to then divert them to some other, politically unauthorized or publicly unacceptable place. This appears to be how the CIA continued to equip both UNITA in Angola and the Contra rebels in Nicaragua during periods when such aid was banned by the US Congress. It merely diverted material from stocks approved for the Afghan mujihadeen. Similarly using the excuse that weapons have been obtained as war booty in the course of combat automatically obviates any need to respect or impose end-user restrictions. This is precisely why, for a decade after its 1982 invasion of Lebanon, Israel could peddle with impunity enormous amounts of weaponry around the world, while claiming they had been captured from the Palestine Liberation Organization (PLO).

Apart from the USA itself, whose open arms bazaar has fed the needs of private paramilitaries, narco-militias, insurgents and terrorist groups across the Americas, as well as Japanese gangsters, Filipino landlord security forces and the Irish Republican Army (IRA), the earliest of these regional supermarkets to emerge was in Bangkok. It dealt first with the spill over of weapons from the Vietnam and related wars in Southeast Asia in the 1970s, and then was stoked further by conflict in Cambodia during the 1980s. In recent years everyone from Tamil separatist guerrillas to Burmese drug armies has turned to Thai arms merchants to replenish their supplies.

Next came Beirut. Within two years of the outbreak of the Lebanese civil war in 1975, and the consequent flocking into the country of arms dealers from all over the world, Lebanon, though itself still at war, became a net exporter of weapons to everyone from French mobsters to Turkish leftist insurgents to the Nicaraguan Contras. And once the civil war ended, Lebanese militias managed to find a new vocation selling surplus arms to the breakaway republic of Croatia, then under international embargo.

Yet another was and is located in the Horn of Africa. Weapons of all sorts flooded into Ethiopia, Eritrea and Somalia during the 1970s and early 1980s, and then began flowing out again in the late 1980s and 1990s, nourishing conflict across eastern Africa without any noticeable diminution of the amount of weaponry in the hands of its own many militia groups.

Next came Afghanistan. During the 1980s at least US$10 billion worth of weapons of all sorts poured in, the USA supplying the anti-government forces and the Soviet Union the government. From the start the USA pipeline began, not merely leaking but spouting, with weapons diverted onto local and regional black markets into which everyone from Sindhi dacoits to Kashmiri rebels to embargoed countries such as Iran could dip. Then, once the government fell, all of the Soviet-supplied weapons went into the same pot, with results that have been felt across Southwest Asia and North Africa and even into the Balkans.

But of all of these supermarkets, there is one that today plays an especially important role, partly by virtue of volume and partly because it has become the epicentre of black market patterns that have transcended the regional to the global, namely the yard sale erected on the ruins of the Warsaw Pact. It started with the re-unification of Germany. With the pullout of the Red Army an enormous amount of military equipment was suddenly thrown onto the second-hand market. Then, with the united German army standardizing around NATO models, the East Bloc equipment of the former East German forces became surplus and was available for a host of destinations. One-third of the East German navy was overtly sold to Indonesia, top-of-the-line tanks were smuggled to Israel in a deal between the West German and Israeli intelligence services, while 250,000 AK-47s were covertly shipped to Turkey: since Turkey itself uses NATO standard equipment, the Soviet weapons are likely to be used to equip pro-Turkish paramilitary forces throughout the former Soviet Union.

However large these stocks were, they were a pittance compared with those freed, first by a Soviet-American arms reduction treaty (that, among other things, made no less than 10,000 tanks surplus), then by the collapse of the Soviet Union itself, the Red Army along with it. Together they meant the greatest stock of military surplus in history was suddenly dumped on the market.

It was a free-for-all. Desperate individual soldiers and entire military units sold their weapons in exchange for basic supplies. The emerging republics grabbed control of any material in their reach – often it was the very best which the Soviet Union had sent to guard the frontiers. Cities in Russia took over local arsenals and announced they were open to offers. The Ukrainian-Siberian Commodity Exchange switched from dealing in grain and oil to selling fighter planes, tanks and anti-aircraft systems. Fully US$2 billion worth was put on the auction block with the only restrictions that the buyers show an arms dealer's license, guarantee to take their purchases out of the territory of the ex-Soviet Union and prove they had the means to pay. Then there was the Kaliningrad yard sale: up to seven train loads a day arrived during 1992 to dump enormous amounts of weapons from across Eastern Europe into a compound with no accounting system and protected only by barbed wire and underpaid or unpaid soldiers. Not least, downsizing and drastic pay cuts put thousands of top Russian military engineers and research scientists on an international market for military expertise in which the respectability of the destination was less important than the size of the pay cheque.[18]

While some of this mass of weaponry stayed in Russia and fell into the hands of heavily armed criminal gangs, ethnic insurgent forces and private security firms, inevitably much of it poured onto the world market. Everyone from Italian Mafia hit men to the Iranian government came shopping. Added to the stock was the continued flow of newly produced arms. After a failed attempt to promote conversion of factories to civilian production in the final days of the Soviet Union, Russia decided to encourage its arms manufacturers to seek foreign sales. While some weapons continued to be supplied for political reasons – to the former republics like Tajikistan to sway the balance in its civil war, or to Serbia and Serbian forces in Bosnia and Croatia – the watchword became commercial sales. And with Russia in the unique position of having flows of new material from its factories competing directly with stocks sold by its military, the result was top-of-the-line material at unbeatable prices.[19]

The emergence of all of these second-hand weapons supermarkets, particularly the one in the ex-Soviet Union, meant that the historical weaknesses of the arms black market were rectified: it could easily ensure continuity of supply, even of fairly sophisticated weapons; it could serve a global rather than just regional market; and with prices falling in the face of the glut, the cost disadvantage black market sales used to face compared with formally controlled ones began to vanish. Moreover, with both the commercialization of sales of new equipment along with the progressive growth of second-hand stocks, prices now reflect quality and cost in a much more reliable way. Moreover, the growing potential for upgrades, which eliminates much of the generation gap between models, facilitates greatly comparison between different types of equipment. And the probability of a customer getting fleeced, something commonplace in a secretive and highly segmented black market, is that much smaller. For the first time in history, black market weapons could be not only cheaper than their legitimate counterparts, but have just as firm a guarantee of quality and reliability for the customer. Finally, in terms of the logic of operation of the arms market, the old distinction between 'light' and 'heavy' weapons became irrelevant.

THE COMMERCIALIZATION OF DEMAND

Despite the massive supplies, the amount of weaponry officially entering the world marketplace seems to have been dropping substantially. Recorded arms transfers fell from a peak of US$46.5 billion in 1987 to a mere US$18.5 billion in 1994. That should be good news. There are several reasons, however, why it may not be.

One is that these numbers have to be adjusted upward to take account of the trade in dual-use technology and in upgrading services. A second is that, in response to the many attempts to restrict illicit transfers, production capacity has proliferated. When weapons cease to be transferred from country to country, where they have at least the potential to be monitored and controlled and instead are produced at home, where they can be deployed and employed at the behest of the producing country without restrictions, it is scarcely a cause for relief that much of the reduction may be the result of the proliferation of production capacity around the world. A third is the fact that in the international arms trade, the value of the merchandise traded is a poor guide to its potential for damage. Value is determined by multiplying price by quantity, and much of the recent fall in value can be imputed to price cuts. A fourth is that the measured values obviously fail to capture unrecorded, unreported and illegal sales, which may well be on the rise. A fifth is that, even if the numbers do show a substantial drop, they do not take into account a subtle, but dangerous shift in the nature of the demand for weapons.

Apart from the role of weapons manufacturing to bolster employment and economic growth at home, the former Cold War arms boom involved an attempt by the West, led by the USA, not so much to prepare for a physical confrontation with the Soviet Union as to try to drive it into bankruptcy.[20] The strategy was to lock the latter into a spending spiral in which the two camps would competitively waste as much of their national product as possible in stockpiling weapons they assumed would not be used. Although in the final analysis internal factors were much more important in bringing about the actual fall of the Soviet Union, the strategy of war-through-inventory accumulation actually contained a twisted logic. Since the main danger facing advanced capitalist economies was assumed to be a deficiency of the economy's ability to absorb the enormous volume of civilian production of which the economy was capable, military spending to inflate demand was one way of taking up the slack. On the other side, since the main problem facing the Socialist Bloc was a deficiency of total supply to fill the enormous gap in civilian demand, forcing it to waste resources in arms production would have the advantage of exacerbating the problem.

As a result, much of the weaponry being turned out, whether absorbed into the military inventories of the producing country or sold to its major allies, represented an appalling waste of resources and caused incalculable environmental damage in the process of production, though posing little immediate threat to human life. But now, with Cold War restraints gone, acquisition and use tend to go hand in hand, a shift rendered all the more dangerous by the release of accumulated Cold War stocks into the international arena.

This dangerous development has been reinforced by the second change taking place on the demand side of the market. In the weapons market, wishing will not automatically make it so. Demand is only effective if it can be translated into an ability to pay. In the past the payment methods in the international arms trade were relatively straightforward. States would provide arms to other states, legally and openly, either through gifts or by providing state-subsidised credit or by sometimes accepting payment in local (soft) currency. Since the fundamental reason for making the transfer was political, the fact that such sales were not commercially profitable was irrelevant; and the purchaser usually had little problem financing what was allocated. States would also covertly provide arms, either directly or by acting through the international weapons black market, to non-state actors, especially guerrilla and insurgent groups active against a political rival. Here, too, payment would take the form principally of political action. The closest states got to purely commercial considerations was when they sold arms illegally to embargoed states, although even then there might be a secret political agenda involved as well.

Thus, all these transactions were subject to political control. In the case of legal sales, that control was overt. When arms transfers took the form of illegally supplying an embargoed country or smuggling arms to non-state actors, control was covert. In these instances the intelligence agencies of the supplying country were generally on hand to arrange the deals, move the money and sometimes take a cut of the proceeds, a process facilitated by the fact that the actual gun-runners were so often retired former intelligence officers or veteran military men.[21]

Historically such constraints worked to limit, at least partially, the propensity of social, political and economic tensions to translate themselves into violent conflict. But in current market conditions embargoed states and ethno-sectarian insurgents alike have had surprisingly little trouble replenishing their arsenals, partly because the commercialization of the trade eliminated most of the political constraints and partly because the rise of global underground economy has made it much easier to find the money to pay the bills. This is a factor particularly important in assuring that non-state actors can pay for what they need.

There are actually two major ways in which insurgent groups have been able to raise money to finance their activities, including their weapons purchases. One is through the use of external sponsors. During the Cold War these sponsors were usually political in nature. A country would quietly provide money to an insurgent group making trouble for a rival. Most of this occurred on the Western side. Although there was a popular misconception that the bulk of anti-state insurgencies were a product of a Moscow-based conspiracy, in reality most of the covert financial support provided by the Soviet Union to political dissidents went to Communist parties legally contesting elections. Even China confined its sponsorship of insurgencies to a handful of groups operating in countries on its immediate borders. However, the USA, Britain, France and Saudi Arabia provided a veritable cornucopia of aid to insurgent forces opposing Soviet-backed regimes. The main difference today is that the major powers provide little such aid; while the opportunities for independent fund-raising are far greater.

Even during the Cold War, not all of the outside support came from sympathetic or opportunistic governments. Ethno-religious solidarity also could play a role, as with the Irish in the USA pumping arms and money to the IRA, or the Turkish diaspora in Germany sustaining the Grey Wolves back home. As the 1980s wore on and the 1990s dawned, this phenomenon became more widespread. Sikhs in Canada, Croats in Chile, Tamils and Kurds in Europe, Armenians almost everywhere, and many more all raise funds and arrange arms shipments to their co-religionists or ethnic kin. They do so in two distinct ways. Some of the money is raised from legitimate business and donors using methods that are legal, even if the money is subsequently diverted to illegal uses. And some of it is raised through extortion, racketeering and smuggling. For along with the unparalleled expansion of international migration in the last two decades has come the formation of underground trade diasporas, regional and global networks based on extended family or ethno-sectarian loyalties that are well positioned by virtue of their contacts with the underground economy to smuggle everything from diamonds to designer jeans, from cigarettes to heroin, with at least part of the profits recycled back into arms.

The result is that a modern covert arms deal is likely to take place within a matrix of black market transactions. Weapons might be sold for cash, exchanged for hostages, bartered for heroin or religious artefacts, or counter-traded for grain or oil. The transactions, formerly dominated by veteran military or intelligence people, are now more likely to be handled by middlemen equally at home in smuggling rubies from Burma, sneaking counterfeit computer chips into the USA or dumping toxic waste in Lebanon. The transportation can be entrusted to a company whose headquarters is designated by one of several dozen brass-plates on the door of a small Cayman Islands office, staffed by one secretary who sits watching American soaps for the whole working day. To haul the arms such companies in turn will hire ships registered in one of the many flag-of-convenience centres that are so much the bane of seafarers' unions, marine insurance companies and government officials attempting to enforce arms trade embargoes. And the payments can move through a series of coded bank accounts in the name of a network of shell companies, protected by the banking and corporate secrecy laws of one or several of those financial havens.

Meanwhile, those engaged in the struggle on the home front usually evolve their own methods of financing, which in turn are closely linked to the military stage an insurgency has reached. In the earliest stage, a guerrilla group usually engages in hit-and-run operations against individual symbols of the state, either officials or isolated institutions such as police stations and army outposts. At that stage the group's expenditure requirements are relatively small and mainly military. Hence, it can rely on fundraising activities based on similarly sporadic and predatory actions such as bank robbery and ransom kidnapping.

In the next stage the guerrilla group begins openly disputing the political power of the state, mainly through the conduct of low intensity warfare against the infrastructure of the formal economy. Confrontations are more intense, and the logistical requirements heavier. The guerrilla group's expenditure obligations are not only much greater in absolute amounts, but also include a rising social security component for the care of dependents of its militants, as well as providing some assistance to the population whose support it is attempting to win. Fundraising therefore shifts from once-for-all predatory operations to parasitic ones that yield a steadier and more dependable flow of income at the expense of the formal economy. The most important will be the 'revolutionary taxation' of income and wealth, sometimes voluntary, more often pure extortion.

In the third stage the guerrilla movement succeeds in implanting itself firmly on a piece of territory from which the state is effectively excluded. At that point it may well need to upgrade its arsenal to include material essential for defending its gains. And to its obligations for military operations and social security for dependents of its militants are added those arising from the provision of social services to the general population of the controlled area, and the building of the infrastructure necessary for the growth and development of a parallel economy. Fundraising ceases to be parasitic with respect to the formal economy controlled by the state and instead becomes symbiotic with the parallel economy being developed by the insurgent group.[22]

In this advanced stage, the most important sources of revenue come from indirect taxation – sales taxes on domestic commerce and/or export and import taxes on foreign trade that are not only lucrative but produce their revenues in the form of the foreign exchange so crucial to tapping the international arms black market. While taxing the growth and/or transit of 'recreational drugs' has been playing an increasingly important role in such financing almost everywhere in the world,[23] none the less the income from taxing commodities that are inherently legal –

226

everything from tea to teakwood – is likely much greater. Across Southeast Asia and sub-Saharan Africa, throughout Central Asia and the Indian subcontinent, this pattern is repeated.

During the Cold War era, this third stage was usually a prelude to a final assault on the state. However, one of the main ways in which the current round of insurgent wars differs from its predecessors is that there is often no incentive to capture control of the existing state, a need that decreases as ethno-sectarian concerns replace more strictly political ones, and as the old state structure gets closer and closer to financial and political bankruptcy. Instead, the strategic objective becomes the creation of economically differentiated and ethnically homogenous mini-states built around control of one or a few major resources that can be used on world markets to obtain arms of all sorts.

LETHAL DISTINCTION

For several decades it seemed reasonable to treat the arms market as if it could be separated into two components, one dealing in light weapons and the other in heavy. Initially the assumption was that the heavy stuff was the more dangerous, and for that reason arms control regimes gave it almost all of their attention. More recently the view has emerged that far more attention needs to be focused on small arms and light weapons. There are three reasons. One is that light weapons are the characteristic equipment of irregular warfare, of the multitude of ethnic and social conflicts spreading around the world. A second is that in actual conflict situations it is the light stuff that does the killing. A third is that it is light weapons that are most prone to getting loose. Granted the exact line of demarcation between the two have always represented something of a moving target,[24] nonetheless the difference was deemed sufficiently important as to merit policy explicitly formulated to counter light weapon proliferation.

In fact, the problems inherent in the distinction go beyond merely finding an accurate definition of the dividing line. First, the distinction itself seems militarily artificial. It is true that in modern wars artillery, for example, has directly accounted for only about two per cent of battlefield deaths. Nonetheless one of the most important roles of artillery in a conflict is to take out specific targets such as bunkers, leaving enemy troops exposed to the effects of 'light' weapons.

Second, the very concept of a 'light' weapon implies a differentiation based on physical properties – size, weight and mobility. But the relevance of this is ever more dubious at a time when advances in military technology have given some hand-held weapons the capacity to inflict a level of damage formerly restricted to weapons that were decidedly 'heavy'. It is the threat from Stinger anti-aircraft missiles, not from the numerous large anti-aircraft cannons in the region, that causes civilian planes to divert their flight paths away from the Hindu Kush. The fact that so much military science consists of the development of weapons that are smaller and smaller in terms of scale and weight to accomplish larger and larger jobs in terms of explosive force and killing power suggests that this ambiguity in the light–heavy distinction will only become more problematic.

Third, it is unclear if the point of the definition is the actual weapon or the delivery system. A tank, for example, would fall into anyone's list of 'heavy' weapons. Yet its cannon and armour exist to deal with other tanks. Once that intermediate function has been carried out, the real role of the tank comes into play – namely bringing its machine-guns to bear on unprotected or lightly protected infantry. At that point, with both its armour and its cannon redundant, the tank becomes militarily little different from a truck-mounted machine-gun or even one man-handled from behind a concrete barricade, items which are usually classed as 'light'.

Fourth, the distinction threatens to throw the focus onto a technical issue of delivery systems rather than on impact. Land mines, for example, fall into the category of 'light', since it has become standard in some bush wars to equip each infantry soldier with several of them. The land mine is a weapon that has been singled out for special opprobrium because it maims and kills indiscriminately and remains actively dangerous to civilians long after the conflict has moved on to other locations. On the other hand, the projectiles used to scatter cluster bomblets are either dropped from aircraft or fired from artillery, placing them firmly in the 'heavy' category. But spread widely across an area, primed for delayed detonation, and used in brush or desert conditions where nature quickly conceals them or, as during the Israeli siege of Beirut, hidden in urban debris, the actual cluster bomblets are difficult to differentiate from land-mines in terms of their ability to maim and kill indiscriminately long after the scene of battle has moved elsewhere.[25]

Fifth, it may be a mistake to attempt to formulate arms control strategy on the basis of a distinction that comes down to an issue of military tactics. During the siege of Sarajevo, for example, the fact that the Serbs used mortars (which are 'light') for random shelling and terrorizing of the civilian population reflects not the special importance of the equipment *per se*, or the absence of heavier weapons in the Serb arsenal – they had plenty of those. Rather it was because the defenders had limited capacity for long-distance defence, permitting the Serbs to approach close enough to leave the job to mortar teams. The impact on the population would have been little different if barrages of accurate artillery fire had been used instead.

Sixth, since weapons are demanded not according to their inherent nature but for what they will accomplish, a conflict such as the Lebanese civil war might start with weapons that are unambiguously light. But in that case each successive escalation induced the belligerents to move further up the light–heavy continuum until tanks threatened to become a hazard to automobile traffic in Beirut streets. In short, what is in demand depends not on a technical light–heavy distinction, but rather on what material one side has already obtained, and what, in response, the other side needs and can afford to acquire.

Seventh, the insistence on the difference between 'light' and 'heavy' weapons reflects in some degree the simplistic dichotomy between informal and formal warfare, and the accompanying assumption that light weapons characterize the first, and heavy the second. In reality there is a continuum, revealed in, for example, the Horn of Africa, where irregular forces started with hit and run tactics, graduated to sustained guerrilla actions and then went on to large-scale insurgency before evolving into a state of full civil war – at which point the distinction between formal and informal warfare largely vanished. That continuum in tactics will also dictate a continuum in choice of optimal weapons, something further reinforced by the nature of the terrain on which conflict is undertaken. If a small guerrilla force needs mobility, it avoids heavy material that is not only burdensome but also difficult to hide. Similarly, inside a crowded urban area, co-inhabited by both sides, where the targets must be selective, 'light' weapons might well do the job. But as the degree of security of the insurgent force increases, so too will its territorial hold; and that will raise its requirement for major weapons systems to defend its gains, along with its capacity to raise money to purchase those weapons. Furthermore, the implicit equation of irregular war with light arms seems to be based on a notion of the inherently limited size of irregular forces. In fact 'guerrilla' armies can swell, as in Afghanistan, to number in the hundreds of thousands and move about in armoured personnel carriers while settling scores with multiple-barrel rocket launchers. Indeed, the Taliban who now dominate Afghanistan started as a lightly armed insurgency-within-an-insurgency and were soon flying MiG fighters against other factions. Thus, any perceived proliferation of struggles waged overwhelmingly with light weapons might well reflect not so much a matter of a firm choice of tools per se, but rather of the relatively early stage (in military-strategic terms) that the conflict has reached or the precise nature of the terrain on which it is fought.

Eighth, the notion that reliance on 'light' weapons is more characteristic of irregular warfare and reliance on 'heavy' inherent in the nature of formal warfare may not only be based on a static view of the former, but may represent a technical oversimplification as well. Given the direction of military technology, the 'formal' conflicts of the future may well involve regular forces that are very widely dispersed, highly mobile and dependent on extremely good intelligence about their terrain and target.[26] In form they will differ little from today's guerrilla war, the difference being largely a technological one. While irregular forces score intelligence successes by keeping their ears to the ground, the future regular soldier will do so by keeping his or her eyes on the screen. Who knows to what degree modern heat- and sound-sensing equipment, and the digital information processing technologies that go with it, are really an 'advance' so much as a means of permitting humans raised in a modern urban environment to catch up with their more 'primitive' counterparts who are well tuned in to the terrain and environment in which they have always lived?

Ninth, even if the logistical difference between the two forms of warfare is a reasonable approximation, the special attention given to light arms also presumes that the principal problem will remain, for the foreseeable future, internal civic strife rather than state-to-state conflicts. This assumes that internal wars have exclusively internal causes, whereas many can be stirred up by external forces for political gain, just as in the Cold War era. No better example exists than in the current conflicts in Central Africa, Uganda and Angola who are really at war without any need for formal armies to push past frontiers. And such ethno-sectarian based strife, even if initially internal, has the potential to spill over borders and, as in the Balkans, draw in other countries who choose to come to the defence of their ethnic kin or co-religionists.

Tenth, the entire distinction rests on a view of the international arms market that is decidedly passé. Certainly the distinction had its uses in the past because the 'heavy' material assumed destined largely for formal armies was subject to political control and the 'light' material to equip irregular forces seemed much more susceptible to black market transactions. However, today the arms market is glutted, not just with 'light' weapons, but also with second-hand artillery, recoilless rifles, missiles and tanks. On that market the primary issue is not whether the material sought is light or heavy but how much the order is worth and whether would-be purchasers have the necessary connections and money, two things that are improving all the time.

CONCLUSION

There has been a tendency to give credit for the Cold War peace to the fact that, thanks to the strength of their armed forces, each side had too much to lose to engage in a shooting war. In reality, most of the credit should have been given to memories of the carnage of the Second World War; the development of international institutions that could mediate disputes; the ability of Europe, albeit divided, to play a conciliatory role with both sides; the relative economic self-sufficiency of the two major protagonists that reduced international competition for resources; and the fact that, since the stakes were less territorial than political, much of their competitive energies could be channelled into bribing or bullying other countries into lining up, however temporarily, on one side or the other.

Thus, the massive production of arms during the Cold War deserves little credit for keeping the peace. But it does deserve a large part of the blame for laying the foundations of today's glut of arms. Although the ready availability of weapons is not the primary cause of the current epidemic of political and social conflict, it does considerably exacerbate it. It also bears much of the responsibility for the upsurge of criminal violence – biker gangs in northern Europe settle disputes with bazookas, ivory poachers hunt elephants with machine-guns and helicopter gunships, and the last 15 years have seen a dramatic upsurge of incidents of armed piracy-at-sea, some of it conducted by men with military training and equipment.

The problem of the enormous volume of arms production and its steadily increasing rate of dispersion is clear enough. What to do about it is far less so. Policy can be directed at three logically distinct, though not mutually exclusive, levels. The first is to attack the actual trafficking.

231

This runs afoul of a number of obstacles – apart from the obvious fact that, in the absence of measures to simultaneously reduce demand, restrictions on the flow of weapons merely lead to countries developing their own production capacities. The machinery for smuggling today is extremely sophisticated. Nor is it limited to small, precious items such as diamonds. Today oil, grain, lumber and containers of consumer goods are smuggled all over the world with virtual impunity. Even if the traffickers in guns get caught, they are, like those in narcotics, easy to replace. And the real problem is not the greed of the trafficker who is merely an intermediary. Before a trafficker can do the job, it is necessary to have something to sell and someone to sell it to.

Therefore the second level of possible attack is on the supply side, which must be further subdivided into primary (the production of new equipment), secondary (the distribution of old stocks) and tertiary (the dispersion of arms into the hands of the user population) levels. With all three the obstacles to control are formidable. Perhaps the greatest impediment to primary supply control is governments whose behaviour, with respect to the world weapons trade, is based on equal portions of short-sighted financial expediency and sheer hypocrisy. Those who put their faith in primary supply control insist that it has never really been tried, and cite as proof all the holes in the existing regulations. But those holes have been deliberately created by governments precisely to let certain deals get through. The issue, then, is not how to reform the rules but how to change the attitude of the states supposedly enforcing them.

And this lack of enthusiasm shown by so many governments for genuine policing from the supply side reflects something even more dangerous. For decades governments in the West used military expenditure as the central instrument for pump-priming economies in recession, therefore increasing the productive capacity of the arms industry and the flow of new material. Even now, in spite of the loss of the legitimization formerly provided by the Cold War, economic pressure on politicians to maintain extremely elevated levels of military spending has proven hard to resist.

That has been complicated by the fact that, unlike the situation just after the Second World War, conversion today is difficult. The reasons are partly technical and partly the absence among arms producers of a corporate culture and infrastructure for success in the civil sector. Nor has there been any evidence of governments' willingness to allocate sufficient funds to cover the huge overhead costs of conversion. Hence, even if fiscal pressures finally force the governments of the main industrial countries to slash military spending, they will also constrain governments' willingness and ability to pay for alternatives.

Failing any broad-based commitment to industrial restructuring, the only result of reducing domestic expenditures for arms procurement will be arms manufacturers pushing export sales all the harder. They will then run up against competition from a whole host of other eager producers. For many developing countries stimulating weapons production is a deliberate tool of industrial development. And for ex-Socialist countries it is often the most immediately viable source of desperately needed foreign exchange.

Thus, genuine supply-side control requires weaning industrial and industrializing economies off their addiction to war industries for jobs, technical change and money. That is a tall order. Nor is it enough. For effective supply-side control also requires addressing the problem at the secondary level and doing something about the accumulated stocks. After the Second World War that seemed briefly possible. But today it is difficult to see a new Sam Cummings on the horizon, not least because his role would be to remove (permanently, in this case) from the multitude of second-hand markets, not only the light weaponry as of old, but all the stockpiled tanks and planes and artillery pieces. Apart from the huge cost, the logistics of such an operation would be awesome.

Finally, no measure of supply-side control can be truly effective without addressing the tertiary level – the arms already in the hands of the public at large, including criminals and insurgents. Efforts can be made to do so through increased policing. But rarely, if ever, in the face of a pressing need for the weapons, have repressive tactics had much success. Israel turned the Gaza region of Occupied Palestine into the world's largest concentration camp, policed through the most *avant garde* of surveillance technology bolstered by networks of paid informants, mass deportations, collective punishments and free-wheeling death squads. Yet, at the end of the 27 years of military rule, weapons in the hands of the population were far more abundant than at the beginning.

The alternative is buybacks and amnesties to encourage the voluntary handing in to the authorities of illegal weapons. The record of success is spotty and geographically very limited. All too often it is only the worst junk that is handed in. Furthermore the most dangerous elements in society, those most prone to using their weapons, are the last to surrender them, if they ever do. Tertiary supply-side control ultimately bumps up against the fact that the arms supply business is subject to the law of entropy – the further the material moves away from the primary source and the greater the degree of dispersal, the greater the problems of putting the process in reverse.

Any global solution will, of course, require paying considerable attention to all three levels on the supply side: encouraging conversion, tightening regulations and encouraging the voluntary disarming of populations. But none of this will work miracles, or even have any discernible long-term effect unless attention is simultaneously focused on the demand side of the market. Contrary to the conviction of those who still hold the 'merchants of death' responsible for conflict and war, the arms market has been, and always will be, driven from the demand side.

Attacking the problem of arms proliferation from the demand side requires addressing squarely the other main causes of the current wave of violent conflict. It requires shifting loyalties back, away from clan, sect and tribe in favour of rebuilding civil societies. It also requires that something be done to rectify the current gross inequities in the global and local distribution of income, wealth and ecological capital. In short, the best way to attack the economy of weapons production and the infrastructure for arms distribution may well be to render the weapons that do exist irrelevant.

NOTES

1. This analysis was previously published in Virginia Gamba (ed.), *Society Under Siege: Crime, Violence and Illegal Weapons*. Towards Collaborative Peace Series; Volume 1, by the Institute for Security Studies in South Africa. It is published here with permission of the Institute for Security Studies
2. This paper is the offshoot of research conducted over several years on the emergence and operation of modern black markets, including those for arms. It has benefited from the critical input of many persons and from the financial support, in the past, of the Social Sciences and Humanities Research Council of Canada; at present it is assisted by the John D. and Catherine T. MacArthur Foundation. Some of the arguments were initially published in 'The Structure and Operation of the Modern Arms Black Market', in J. Boutwell *et al.*, *Lethal Commerce: The Global Trade in Small Arms and Light Weapons* (Cambridge, MA.: American Academy of Arts and Sciences, 1994) and in 'Loose Cannons: Covert Commerce and Underground Finance in the Modern Arms Black Market', *Crime, Law and Social Change*, Vol.25 (1995). The main themes have been developed into a book-length study entitled, *Loose Cannons: Inside the Modern Arms Black Market*.
3. This point is well made by Virginia Gamba in the introduction to a series of case studies, *Managing Arms In Peace Processes* (Geneva: United Nations Institute for Disarmament Research, 1995 and 1996).

4. The theme of ecological causes of conflict has been convincingly treated by Thomas Homer-Dixon. See especially, 'On the Threshold: Environmental Changes as Causes of Acute Conflict', *International Security*, Vol.16, No.2 (Fall, 1991); and 'Environmental Scarcities and Violent Conflict: Evidence from Cases', *International Security*, Vol.19, No.1 (Summer 1994).

5. See T. Dale and V. Carter, *Topsoil and Civilization* (Norman, OK: Oklahoma Press, 1955). They point out that the sole important exceptions – and therefore the real birthplace of civilization – are the areas served by the Nile, Indus and Tigris–Euphrates river systems whose annual flooding replenished the soil. Also interesting in this regard is C. Ponting, *A Green History of the World* (London: Sinclair-Stevenson, 1989).

6. This *de facto* merger of the political and criminal is commonly referred to as a 'grey area phenomenon'. See, for example, P. Lupsha, 'Grey Area Phenomena: New Threats and Policy Dilemmas', paper presented to the High Intensity Crime/Low Intensity Conflict Conference, Chicago, 27–30 September 1992.

7. The classic work, highly influential at the time, was by H.C. Engelbrecht and F.C. Hanighen, *Merchants of Death: A Study of the International Armament Industry* (New York: Dodd, Mead, 1934).

8. This history is reviewed in J. Stanley and M. Pearton, *The International Trade in Arms* (New York: Praeger, 1972).

9. For background see J. De St Jorre, *The Nigerian Civil War* (London: Hodder and Stoughton, 1972).

10. Sam Cummings' career is traced in P. Brogan and A. Zarca, *Deadly Business: Sam Cummings, Interarms and the Arms Trade* (New York: Norton, 1983).

11. These points are well made in R. Kaufman, *The War Profiteers* (New York: Bobbs-Merrill, 1970), p.26; and R.W. Howe, *Weapons: the International Game of Arms, Money and Diplomacy* (New York: Doubleday, 1980), pp.xxiii–xxxv.

12. There had been a very active debate in the USA concerning the extent to which the military–industrial system really has contributed to American prosperity. For the negatives the finest research has been by S. Melman in *Pentagon Capitalism* (McGraw Hill: New York, 1970); *The Permanent War Economy* (New York: Simon & Schuster: New York, 1974); *Profits Without Production* (New York: Knopf, 1984); and *The Demilitarized Society* (Montreal: Harvest Books, 1988). There is a useful summary of his views in *The Nation* 20 May 1991. There is also a large body of literature strongly influenced by Melman. See, for example, A. Markusen and J. Yudken, *Dismantling the Cold War Economy* (New York: Basic Books, 1992). But see also the interesting critique by D. Henwood in *Left Business Observer*, 17 April 1991, 3 June 1991.

13. In fact, this could well be exaggerated by partisans of arms exports. A study done in Sweden in the mid-1980s showed that eliminating arms exports would raise unit costs for the Swedish military by a mere 1 per cent per year. See *Inside Sweden*, 3–4 September 1987.

14. This refers to the trade in conventional arms. Clearly the capacity of nuclear weapons to inflict awesome destruction has varied little in the past three decades.

15. This 'stars' analogy is from W. De Bock and J-C. Deniau, *Des Armes pour l'Iran* (Paris, 1988), p.41.

16. G. Thayer, *The War Business* (New York, 1969) p.133.

17. *Observer*, 16 August 1992; *World Press Review*, November 1993; C. Smith Light, 'Weapons and the International Arms Trade', in United Nations Institute for Disarmament Research, *Small Arms Management and Peacekeeping in Southern Africa* (Geneva: UNIDIR, 1996), p.9.

18. *Financial Times* (London), 24 January 1992, 6 February 1993; *Observer* (London), 16 August 1992, 28 February 1993; *Sunday Times* (London), 26 January 1992; *The Moscow Times*, 31 March 1994.

19. *The Washington Report on Middle East Affairs*, August/September 1992; C. Petersen, 'Moscow's New Arms Bazaar', *Orbis* (Spring 1994); *Sunday Times* (London), 30 May 1993; *Washington Post*, 25 October 1992.

20. This strategy was a factor in USA arms policy from at least the late 1960s. However, it has been claimed by boosters of the Reagan administration that it was in the 1980s, under the sponsorship of CIA chief, William Casey, that it really locked in, together with a whole host of other instruments of economic warfare. See P. Schweizer, *Victory: the Reagan Administration's Secret Strategy that Hastened the Collapse of the Soviet Union* (New York: Atlantic Monthly Press, 1994).
21. For an analysis of how the process worked, see Naylor, 'Loose Cannons: Covert Commerce and Underground Finance in the Modern Arms Black Market', op. cit.
22. See ibid.
23. See the various issues of the Paris monthly, *Observatoire Géopolitique des Drogues*, besides its annual report, *Géopolitique des Drogues* (Paris: OGD, 1995).
24. See the list of possible definitions of 'light' weapons in A. Karp, 'The New Major Weapons', *Ploughshares Monitor* (September 1995).
25. Interestingly, even the especially macabre and inhumane character of mines may reflect not the mine *per se*, but the way in which it is employed. In the hands of insurgents with a clear ideology locked in a politically motivated combat against a defined opposing force, as was typical in Central America in the 1980s, for example, mines are deployed in a reasonably disciplined way against military targets; whereas when the purposes of the conflict involves ethnic cleansing and mass terrorism they are scattered without discipline or restriction. This was documented by the International Committee of the Red Cross (ICRC) in their *Anti-Personnel Mines in Central American Conflict and Post-Conflict* (Geneva: ICRC, 1996). I am indebted to Dr Peter Lock for bringing this to my attention. Ironically, in this respect, the 'heavy' cluster bomb is less susceptible of being used in a restrained way than is the 'light' land mine.
26. See *The Economist*, 8 March 1997, for a survey of some of these developments.

Trafficking and Sexual Exploitation of Women and Children

LIVIA POMODORO

Some time ago, Italy began efforts to arrive at a definition of so-called 'persons in need of protection'. This process led to the realization that, for many people, being at risk is the result of a series of external factors or obstacles that, when aggravated by uncaring social structures and inadequate social policies, prevent such people from attaining due autonomy and self-fulfilment. This problem has assumed particular importance in relation to migration. Migrants may be considered in need of protection because of their extreme vulnerability, especially where there exist markets that encourage their exploitation. Recent classifications of persons in need of protection include women who have been recruited with false promises of employment but who are destined, in practice, to be coerced into prostitution and unpaid labour. Such a dramatic situation is aggravated by the fact that these victims, in the countries to which they migrate, have little chance of assistance and even less of being able to communicate and denounce the abuses to which they are subjected. Regrettably, at the head of the list stand young persons, who have been exposed to abuses such as abduction, sale into slavery and forced prostitution (a phenomenon that is becoming more prevalent as a result of a growing demand throughout the world for children as sexual partners).

There are also those asking for asylum. In recent years, asylum seekers have become a massive presence, especially in Italy, largely because of deteriorating situations in other countries, some of which are actually in a state of war. Finally among the category of defenceless subjects should be included so-called migrants, or those who move from one region of the world to another, and invariably experience greater difficulties of communication and comprehension than those who move within their own region.

DEFINITIONS

Such a situation has many aspects requiring more detailed definition and analysis. For instance, one needs to identify precisely the meaning of the expression 'traffic' in relation to persons at risk. The word does not immediately indicate the aims of the traffic (be they prostitution, pornography, illegal adoptions, sale of human organs or exploitation of migrant labour), but relates to the phenomenon produced when there are illegal entries into the country of people who manage to avoid border controls and use false, stolen or forged documents.

One may identify two definitions contained in legislation in Europe. The first refers to the illegal smuggling of foreigners as an activity that deliberately intends to facilitate, in order to gain entry, the possibility of permanent residence and employment in a given country in such a way as to infringe the legal provisions of that country. The second, on the other hand, relates to the traffic in human beings as an activity whose main aim is not only to facilitate and encourage illegal entries but that is also directed, through extremely serious means of coercion (such as violence, threats and abuses), towards the commission of crimes or the exploitation of the subjects concerned.

Clearly this is not only a conceptual contrast. Nevertheless, there is some overlapping between the two levels and they are often lumped together in a numerical or a quantitative context. There is also some confusion between 'generic' legal immigration (to avoid using the conventional term) and the traffic in human beings aimed at the exploitation of prostitution. In fact, these and other cases are frequently confused and superimposed, so that students of these phenomena find that the statistics available to them in relation to some parts of the world are not easy to interpret and also contain a high measure of diversity.

Nevertheless, the statistics reveal the broad scale and scope of the problem. An example concerns Italy. According to a report by End Child Prostitution in Asian Tourism (ECPAT), a non-governmental organization (NGO) that concerns itself with these matters, the data are extremely alarming: ten per cent of the prostitutes in Italy, and especially in the north of Italy are between 10 and 15 years of age, a proportion which increases to 30 per cent for the 16–18 age group; this means that all these are below the age of adulthood. It should also be added that in many countries of the world the traffic and exploitation of women and minors assume dimensions that are even more alarming. For example (again using ECPAT data) it is estimated that there are

200,000–500,000 minors engaged in prostitution in China; in Vietnam, Laos and Sri Lanka there are some 10,000 children between 6 and 14 years of age engaged in prostitution, a situation that is also mirrored in other countries.

These figures also show something else: supply and demand assume different connotations from one country to another. It is not merely a case of strong demand and weak supply, such as, for example, sex-oriented tourist culture, but phenomena that are implanted in the markets that produce them. As these statistics illustrate, in the very poorest areas there are strong markets for the exploitation of women and minors.

Hence one can identify a *continuum* between traffic and exploitation, a link that, in the view of some Italian sociologists, proves the existence of a single market, whose efficient operation is guaranteed by the entrepreneurial management of criminal organizations.

The factors helping to expand trafficking in women and minors are various and derive from multiple causes: some are found at the origins of the traffic, while others act as phenomena attracting migrants to their intended country, and so on. In trying to give some order and meaning to this system (for which it is hard to provide a theoretical construction) it is helpful to refer to the international conference, which took place in June 1996, on trafficking in women for sexual exploitation. In the course of this conference several factors were identified that, regrettably, encourage and facilitate the exploitation of women: greater freedom of movement within the whole of Europe, East and West; the demand for manual labourers under illicit payment arrangements in developing countries; the great gap in living standards between developed and developing countries; the virtual lack of serious penalties for certain types of crime; and the growth and internationalization of organized crime.

It is worth reiterating that each of the two phenomena – traffic and exploitation of women on the one hand and of minors on the other – has its own special characteristics. For example, significant dimensions have been identified that are incorporated in the typology of the women who are exploited and introduced into the prostitution market. Some of these women have been attracted by the prospects of a comfortable existence while many others have been impelled by a need to find means of sustenance, and yet others seek to escape from serious domestic conditions, perhaps from ethnic persecution or conflict situations. In relation to the exploitation of minors, it cannot be overemphasized that they are thrown into the conditions of human traffic and exploitation generally as a result of violent coercion. This is even less acceptable to the civilized community because it concerns children and young people who incur a double violence: not only are their fundamental rights violated but they suffer a loss of trust in the world of adults and a subsequent inability to reconstruct their own personalities. This may be the most significant aspect of all such forms of violence towards minors.

The forms of brutality, however, traverse every form of coercion towards children, and it is appropriate to classify them with other forms of coercion from which at first sight, they appear to differ. It is appropriate to begin with illegal adoptions that are often forms of violence and a violation of the fundamental rights of minors, and go on to other more serious forms, such as the traffic in human organs and exploitation for sexual purposes. It should not be forgotten that if one commences with definitions that are accurate at a conceptual level, one cannot fail to associate them with this 'packet' of violence towards the most defenceless individuals – those who are incapable of expressing their own wishes.

These forms of violence and exploitation may result either from a demand from developed countries or from the response to an exigency identified in the country of origin. Poverty in certain areas of the world is not a bar to phenomena of this sort and can even encourage it. Even more serious, of course, is the phenomenon given the name of 'sexual tourism'. There are conditions of vulnerability among minors and women in some regions of the world, the exploitation of which is reflected in the demand that has come to be known as sex tourism. This is a very serious and widespread abuse, because of the ease of access to children who live in extremely poor conditions in their own countries, with little knowledge of their own rights. In some countries there are well-organized criminal enterprises that are easily able to replace their traditional illegal activities (linked, for instance, with drugs trafficking) with the traffic in human beings. The system within which such events occur is bound by *omertà*, a covert system and one that from time to time transforms its operational capacity within a mechanism that is exclusively known to those whose business it is to track down children to satisfy the demands of foreign paedophiles or foreign sexual tourists. Sometimes the systems employed to find the victims are very sophisticated: one thinks, for example of information technologies that enable paedophiles to keep in touch with the whole world in real time. Although law enforcement agencies have identified some of these criminal webs, far greater attention is needed throughout the world if these achievements are not to remain isolated successes.

COMBATING TRAFFICKING AND SEXUAL EXPLOITATION

Counter-actions to these phenomena should be conducted with highly developed instruments, which must be progressively updated, since it is clear that criminal organizations are always able to equip themselves to counteract effectively once they have been detected. This, of course, only includes what is needed in a repressive sense. There is another critical aspect, which is the need to indemnify or restore adequate living conditions to the children or women who are the victims of such exploitation. This objective necessarily calls not only for national but international legislation, which must go beyond a merely repressive tenor. The need is to create and activate a global system that will include serious penalties, but avoid a situation where women and children victims are simply avenged (and even this does not occur in 90 per cent of the cases) and is able to give assistance to the victims. To this end it is necessary to create in public opinion a serious cultural movement to combat and reject such forms of exploitation of the defenceless subjects.

Many measures along these lines could be initiated by the international community. Every country should identify actions that are common to them all, if it is true that the future of civilized society must be safeguarded with a recognition of the rights of every individual in its midst. This aim is reflected in the initiatives of the European Union while the implementation of such a programme is one of the priorities indicated by the United Nations.

It is also necessary to quantify more carefully illegal migrations in Europe, analysing the ways such flows have changed over the years, focusing on the traffic in migrants and especially the circuit involving both 'traffic and exploitation of migrants'. It is necessary to understand how these circuits are formed and to identify the new forms of criminal organizations that seem to be active in this sector. Finally, we should determine whether the subjects in question are recycled from other criminal experiences or whether we are dealing with new organizations – as target-oriented as they are sophisticated in developing these types of crime. It is essential to map out the routes employed by traffickers that require international cooperation, so as to assess the interdependence between the traffic and other crimes, and thereby improve the strategies currently being employed. Equally useful is research into the causes of exploitation of certain vulnerable subjects within the traffic, and this will require a study of legislative innovations recently introduced by various states. In this connection, legislative innovation in Italy is represented by the law, which came into force in August 1998 (Law No.269 of 1998) entitled 'Norms against the exploitation of prostitution, pornography and sexual tourism to the prejudice of young persons as new forms of slavery'. By introducing the element of reducing people to slavery, the law makes it possible to administer effective penal measures.

One would also wish to see the international community face up to the problem by updating the norms and conventions already existing in this field. In addition, it is necessary to monitor law enforcement in various countries, with regard to illegal immigration and trafficking in human beings, to study the process of international cooperation both between Western and Eastern countries and among other countries in the world, and to identify measures that are not only repressive but also, and especially, preventive in nature.

In conclusion, we have to develop and activate centralized instruments that can constantly monitor and verify what is happening, and bring the data together in order to understand the phenomenon. This calls for coordination and an indispensable fund of data on which to base counter-measures against this type of criminality. In this field of crime, we can no longer permit a generic term such as that of prevention to be used unless it includes a genuine civil and humane content.

Trafficking in People: The Human Rights Dimension

OFFICE OF THE HIGH COMMISSIONER FOR HUMAN RIGHTS (OHCHR)

The date 1998 was the year in which the international community commemorated the 50th anniversary of the Universal Declaration for Human Rights. The year 1999 was 50 years on from the signing of the 1949 Convention for the suppression of the traffic in persons and of the exploitation of the prostitution of others. Yet it has been estimated that some four million people are trafficked annually, worldwide. Indeed, organized trans-border criminality of all types is thriving, and trafficking in people for diverse purposes has been on the increase, generating huge profits for the traffickers and international crime rings. People are literally being bought and sold around the world, in most cases with impunity, in violation of their most fundamental human rights. As a matter of grave concern, the Office of the High Commissioner for Human Rights has made the eradication of trafficking a priority.

It is generally recognized that the lack of consensus with regard to establishing a definition constitutes one of the difficulties in effectively addressing the trafficking problem. There is a need for a comprehensive definition of trafficking, based on accepted international standards and more in keeping with modern manifestations of trafficking. For a long time trafficking was considered as only constituting forced prostitution. The 1949 Convention for the Suppression of the Traffic in Persons and of the Exploitation of the Prostitution of Others adopted this type of approach. It is now clear that trafficking in people requires the adoption of a broader definition to clarify the modern sense of the term: those that are subjected to trafficking are not only exploited through prostitution or other forms of sex work, but also through manual or industrial labour (that amounts to slavery), marriage, adoption, domestic servitude, begging or for criminal purposes.

In this regard various propositions have been made. In General Assembly resolution 49/166 of 23 December 1994 trafficking was defined as:

> the illicit and clandestine movement of persons across national and international borders, largely from developing countries and some countries with economies in transition, with the end goal of forcing women and girl children into sexually or economically oppressive and exploitative situations for the profit of recruiters, traffickers and crime syndicates, as well as other illegal activities related to trafficking, such as forced domestic labour, false marriages, clandestine employment and false adoption.

During the Transnational Training Seminar on Trafficking in Women held in Budapest in June 1998, it was agreed that:

> Trafficking consists of all acts involved in the recruitment or transportation of persons within or across borders, involving deception, coercion or force, debt bondage or fraud, for the purpose of placing persons in situations of abuse or exploitation, such as forced prostitution, slavery-like practices, battering or extreme cruelty, sweatshop labor or exploitative domestic servitude.

All of the proposed definitions, including these, do not take into account people who voluntarily decide to leave their country and work in another one. Although the two are related, the definition of trafficking should not be widened to include all forms of illegal migration for the purpose of working. A comprehensive distinction could be made in terms of the purpose for which borders are crossed and whether movement occurs through the instrumentality of another person. The use of such a distinction would enable trafficking cases, which start with consent and later become a matter of force and deception to come within the scope of the definition.

THE ROOTS OF THE PROBLEM

Various socio-economic factors are instrumental in the development of trafficking in people, in particular the economic inequality between and within countries. Poverty is always shown as the first factor to lead to prostitution. The combination of the pursuit of better opportunities, diminished legitimate migration possibilities and the demand of the industry, has resulted in a dramatic increase in trafficking of people. Traffickers have exploited the vulnerability of would-be migrants to lure them into situations of abuse and exploitation.

Victims are procured by kidnapping or purchase, or with fraudulent inducements for jobs and a better life. People are often deceived about the nature of the work they or their children would finally do or about the conditions they would encounter. They are enticed by false promises, misled by information concerning migration regulations or compelled by economic despair. Victims of trafficking find themselves in exploitative situations where they are particularly vulnerable to numerous human rights violations, although the form the abuse takes varies depending on the purpose of the trafficking. Once the victims are in the destination country their documents are confiscated. Given their illegal status, this makes them more vulnerable and constitutes a major obstacle to efforts to escape. Furthermore, when they do approach the authorities, officials often do not recognize or consider them as victims (this is particularly the case for commercial sex workers) but as individuals in illegal situations or even as criminals who have to be prosecuted as such. Indeed, they are often subjected to further abuse and re-victimization by corrupt officials. People who are trafficked are subjected to discrimination because of their gender, the stigma attached to their status as sexually exploited women and children, illegal immigrants or sometimes because of their indigenous origin.

The involvement of a criminal element in trafficking of people generates a variety of interlinked criminal activities. Collaboration with local and international crime networks facilitates the provision of transport, safe houses, local contacts and documentation. It also ensures that the traffickers are well informed so they can divert their routes at very short notice. Traffickers are well organized and powerful. With enough money to bribe important officials, they profit from relatively lax sanctions, as well as from uncoordinated and ineffective measures taken to eliminate the practice. Compared with other forms of trafficking – which have provoked efforts by states to crack down by improving detection capabilities and imposing harsher sentences – the risks involved in people trafficking are modest. The low-risk factor coupled with the profits that can be made have led to a dramatic increase in this particular form of trafficking in recent years. Trafficking rings have changed their merchandise, but the network continues to work as before.

Trafficking has an impact on men, women and children, although studies show that the phenomenon has a disproportionate impact on women and girls, owing to their already marginalized position in society. As violations suffered by victims of trafficking are often regarded as gender specific, many studies have investigated the phenomenon from a women' and girls' perspective. Consequently, the trafficking of men requires more research as to date there is little information on the subject.

Since the beginning of the 1990s, trafficking of Central and Eastern European women has increased dramatically. According to experts, Central and Eastern European women constitute the last wave of women trafficked from different parts of the world to Western Europe, especially Germany, the Netherlands, Belgium and Switzerland. The first waves came from Southeast Asia in the 1970s, the second from Africa and the third from Latin America. The more recent phenomenon can be understood as a direct result of the economic crisis and unemployment in the states of Central and Eastern Europe.

In the case of trafficking for prostitution, studies have shown that women and children enter prostitution by voluntarily, bonded, or involuntary means. The term voluntary suggests free will. When driven by economic despair or large-scale violence, however, a person's freedom of choice is so limited that the voluntariness of engagement in this means of livelihood must be questioned. Many are victims of deception as to the conditions the work will be carried out under, and they often arrive with debt-bondage contracts so that they earn no money until the debt is paid back. In the case of bonded prostitution, poverty stricken relatives sell a child or a young woman to a person for promised employment in return for money or to repay a debt. The historical practice of selling women that can be found in Southeast Asia provides an important precedent for the current practice of selling young women for the purpose of prostitution. Prostitution has become a way in which a daughter can fulfil her role of providing financial support for the family. Involuntary prostitution describes when women are lured, kidnapped or tricked by any other way into prostitution. Once they are in the destination country, their passports are confiscated and they are sold to a brothel where they are forced to work as a prostitute. Women and children who are sold into slavery suffer both physical and emotional harm, they are forced to work in degrading and sometimes life-threatening situations, and many suffer from AIDS and other sexually transmitted diseases.

Rapid population growth, coupled with social and cultural norms that discriminate between male and female children, has created an environment for trafficking in children for labour or prostitution in developing countries. Trafficking in people for the purpose of begging is also growing. The target groups for this form of traffic are children, the elderly and the handicapped – the more pitiful and sick they look, the more money they will be given. Indeed, it is believed that some of them have been mutilated specifically for that purpose.

THE ANTI-TRAFFICKING REGIME

Various international human rights instruments explicitly prohibit trafficking of peoples. The 1949 Convention for the Suppression of the Traffic in Persons and the Exploitation of the Prostitution of Others specifically addresses the issue, albeit by linking it to prostitution only. The Convention on the Elimination of Discrimination against Women obliges all states to enact legislation to suppress all forms of traffic in women (Article 6). The Convention on the Rights of the Child obliges all states to take all appropriate national, bilateral and multilateral measures to prevent the abduction of, the sale of or traffic in children for any purpose or in any form (Article 35).

When trafficking is broken into its component parts, many generally accepted principles lend support to an international legal regime against trafficking. Under various general human rights instruments, freedom from slavery and slave-like practices is explicitly guaranteed in all situations and under all circumstances. The concept of slavery is given a broad interpretation to include contemporary practices involving women, debt-bondage, exploitation of child-labour, forced labour, illicit traffic in migrant workers, exploitation of hard drug addicts and traffic in children. The Universal Declaration of Human Rights states that everyone has the right to life, to liberty and to security of persons (Article 3) and specifically prohibits slavery: no one shall be held in slavery or servitude; slavery and the slave trade shall be prohibited in all its forms (Article 4).

The issue of trafficking has also been addressed in numerous regional and international fora. The plans of action that were produced serve as useful tools for states as legislative and policy recommendations as well as guidance on how to coordinate their efforts. The Vienna Declaration and Program of Action adopted by the World Conference on Human

Rights (A/CONF.157/23) affirmed that gender-based violence and all forms of sexual harassment and exploitation, including those resulting from cultural prejudice and international trafficking, are incompatible with the dignity and worth of the human person and must be eliminated.

The OHCHR has various mechanisms that work in a direct or indirect way towards the eradication of trafficking in people: the Working Group on Contemporary Forms of Slavery, the Voluntary Trust Fund on Contemporary Forms of Slavery, the Special Rapporteur on the sale of children, child prostitution and child pornography, the Special Rapporteur on violence against women, and the Committee on the Rights of the Child.

The Working Group on Contemporary Forms of Slavery was established to review the developments in the field of slavery, the slave trade and the slavery-like practices of apartheid and colonialism, the traffic in persons and the exploitation of the prostitution of others. The working group has drafted a programme of action on the traffic in persons and the exploitation of the prostitution of others. This was adopted by the Commission on Human Rights in 1995. The next session of the working group will be devoted to the question of traffic in persons, and is preceded by a non-governmental organization's seminar on traffic in persons and the exploitation of the prostitution of others. The Working Group is particularly concerned with the status of ratification of the 1956 and 1949 Conventions. It requests each year that the Secretariat approach a number of selected countries that have not ratified the conventions in order to establish an informal dialogue as to the reasons why they have not done this. There has been discussion of the drafting of an optional protocol to the Convention, of the issue of explanatory documents clarifying the provisions of the conventions and of creating a mechanism of control for implementation. As yet, however, no agreement has been reached on these matters.

The Voluntary Trust Fund on Contemporary Forms of Slavery, created in 1991, assists victims of contemporary forms of slavery and allows representatives of NGOs to participate in the debate of the working group.

The Special Rapporteur on the sale of the children, child prostitution and child pornography has paid particular attention to the question of trafficking in children. The Special Rapporteur carried out a fact-finding mission to the Czech Republic to study the issue of sale of children and trafficking for the purposes of prostitution and pornography (E/CN.4/1997/95/Add.1). Based on this study, she recommended that consultation and information services be established in countries of origin, as preventive measures for children likely to fall victims of trafficking. The Special Rapporteur has noted with concern the growing number of allegations of traffic in children she receives, in particular trafficking by paedophile international rings. As a result she has given particular attention to the question of trafficking in children – in Asia and elsewhere.

The Special Rapporteur on violence against women, in her report to the Commission on Human Rights focused on the issue of violence against women in the community, including trafficking and forced prostitution of women and girls (E/CN.4/1997/47). The Special Rapporteur also undertook a fact-finding mission to Poland to study in-depth the increasing phenomenon of trafficking in the Central and Eastern European region (E/CN.4/1997/47/add.1). The Special Rapporteur emphasized that violations of human rights associated with trafficking occur in both countries of origin and countries of destination, and is complicated by the international cross-border character of trafficking, making the protection of women's rights a difficult task.

The Committee on the Rights of the Child is also considering the question of trafficking along with questions of sexual exploitation and abuses and intercountry adoption when examining country reports.

ADDITIONAL MEASURES

In order to improve implementation and coordination a comprehensive definition of trafficking is required. Measures taken by states to combat trafficking must focus on the promotion of human rights, and must not further marginalize, criminalize, stigmatize or isolate victims of trafficking, thereby making them more vulnerable to violence and abuse. Prostitution should be decriminalized, and women who are willing to work in prostitution should not live in slave-like conditions or be banned from moving freely.

States should address prevention with effective information campaigns in countries of origin to inform potential migrants of the risks of irregular migration, and also for other concerned parties such as consular and embassy staff.

States should fortify their laws and policies against trafficking by ratifying the 1956 Supplementary Convention on the abolition of Slavery, as well as other relevant conventions including the Convention for the Elimination of Discrimination against Women, the Convention on the Rights of the Child and the Convention Against Torture and Other Cruel, Inhuman and Degrading Treatment or Punishment.

Trafficking must be battled with a multi-dimensional approach that recognizes the most frequent root cause is poverty. The economic consequences of poverty cause women to migrate to urban areas and to foreign countries, making them susceptible to sexual exploitation, including trafficking and sex tourism. Affirmative measures should be made to support women's efforts to break the cycle of poverty (for example through micro-credit programmes) and states should incorporate a gender perspective in all poverty eradication efforts.

States must conduct training of governmental authorities, in particular officials from immigration and consular affairs offices, customs services, border guards and migration services, and representatives of the Ministry of Foreign Affairs, regarding the assistance that victims of trafficking require as well as in ways to prevent trafficking in people.

States must take all necessary steps to ensure that the victim may press criminal charges and/or take civil action for compensation against the perpetrators if they choose to do so. States should implement asset forfeiture from criminal operations that profit from trafficking with funds set aside to provide compensation due to victims of trafficking. Measures should include free legal assistance and legal possibilities of compensation and redress for the economic, physical and psychological damage caused to them by trafficking and related offences.

Governments must implement stays of deportation and an opportunity to apply for permanent residency. As well as witness protection, relocation, repatriation and reintegration assistance for trafficking victims are essential. Victims should also receive adequate, confidential and affordable medical and psychological care. Confidential HIV tests should be available for women, and should be accompanied by appropriate pre- and post-test counselling.

In the effort to combat trafficking in people, international cooperation is also vital. States should pursue bilateral agreements and cooperate in multilateral efforts to reduce and eradicate trafficking in people. This is essential from both a human rights perspective and as part of the broader effort to combat transnational organized crime.

Money Laundering in Italy

ALESSANDRO PANSA

Money laundering is a particularly complex phenomenon, which influences different areas at the same time. The salience of money laundering reflects its incredible importance within the criminal world, especially now that economic-related crimes are the most widespread. At the same time, money laundering is strategically important since its international scope obliges criminal organizations to develop transnational networks, as well as to connect with criminal environments of different origins.

Several characteristics make money laundering particularly important and influential. First of all, the effects of money laundering have an impact on organized crime itself, encouraging the development of more and more sophisticated criminal groups and greater professionalism. Furthermore, top-level positions in the Mafia hierarchy are achieved more rapidly by people with personal skills in the economic and financial sectors. Thus, more and more often, we find managers rather than killers at the top of criminal syndicates.

More primitive criminal groups, characterized by a low level of professionalism and a capacity to exert violence more or less indiscriminately, have to cope with less numerous but more sophisticated criminal groups, that are able to move and operate in different countries, develop contacts with other organizations, including those who operate legally, and are familiar with technology, finance and international trade. Generally, these more sophisticated criminal groups prevail over others. By providing the less developed organizations with services that are essential for their survival, they make them subordinate and deprive them of their autonomy in handling their illegal profits.

In the early 1970s, high positions in the criminal hierarchy were reached by Mafia members who, for the organization, represented the most powerful source of wealth. Drug traffickers, in fact, tried to remove old bosses from high-ranking positions, still linked to archaic criminal mechanisms and values such as 'respect', 'trust' or 'honour'. Now that wealth production capacity has improved and is more available to criminals, a strategic role is played by those who are able to launder profits of illegal origin and reinvest them in legal circuits, thus making them spendable by owners.

Moreover, money laundering causes destabilizing effects in other sectors, too, that is in labour, financial and business markets. Among launderers, there are increasingly more who exploit criminal resources to gain access to new markets, make use of commercial opportunities and take advantage of certain juridical and economic systems. With time, it is even more evident that typical money laundering activities, such as just interrupting the trace that links the profit of a crime to the person that committed it, are outdated when compared with the transformation of dirty money into laundered money. The latter, in fact, is directly introduced into the commercial circuit. From many investigations it has become clear that criminals use dirty money to purchase consumer goods in different areas from those where this money was produced.

THE LIMITS OF KNOWLEDGE

Also worth mentioning are the effects of money laundering on the legal systems of many countries and, above all, on their financial systems, that is the issuing of new and constantly changing laws, the setting up of new entities that operate both domestically and at the international level, and the introduction of new rules for banking institutions, both for internal regulation and for their mutual relationships. Partly because of these initiatives the general situation is now one in which the financial sector is no longer at the forefront of many money-laundering schemes. The implication is that an analysis of money laundering from an exclusively financial perspective would not be exhaustive, and would not succeed in illuminating many aspects critical to the criminal environment. Such an analysis produces an abstract idea of money laundering that is very far from the one found in reality.

Indeed, it is now clear that past assessments of this phenomenon – on the basis of which most countermeasures were developed – fail to take into consideration salient components of today's criminal world. An example thereof, in Europe, is the impact of the expansion of Eastern European organized crime on the Western side of the continent. Do we really believe we know what the so-called 'Russian Mafia' is?

The impact of transnational organized crime on the old continent is not only internal, but stretches well beyond. Far East criminal organizations are increasingly involved in illegal activities with direct consequences for Western countries. People smuggling, illegal immigration, drug trafficking and corruption in financial aid to less developed countries are all criminal phenomena that yield very high proceeds, which we are not completely aware of and are not taken into consideration when countermeasures are set up. There are also limits to our understanding of the geographic scope of organized crime. We do not have much knowledge, for example, of what is happening in Africa in terms of organized crime and money laundering. Yet, we do not really need to look so far away to find out how limited our understanding of the criminal reality is. Are we really sure that Italian organized crime is the same we knew in the early 1990s? Is the Sicilian Mafia still structured according to the American pattern, where the 'cupola' decides strategies and settles conflicts within the whole organization? Are the Sicilian groups still the most powerful criminals in Italy? Is the 'Ndrangheta still subordinate to the Sicilians?

If there are so many doubts and outstanding questions about the internal organization of Italian criminal groups operating within Italy itself, just think how low is the level of understanding of the international dimensions and ramifications of these organizations. In some countries, for example, they have invested their criminal funds and laundered not only their illegal profits but also themselves, by infiltrating new realities, acting legally and becoming fully integrated into society. In spite of the importance of these developments our understanding of them is very limited. This is why an exclusively financial approach to money laundering would be very limiting.

INSIGHTS FROM INVESTIGATIONS

The analyses carried out as a result of specific criminal investigations have highlighted the need to ensure the fight against money laundering and the proceeds of crime is fought with rapid and flexible tools, always in keeping with actual criminal reality and the different market sectors wherein criminals act. These analyses also suggest that, although an analysis of the financial aspects of the phenomenon is essential, a focus on the financial system alone cannot be considered positive in terms of effectiveness. In fact, the results of the fight against money laundering

253

based on a repressive and preventive system, with a mainly financial approach, are not encouraging. This is clear in the following tables, which relate to Europe and are drawn from the second report of the EC Commission on the implementation of the Directives relative to the laundering of the proceeds derived from illegal activities, issued in Brussels on 1 July 1998.

TABLE 1
EUROPE

Countries	Year	Suspicious Transactions	Reported Offences	Pending Prosecutions	Convictions
Belgium	1994		117		
	1995		149		From 94 to 97
	1996		321		48
	1997		495		
Denmark	1994				7
	1995				5
Germany	1994				16
	1995				15
	1996				24
Greece	1995/97	38	13		
Spain	1995	19			
	1996	165			
France	1994		22		
	1995		30		From 93 to 96
	1996		47		34
	1997		75		
Ireland					
Luxembourg					
The Netherlands					
Austria	1994				1
	1995				2
Portugal	1994		12		
	1995		49		
	1996		53		1
Finland	1994/97		119		
Sweden	1994/97	66			
UK	1993/96				25

TABLE 2
ITALY: NUMBER OF CONVICTIONS FOR MONEY-LAUNDERING, AS SET
FORTH BY ARTICLE 648 BIS C.P., AND REINVESTING, AS SET FORTH BY
ARTICLE 648 TER C.P.

Year	ART. 648 BIS C.P. 72	ART. 648 TER C.P.
1993	72	1
1994	58	4
1995	62	3
1996	116	9

Reports of suspicious transactions initiated 85 criminal proceedings: 16 on money laundering charges and 69 on other offences.

The limited number of traced cases reveals that repressive actions and the so-called active cooperation of financial intermediaries have had very limited impact and do not contribute significantly to the detection of the areas and ways in which organized crime seeks to convert illegal profits and reinvest laundered funds. There is no doubt, however, about the magnitude of the proceeds of crime, and even if these proceeds have been hidden within complex money laundering schemes and successfully laundered, they must surface somewhere – it is there that action should be undertaken.

Thanks to the capacity to cross the borders of many countries and escape controls, money laundering schemes create many difficulties for national law enforcement agencies and magistrates in single jurisdictions – both in identifying unlawful money transfers occurring domestically and in tracing them back, once their illegal origin has been detected. Yet, sooner or later the money laundering process is exhausted and the laundered money is brought to light. Wealth shows up again and, somehow, it has to be traced back to the owner. It is here that our efforts should be concentrated, by seizing illegal assets and properties. The criminals' impoverishment is one of the most effective ways of fighting organized crime.

In Italy, this approach has been encouraged, with some very positive results. Moreover, an analysis of what has been seized so far facilitates a better identification of the kind of assets that criminals utilize to convert their illegal proceeds. This awareness facilitates further investigations on money laundering and, above all, on the offence set forth in Article 648 TER of the Italian Penal Code: the reinvestment of laundered funds. An overview of the assets seized in Italy explains how important it is to prosecute organized crime in this way. For evaluation purposes, and to have a wider reference sample, we consider only seized assets that have not yet been confiscated by the Judicial Authority, since this final order is particularly laborious and currently the number of confiscated assets is lower than the total of seized assets. Significantly, Italian legislation is being up-dated, with a view to streamlining confiscation procedures and making them more effective. The details are provided in Tables 3 and 4.

TABLE 3
OVERVIEW OF SEIZED ASSETS IN ITALY

Year of seizure	Total seized assets	Value in millions (lire)	Non-evaluated assets
1982	15	516	2
1983	892	183,969	193
1984	1456	318,400	211
1985	977	256,410	154
1986	707	136,729	144
1987	488	85,750	47
1988	376	203,147	25
1989	408	172,458	18
1990	278	70,873	47
1991	692	272,081	112
1992	3273	1,084,109	356
1993	4727	1,321,664	415
1994	3895	1,389,923	801
1995	3116	917,313	1201
1996	2880	449,752	1469
1997	2562	291,031	1505
1998	852	122,387	531
TOTAL	27,594	7,276,512	7231

The over seven thousand billion lire worth of seized assets represents only part of the criminal wealth accumulated in Italy, but the high social and educational impact of this course of action is much higher than its economic value. When a local 'boss' is deprived of his high-powered sports car or highly polished motorcycle, or the villa of a kingpin figure is transformed into a relief centre for the poor, for example, police activity has had an impact far beyond the seizure and confiscation of properties of illegal origin.

What has been said so far and the data in the tables highlight the need for a thorough reappraisal of the phenomenon of money laundering while also pointing to two main issues:

• the repressive system, in spite of efforts to perfect through further

TABLE 4
BREAKDOWN OF SEIZED ASSETS IN ITALY

Year of seizure	Real Estate	Valuables	Corporate Property	Securities	Other	Total seized Assets	Value in millions (liras)
1982	4	11				15	516
1983	492	151	7	242		892	183,969
1984	837	377	18	224		1456	318,400
1985	543	201	5	227	1	977	256,410
1986	421	160	8	118		707	136,729
1987	300	129	14	43	2	488	85,750
1988	246	69	10	51		376	203,147
1989	220	101	44	38	5	408	172,458
1990	98	80	6	94		278	70,873
1991	308	161	41	182		692	272,081
1992	1216	1158	117	779	3	3273	1,084,109
1993	2052	1783	147	740	5	4727	1,321,664
1994	1863	1159	158	710	5	3895	1,389,923
1995	1247	604	101	1162	2	3116	917,313
1996	1473	665	34	706	2	2880	449,752
1997	1281	529	38	714		2562	291,031
1998	441	234	29	148		852	122,387
Total	13,042	7572	777	6178	25	27,594	7,276,512

developments and initiatives, cannot produce, by itself, positive results in the fight against money laundering, especially if a mere financial perspective prevails;
• the preventive system, which is by no means perfect, is made up of a number of prohibitions and control barriers that are limited almost exclusively to the financial sector. Most of the trade market is not included, yet this is an area where real and effective transparency and efficient prevention mechanisms can be reached only by means of direct involvement of the participants themselves.

There are trading areas that escape any kind of control behind tax havens and offshore centres. An example – taken from the specific investigative experience of the Italian National Police and US law enforcement agencies – is the gold market, where Italy occupies, particularly with respect to gold products, an important position at world level. In order to purchase hard currency and dodge taxation, gold buyers, especially those in free zones such as Panama, resort to money exchange offices and buy credit instruments or make payments through compensation mechanisms that are completely uncontrollable.

So, it happens that jewellery coming from an Italian gold firm is supplied, through a reseller in Panama, to a South American retailer, who pays for the purchase in US dollars, with a bankers' draft issued by an Israeli bank and bought in Cyprus with money coming from Eastern Europe. It is very hard to develop efficient repressive systems against such a scheme. Furthermore, it is essential that any effective prevention or control programme take into consideration the direct cooperation of single individuals involved.

CONCLUSION

In conclusion, there are three ways to respond more effectively to the challenge posed by transnational organized crime: the improvement of the repressive system against money laundering by enhancing investigators' operative capacity at the international level and beyond the limits of the mere financial system; increasing resort to the seizure and confiscation of assets whose origin cannot be proven by criminals; and the involvement of the international economic system, making it feasible and favourable for legally operating subjects to reject dirty money by refusing to cooperate with money launderers and to deny any assistance to mafia entrepreneurs.

Strengthening the International Legal System in order to Combat Transnational Crime

GIUSEPPE DI GENNARO

Over the last 20 years there has been a growing preoccupation with transnational crime. Initially, it was only the criminologists who gave it their serious attention, but in those early days the phenomenon had not acquired the gravity characterizing it in recent years. Today, public opinion, alerted by its grave and flagrant manifestations, is keenly aware of it. The media focus strongly upon it and politicians declare an intense concern about it.

Such a level of preoccupation has mobilized various international authorities and numerous initiatives have been taken within Europe by the Council of Europe and the European Union, while comparable steps have been taken in other parts of the world, and most notably by the United Nations (UN). The UN has studied the subject at a number of important meetings, and particularly at the Ministerial Conference on Transnational Organized Crime, held in Naples on 21–23 November 1994.

In preparing this paper, use has been made of the copious materials produced for that conference and subsequent to it, as well as an impressive weight of scientific documentation dealing with the various aspects of the phenomenon during the past few years. Much of the content has already been stated, and it is extremely difficult, if not impossible, to add anything new. At the same time, however, it is legitimate to ask one question, namely: after so many authoritative contributions, after the pressing exhortations to governments by international bodies, and especially the UN, and after the many initiatives taken by the latter, what has been the practical outcome?

The answer is rather depressing: the situation has constantly deteriorated. The network of organized crime has become ever wider, invading areas that were previously immune from it. Criminal organizations have increased in quantity and type, the links between criminal powers and the management of the economy, conduct of business, and public and political authorities, have become ever more complex and shadowy. One gains the impression that the endeavours to contain and combat such contagion have, for the most part, been futile. There are many reasons for disquiet, but it is also clear that this is no time to surrender.

First of all, we must acknowledge that, however bad the situation, it would have been far worse without the efforts that have been made to combat it. We must also convince ourselves that the failure to achieve the desired success in the past does not mean that we will be unable to obtain it in the future.

INVIGORATING THE INTERNATIONAL LEGAL SYSTEM

My task is to put forward some reflections on possible ways of giving greater vigour to the international legal system in combating the forms of crime at work on a transnational basis. To do this, we need first to be clear about the particular *phenomenon* to which we refer and what we mean by *legal system*.

In the former case, we must have a common understanding about the objective. Tackling this question of definition is essential insofar as many of the problems attending the mobilization of an effective counter-system have derived from the lack of agreement on the relevant definition. Here the natural characteristics of the phenomenon and their individual features are less important than the juridical formulae used to identify them with the precision demanded by the need for certainty in the law, respect for which is the guarantee for the proper application of the relevant laws and regulations, and for clarity in international relations.

As we shall see, however, the search for a common definition runs into serious conceptual problems that are not easy to resolve. In fact, these problems, of which we are so conscious today, were not considered equally important by the draftsmen of the 1961 New York Consolidated Convention on Drugs. At that time no opposition or misgivings appeared with regard to the formulation of Article 36.2(a)(ii), which sets out a definition, as follows: '*the participation by any person in the said offences* [listed in para.1], *the association in or intent to commit such offences, or the intent to commit them, and preparatory acts or financial operations unlawfully undertaken with regard to the offences set out in this Article, will be considered as offences punishable as prescribed in para.1'*. Nor, it seems, did this definition provoke any problems subsequently, since it is faithfully reproduced in Article 14.2(a)(ii) of the amending Protocol of 1972 and in Article 22.2(a)(ii) of the 1971 Vienna Convention on Psychotropic Substances. Despite some difference in words, the definition in Article 3.1(b)(iv) of the 1988 Vienna Convention is along the same lines, where it prescribes that each participating state must consider as an offence *'the participation in any of the offences as described in the present Article, as well as any association, agreement, attempt or complicity through the provision of assistance or advice aimed at perpetrating the same'*.

We can now see that the aggravated manifestations of organized crime have subsequently required a more careful examination of the theme, revealing its inherent complexities. The need to adopt a consistent definition for use at the international level is now perceived as a matter of priority.

In the Report on the Meeting in April 1998 of the Working Group 'On the implementation of the Naples political declaration and global action plan against organized transnational crime', established by the 'Committee on the Prevention of Crime and Criminal Justice' at its Seventh Session, one reads that the problem had been raised at the very outset by the Representatives from Colombia, Pakistan and Turkey. In their respective ways, these Representatives maintained that only a clear juridical definition of 'transnational organized crime', underlying an international legal instrument, can ensure effective cooperation and mutual assistance in full respect for the principles contained in the United Nations Charter and international and national legislation on human rights.

As a result, the Group attempted a definition of 'organized crime' to serve as a foundation for an International Convention. This had originally been drafted by an 'Inter-Governmental Group of Experts' who met in Warsaw in February 1998, with later amendments proposed by the Russian Representative.

The resulting text is as follows: *'by "organized crime" is meant activities by groups of three or more persons, bound by hierarchical bonds or personal relationships, which permit those at their head to gain profits or the control of territories or markets, whether domestic or foreign, through the use of violence, intimidation or corruption, either to support the criminal activity or to infiltrate the lawful economy'*.

261

Another definition to which Representatives in the same Group have referred, is the one contained in the 'Draft Joint Action' adopted by the Council of Europe on the basis of Article K.3 of the European Union Treaty. Article 1 of that 'Draft' reads as follows:

> For the purposes of this Joint Action, 'criminal organization' is defined as a permanent and structured association of more than two persons who act in concert with the intent to commit crimes or other offences punishable by imprisonment or with a detention order not exceeding four years or more severe penalties, whether such crimes or offences are an end in themselves or a means to obtain present or future material benefits through influencing improperly the operations of public authorities.

The difficulty in reaching a unanimously acceptable decision is reflected in particular by a document submitted by the Japanese delegation to the same Working Group (Japanese non-paper), saying:

> in the course of drafting an International Convention against transnational organized crime, it became clear that the task of giving a precise definition of 'transnational organized crime' or of crime with a 'transnational' or 'organized' nature is extremely difficult. In the light of this difficulty, we would be minded to propose that the Convention relate to serious crimes punishable with imprisonment or other forms of custodial sentence exceeding a (given number of) years.

The Japanese delegation observed that this position could be criticised for prompting an, 'International Convention against Serious Crimes', which was very broad. However, in its opinion, the aim of combating transnational organized crime might still best be pursued in this way since, apart from the problem of a precise definition of 'transnational organized crime', the inclusion of the terms 'organized' and 'transnational' in a uniform way in the text might lead to a serious weakening of the efficacy and objectives of the Convention.

It is interesting to note that the European states, who have a greater homogeneity in their systems than other regions, tackled the definition problem in the June 1990 Convention to apply the Schengen Accord of 14 June 1985. At the conclusion of a lengthy debate on this subject, it was decided not to proceed for the present with a definition either of criminal organization or the international extension of criminal activity, but to make a list of the offences to be the subject of collaboration between the interested states, as follows:

- assassination,
- homicide,
- rape,
- arson,
- counterfeiting,
- grand larceny and receiving,
- extortion,
- kidnapping and hostage-taking,
- trade in humans,
- illicit trafficking in drugs and psychotropic substances,
- breach of regulations on arms and explosives,
- illicit transportation of toxic and dangerous waste.

From the context of the Convention it is clear that in every case it is a matter of transnational crime, while the element aggravating the offence, provided by the organized structure, is implicitly taken into account so as to amount to something more serious than a crime committed on an individual basis. This solution adds weight to the Japanese position mentioned above.

A different approach was taken in the EU Convention of 26 July 1995 between the member states of the European Union, which established Europol. Article 2 of the Convention provides that cooperation between the member states is aimed at 'preventing and combating terrorism, illicit trafficking in drugs and other serious forms of international crime, wherever concrete evidence exists of an organized criminal structure such that the scope, seriousness and consequence of the crimes, shows the need for common action between the member states'. One might demur that, while reference is made to the elements of the organization and to the involvement of two or more states, these elements are simply enunciated without being described.

Perhaps no more remains to be added to underline at the same time the difficulty, already mentioned, of reaching an agreed definition and the efforts still being undertaken at the appropriate international levels to find a solution.

In view of all this, it might be presumptuous of me to advance a proposal of my own. It is worth mentioning that in the Italian Penal

Code, under the heading 'association to commit offences', an addition was made in 1982 to define a 'Mafia-type association' (Article 416 bis). The legislation provided a very detailed description, although subsequently it has been subject to many, and not always consistent, interpretations. Yet it is possible that the close attention given to this question, both in the courts and in legal doctrine, may to some extent have paved the way towards agreement.

THE LEGAL SYSTEM

When speaking here of the international legal system, we have in mind the whole complex consisting of the various national systems when they operate in correspondence with each other, and also of legal machinery of a specifically international nature, such as Europol, Interpol and the International Courts of Justice. The linking between the national systems is the result of accords, which, although they do not cover the whole system of penal justice, do embrace the judicial and police sub-systems.

Traditionally, in order to facilitate judicial action for the pursuit and punishment of offenders who are beyond the jurisdiction of the authority for the place where they committed their offence, recourse has been made to Treaties for Mutual Judicial Assistance and Extradition. In the past, these have been bilateral in nature, where individual states have reviewed from time to time the advantages of reaching an accommodation with one or other foreign government. Such an assessment took into account the safeguards offered by the other's juridical system, seen as its degree of 'juridical civility'.

In fact, Accords of Mutual Assistance and Extradition embody a reciprocity of obligations and so it is inconceivable that a state enjoying a system with appropriate legal safeguards for the individual would remit someone to the judicial machinery of another state that does not provide similar safeguards, whether as a suspect or condemned person, or would even assist his pursuit. In short, one can say that such accords are only possible between equals. Moreover, the effective implementation of the accord requires similar concepts between the participating states of the crime in question and hence the need for the harmonization of substantive norms.

Similarity between the judicial systems of states located in the same region, and with democratic traditions, permits the adoption of multilateral conventions. A typical example is Europe, which, within the forum of the Council of Europe, adopted in 1957 a Regional Extradition Convention, which has had excellent results.

Subsequently, within the framework of the United Nations, confronted with concern at the relentless spread of drug trafficking, an endeavour was made to offer to every country in the world, though purely in the drugs sector, an instrument of accord so as to enable every participating state to secure from another the extradition of drug-traffickers. This concept was embodied in the Amending Protocol to the 1961 Consolidated Convention on Drugs, which was concluded in Geneva in March 1972. Article 14.2(b)(ii) of this convention provides: '*where one Party which requires matters of extradition to be covered by a treaty receives an extradition request from another Party with whom it does not have an extradition treaty, it may consider this Convention as juridical authority for permitting extradition for the* [most serious drug-connected] *offences*'. A similar provision is found in Article 6.3 of the 1988 Vienna Convention on Drugs.

For the police sub-system there are numerous bilateral accords. In recent years these have been based not only on formal conventions between governments, but also on 'protocols of understanding' between the ministers directly interested. But, in this area, multilateral cooperation has made major advances. A typical example is the Convention to apply the Schengen Accord of 14 June 1985, adopted in November 1990, which devotes a whole chapter to 'cooperation between police forces' (Articles 39–47). Such provisions aim to intensify and strengthen common action between the police forces of the various European countries. It is appropriate to mention the possibility for the police of one state, who are keeping under observation in their own territory people suspected of serious crimes, to continue their surveillance in another state; also, the confirmation of the so-called *right of hot pursuit*, which enables police officers under certain conditions to carry out operations in another state to identify and arrest the perpetrators of serious crimes.

Still on the subject of direct collaboration between police offices of different states, one should mention the important innovations introduced at a global level by the 1988 Convention against Drugs Trafficking, which, going beyond the opportunities available under previous conventions in this field for the deployment of informants in foreign states, provided for the establishment of 'mixed squads' of police consisting of members from different states (Article 9.1(c)) and so-called 'controlled delivery' (Article 11), which, to assist the identification of various members of criminal organizations, permits agreement between the police forces to undertake surveillance of the passage and destination of drugs consignments.

Indeed, it is precisely in the police sector that the first initiatives have emerged to give life to machinery of a specifically international nature. To some extent Interpol anticipated this trend, which has appeared with greater decisiveness and clarity in the European context with the creation of a 'European Office of Police' (Europol). This first initiative seems capable of further development, and opens up prospects of major interest. The body in question derived from the provision in the 1992 European Union Treaty for the institution of a European Office of Police, and this decision was followed in July 1995 by the adoption of the Brussels Convention to implement it.

In this Convention, the objective of Europol was defined as the improvement of:

> the efficacy of the competent services of the Member States and cooperation between them ... in order to prevent and combat terrorism, illicit drugs-trafficking and other serious forms of international crime, wherever there is concrete evidence of a criminal structure or organization and two or more Member States harmed by the above-mentioned types of crime so as to indicate the need, given the scope, seriousness and consequences of the crimes, for common action between Member States.

In taking the first step towards a firm integration between the national police forces, which could anticipate a genuine functional integration between them, Europe has shown both caution and practicality. This is borne out by the description of the programme for common action, which is articulated in successive phases, with an implicit commitment to experimentation and verification.

Thus the second paragraph of Article 2 reads:

> in order progressively to realise the objective ... Europol is initially made responsible for the prevention of, and fight against, illicit trafficking in drugs and nuclear and radioactive materials, clandestine immigration organizations, trade in human beings and trafficking of stolen vehicles. Europol will also, not later than two years after the coming into force of the present Convention, concern itself with crimes committed, or which may be

committed, in the course of terrorist activity, which represent offences against life, physical safety and the freedom of persons and property.

At present, it is too early to evaluate the real potential of this organization, although its development is being followed closely since it could indicate features that might be extended. Indeed, the strengthening of the international legal system to combat transnational crime should have a special focus upon the police organization. In fact, all the initiatives that have been, or may be, undertaken with regard to judicial organization, however important they may be, do not have a direct impact on the control of this type of crime. Mutual judicial assistance assists the execution of direct operations to obtain evidence and impound illicitly obtained assets; conventions for extradition will assist proceedings to bring to court those accused of serious crimes who are now outside the jurisdiction of the judicial authority intending to take action against them or to carry out sentences imposed upon them; international courts make it possible to attempt to sentence those who otherwise might escape from national jurisdictions; but the functioning of such machinery presupposes an investigative capability, at an international level that can obtain the essential data for the discovery of crimes that have been committed and the identification of their perpetrators. Such a capability is possessed only by the police organizations.

Crime has profited, with great opportunism, from every opening provided by technological progress for moving men, goods and moneys across national frontiers. It employs widespread organizational networks and trafficking facilities throughout the world. To combat this phenomenon, the international community must organize itself so as to have a comparable capability in the hands of the police. Collaborative accords between the various national police forces are a first step towards this goal, although further advances are needed to attain the efficiency that can only be achieved by a genuine internationalization of the police.

At this time, the most important on-going initiative to tackle organized international crime lies within the ambit of the UN under the guidance of the Commission for the Prevention of Crime and Criminal Justice. It calls for the drafting of the Convention, mentioned earlier, on which the Inter-Governmental Group of Experts is keenly working under the directives contained in the 'Naples Policy Declaration' and the 'Global Plan of Action against Transnational Organized Crime'.

The Convention covers:
1. definition of 'transnational organized crime';
2. scope of application;
3. participation in criminal organizations;
4. money laundering;
5. the criminal liability of business undertakings;
6. efficiency of judicial proceedings and sentences;
7. confiscation;
8. transparency of transactions;
9. jurisdiction;
10. extradition;
11. mutual assistance.

These subjects include money laundering and confiscation. The proposed harmonization of legislation on these matters can certainly help to strike at the resources of organized crime, so affecting its operational abilities and its capacity to enjoy its illicit profits. Nevertheless, there is the impression that, for the rest, even if useful to improve institutions for cooperation that already exist, no decisive effect will be achieved in the fight against transnational crime. Simultaneously a parallel initiative should be taken to promote the real internationalization of police forces, although this is a difficult task. Probably the climate is not yet ripe to realize it. The creation of Europol, which is a first step in this direction, must be warmly welcomed and its work must be followed and evaluated with great care, having in mind its possible future extension.

Responding to Transnational Crime

RAYMOND E. KENDALL

Transnational crime is a major challenge facing the world community in general and the global law enforcement community in particular. Today, its corrupting effects reach into every segment of our society.

When one examines transnational crime closely, it is readily apparent that only a small portion of it is random crime. The vast majority is highly structured organized crime. At Interpol we have defined organized crime as 'any enterprise or group of persons engaged in a continuing illegal activity which has as its primary purpose the generation of profits irrespective of national boundaries'. Succinctly, the aim of each and every organized criminal group is the realization of large financial profits through any means, as quickly as possible. Financial profit is derived from every possible source of illegal activity, including trafficking in securities, arms deals, smuggling, the theft and fencing of stolen property, corruption, prostitution, gambling and, in particular, trafficking in and distribution of drugs.

The International Monetary Fund estimates that within the world criminal fraternity approximately US$500 billion in ill-gotten gains change hands annually. Ten years ago that figure was US$85 billion. Contrary to the old adage, it seems that crime does, in fact, pay.

Transnational organized crime is a sophisticated, diversified and widespread activity that annually drains billions of dollars from the world's legitimate economy by unlawful conduct and the consistent use of force, fraud and corruption. Much of this untaxed wealth derived from criminal enterprises is being laundered through ostensibly legitimate businesses. The 'business strategy' of such groups is the corruption of both public officials and private citizens and 'business competition' is eliminated by any means. We are all victims as the costs of this corruption are inevitably passed on to the public sector, causing an additional burden on state social and economic programmes. Organized criminal gangs have become increasingly sophisticated in using their profits, power and influence to insulate and protect their hierarchy from discovery and prosecution.

269

TRENDS IN TRANSNATIONAL ORGANIZED CRIME

Transnational crime continues to expand and grow exponentially. In my earlier years with Scotland Yard, and even with Interpol in the 1970s, drug and organized crime investigations were focused primarily on the Sicilian Mafia. Today, Interpol receives messages concerning investigations of the Sicilian Mafia, the Camorra, the 'Ndrangheta, the Chinese Triads, the Japanese Boryokudan, the various Colombian and South American cartels, the outlaw motorcycle gangs, the West African criminal enterprises and criminal organizations of East European/Asian origin. All of these organizations conduct a myriad of criminal activities, usually including cocaine and heroin trafficking and money laundering.

Law enforcement around the world is finding that investigations of organized crime organizations are much more complicated than investigations of traditional crime groups operating in one area or country. As we have seen in the last few years, crime is no longer bound by the constraints of national borders. The widespread political, economic, social and technological changes that have occurred within the last two decades have allowed organized criminal groups to become increasingly active in the international arena.

These groups use the increased ease of international travel, liberalized emigration policies, expansion of free trade, high-tech communications equipment and sophisticated money laundering techniques to enhance and further their criminal efforts. For instance, in just one message we receive concerning an East European organized crime group, that investigation might involve telephone information from Spain and the USA, bank records in Switzerland, addresses of residences and businesses in Germany and Poland, and passport information from Russia and Israel.

To quote one example, the Interpol General Secretariat is currently assisting in an international investigation, known as Operation 'Black Powder', which includes Colombia, Panama, Germany, the Netherlands, Belgium, Albania and Lithuania. The investigation centres around a well-financed Colombian organization whose members operate in Bucamaranga and Bogotá, Colombia, where they have developed the technology or chemistry to mix cocaine hydrochloride (HCL) with other substances such as iron filings or red scarlate pigment so as to render the compound very difficult to detect by conventional means. Through analysis of seizure data communicated routinely through Interpol channels, the General Secretariat has established strong links between six significant seizures in Colombia and Europe that have given investigators in each of the above-mentioned countries the knowledge that the seizures in their countries are not isolated cases but form part of a global smuggling and marketing strategy devised by the Colombian traffickers. It is worth mentioning here that as a result of an immediate response by the Interpol General Secretariat to intelligence received from the Netherlands, Interpol Bogotá was able to isolate a suspect shipment of so-called 'black cocaine' before it could be exported by air freight. The shipment contained 193 kg of cocaine. The ensuing investigation in Colombia resulted in three arrests, including one of the chemists recruited by the trafficking organization. This is an excellent example of the coordinating role the General Secretariat can play in such investigations.

East European organized crime has been commonly, but incorrectly, labelled by the media as 'Russian organized crime'. These crime groups emanating from the former communist countries of Eastern Europe and the republics of the former Soviet Union pose a deadly threat internationally as the number of crime syndicates rise steadily. The latest estimates are that about 1,000 Russian organized crime groups are operating internationally, excluding the 8,000 to 10,000 operating in the area of the former Soviet Union itself, which range in size from 50 to 1,000 members. All are engaged in systematic criminal businesses, often protected from the law with the help of corruption. It is estimated that more than US$25 billion of Russian capital is in circulation outside Russia, and most of this money is in the control of these crime syndicates.

In Russia itself, the police authorities have struggled to keep pace with the takeover of legitimate businesses by crime syndicates. The latest Russian police figures state that 41,000 companies are now run by these crime groups, as well as 50 per cent of the banks and 80 per cent of the joint ventures with foreign capital. Nearly 30 Russian bankers have been murdered in the past few years, allegedly for failing to comply with the requirements of the Russian 'Thieves in Law'.

The 'Thieves in Law' are a loosely organized group of 'elite criminal leaders' whose roots stem from gangs in former Soviet prisons. They are selected by their prison peers for membership and observe strict codes of conduct. It is believed that top-level 'Thieves in Law' have been given responsibility by others for overseeing operations in Western Europe, the USA and Canada. These criminals are generally better educated and more technologically skilled than the typical organized crime leader from groups such as the Colombian cartels or the Italian Mafia.

Nigerian trafficking organizations control the drug markets of sub-Saharan Africa and operate drug distribution networks from strategic locations throughout the world. Nigerian couriers or individuals from other countries recruited by the Nigerians, transport a large portion of the heroin abused in the USA; they smuggle South American cocaine to Europe and Africa, especially South Africa; and they export marijuana – the only narcotic cultivated in Nigeria – to Europe and other countries in West Africa.

Nigerian trafficking organizations are established in the opium-producing centres of Asia and in the markets of every heroin-consuming nation. They have forged connections with cocaine producers in South America and created permanent distribution networks not only in Africa, but also in Europe, East Asia and countries of the former Soviet Union.

One unusual aspect of both the Nigerian traffickers and the East European crime syndicates has been their willingness to cooperate or make business arrangements with other organized crime groups, such as La Cosa Nostra and the Colombian cartels. This ability and willingness to form alliances and negotiate for territories again demonstrates the adaptation of these crime groups and the similarities to the trends in legitimate multinational corporations. For example, Russian crime groups working with the Colombian cartels have resulted in a sharp increase in the flow of Russian weapons to Marxist guerrillas in South America and right-wing paramilitary groups in Colombia and a surge of cocaine flowing into Russia.

This need to facilitate laundering operations has also resulted in the emergence of significant organized crime influence and corruption in countries in the Caribbean, with weaker economies or economies reliant on supplying financial services. A recent study of the Cayman Islands found 450 banks on the island, with assets of about US$400 billion, or about US$15 million for each of the nation's 26,000 residents. Antigua has authorized the opening of 27 offshore banks in the past few years. Four Russian-owned banks and one Ukrainian bank have opened on this island of 63,000 people. With profits, these increasingly powerful crime syndicates are now laundering money on a grand scale in London and other European capitals. This money has been acquired not only through drug trafficking but also prostitution, extortion, illegal immigration and fraud operations.

Money laundering is one of the huge challenges facing law enforcement agencies as they try to counter the rising threat from organized crime. In London and other cities in Europe, Russian criminal money is suspected of being behind a number of large property deals. This is all part of the process to make dirty money 'legitimate' through a three-stage process:

- *placing* – where money is removed from a criminal organization to a legitimate business, such as a bank or small firm;
- *layering* – when it is mixed with the legitimate funds of that bank or firm;
- *integration* – where it is moved on to other legitimate assets such as stocks and bonds, bearer shares and large property developments, and thus hidden from law enforcement.

With the explosive growth in the development and use of advanced information technologies such as the Internet, the global information infrastructure is now a reality and national and international borders are effectively disappearing. Although advances in communications and computer technology are creating unprecedented international business opportunities, these technologies are also having an impact on the effectiveness of law enforcement worldwide in performing its mission. The same technologies that have transformed the globe into the 'global village' for legitimate commercial purposes are also being used by groups engaged in drug trafficking, terrorism, economic crime, trafficking in weapons and the smuggling and trafficking of human beings.

INTERPOL

With the vast changes in the world today, where does Interpol fit in and what is its response to transnational crime? As an organization, Interpol has undergone dramatic changes during the past ten years. Every effort is being made to take advantage of development in terms of information technology, and structures are being created to ensure the delivery of a service that is focused upon the needs of its member countries.

With a current membership of 177 countries, Interpol has been faced with an enormous challenge to develop a system that will operate quickly and efficiently so that any of these member countries may communicate with each other. It was not so long ago that in some countries the medium for communication was Morse code! Today Interpol boasts an efficient, secure and reliable telecommunications system that links each of the Interpol National Central Bureaus by e-mail and gives automated access to a central database of information on international crime and criminals. There remains, however, much to be done.

First, we must undertake a worldwide coordinated and cooperative law enforcement response that is consistent with the fundamental democratic principles of justice. That means attacking organized crime groups strongly and lawfully within the boundaries of each affected country's jurisdiction and then, where appropriate, sharing the resulting criminal information with other affected countries.

In addition to exchanging investigative data, we must explore ways in which to increase the exchange of law enforcement-related technology and forensic methods. Interpol continues to explore initiatives to standardize how law enforcement agencies collect, analyse, store and utilize evidence of criminal acts. We continue to strive to improve the level, intensity and quality of investigative cooperation and information-sharing among law enforcement agencies around the world.

Interpol has and must continue to serve as a bridge that links the law enforcement agencies of the world. Only with the enhanced cooperation of the law enforcement agencies of the world using laws that meet the challenge of the crime will there be a meaningful impact upon the criminals and crime groups that now call the entire globe their home. Can we continue to ignore proven investigative methods, such as undercover penetrations, electronic monitoring, controlled deliveries and informant statements? The answer is no. The problem has evolved and so too must our ability to apply appropriate counter-measures.

In the context of its general efforts to supply member countries with information about various criminal enterprises and individuals, the organized crime branch at the general secretariat, in operation since 1986, is studying all aspects of the organized crime issue. The long-term aim of the branch is to create an extensive database of enterprises and groups of persons engaged in continued illegal activity in order to generate illicit profits. In concrete terms, this means that the branch's objectives are:

274

- to establish and continuously update a computerized file of information on individuals, associations and groups with international ramifications that engage in continuous criminal activities;
- to cross-check and analyse all information on organized crime supplied by member countries;
- to pass on all relevant information by way of circular letter, bulletins, reports, international notices, etc.;
- to plan coordinated action and organize conferences, symposia and working groups on particular topics relevant to organized crime.

In order to extract and analyse data from the organization's centralized database, a number of officials at the general secretariat have been trained in crime analysis and now form the analytical criminal intelligence unit (ACIU). Utilizing state-of-the-art analytical software, this unit has been designed to ensure that full advantage can be taken of the wealth of information that is stored in Interpol's criminal information system. For example, by establishing the links between crimes and offenders and disseminating that information for exploitation by its member countries, Interpol provides law enforcement with valuable and actionable criminal intelligence.

One on-going project of both the organized crime branch and the ACIU is the go-west project that deals with collecting and analysing information concerning the East European crime syndicates mentioned previously. In that vein Interpol has begun several new projects on specific groups that we feel will assist various affected countries in their investigations of these groups.

The over-riding priority of the law enforcement community must be the dismantling of international organized crime groups by coordinating international and domestic investigations. This requires law enforcement agencies to provide advice, assistance, operational planning and investigative support to each other in order to combat international organized crime. Criminals work together – law enforcement must do the same.

Transnational Organized Crime and Institutional Reform in the European Union: the Case of Judicial Cooperation

CYRILLE FIJNAUT

In recent years, the European Council, the European Parliament and the European Commission have frequently emphasized the importance of police, customs and judicial cooperation among the member states in controlling organized crime in the European Union (EU), particularly where protection of the financial interests of the European Communities (EC) is concerned. Furthermore, the European Parliament and the European Commission have highlighted the need for a more supranational approach because existing forms of cooperation, despite all kinds of measures to make them more effective, have insufficient impact. The Parliament and Commission have been unwilling to hold back with the orchestration of this approach until there is no longer any disagreement about the need for it. On the contrary, these bodies, for some time, have been advocating not just the establishment of communitarian customs but also the creation of a European Prosecutor's Office and, separately from the continued development of Europol, the transformation of the *Unité pour la coordination de la lutte anti-fraude* at the European Commission (UCLAF) into a communitarian bureau of investigation. The progression of judicial cooperation in the EU, therefore, clearly forms part of a more general development: the creation of a targeted and integrated policy in the EU against organized crime, whether this jeopardizes the financial interests of the Communities or not.

In order to be able to adopt a position in this debate on the continued development of judicial cooperation in the EU *versus* the expansion of a communitarian criminal justice system, it is obviously appropriate to assess the problem of organized crime in the EU and the differing ways of tackling this problem. Obviously ...? The proponents of a more communitarian, that is to say supranational, approach to this problem usually argue from the premise that organized crime has already assumed such proportions that it can no longer be curbed by intergovernmental cooperation alone, even with more and better forms of such cooperation. But is it really necessary, in view of the seriousness of the problem, to supplement the existing forms of cooperation between the member states with supranational police, justice and customs? How serious is the problem of organized crime? And are there no any other ways of controlling this problem, if it is so serious?

A specific examination will then follow of the laborious and complex progression of judicial cooperation as given shape in the EU, both in the context of the Third Pillar and in the context of the First Pillar (but not forgetting Schengen, prior to the adoption of the Treaty of Amsterdam in the summer of 1997). In discussing the development of judicial cooperation we will assess the claims that existing forms of judicial cooperation are no longer sufficient (as a complement to police and customs cooperation) to control the problem of transnational organized crime and should be supplemented with, or replaced by, supranational institutions and mechanisms.

The provisions of the Treaty of Amsterdam directly related to the judicial approach to organized crime in the European Union form the subject of the third part of this paper. Reference is naturally made in discussing them to the *Action plan to combat organized crime* adopted by the European Council in spring 1997. The extent to which this plan has already been incorporated into the development of EU policy against organized crime is also considered.

THE PROBLEM OF ORGANIZED CRIME IN THE EU

The Nature of the Problem

This is not the appropriate place to discuss the many obstacles to providing an adequate picture of the nature and extent of organized crime in the EU.[1] On the basis of reports made by Europol and police services in countries such as Germany, Italy and Belgium, as well as (unfortunately, not particularly numerous) academic studies it is possible to assess the seriousness of this problem.[2] In this connection, the following observations are particularly pertinent.

First, organized crime is still a highly differentiated phenomenon in the EU. There are not only significant differences between countries such as Italy and Germany, for example, but also between the

Scandinavian countries and the Benelux. While the Scandinavian countries appear to have particular problems with motorcycle gangs, the Low Countries are faced with groupings of many different kinds (Dutch, Turkish, Yugoslav, etc.), active in a widely diverse areas of illegality – trafficking in drugs, trading in weapons, trading in women, etc.

Second, the groups that perpetrate organized crime are organized in widely differing ways. The 'Dutch networks', for example, in many respects have a different appearance than the Italian Mafia families: not only are they usually far smaller, they are also far less closely knit; in addition, they do not appropriate particular territories for themselves and they use violence on a far smaller scale to screen their illegal activities.

Third, in by far the majority of the member states, organized crime groups to date have not controlled any legal economic sectors, although they usually have import and export firms at their disposal to screen their smuggling operations. Only in certain parts of Italy do such groups control significant sectors of economic life.

Fourth it is only in Italy that organized crime actually has a grip on politics and public administration in particular towns and cities or regions of the country. This takes nothing away from the fact that, in recent years, every member state has suffered from corruption scandals, which suggest that there are some disturbing trends.

To sum up, in virtually none of the member states does organized crime pose a real threat to the democratic constitutional state and the free market economy. Rather, it represents a greater or lesser challenge to the authorities.

It is also important to point out that the European Commission, in the form of the UCLAF, has been hammering the message since 1995 that organized crime has also been targeting the financial resources of the Communities. It is stated in the 1997 annual report, for example, that

> more than 50 crime networks have been identified in the course of large-scale investigations which have revealed the attacks being made on Community expenditure and revenue. The networks work with each other and are involved in other criminal activities as well as financial crime against the Community finances. Organised crime has its sights trained on high-risk products in which trafficking brings in huge profits, such as alcohol and cigarettes: customs duties are evaded at the expense of the Community's financial interests, while excise duty and VAT are evaded primarily at the expense of national interests. In

agriculture, investigations by the specialist national departments and the Commission more and more often uncover evidence of involvement by organised, international crime networks.[3]

If it cannot be disputed that large-scale EC fraud is partly perpetrated by organized crime, however, the extent of organized crime's role in the perpetration of this fraud is less clear. Not only is there no good definition anywhere of what is to be understood by organized crime, but also there is no clear account of the number of cases each year in which organized crime played a part. Precisely because the involvement of organized crime in the perpetration of EC fraud is one of the leading arguments for a supranational penal approach to this fraud, there is an urgent need for greater clarity on its role. Such a radical reorganization of relations within the EU cannot be made on the basis of general impressions, sprinkled with hard cases. And do 50 criminal networks really pose such a huge threat to the EU as such? Probably not. This number is not high when set against the numbers of investigations into organized crime launched annually in the member states: 841 investigations in Germany in 1997, 162 in Belgium in 1996.[4] Furthermore, the European Court of Auditors in a recent report on the UCLAF established that the annual reports of the European Commission on the fight against fraud are not reliable, neither with regard to the numbers of cases of fraud which have come to light nor with regard to the extent of the financial or economic damage inflicted.[5]

In addition, organized crime – and therefore also organized EC fraud – is always regarded as crime that is organized internationally. To the extent, however, that organized crime involves, above all, the supply of illegal goods (whether it be drugs or cigarettes and alcohol) and/or illicit services (prostitution, gambling) in black markets, it is a problem that, almost by definition, is international in nature. Yet this dimension relates primarily to the transportation of these goods and services to the markets where they are distributed – this applies equally to hash shipped from Morocco to the Netherlands or cigarettes transported from the port of Antwerp to Italy. Organized crime, as most member states know it, is, for the most part, not international in nature but a local problem. Production of illegal goods, for example, is usually in the hands of those who, on the spot, are able to exercise control over the raw materials required and the associated means of production or can exert influence on the recruitment of the people required. Also, so far as distribution is concerned, this can only be organized by individuals or groups with access to a network of channels to reach the customers in the vicinity of the black markets. This presupposes that they are at home in these places, have fixed distribution points at their disposal, know what else is going on in the underworld and have some familiarity with the upperworld, especially with applicable legislation and the ways in which it is enforced, and with specialists who can be called in when problems arise with the police and the judicial system.[6]

Organized Crime and Judicial Cooperation

Following from all this, it can be argued that the significance of international cooperation in criminal law, and in particular judicial cooperation, in the control of organized crime is overestimated both in official publications and in much scientific literature. Because organized crime is to a significant extent a local issue, the control of this crime is first and foremost a responsibility of local and national authorities: the task of keeping the production or consumption of illegal goods and services in check (by both prevention and control) rests on their shoulders. It is up to the authorities in the countries of origin, for example in the area of the trade in women, to prevent women being recruited for the sex industry in the West, and it is up to the authorities in the West – on the basis of the necessary legislation – to make their shameless exploitation impossible. The idea that organized crime in the first instance must be fought at the local level and through administrative and preventive means is not old-fashioned. The importance of such an approach has been recognized for some years in the USA and is evident in the policy conducted by Mayor Giuliani in New York of barring the Cosa Nostra from the city's food markets, the building industry and waste processing. Completely new licensing systems have been developed for these economic sectors, and compliance with the terms of the licences that have been granted is enforced with tough sanctions.[7] Similarly, the municipal administration of Amsterdam in the late 1980s approved an action programme with more than 70 administrative measures to deal with (organized) crime in the city.

The penal fight against organized crime must also be organized primarily by local and national authorities – the reason being that organized crime, in many respects, is a local phenomenon, whether perpetrated by indigenous criminal groups, by immigrants or by known transnational criminal organizations. If the authorities wish to fulfil their task of repression in an appropriate manner, various prerequisites must be met: proper legislation with a view to the application of special methods of investigation, expert training of investigators and magistrates, adequate infrastructure in the institutions involved, etc. On all these points the organization of police and justice, so far as possible, should be compatible with that in the surrounding countries, because this appreciably simplifies cross-border cooperation in criminal justice.

The implication is that the latter form of cooperation must be the keystone of national and local measures for prevention and repression of organized crime. It serves the purpose, where necessary, of making possible or facilitating repressive action by local and national authorities. The question naturally arises, however, as to whether this cooperation has been organized in a way that satisfies current requirements. Are the conventions on mutual assistance of the Council of Europe suitable for efficient and effective cooperation between the signatories in combating organized crime? What is the practical significance of the Convention applying the Schengen Agreement in this context? And what can be expected from the supplementary agreements that have been or are being brought about in the European Union's Third Pillar? These and other questions are impossible to answer well in the absence of empirical research on the actual working of international cooperation in the field of criminal justice.[8] Rather like the question about the degree to which EC fraud is perpetrated by organized crime, however, they would have to be answered very negatively before a decision should be taken also to combat organized crime (including that in which the financial resources of the EU are jeopardized) at a supranational level, as the European Parliament and the European Commission wish.[9]

JUDICIAL COOPERATION BEFORE THE TREATY OF AMSTERDAM

The Role of the Council of Europe

It is to the credit of the Council of Europe that some mutual legal assistance conventions have been created that have continued to prove of great benefit for interstate criminal justice cooperation between the countries (including but not confined to most of the member states of the EU) that ratified them. These conventions include the European Convention on Extradition (1957, with supplementary protocols from

1975 and 1978), the European Convention on Mutual Assistance in Criminal Matters (1959, with a supplementary protocol from 1978) and the European Convention on Money Laundering (1990).[10]

The first two conventions regulate traditional forms of mutual assistance such as extradition; the exchange of information; the transmission of objects and documents; the questioning of witnesses and experts; the conducting of investigative actions, such as seizures and the searching of premises; and the appearance of suspects. In these regulations, not only are the conditions under which mutual assistance may be rendered quite strict (think, for example, in the case of extradition of double punishability and the principle of speciality), but also there are many grounds on which mutual assistance may be refused (extradition, for example, may be refused in the case of political and fiscal offences, in the case of nationals and in the case of double prosecution and limitation). Furthermore, those countries wishing to become a party to these conventions in many places are given an opportunity to make one or more reservations and/or to issue declarations. The reason why the regulation of these forms of mutual assistance are so complex is not difficult to find: the countries involved in its development were prepared to harmonize existing forms of cooperation a little but wanted to retain sufficient freedom and flexibility to be able to decide, from case to case, whether they should or should not honour a request for mutual assistance.[11]

During the 1980s there was also a realization within the Council of Europe that the existing conventions were no longer entirely appropriate to new requirements. This led to the plan for various conventions (relating to extradition, concerning mutual assistance and with regard to the transfer of criminal proceedings) to be integrated into a single mutual assistance convention that was simultaneously modernized. The draft, which was tabled in 1987, provided, among other things, for a right of cross-border pursuit, cross-border surveillance and the confiscation of goods. However, some participants in the discussion wanted to go further and, for example, include a provision for the interception of calls and the direct transmission of documents. In addition there was talk of broadening the conditions under which mutual assistance could be provided and of discussing the grounds on which mutual assistance could be refused. It was probably these discussions that explain why this topic eventually died a gentle death: no agreement could be reached on this and other questions.[12]

The result was that the Council of Europe, in effect, put itself out of contention in the reorganization of international mutual assistance in Europe. It was incapable of continuing to give practical form to its leading role at this level in Europe – and this was definitely a weak point in the light of the expansion of the European Communities taking place at the same time.[13] The idea that there should be radical intervention in the European system of mutual assistance was becoming ever stronger, not least in the member state that was pushing like no other for further unification of Europe – Germany. The German State Secretary Schomburg openly declared at an international congress in 1990 that it was high time for international mutual assistance to be modernized and that, at the level of the member states involved, there was no longer any place for the principle of speciality, the principle of double punishability or grounds for refusal.[14]

Schengen and Judicial Cooperation

The conclusion of the Schengen Agreement in 1985 was dictated by the plan of the member states of the EC to organize, by 1 January 1993, a common internal market and consequently to abolish controls at internal borders. The countries that took the initiative for this step in 1984, Germany and France, were at the same time convinced (and the Benelux countries soon latched onto this idea) that these controls could only be abolished if a large number of accompanying measures were taken, particularly in the area of police and security.[15]

The texts of the Schengen Agreement and of the Convention applying the Schengen Agreement demonstrate that the countries involved were thinking much more about strengthening police cooperation (to the extent of setting up a joint centre for the fight against drugs) than the expansion of judicial cooperation. Nevertheless, the parties to the Convention applying the Schengen Agreement achieved something that the Council of Europe, at the same time, proved incapable of achieving – an integrated scheme for the provision of police cooperation and judicial mutual assistance. Not only are various forms of police cooperation regulated in this agreement, but also it incorporates provisions that simplify or broaden the application of some European conventions on mutual assistance. It is in the nature of this agreement that this chiefly involves application of the European Convention on Mutual Assistance in Criminal Matters.

More specifically, thought must be given to broadening the type of offences for which the granting of mutual assistance is possible (now also *Ordnungswidrigkeiten* – contravention of regulations), expansion of the categories of procedures where this is possible (civil procedures that are linked to criminal procedures), easing of the conditions for the searching of premises and seizure (lowering the criminal threshold) and the normalization of the direct exchange of requests for mutual assistance between judicial authorities. All in all, these supplementary provisions are not very radical, proving once again that it is not so simple (even between countries with significant common interests) to change radically the existing organization of cross-border judicial assistance.[16] This is even more obvious because it would have been possible via the Convention applying the Schengen Agreement to institutionalize judicial cooperation between the member states in some way (for example in the form of regular consultation between representatives of the prosecutor's offices in different states).

Judicial Cooperation in the 'espace judiciaire européen'

Since the establishment of the EC there has been discussion about whether or not these institutions ought to have some power in the area of criminal justice. One form of this question was whether the EC ought not itself (that is to say separately from the member states), be responsible for the penal enforcement of their legislation. This question has been answered in the negative by the member states. A more limited issue concerned the possibility of the EC itself being enabled to take penal action against persons and firms that targeted its budget. The member states also rejected this proposal: the penal enforcement of the communitarian legal system in each area was a matter for the member states themselves and in no way for the EC, specifically the European Commission. When it became clear during the course of the 1960s, however, that EC fraud did, in fact, represent a problem, there was some discussion on increasing the opportunities for closer cooperation between the member states in combating this fraud.[17]

This discussion culminated in the mid-1970s in a Commission proposal to organize better the penal protection of the financial interests of the EC by amending the EC Treaty through a protocol. This discussion was not entirely fruitless and in 1976 the proposal was even published in the Official Journal.[18] It came down chiefly, on the one hand, to an undertaking by the member states to adapt their criminal legislation with regard to fraud to encompass EC fraud and, on the other, to supplementary regulations in connection with the transfer of criminal proceedings and the provision of mutual assistance in general. Ultimately, though not much came of this apart from a discussion in the European Parliament in 1979. The member states were clearly not willing to continue along this path, partly because they did not want the Court of Justice to acquire any power in relation to combating fraud as a result of an amendment to the Treaty.[19]

However, this failure must not cause us to lose sight of the fact that the member states at virtually the same time (in 1976, one year later than the year in which the police cooperation in combating terrorism between the member states was organized in a totally new way under the name of TREVI) launched a *Coopération Judiciaire* working party in the framework of European Political Cooperation (EPC). But although French President Giscard d'Estaing, from 1977 on, openly advocated the expansion of an *espace judiciaire européen*, this working group too achieved little. It was ready with a draft convention relating to cooperation in criminal matters in 1980, but this proposal was not even presented for signature owing to lack of agreement. In short, more detailed regulation of international mutual assistance proved not to be a sinecure at EC level either.[20]

Evidently under the influence of the plans to bring about an internal market, the working party from 1985 onwards made another attempt to modernize the provision of mutual assistance in criminal matters, on the basis of the conventions of the Council of Europe. This time the effort was more successful – largely because the economic and political interests at stake were not compatible with another failure. Five supplementary conventions were signed between 1987 and 1992, in order to promote judicial cooperation, among other things on the transmission of extradition requests and the transfer of criminal proceedings between the member states. Yet, there is a down side to this success: the conventions have remained a dead letter up to the present day because they have been ratified by only a few member states.[21] This underlines yet again that states are loath to relinquish even a fragment of their freedom of action in the field of judicial cooperation – even where they have large common interests in many other fields, as in the case of the EC. This makes it easier to understand why the Council of Europe in 1987 did not succeed in drawing up a contemporary and integrated (draft) convention on mutual legal assistance: not only do more countries have to be brought into line than in the EC but also these countries are a long way from all sharing economic and political interests. Not surprisingly, therefore, for many years little has come of the *espace judiciaire européen* envisaged by Giscard d'Estaing.[22]

The Treaty of Maastricht and Judicial Cooperation

The deliberations in the context of EPC with regard to judicial cooperation between the member states were incorporated in the Treaty of Maastricht into what is known as the Third Pillar of the EU. In Article K.1 of Title VI (Provisions relating to cooperation in the field of justice and home affairs) of this Treaty, judicial cooperation in criminal matters (item 7) – alongside customs cooperation (item 8) and police cooperation (item 9, Europol) – is fully identified as common interest for the member states. In other words, it became an intergovernmental question in which according to Article K.3 only the Council, and then only on the initiative of a member state, was entitled, in principle by unanimous vote, to establish joint positions, decide on joint actions or draw up conventions.

In the working plans approved in 1993 and in 1996 by the Council of Ministers of Justice and Home Affairs, a modest but not insignificant role was allocated to judicial cooperation,[23] specifically the drawing-up of a convention on extradition and a convention on mutual assistance in criminal matters, and the launching of a network of contact and liaison magistrates, with a view to smoother cooperation in the provision of mutual legal assistance. The conclusion of a convention on Europol was also at the top of the agenda. Also it is impossible not to conclude that the Council, and therefore the member states, kept their word on a number of points. At the end of 1996 not only was the Europol Convention (26 July 1995) signed, so too were the Convention on the Simplified Extradition (10 March 1995) and the Convention on Extradition (27 September 1996).[24] In addition, a formal start was made via 'joint actions' of 22 April 1996 and 14 October 1996 on the exchange of liaison magistrates.[25] The only promise not kept at that time (although dealt with subsequently), was the drawing-up of a convention relating to mutual assistance in criminal matters. Substantially more has been achieved via the Third Pillar, therefore, than through the EPC.

There was nevertheless some criticism in 1995–96 (particularly with a view to the Intergovernmental Conference on the revision of the Treaty of Maastricht) of the way in which the Third Pillar works. Part of the problem was the purported institutional deficiencies of this Pillar (the lack of parliamentary control, the absence of the Court of Justice, the power of intergovernmental bureaucracy) but operational deficiencies were also highlighted, especially in the context of rapidly escalating organized crime.[26] It was argued above all by officials in the European Commission and the European Council that:

- the rule of unanimity made it impossible for the Council to take decisions quickly;
- the decision-making structures on the basis of Article K.4 were far too cumbersome;
- the instruments at the disposal of the Council were not suitable for operating effectively in this context;
- the national bureaucracies worked far too statically; and
- almost unbridgeable cultural gulfs existed between the member states.

In the view of the critics, police and judicial cooperation was still unjustly caught up in national frameworks, while the political, economic and monetary integration of the member states was progressing steadily.[27] The results that, up to that time, had been achieved in this area in the Third Pillar did not amount to much. Accordingly, more far-reaching communitarization of cooperation was needed to achieve better results. Precisely how far this should go was usually left vague. Would greater Commission involvement be sufficient? Would the rule of unanimity have to be dropped altogether? The issue of whether organized crime was actually starting to pose such a threat to the EU that structural intervention in relationships just created was urgently required was never asked, even though it was fundamental.

Criticism of the decisiveness of the Third Pillar must also be questioned for other reasons. Certainly, prolonged negotiations on a convention relating to mutual assistance in criminal matters without much being achieved do not provide a model of decisive action. At the same time, the convention is concerned with politically very awkward problems. Further, the draft that was completed in spring 1998 did make arrangements on thorny issues, including the interception of communication, the organization of controlled deliveries, the questioning of people by satellite and the practice of infiltration. Nor is it surprising that it has taken a long time for member states to fall into line: application of this convention necessitates great trust on both sides in the integrity and effectiveness of each other's criminal justice system.[28]

It must also be noted that the Europol Convention, which in view of the Treaty of Amsterdam is also becoming increasingly significant for judicial cooperation (see below), is nothing more but also nothing less than a silent revolution in the history of international police cooperation in Europe. Never before have so many forms of cross-border police cooperation been regulated in such detail by convention. Although it took a few years of negotiations to bring about this convention, this is perfectly normal for a radical project on which there has been a lot of discussion in many member states and in the European Parliament.[29] Moreover, the Convention on Extradition is regarded in academic circles as a 'quantum leap' in international mutual assistance, particularly because in the case of participation in organized crime the principle of double punishability in principle is not a factor, and because the effect of the principle of speciality is also considerably limited.[30]

The Treaty of Maastricht therefore is not, at least as far as the Third Pillar is concerned, the failure that the Brussels' bureaucracy proclaims it to be. Given the politically sensitive nature of judicial (and police) cooperation between the member states and the EU, and the consequently highly complex decision-making structure in the Third Pillar, a great deal has been achieved.

Judicial Cooperation and the Fight against EC Fraud
Developments in 1994–95

The Treaty of Maastricht was one reason why the European Council, in June 1993, had the European Commission look again at how the fight against EC fraud might be organized better through the First and Third Pillars. The Commission, which had not in fact been idle in the meantime and had already moved to set up the UCLAF in 1988, took on this challenge to reformulate its anti-fraud strategy. It published an action plan in 1994, which broadly comprised four items:

- a more operational approach to fraud by the Commission in cooperation with the member states;
- intensification of the cooperation between the Commission and the member states, particularly in the area of the exchange of information;
- a tightening of communitarian legislation on a number of points; and
- in view of the outcome of the comparative study which the Council had requested in 1991, some harmonization of the criminal legislation of the member states so that 'fraud against the financial interests of

the Community is treated by the member states as a criminal offence and that an adequate legal framework exists to bring those responsible for fraud to account'.[31]

It was immediately apparent in the implementation of this programme that the member states were unwilling, in the context of the First Pillar, to relinquish much of their sovereignty, even to benefit of the fight against fraud. While the European Commission initially was of the view (and had already informally drawn up new proposals for this purpose as long ago as 1992) that a Community administrative/penal framework could be created via regulations to curb cases of EU fraud, it had to acknowledge in 1994 that this was not politically feasible. For this reason in June 1994 it stopped at a proposal for a regulation making provision both for the imposition of administrative fines by the Commission and the member states in the case of fraud (in the broad sense) and for the conducting of on-the-spot checks and inspections by employees of both of them. Significantly, the Commission also submitted a proposal for a convention, based on Article K.3(2) of the Treaty of Maastricht, in which the member states not only undertook to introduce a specific penal provision relating to EU fraud but also to intensify their mutual judicial cooperation and their cooperation with the Commission.

With regard to judicial cooperation, it was proposed among other things in Article 7 that the member states should no longer be able to refuse extradition on the basis of the argument that it was not a case of double punishability or the argument that a fiscal offence was involved. Also in Article 8, judicial cooperation was expanded to include the actual investigation at the crime scene, the handing-over of evidence, the exchange of criminal and police information, the conducting of searches of premises and seizures and the collection of fines.[32]

The European Council appeared, according to a Resolution of 6 December 1994 on the fight against EC fraud, broadly to side with these Commission proposals. On this occasion, however, it did not express a view on several controversial points especially those in the area of judicial cooperation. The Council merely made the general statement that, when fraud affected two or more member states, these states 'should cooperate effectively in relation to such an offence, for example through mutual assistance, extradition, the transfer of criminal proceedings or the enforcement of foreign criminal sentences'.[33]

Certainly in hindsight this was an ominous sign. This silence was a clear indication of the resistance of the member states to the proposals. In the Convention on the Protection of the Financial Interests of the EC, which dates from 26 July 1995, the proposals were watered down with the provisions relating to extradition largely reduced to re-affirming the *aut dedere aut judicare* principle (Article 5). Similarly, the proposals in the area of mutual assistance were weakened to the non-committing phrase that the member states in relevant cases 'shall cooperate effectively in the investigation, the prosecution and in carrying out the punishment imposed by means, for example, of mutual legal assistance, extradition, transfer of proceedings or enforcement of sentences passed in another member state'. There is no longer any mention at all of cooperation with the Commission (Article 6).[34]

This minimization of the Commission's proposals ran directly counter to the positions the European Parliament had adopted in March 1995. The net effect was the proposal for a convention having to be withdrawn and the Commission instead having to produce a draft directive on the basis of Articles 100A and 209A of the EC Treaty. The intended directive had to make possible not only clear strengthening of cross-border cooperation but also harmonization of the national penal provisions on fraud. And the proposed regulation was heavily amended by the European Parliament. In Article 11, for example, a new paragraph 6 was introduced stating that the members of the UCLAF are obliged to notify the judicial authorities of the state where they carry out the check or verification of any offence that they have come across in exercising their function, and that their report has the same evidential value as that of the government officials of the state concerned. However, these and other amendments had little or no effect. In the final text of the regulation as eventually adopted on 18 December 1995, there is no mention whatsoever of such obligations and rules of evidence. It merely creates a common judicial framework for the application of administrative measures and sanctions in the event of irregularities in relation to compliance with Community law.[35]

Developments in 1996–97

The policy that was conducted in 1996–97 in relation to the containment of EC fraud can justly be termed a catching-up operation with respect to the policy in 1994–95 – much of what earlier was deemed not feasible was now aimed for and, at least in part, accomplished.

An example of this is Regulation 2185/96 of 11 November 1996 concerning on-the-spot checks and inspections by the Commission with a view to preserving the interests of the EC against fraud and other irregularities. This Regulation, based on Article 10 in the Regulation of 18 December 1995, reflects the principle that the member states themselves are no longer capable of effectively combating serious forms of EC fraud ('which is not confined to one country and frequently involves organized rings', the preamble says) and that this can be done better at the level of the EC. Although it is noted – and this is repeated in as many words in Article 1 – that this regulation does not affect the powers of the member states in relation to the prosecution of offences or the rules applicable to mutual judicial cooperation between them, this does not take away the fact that in this regulation (entirely in line with the draft Regulation which was found in 1994 not to be feasible), the foundation is laid for a special communitarian bureau of investigation in the form of a new-style UCLAF.[36] Article 6 states quite plainly that the on-the-spot checks and inspections shall be carried out on the authority and under the responsibility of the Commission by its own inspectors. According to Article 7, the Commission's inspectors are to have access under the same conditions as national inspectors to all necessary information and documentation relating to the cases they are investigating. In particular, the actions of the UCLAF may include the following: access to official documents, computer data and accountancy documents, and also physical checks, assessments of the status of projects and the taking of samples. If the Commission so requests (Article 7 (2)), the member states are additionally obliged to take appropriate measures with a view to preserving evidence.

The significance of this last obligation becomes clear in Article 8. In the second paragraph of this article a requirement is imposed on the Commission to inform the proper authorities of the state in which it operates of 'any fact or suspicion relating to an irregularity which has come to its notice in the course of the on-the-spot check or inspection'. The third paragraph adds that the reports of its inspectors 'shall constitute admissible evidence in administrative or judicial proceedings of the member state in which their use proves necessary, in the same way and under the same conditions as administrative reports drawn up by national administrative inspectors'. Under this Regulation, the UCLAF can be directly transformed from a coordinating administrative unit to an executive communitarian police body that acts as a bureau of investigation for the judicial authorities in the member states, although it is not in any way under their authority.[37]

Anyone who finds this future projection of the UCLAF exaggerated would do well to read the annual reports and working plans of the Commission on the fight against fraud for the years in question. These documents leave no room for misunderstanding that it is indeed the ambition of the Commission genuinely to build the UCLAF up into an executive communitarian police service that acts both as a central coordinating information service and an operational bureau of investigation. The 1997 annual report, for example, mentions the establishment of a 'criminal law expertise unit'.[38] It is stated in the explanation that the powers granted under Regulation 2185/96 to the employees of the UCLAF 'will lead to an increasing need for judicial follow-up', and that partly for this reason it is important to have a unit which is able 'to have cases speedily referred to the relevant prosecutors and magistrates as well as to identify the factual and legal aspects relating to the cross-border dimension of the proceedings in order to facilitate the coordination of judicial cooperation procedures in real time'. Nor does the Commission make any secret of the fact that the coordinating role which the UCLAF will fulfil in the transnational fight against EC fraud results from its judgement that the existing forms of judicial cooperation are no longer suitable for a decisive approach to this fraud, certainly not in those cases in which organized crime plays a role. This argument is repeated in one annual report after another. It is stated in the 1995 report, for example, that the instruments at the disposal of the member states for cooperating in the area of criminal law against cross-border financial crime are no longer appropriate and that, alongside cooperation and coordination, action at communitarian level is required.[39]

This aim of a communitarian police bureau coincides totally with the *Corpus Iuris* project of the European Parliament and the Commission. This project – launched in 1995 and completed at the beginning of 1997 – is intended finally to give practical form in the field of the fight against EC fraud to the old idea of an *espace judiciaire européen*. Unlike earlier efforts, this time no attempt is made to expand existing judicial cooperation between member states, because this cooperation is now regarded as an obstacle to effective combating of EC fraud through repression. The initiative focuses on the elaboration of a legal and institutional framework for a supranational penal approach to EC fraud

292

that would make intergovernmental efforts unnecessary. The proposal is to create a European Prosecutor's Office that is directed at European level by a European public prosecutor general and in the member states by deputy public prosecutors general who sit in the capitals of their countries. This Prosecutor's Office will be responsible throughout the territory of the EU for the investigation and prosecution of EC fraud offences, which are defined in detail in the text of the proposal. Following this corpus of EC crimes, a listing of procedural rules has been compiled which must be taken into account in the investigation and prosecution of these crimes, anywhere in the EU.[40]

This project is based on two contestable assumptions. The first is that judicial cooperation in the EU works inadequately and, even after expansion, will continue to work inadequately in dealing decisively with serious cases of EC fraud. This is regularly claimed on the side of the Commission and the Parliament, but no in-depth empirical analysis has demonstrated that it is really the case. Indeed, available documents indicate that this is largely an ideological question. The second – equally questionable – assumption is that the organized forms of EC fraud occur on such a large scale that only a supranational criminal justice approach is now equal to the task. The Commission's reports on the fight against EC crime provide insufficient proof of this. This raises several serious doubts about resorting to a supranational approach when less radical, intergovernmental means might still be sufficient. In addition, there are snags in this project that make rapid implementation impossible: who is politically responsible for the actions of this European Prosecutor's Office? What is the authority of this body over the UCLAF and over the national regulator and special police services? The existing text of the proposal does not provide any answers to such fundamental questions. They could also be formulated differently: is this proposal not based on an EU that does not exist at all – a truly federally organized Union?[41]

THE TREATY OF AMSTERDAM AND JUDICIAL COOPERATION

With reference to this question, the *Corpus Iuris* project appears to have little chance because the Treaty of Amsterdam does not offer any scope for the realization of the proposals in this project. Although the position of the European Commission is strengthened in this convention with regard to the organization of the penal fight against EC fraud, there is no mention of a supranational approach to this fight. For the time being member states are strongly in favour of strengthening mechanisms for police and judicial cooperation and a certain degree of institution-alization of cross-border relations between judicial authorities.

The Action Plan to Combat Organized Crime

It was already clear from the action plan to combat organized crime adopted by the European Council in 1997 that the Treaty of Amsterdam would not, even in the fight against organized or financial crime, lead to the construction of the Union that the European Commission and the European Parliament want.[42] This plan made no mention of the need for European criminal law, the establishment of a European Prosecutor's Office or of the transformation of the UCLAF into a communitarian bureau of investigation. What, then, are the lines of force in this plan with regard to judicial cooperation in the European Union?

First, it stated that, by the end of 1998, all the member states must not only have ratified the conventions of the Council of Europe discussed above but also the EU conventions identified previously. It also emphatically stated that the draft Convention on Mutual Legal Assistance must be completed as quickly as possible.

Second, the basic principle that judicial cooperation must be brought up to the same level as police cooperation in the EU is formulated. For those who have drawn up the plan this means the creation of a network for judicial cooperation with ties between the central contact points that would be set up and made responsible for the exchange of information between national judicial authorities. It was recognized, however, that further thought should be given to the specific terms of reference of this network and that it would have to be manned by 'practitioners having extensive practical experience in fighting organized crime'. In addition, an in-depth study would have to be conducted on 'the place and the role of judicial authorities in their relations with Europol', chiefly in connection with the expansion of the powers of this bureau; and 'whether it should in the long term be transformed into a more permanent structure, which could become an important interlocutor of Europol'.

Third, it is regarded as self-evident that the member states regularly consult the competent services of the Commission on both specific cases of EC fraud and on the *modi operandi*. But it is added succinctly here that 'if necessary, additional mechanisms shall be put in place with a view to arranging such consultations on a regular basis. In this context,

294

future relations between Europol and the Commission's anti-fraud unit (UCLAF) should be taken into account'.

It is clear, therefore, that this action plan offers no scope for the realization of any important component part of the *Corpus Iuris* project. The penal fight against organized crime is still regarded as a primary responsibility of the member states, in themselves and jointly in the Third Pillar. It is significant that the emphasis is not so much on police cooperation (and this is no longer necessary now that the Europol Convention has been ratified by all member states) but on judicial cooperation. Its cautious institutionalization is evidently regarded as a necessity now that the instruments for cooperation are expanding and Europol will have what are referred to as operational powers at its disposal.[43]

The Text of the Treaty

The extent to which the action plan foreshadowed the Treaty of Amsterdam in terms of content is clearly apparent from the text of this Treaty, especially with regard to the strengthening of judicial cooperation.[44] This form of cooperation, like police cooperation, is dealt with in the revised Title VI of the EU Treaty, which is now purely and simply devoted to police and judicial cooperation in criminal matters. Article 31 contains a non-exhaustive enumeration of topics counted as being related to judicial cooperation:

- the promotion of cooperation between competent ministries and judicial authorities with regard to procedures and the implementation of decisions;
- the simplification of extradition between member states;
- making the legislation in member states compatible insofar as this may be necessary with a view to judicial cooperation;
- the avoidance of conflicts of jurisdiction between member states; and
- the acceptance of measures by which minima are stipulated with regard to the essential constituents of criminal acts and of punishments in the area of organized crime, terrorism and illegal trafficking in drugs.

This enumeration of topics in fact parallels the intentions specified in the action plan: harmonization of legislation, ratification of agreements and institutionalization of cooperation. The last item ties in with the provision in Article 30,2,c that in close cooperation with

Europol the relations between police and prosecutors specializing in the fight against organized crime must be promoted. There is, therefore, no mention of an arrangement for one or other form of judicial control over Europol. Furthermore, Article 32 explicitly obliges the Council to draw up an arrangement for the action of judicial (and other) authorities on the territory of another member state with the consent of the authorities in that state.

With specific reference to the organization of the fight against EC fraud, the new Title VI of the EU Treaty explicitly does not contain any provisions of direct relevance to this problem. A relatively significant point, however, is that under Article 34,2 the Council can employ all kinds of (new) instruments to promote cooperation for the sake of the security of the citizens no longer purely on the initiative of a member state but also on the initiative of the Commission: joint positions, framework decisions, decisions and agreements. This means that the Commission now has slightly more scope in attempting to improve the fight against EC fraud according to its own understanding.

On the other hand, it would be wrong in this connection to disregard the new Article 280 (replacing 209A) of the EC Treaty. The first paragraph now states, far more emphatically than in the old article, that not just the member states themselves but the Community as such has a duty to combat EC fraud and other irregularities that affect the financial interests of the Community in an effective and deterrent manner. This is embroidered in the third paragraph: the member states shall mutually coordinate their actions in this regard and, in cooperation with the Commission, organize closer cooperation between the competent authorities. The fourth paragraph adds that the Council, on the proposal of the Commission and in consultation with the Parliament and the Court of Auditors, in order to prevent and combat EC fraud will take measures necessary to protect the financial interests of the Community in the member states. It is explicitly noted that these measures 'shall not concern the application of national criminal law or the national administration of justice'. It is not so clear what this precisely means for judicial cooperation in the EU. It may be very important in order to combat EC fraud effectively to intensify this form of cooperation, but is it not in Title VI that initiatives for this purpose must be taken? Or must thinking in terms of separate 'Pillars' (First and Third Pillar) not be regarded in this area as outmoded and must the possible overlapping of powers between Article 280 of the EC

Treaty and Article 34 of the EU Treaty be viewed as an opportunity to develop a 'pillar-wide' anti-fraud policy? However that may be, Article 280 does not offer scope for the development of European mini-criminal law and a European Prosecutor's Office, because putting this into effect would be contrary not just to the third paragraph of Article 280 but to the fourth paragraph as well.[45]

The Implementation of the Action Plan

Although implementing the Treaty of Amsterdam requires prior ratification by all the member states, this Treaty is already casting shadows through the implementation of the action plan to combat organized crime. It is not precisely known at present how far the ratification of the various conventions (extradition, protection of financial interests) by the member states has advanced – apart from the Europol Convention, which has been completed – but the number of member states ratifying them, according to internal reports, has increased. The draft of the Convention on Mutual Assistance was more or less ready but had not been published by September 1998.[46] A joint action was also in preparation to improve and speed up the execution of letters rogatory (item 16 of the action plan). The relevant proposals contain among other things an improvement in communication between the authorities concerned, appropriate prioritization for requests for mutual legal assistance and a duty to submit an annual report on the provision of mutual legal assistance.[47]

There is also a proposal for a joint action with a view to the establishment of the judicial network. This proposal contains provisions relating to the composition of the network ('central authorities responsible for international judicial cooperation and the judicial and other competent authorities with specific responsibilities within the context of international cooperation'), the tasks of the national contact points ('facilitating judicial cooperation', 'coordination of judicial cooperation', 'legal and practical information'), their contact meetings, and mutual telecommunications links.[48]

Third, reference can be made here to the Falcone programme, which the Council adopted for the period 1997–2001 and which was intended in particular to promote the action plan by updating the knowledge of prosecutors, judges, police officers and so on in, all kinds of ways: training, joint study projects, exchange of information, work experience placements, etc.[49] Although this was not being implemented as quickly on all points – including judicial assistance – as those who drew it up had hoped, some progress is certainly being made.

CONCLUSIONS

The difference between the First Pillar and the Third Pillar is in fact no more than a distinction. Institutionally, procedurally and functionally the two pillars form part of the same political construction: the European Union. The unbreakable link that exists between the First and Third Pillars is also expressed very well in the anti-EC-fraud policy; this policy is conducted both using instruments (regulations) that belong in the First Pillar and those specific to the Third Pillar (conventions). On the other hand, there are tensions and conflicts between the two pillars, particularly between the different institutions and member states that have a say in these pillars. The discussion on the question of whether (judicial) cooperation within the Third Pillar with regard to combating organized crime, particularly EC fraud, must be replaced or supplemented by a communitarian approach to the relevant problems is an outstanding illustration of this.

As far as the development of judicial cooperation in the EC and the EU is concerned, not much progress was actually achieved until the mid-1990s. Initiatives were taken to modernize this cooperation in supplementing the basic conventions of the Council of Europe from the 1950s, but these (with the exception of the Convention applying the Schengen Agreement) did not bear any fruit. Since 1995, however, there has been more impetus, and judicial cooperation appears to have been boosted as much as police cooperation. Not only have important mutual assistance conventions been signed or are in preparation in the context of the Third Pillar, but work is finally also being done on building up a network to substantially improve the application of the conventions. Some 20 years after it was first mentioned, the *espace judiciaire et policier européen* is finally becoming reality – at least if the member states keep to the agreements laid down in the action plan to combat organized crime and, following ratification of the Europol Convention, now also ratify the conventions with a judicial element.

It is important that their ratification is completed within the foreseeable future, because otherwise the idea that organized crime in the EU can only be effectively controlled through communitarization of the administration of justice (starting with the combating of EC fraud through the UCLAF in cooperation with a European Prosecutor's Office) will be nurtured again. The position here is that such a radical supranational approach should only be employed if it has both been clearly demonstrated that the problem of organized (economic and financial) crime is really so serious that a communitarian approach is called for and that intergovernmental, judicial (and police) cooperation, despite improvements, is no longer really suitable for bringing and keeping this crime under control.

In addition, it was indicated that a choice in favour of communitarization of the penal fight against organized crime must also not be made too hastily for other reasons. First of all, however, clarity will have to be created on how communitarian criminal justice bodies fit into both the constitutional construction of the EU and how it fits into the organization of criminal justice in the member states; if not, state actions will be a source of immense problems, both structurally between institutions and operationally in specific investigations.[50]

Second, it is necessary to assess to what extent the build-up of a communitarian criminal law system with the bodies mentioned might not be at the expense of the preventive combating of organized crime, including at communitarian level, by the Commission, using supervision and control. The Commission's fixation (strengthened in this regard by a Parliament bent on acquiring more power) with having its own criminal justice apparatus is already causing it to lose sight of the fact that its first and primary task lies in the sphere of prevention.

Third, a solution must first be found to the smouldering conflict between the Commission/UCLAF on the one hand and the member states/Europol on the other, especially now that the UCLAF no longer counts the combating of EC fraud as its sole task. With Europol having operational powers at its disposal the integration of UCLAF and its repressive functions into Europol is a natural step.

NOTES

1. C. Fijnaut, 'Empirical criminological research on organised crime: the state of affairs in Europe', in *L'évolution de la criminalité organisée* (Paris: La Documentation Française, 1996), pp.47–60.
2. The following is based on C. Fijnaut, 'Georganiseerde misdaad: echt een bedreiging voor de Europese Unie?', in B. Raymaekers and A. van de Putte (eds.), *Denken voor Morgen; Lessen voor de Eenentwintigste Eeuw* (Leuven: Universitaire Pers Leuven, 1998), pp.165–85.
3. European Commission, *Protection of the Financial Interests of the Communities; Fight Against Fraud; Annual Report 1997* (Brussels: COM, 1998) 276 final, pp.13–14. See also European Parliament, Committee of Inquiry into the Community Transit System, *Final Report and Recommendations* (Brussels, 1997), pp.55–75 (A4-0053/97-PE220.895/FIN).

4. Bundeskriminalamt, *Lagebild Organisierte Kriminalität Bundesrepublik Deutschland 1997* (Wiesbaden 1998); *Georganiseerde Criminaliteit in België in 1996* (Brussels, 1997).
5. European Court of Auditors, *Speciaal Verslag nr. 8/98 over de Diensten van de Commissie die Specifiek zijn Betrokken bij de Fraudebestrijding, met name de 'Unité de Coordination de la Lutte Anti-fraude' (UCLAF), Vergezeld van de Antwoorden van de Commissie* (PB, 22-7-1998, C230/1-C230/44).
6. See C. Fijnaut, 'De mobiliteit van daders en de internationale strafrechtelijke samenwerking in de Europese Unie: een schets van het probleem' (unpublished).
7. C. Fijnaut, 'Nieuwsbrief uit voormalig Nieuw Amsterdam', in D.W. Steenhuis *et al.* (eds.), *Greep op de Misdaad* (Den Haag: Openbaar Ministerie, 1997), pp.74-83. As far as Amsterdam is concerned, reference has to be made to *De Bestuurlijke Aanpak van de (Georganiseerde) Misdaad in Amsterdam; de Ontwikkeling van een Effectief Instrumentarium* (Amsterdam, 1998).
8. It is indeed remarkable that far more empirical research has been done on international police cooperation than with respect to international judicial cooperation. Compare G. Vermeulen, T. van der Beken, P. Zanders and B. de Ruyver, *Internationale Samenwerking in Strafzaken en Rechtsbescherming* (Brussels: Politeia, 1995), pp.91-102.
9. European Commission, *The Commission's Anti-fraud Strategy; Work Programme for 1994* (Luxemburg: Bureau voor Officiële Publicaties, 1994).
10. The text of these and other Treaties is included in Ch. Van den Wyngaert and G. Stessens (eds.), *International Criminal Law; A Collection of International and European Instruments* (The Hague: Kluwer Law International, 1996). See also D. Schröder, 'Polizeirelevante Formen der Zusammenarbeit im Rahmen des Europarats', *Die Polizei*, No.1 (1998), pp.56-62.
11. H.-J. Bartsch, 'The Western European Approach', *International Review of Penal Law*, Vol.62, Nos.1-2 (1991), pp.499-510.
12. P. Wilkitzky, 'Development of an effective international crime and justice programme - a European view', in A. Eser and O. Lagodny (eds.), *Principles and Procedures for a New Transnational Criminal Law* (Freiburg i.B.: Max Planck Institute for Foreign and International Criminal Law, 1992), pp.267-91. Also J. Schutte, 'Europese samenwerking inzake justitie en veiligheid', *Panopticon*, Vol.13, No.6 (1992), pp.534-7.
13. C. Fijnaut, 'De criminele politiek in de Europese Gemeenschap', *Panopticon*, Vol.13, No.6 (1992), pp.572-89.
14. W. Schomburg, 'Problems arising in connection with extradition in Europe in the process of growing together', *International Review of Penal Law*, Vol.62, Nos.1-2 (1991), pp.511-14. However, Schomburg was not alone in heavily criticizing the existing situation. Particularly in Germany, many authors pinpointed the problems in the field of judicial cooperation with respect to the fight against organized crime. See, among others, S. Heitmann, 'Grenzüberschreitende Zusammenarbeit im justiziellen Bereich', *Die Polizei*, No.6 (1993), pp.154-8; R.A. Martin, 'Dual criminality in organized crime cases', *International Review of Penal Law*, Vol.62, Nos.1-2 (1991), pp.175-81; Th. Vogler, 'The rule of specialty in extradition law', *International Review of Penal Law*, Vol.62, Nos.1-2 (1991), pp.231-47; Th. Diallo, 'L'entraide répressive internationale en matière pénale: esquisse d'une problématique', *Revue de Science Criminelle et de Droit Pénal Comparé*, No.3 (1992), pp.541-52.
15. C. Fijnaut, 'Naar een "Gemeenschappelijke" regeling van de politiële samenwerking en de justitiële rechtshulp', in C. Fijnaut, J. Stuyck and P. Wytinck (eds.), *Schengen: proeftuin voor de Europese Gemeenschap?* (Antwerp-Arnhem: Kluwer Rechtswetenschappen-Gouda Quint, 1992), pp.89-117.
16. Ch. Van den Wyngaert and G. Stessens, 'Mutual legal assistance in criminal matters in the European Union', in C. Fijnaut *et al.* (eds.), *Changes in Society, Crime and Criminal Justice in Europe* (Antwerp: Kluwer Rechtswetenschappen/Kluwer Law International, 1995), Vol.II, pp.137-79.
17. A. Mulder, 'Europees strafrecht; het verslag van een trieste geschiedenis', *Sociaal Economische Wetgeving*, Vol.27 (1979), pp.466-8; E. Packe, *Der Schutz der finanziellen Interessen der Europäischen Gemeinschaften* (Berlin: Duncker & Humblot, 1994).

18. *Official Journal of the European Union* [hereafter *Official Journal*], Pb, 22-9-1976, C222/2-222/17.
19. Ch. Van den Wyngaert, 'De internationale strafrechtelijke samenwerking bij de bestrijding van de E.FOR EXAMPLE-fraude', *Rechtskundig Weekblad*, Vol.56, No.13 (1991-2), pp.417-24.
20. See Wilkitzky, op. cit.
21. For the actual ratification rate, see Van den Wyngaert and Stessens, op. cit., pp.177-9, and W. Schomburg and O. Lagodny (eds.), *Internationale Rechtshilfe in Strafsachen* (München: C.H. Beck'sche Verlagsbuchhandlung, 1998), pp.767-910.
22. Compare S. Oschinsky and P. Jenard, *L'espace juridique et judiciaire européen* (Bruxelles: Bruylant, 1993).
23. M. Bonn, 'Judicial cooperation under Title VI EU: a first assessment in the light of practical experiences', in R. Bieber and J. Monar (eds.), *Justice and Home Affairs in the European Union: The Development of the Third Pillar* (Brussels: European Interuniversity Press, 1995), pp.211-6; D. Flore and R. Troosters, 'Maastricht in beweging; enkele bedenkingen na het Belgisch Voorzitterschap van de Europese Unie', *Panopticon*, Vol.14, No.4 (1994), pp.301-22; Council of the European Union, *Resolution of 14 October 1996 Laying Down the Priorities for Cooperation in the Field of Justice and Home Affairs for the Period from 1 July 1996 to 30 June 1998, Official Journal*, 26-10-1996, C319/1-319/6.
24. The named conventions have been published in *Official Journal*, 27-11-1995, C316/2-316/32; 30-3-1995, C78/1-78/5; 23-10-1996, C313/11-313/23.
25. See *Official Journal*, 27-4-1996, L105/1-105/2; 29-10-1996, L268/2-268/4.
26. Compare D.M. Curtin and J.F.M. Pouw, 'La coopération dans le domaine de la justice et des affaires intérieures au sein de l'Union européenne: une nostalgie d'avant Maastricht', *Revue du Marché Unique Européen*, No.3 (1995), pp.13-34; P.-Ch. Müller-Graf, 'The legal bases of the Third Pillar and its position in the framework of the Union Treaty', *Common Market Law Review*, Vol.31 (1994), pp.493-510; D. O'Keeffe, 'Recasting the Third Pillar', *Common Market Law Review*, Vol.32 (1995), pp.893-920.
27. See G. de Kerchove, 'Les progrès des groupes de travail du troisième pillier en matière de coopération judiciaire', in M. den Boer (ed.), *Schengen, Judicial Cooperation and Policy Coordination* (Maastricht: European Institute of Public Administration, 1997), pp.101-14; J.A. Fortescue, 'First experiences with the implementation of the Third Pillar provisions', in Bieber and Monar, op. cit., pp.19-27; B. Knudsen, 'La fraude au détriment du budget de la Communauté', *Revue de Science Criminelle et de Droit Pénal Comparé*, No.1 (1995), pp.65-74; H. Labayle, 'L'application du titre VI, du Traité sur l'Union européenne et la matière pénale', *Revue de Science Criminelle et de Droit Pénal Comparé*, No.1 (1995), pp.35-64; M. Lepoivre, 'Le domaine de la justice et des affaires intérieures dans la perspective de la conférence intergouvernementale de 1996', *Cahiers de Droit Européen*, Vol.31, Nos.3-4 (1995), pp.323-43; J. Lipsius, 'La conférence intergouvernementale de 1996', *Revue Trimestrielle de Droit Européen*, Vol.31, No.2 (1995), pp.175-206; A. Lo Monaco, 'Les instruments juridiques de coopération dans les domaines de la justice et des affaires intérieures', *Revue de Science Criminelle et de Droit Pénal Comparé*, No.1 (1995), pp.11-21.
28. These comments are based upon the draft of 3 March 1998, No.6414/98, Justpen 27.
29. C. Fijnaut, 'International policing in Europe: its present situation and future', in J.-P. Brodeur (ed.), *Comparisons in Policing: an International Perspective* (Aldershot: Avebury, 1995), pp.115-34.
30. Compare J. Vogel, *Combating International Organized Crime by International Cooperation: the German View* (Freiburg, 1998). See also G. Vermeulen and T. Van der Beken, 'Extradition in the European Union: state of the art and perspectives', *European Journal of Crime, Criminal Law and Criminal Justice*, Vol.4, No.3 (1996), pp.200-25.
31. See note 10.
32. These proposals were published on 15 June 1994 in Commission (94) 214 final.
33. Council Resolution of 6 December 1994 on the legal protection of the financial interests of the communities, *Official Journal*, 14-14-1994, C355/2.
34. See *Official Journal*, 27-11-1995, C316/48-316/52.

35. See European Parliament, *Verslag over het Voorstel voor een Besluit van de Raad van de Europese Unie tot Opstelling van het Verdrag Betreffende de Bescherming van de Financiële Belangen van de Gemeenschappen* (rapporteur: R. Bontempi, A4-0039/95, PE 210.527/def.), and European Parliament, *Verslag over het Voorstel voor een Verordening (EG, Euratom) van de Raad Inzake de Bescherming van de Financiële Belangen van de Gemeenschap* (rapporteur: D. Theato, A4-0040/95, PE 211.096/def.). The relevant regulation dates from 18 Dec. 1995 and was published in Pb, 23-12-1995, L312/1-312/4. Concerning these problems, see L. Kuhl, 'The criminal law protection of the Communities' financial interests against fraud', *Criminal Law Review* (1998), pp.259–69, 323–31.

36. This regulation has been published in *Official Journal*, 15-11-1996, L292/2-292/5.

37. A highly critical article on this development has been written by U. Nelles, 'Europäisierung des Strafverfahrens-Strafprozessrecht für Europa?', *Zeitschrift für die gesamte Strafrechtswissenschaft*, Vol.109, No.4 (1997), pp.727–55.

38. European Commission, *Protection of the Financial Interests of the Communities; Fight against Fraud; Annual Report 1997*, op. cit., p.35.

39. European Commission, *Protection of the Financial Interests of the Communities; Fight against Fraud; Annual Report 1995* (Brussels: COM 1996), 173 final, pp.18–19.

40. M. Delmas-Marty (ed.), *Corpus Juris; Introducing Penal Provisions for the Purpose of the Financial Interests of the European Union* (Paris: Economica, 1997).

41. C. Fijnaut and F. Verbruggen, 'The eagle has not landed yet; the federalization of criminal investigation: precedents and comparisons', in M. den Boer (ed.), *Undercover Policing and Accountability from an International Perspective* (Maastricht: European Institute of Public Administration, 1997), pp.129–42.

42. See *Official Journal*, 15-8-1997, C251/1-251/18.

43. Europol advocates the reinforcement of its relationship with the judicial network. See W. Bruggeman, 'A castle or a house of cards', in A. Pauly (ed.), *De Schengen à Maastricht: voie royale et course d'obstacles* (Maastricht: European Institute of Public Administration, 1996), pp.17–32.

44. The Treaty has been published in *Official Journal*, 10-11-1997, C340/1-340/144.

45. For some comments on the new-style Third Pillar, see J.P.H. Donner, 'De derde pijler en de Amsterdamse doolhof', *Sociaal-economische Wetgeving*, Vol.47, No.10 (1997), pp.370–8; H. Bribosia, 'Liberté, sécurité et justice: l'imbroglio d'un nouvel espace', *Revue du Marché Unique Européen*, No.1 (1998), pp.27–54; S. Glesz and M. Lüke, 'Strafverfolgung über die Grenzen hinweg', *Jura*, No.2 (1998), pp.70–9; A. Klip, 'Amsterdams uniestrafrecht', *Nederlands Juristenblad*, Vol.73, No.18 (1998), pp.811–6; J. Monar, 'Schengen and flexibility in the Treaty of Amsterdam: opportunities and risks of differentiated integration in EU Justice and Home Affairs', in M. den Boer (ed.), *Schengen, Judicial Cooperation and Policy Coordination* (Maastricht: European Institute of Public Administration, 1997), pp.9–28; G. Soulier, 'Le Traité d'Amsterdam et la coopération policière et judiciaire en matière pénale', *Revue de Science Criminelle et de Droit Pénal Comparé*, No.2 (1998), pp.237–54.

46. See note 28.

47. European Council, *Draft Joint Action on Good Practice in Mutual Legal Assistance in Criminal Matters*, 10-12-1997, Crimorg 33.

48. European Council, *Proposal for a Joint Action to Create a European Judicial Network*, 14-10-1997, Crimorg 1.

49. See *Official Journal*, 30-05-1998, C165.

50. On the actual constitutional profile of the European Union, see K. Lenaerts, 'Federalism: essential concepts in evolution; the case of the European Union', *Fordham International Law Journal*, Vol.21, No.3 (1998), pp.746–98.

Responding to Transnational Crime – the Role of Europol

EMANUELE MAROTTA

CHALLENGE AND RESPONSE

The response to international crime involves two aspects that could also be defined as 'phases', differing in their conception but closely related to each other: the perception and precise evaluation of the criminal phenomenon; and the development of the necessary means – institutions, procedures, people, resources, technologies – to combat this phenomenon. This paper will try to respect this distinction. It first seeks to identify, in their essentials, the character of the new challenges presented by international organized crime. It then focuses mainly on the situation in the EU countries, with particular emphasis on the role, competencies and the activity of Europol.

When referring to 'new' challenges posed by organized crime, there are at least three different aspects relating to the criminal attack on our society:

- novel elements in criminal behaviour often in relation to the use of new technologies;
- the spread of the criminal environment to new fields of activity;
- a better understanding and assessment of already existing criminal phenomena, that have been investigated and revealed more fully than in the past.

All three are examined below.

The first development is criminal exploitation of new information technologies and the great opportunities stemming from the extraordinary developments in the means of communication and transportation. The already common use of advanced technology by internationally acting criminal groups is only likely to expand thanks to the possibilities that new communication media – such as the Internet and mobile cell phones, pagers and other electronic equipment – have to offer in the fast and secure exchange of information, not to mention the ever-increasing possibilities of using these capabilities to commit crimes. For communications, criminal organizations not only use Internet Conferencing Software, such as Microsoft NetMeeting or Netscape's Cool Talk, but also use much more powerful software, such as ICQ, which can be easily downloaded from the Internet. In one European country organized criminals even recruited young, unscrupulous programmers to follow the data transfer of police officers via Eurosignal to discover and draw moving pictures of the police in order to set up counter-surveillance. Another important area being exploited by organized criminals is encryption. The result is that police can only obtain information about the connections, junctions and nodes, but not about the content of communications.

In 1998 there were on the Internet approximately 40 million computers, 60,000 Intranets and more than 100 million users, with a growth rate of 100 per cent per year. This offers organized crime, in Europe and worldwide, new means and new media for their activities, mainly in fields such as child pornography, drug trafficking, money laundering, gambling, prostitution and even weapons trade. The tools of the technological revolution have not escaped the criminal cartels. Indeed, high-tech protection established by law enforcement agencies, security services, banks and private industry is no longer a defence against crime syndicates who are hiring young hackers and 'phreakers' (telecommunications experts) to do their technical work.

The second important development concerns the criminal spread to new fields of activity. In this connection, it is essential to consider that criminal organizations have a simple principle – 'business is business'. Where it is easy and safe to gain more money (or more economic or political power, that in the end is the same thing) that is where crime settles. Such a diffusion is clearly intended both geographically – this explains certain new criminal settlements, mostly ethnic in character – and in relation to new areas of the economy or society in general. The infiltration of organized crime into legitimate sectors of finance or business, and the criminal management of social phenomena, such as the organization and exploitation of illegal immigration, are good examples of this criminal diversification of business.

The third aspect of the notion of a 'new' challenge is linked to our new perception and understanding of criminal phenomena that previously were hidden but are now more obvious. Among the factors that have contributed to enhanced 'visibility' are:

- improved exchange of information among law enforcement agencies;
- more sophisticated cognitive and investigative tools, such as criminal analysis software, now available to the competent authorities;
- greater attention by the academic research community and the media to criminal phenomena; and, unfortunately
- greater violence and greater bullying by organized crime, that does not hesitate to use violent and spectacular means to impose its threatening presence.

THE THREAT TO THE EUROPEAN UNION

It is appropriate at this point to focus on the principal characteristics and dimension of the threat to the European Union currently posed by organized crime.

Drug Trafficking

The EU ranks drug trafficking as the type of activity most attractive to domestic and ethnic organized crime groups. A wide variety of such groups operating from both inside and outside member states is active in this area of crime. Ethnic Albanian, Nigerian and other West African groups, groups from the former Yugoslavia, Moroccan, Chinese, Central and Eastern European, Russian, Pakistani, Turkish, Colombian and other groups including those composed of EU nationals have all found niches in the market.

The importation and distribution of drugs is, as a rule, undertaken by domestic criminal groups, although wholesale drug trafficking is often also closely linked to ethnic crime groups who have their origin in the drug producing and transit areas. Street distribution levels are generally less clearly linked to particular ethnic or domestic crime groups.

Turkish organized crime groups use the Balkan route to import these drugs into the EU and almost exclusively control the trafficking of heroin. Since the political changes of the recent past, Central and Eastern European countries are increasingly used by criminal organizations as warehouses where large quantities of drugs –

particularly heroin – can be safely held for as long as needed. The drugs can be transported from there in smaller quantities to the target areas at any given moment.

Cocaine is traditionally trafficked by Latin American criminal groups, in particular Colombian. The drug is smuggled into the EU both through couriers – who include EU nationals – and concealed in freight. Germany, the Netherlands, the UK and Belgium are attractive to Latin American cocaine traffickers because of their harbours, Spain and Portugal because of their historical and linguistic links.

The EU has become one of the world's major production regions of amphetamine and ecstasy-type stimulants. Over the last few years, clandestine laboratories – ranging from simple 'kitchens' to professional laboratories – have been detected in nearly all member states. Some have the capacity to produce up to a million pills a day; some are mobile; and yet others are abandoned every few weeks in order to avoid detection by law enforcement agencies. The abuse of synthetic drugs, in particular ecstasy, has increased dramatically in the member states perhaps owing to their 'trendy' image as a dance or love drug and their ready availability. It is clear that there is a constant intra-EU trafficking in these substances and that suppliers exploit the younger generation. Increased publicity in some member states surrounding the deaths of youngsters has heightened the awareness of the dangers, but the popularity of these drugs does not seem to have diminished. The profits to be made in this business are enormous, although prices are dropping, possibly owing to abundant supplies.

Morocco still is the major supplier of cannabis (resin) products destined for the EU market, together with South American and Asian countries. Herbal cannabis originates mainly from South American countries, particularly Colombia and Surinam. The prominent role the Netherlands used to have in artificially cultivated cannabis is appearing to be partly taken over by other member states. The UK and Germany are believed to be the second largest producers after the Netherlands.

There are no signs of a decline in global production of, and trafficking in, illicit drugs and this must affect the EU. To a large degree geographical, cultural, historic and economic factors, such as highly developed international trade and transportation systems, are exploited by criminal organizations, thus influencing the role played by individual member states in providing points of entry or facilitating the transit of drugs.

Fraud

Fraudulent activities are mainly the preserve of domestic crime groups. Italian organized crime groups such as the Mafia, Camorra, 'Ndrangheta and Sacra Corona Unita of Apulia are all heavily involved in fraudulent activities. Particular concerns are organized crime groups obtaining and diverting EU money – which is originally intended for the support of economically weak areas – to their use and benefit, and the misuse of the EU budget for agriculture as a major area of fraudulent activities. The involvement of Asian and Nigerian groups in fraudulent activities impacting upon the UK and other member states, however, indicates that fraud is by no means an exclusively domestic activity.

Organized credit card fraud is developing dangerous dimensions in Europe and worldwide, which could result in a radical change of trade and business habits. There was a period during which credit cards were secure using the 'Card Verification Code' and the production of counterfeits had been reduced. Now the offenders can easily copy the magnetic file (skimming). The technical equipment can be purchased in any specialist shop and via the Internet anyone can download hacker programs ('Wizard' or 'credit master'), which allow the registration number of the credit card to be generated.

Extortion

Extortion is one of the crimes used by criminal organizations either to defend and control their territory or to gain huge profits. In EU member states, the use of – in some cases lethal – violence in extortion is primarily associated with Asian criminal groups and criminal groups of Turkish, Russian and Yugoslav origins. The victims are primarily local entrepreneurs, their family, personnel, guests and property. In many countries Chinese criminal organizations have been active in extorting their compatriots and EU member states often face the phenomenon of Asian restaurant owners being forced to employ illegal immigrants. For their part, Scandinavian motorcycle gangs are suspected of 'profiting' from other criminal groups that are being forced to pay fees on their criminal activities.

Organized Illegal Immigration and Trafficking in Human Beings

Most member states are at the same time both transit and destination country for organized illegal immigration and trafficking in human beings. Moreover, this phenomenon is likely to continue. Given the way in which immigration into the EU has evolved over the recent past, and an evaluation of the reasons that induce the present mass migration, there is no reason to believe that the flow of immigrants into the EU will diminish or even stabilize in the near future. Germany, Italy and other countries face considerable activities by criminal organizations in the area of organized clandestine immigration of Turkish, Iranian and Iraqi, as well as of Albanian, nationals whereas France and Spain suffer from organized clandestine immigration of people from Africa and South America. Clandestine immigration via the Balkan route imposes a problem on the majority of member states. On this Balkan route, Turkish and Kurdish immigrants are smuggled into the EU by Turkish and non-Turkish networks alike. But clandestine immigration networks are normally not limited to a specific ethnic group. So, Turkish clandestine immigration networks smuggle non-Turkish immigrants as well. Travel routes, choice of transport means and *modus operandi* do not seem to differ greatly between the different networks.

Clandestine immigration and trafficking in human beings by criminal groups are closely associated with exploitation of prostitutes and minors. Criminal organizations active in the field of the trafficking in human beings are often suspected of a range of facilitating or related criminal activities such as the use of violence, illegal arms trade, drugs and the forgery of documents. Traffickers in human beings are – apart from looking for prospects in all traditional Asian, South American and African source countries – particularly targeting central and East European countries such as Poland, Russia, Ukraine, Hungary and the Czech Republic for recruitment of prostitutes. The *modus operandi* of such criminal groups consists of luring women from the former Eastern Bloc countries into full dependency by making false promises about work and economic prosperity. Russian and Albanian organized crime groups have established links with EU-based organized crime groups to exploit women working as prostitutes in EU member states.

Money Laundering

Closely associated with drug trafficking and other profitable forms of crime such as fraud, illegal firearms trading and the exploitation of prostitution, is the laundering of illicit funds. Most popular facilitators used in money laundering cases proved to be currency exchange offices and banks, but it also became apparent that other legal entities and commercial structures are misused to hide the origins of money. The misuse of commercial structures includes the use of front companies without any legal commercial activities.

To prevent the financial industry within the EU from being involved in money laundering practices, the EC issued a Directive obliging credit and financial institutions in the member states to notify so-called suspicious transactions to the competent authorities. This forced criminals to bring their cash to those states where controls were less severe or non-existent, or where financial services were delivered by offices or institutions (such as Bureaux de Change) that were not brought within the scope of this Directive. This also resulted in the transportation of large amounts of cash by air. Now, in all member states, Bureaux de Change fall under the anti-money laundering legislation and in 13 of the 15 member states they can be controlled in the same way as the banks. To hamper the criminals bringing their cash cross-border, the Financial Action Task Force (FATF) advised countries to implement measures to detect or monitor the physical cross-border transportation of cash by land, by air and by sea without impeding in any way the freedom of capital movements.

Russian Organized Crime

Besides the typical ethnic-based organized crime mentioned above, several EU member states consider Russian organized crime as an important, if still emerging, factor in their national organized crime environments. The most serious crime category facing the Russian Federation is that of economic crime and money laundering, with a proportional impact upon the European Union. Since 1992 the greatest single long-term threat collectively facing the European Union has been the amount and flow of criminal funds originating from Central and Eastern Europe, particularly the Russian Federation. A further intensification in the flow and amount of such funds was perceived in 1995. Initially the areas nearest the borders of Central and Eastern Europe were particularly affected, as was Austria. Over the following three years, however, Portugal, Spain and Italy increasingly noted laundering of criminal monies emanating from the Russian Federation, while Austrian financial authorities have witnessed a huge increase during this same period.

Estimates of the amount of capital flight and laundered criminal funds vary; at one stage in 1994 the estimated amount of laundered funds stood at U$1 billion per month. In the mid-1990s the annual amounts were calculated to be between US$8 and US$12 billion per year. From 1996 to 1998 the overall crime rates in Russia have shown either a small rise or, during some periods, an overall fall; running directly contrary to such trends is the extreme rise in economic crime and money laundering. This is due, within Russia, to three overall trends as result of developments during the mid-1990s. These are:

- A sudden increase in heroin production within the Central Asian Republics of the former Soviet Union during the period 1995–97. This resulted in a massive inflow of heroin directly into the Russian Federation, generating further criminal funds that ultimately are being laundered abroad.
- Accompanying the illicit movement of monies from the Russian Federation has been a steady shortfall in taxation returns. Being deprived on a yearly basis of the full, necessary taxation yield must, in the long-term, call into question the effectiveness of crime control within the Russian Federation.
- Political and economic developments within the Asiatic and Far Eastern regions of the Russian Federation during the same period further resulted in the diminishing of central government control and anti-crime measures, and made certain sectors of the regional economies vulnerable to criminal investment.

Observers have also perceived an increase in organized prostitution from the Russian Federation in several member states, particularly Germany, Austria, the Netherlands and certain areas of the UK. Such an increase has been accompanied by the laundering of illicit assets within some of these member states. From 1996 onwards more evidence came to light from cases indicating increasing involvement of Russian criminal groups in laundering of large-scale criminal funds into the EU. Trends in Russian organized crime groups include the increasing evidence of cooperation, on an *ad hoc* basis, of organized crime groups in individual member states and Russian organized crime groups in dual criminal ventures, particularly those of money-laundering and prostitution, with Italian groups.

These activities, trends and developments represent only a few select aspects of the challenge posed by organized crime. Nevertheless, they provide a useful basis on which to base the discussion of responses.

THE EU RESPONSE

The fundamental conclusion from this description of the criminal threat appears to be the increasingly international character of the more worrying forms of crime. The appropriate reaction to such a threat cannot be based solely on the resources of an individual state. In the fight against crime the keyword is cooperation, at governmental level and at the level of law enforcement agencies. The establishment of a European Police Office – Europol – is the European Union's answer to organized crime. It is a milestone in the effort to strengthen law enforcement cooperation in a Europe without frontiers.

The real Europol began its operation on 1 October 1998, according to the rules laid down by the Europol Convention signed on 26 July 1995. Prior to that time, it was active through what was called its embryo, that is the Europol Drugs Unit (EDU). Based on an agreement of the Ministers of Justice and Home Affairs concluded in 1993 the EDU began its operation in The Hague in early 1994, laying the groundwork for the creation of the final Europol. After adoption of a Joint Action by the Justice and Home Affairs Council in March 1995, EDU's competence expanded beyond the fight against drug-related crime to include such areas as illicit trafficking in nuclear and radioactive materials, organized illegal immigration, trafficking in stolen vehicles and associated money laundering. In December 1996, the organization's competence was further extended to combat trafficking in human beings, especially where this involved sexual exploitation.

Europol facilitates information exchange between member states. It conducts studies of criminal phenomena in Europe, gathers intelligence and performs analyses – all these activities being carried out to support concrete investigations. One area that was off-limits to EDU, but became possible after the Europol Convention entered into force, is the centralized processing of personal data. This change will play a decisive role in the legal position that the organization is to have. Even prior to this, EDU supported international investigations as well as police and customs operations, such as controlled deliveries, by offering coordination, manpower and technical assistance. Europol has continued to develop new methods to combat crime and to offer training. An important example of this work is the analysis training provided by Europol for officers from member states, thus helping to spread expertise. Europol also provides legal, strategic and technical advice at the political level and/or to top-level officials of the national law enforcement authorities.

Europol will have the role of a European Central Intelligence and Support Service, working on behalf of all EU law enforcement. Europol will maintain a common information system enabling authorities with user access rights to verify whether information is held at Europol or in member states regarding specific criminal organizations, criminals and criminal offences. In other words, EU member states will have at their disposal a more versatile instrument for information and intelligence exchange – the first instrument ever to be founded on a central European database of information intended for the purpose of crime analysis. This will enable central analysis of the development and structures of criminal organizations operating in EU member states and involved in serious forms of international crime. It will also facilitate central analysis of data based on and compiled from numerous sources from outside the member states. Such central analysis will, in turn, serve to prompt or support investigations.

Despite these promising prospects for the future Europol, it must be said that Europol is not designed to function like a European FBI. The Convention does not provide Europol with any executive powers, but limits its tasks to those of a central intelligence and support unit. Despite this restriction of powers, however, Europol can offer the member states valuable support in carrying out investigations at national level.

Europol is conducting international analysis and centralized intelligence work on a pro-active basis. It tries to make the best use of resources, avoiding duplication of effort and following an interdisciplinary approach in the fight against organized crime. Europol brings together the information, the intelligence and the expertise of the European Union member states.

The international exchange of information and intelligence has been improved in quantity, quality and speed owing to the involvement of Europol. In conditions of highest security, Europol bridges the cultural, linguistic and organizational gap between the different national services. The liaison officers seconded by member states have direct access to extensive national databases, intelligence and sensitive data. This guarantees within a matter of hours an information and intelligence exchange between local, regional and national police and customs agencies of member states.

In the coordination of investigations and operations, the European Union has made considerable progress using Europol's facilities. Europol has coordinated controlled deliveries of drugs shipments running through four or more countries. It has also assisted with major investigations, such as the two-year effort that culminated, in summer 1997, in the simultaneous arrest in five countries of 68 Mafia suspects. These arrests followed constant intelligence evaluation and coordination by Europol. Another interesting case, still ongoing in some countries, is a large-scale operation initiated by the Italian authorities against a criminal organization of drug traffickers operating in nine EU member states and another six non-EU countries. Europol was deeply involved in the operation, hosting an operational meeting that united law enforcement officers from ten countries, including three non-EU countries and three magistrates, and by providing analytical support. In particular Europol analysts were able to identify and illustrate links among targets in different countries and find the main reference telephone numbers, from more than 5,000, in order to localize the heads of the organization and dismantle the infrastructure. This operation has already led to the arrest of more than 40 people and the seizure of about 170 kg of heroin in different countries.

It goes without saying that effective international cooperation cannot leave aside adequate standards of cooperation at national level among the different law enforcement agencies, and among specialized branches within the same law enforcement agency. In this regard, the Europol Convention provides that each country establishes a Europol National Unit as the only interlocutor of the European Police Office. Obviously, each country is free to structure its own National Unit as it deems appropriate in respect of its own fundamental laws, its own administrative organization and its own historical tradition. Whatever the case, though, the full efficiency of the Europol system has to be ensured. The structure should be such to avoid any dangerous duplication of work with other international bodies. In this way, the establishment of Europol is not only a response to the challenges posed by transnational organized crime but also itself is another challenge:

- a challenge for law enforcement national bodies to revise their organizational and functional schemes;
- a challenge for EU police officers to look beyond the national border;

- a challenge to work more and more together;
- a challenge to think and to act in a modern, open-minded and European way.

For the battle against organized crime to have any prospects for success, each and every one of these challenges will have to be met.

International Atomic Energy Agency Programme against Illicit Trafficking in Nuclear Materials and Radioactive Sources

ANITA NILLSON

THE PRESENT SITUATION IN ILLICIT TRAFFICKING

At the beginning of the 1990s news media began to report an increasing number of cases in which nuclear materials and radioactive isotope sources were subjects of illicit trafficking. These initial cases contained material emanating from the Former Soviet Union and caused great concern among states and international organizations that nuclear material involved in trafficking might become implicated in weapons production, and that radioactive sources used in an unauthorized way would cause health and safety effects to individuals, the public in general or the environment.

Since then, the illicit trafficking in these materials has continued. The International Atomic Energy Agency (IAEA) monitors the situation by maintaining an illicit trafficking database programme. Indeed, 63 of its member states have assigned contact points for reporting trafficking events to the IAEA. From 1993 to 1998, a total number of 285 events was reported. Over the period a slight majority of the cases involved nuclear material, although the quantities in most cases are small and the usability for weapons production low. Only a few cases (13 confirmed) involve strategic material in the form of highly enriched uranium or plutonium. The potential for the smuggling of large quantities of weapons grade material may be low, but even trafficking of small quantities of such material deserves attention in the context of non-proliferation, since larger quantities of nuclear material of strategic value could be accumulated.

The smuggling of radioactive sources can impose a direct health and safety danger to the public. Some cases have resulted in a fatal ionizing radiation exposure to individuals. One example is the well-known incident of the discarded radiation source in Goiânia, Brazil, a few years ago that caused several deaths and radioactive contamination in a large part of a city of 1 million people.

Although the incidence of trafficking cases has decreased somewhat since the mid-1990s, the fact that the IAEA still receives reports of trafficking from its member states indicates weaknesses in the protection of radioactive materials at their storage locations. However, the database does not reveal evidence that this is a problem concerning only one state or a group of states; conversely, incidents reported to the database indicate that this is a global problem of general concern.

EFFORTS TO PREVENT TRAFFICKING IN NUCLEAR AND RADIOACTIVE MATERIALS

It is generally agreed that the problem of illicit trafficking of nuclear materials and radioactive sources should be addressed first through prevention. The complexity of measures for safety, security, physical protection, accountancy and control (including the control of transborder movements) of these materials constitute the protective system as a whole. Much has been accomplished by way of strengthening this system through the efforts of several member states and by the IAEA.

International legal instruments provide a basis for national arrangements for preventing, detecting and responding to illicit trafficking. Presently 127 states have, in accordance with the provisions of the Non-Proliferation Treaty, concluded safeguard agreements with the IAEA, 63 states are parties to the Physical Protection Convention; and 33 states have declared their intention to apply the Nuclear Suppliers' Guidelines (NSG) for nuclear-related exports. These international undertakings lead to national measures that contribute to the prevention or detection of illicit trafficking. Most exporting states now require that adequate physical protection and accounting and control measures are in place in recipient states as a condition for granting export licences for nuclear material.

Several international organizations have taken an interest in the prevention of illicit trafficking and in mitigating the associated risks. The United Nations, the Commission of the European Union and the World Customs Organization (WCO) are among the organizations that have addressed the problem. These, and others, have joined in the IAEA's information exchange efforts and training activities.

Several member states have assigned significant amounts of resources for bilateral cooperation with Newly Independent States, to support their efforts to establish nuclear material accountancy and control systems, physical protection systems and radiation protection systems. These programmes cover a period of several years, as installation of new equipment and implementation of new techniques often require extensive training and acquisition of experience with the new system.

In summit meetings held in 1996 and 1997, the Eight States[1] underlined the need for the safe management of fissile materials as a barrier against the risk of illicit trafficking in such materials. Cooperative intelligence, customs and law enforcement efforts have been recognized as necessary for preventing the sale and diversion of nuclear materials. Through their programmes for preventing and combating illicit trafficking in nuclear materials, these states have demonstrated their concern and determination to prevent illicit trafficking.

THE IAEA PROGRAMME: SECURITY OF MATERIAL

Information Exchange

By maintaining the illicit trafficking database programme, the IAEA provides a focal point for an exchange of information on trafficking. Presently 63 states participate in the database programme and when a trafficking incident in a state occurs, the Point of Contact in the state reports the incident as soon as possible, often within 48 hours of the event, to the IAEA, which disseminates the information to all member states. The IAEA also collects information on incidents from open sources. For the incidents that are not reported formally, the IAEA may contact the Point of Contact to check the accuracy of this information.

All nuclear materials seized in illicit trafficking are to be covered by safeguard agreements in the state where they were seized. The IAEA undertakes appropriate follow-up actions to this effect.

The IAEA organizes international conferences to foster exchange information. In November 1997 a Conference on Physical Protection of Nuclear Material was organized in Vienna and, in September 1998, a Conference on the Safety and Security of Radioactive Materials was held in France.

During the past four years the IAEA has convened meetings with representatives of international organizations that, through their mandate, have an interest in ensuring the safe and secure transport and

317

use of nuclear material and other radioactive substances. The IAEA believes that regular meetings of this kind will help enhance coordination among the organizations and thereby avoid duplication of effort.

Protection of Nuclear Materials

Nuclear material accountancy and physical protection constitute the first line of defence in ensuring that nuclear materials do not become the subject of unauthorized use leading to illicit trafficking. Although the responsibility for physical protection rests entirely with the state, it is recognized that efforts at the international level are also necessary. The IAEA develops, together with member states, the international standards for physical protection.

To assist states in assessing their needs for implementing effective physical protection systems at state and facility level, the IAEA offers the 'International Physical Protection Advisory Service' (IPPAS) to all states. These peer review missions are carried out by a team of experts from member states. The results of IPPAS missions, which are kept confidential because of security concerns, identify areas, as applicable, where legal, administrative and technical components of physical protection need to be improved. If national resources are not adequate for making the improvements, the Secretariat may assist the state in generating the necessary support through, for example, bilateral cooperation programmes or the IAEA's Technical Cooperation programme.

The Convention on the Physical Protection of Nuclear Material defines the international standards for physical protection of nuclear material during international transport. The IAEA recommendations, 'The Physical Protection of Nuclear Material', are applicable for nuclear material, in peaceful or military use, storage or domestic transport. The recommendations are not legally binding but, as references in other legally binding documents such as bilateral cooperation agreements and export control regimes, they acquire legal status. The IAEA also develops technical documents and guidelines to facilitate international physical protection standards.

The IAEA conducts, often together with member states, national and regional courses in physical protection. The training is adapted to the needs of specific states and regions. The target audience is individuals responsible for administering regulatory systems and for designing and implementing physical protection systems. The training material is available in English, Russian, Chinese and Spanish. These courses or workshops might also address the specific need for physical protection systems in a state or region, current concepts and technology, and programmes for prevention, detection and response to illicit trafficking in nuclear materials and other radioactive sources.

The Secretariat has, together with states offering bilateral support to the Newly Independent States (NIS), established a Coordinated Technical Support Programme (CTSP) designed, *inter alia*, to avoid duplication of effort, identify needs and disseminate information. Such coordinated programmes have been developed for Armenia, Belarus, Georgia, Kazakhstan, Latvia, Lithuania, Ukraine and Uzbekistan, and preparations are being made for such activities in the remaining NIS.

Protection of Radioactive Sources

The IAEA is preparing a Safety Guide on the prevention, detection and response to illicit trafficking in radioactive materials. The Safety Guide, which is expected to serve as a basis for national legislation and to provide practical assistance to customs and other law enforcement authorities, is co-sponsored by the IAEA, the WCO and the International Criminal Police Organization (Interpol). The 'International Basic Safety Standards for Protection against Ionizing Radiation and for the Safety of Radiation Sources' (the Basic Safety Standards), which relate to both the safety and the security of radiation sources, provide the scientific foundation for the Safety Guide.

In May 1998, the IAEA and the WCO signed a Memorandum of Understanding providing for continued cooperation between the two organizations including information exchange, joint training and other activities. The IAEA and the WCO have designed, for customs and other officials, a five-day 'train the trainers' course on the prevention, detection and response to nuclear smuggling. The course was given in 1997 and in 1998.

Together with the Austrian and Hungarian customs authorities, the IAEA is involved in a large-scale study of border monitoring systems and inspection procedures. The results of the study will be made available to states as an aid in selecting and installing border monitoring systems.

Legal and Regulatory Framework

As the national legal and regulatory framework is key to preventing, detecting and responding to illicit trafficking, the IAEA provides, upon request, advice and assistance to member states on their present national legislation related to the safe and peaceful uses of nuclear energy. As part

319

of this programme, a 'Model Law' is being developed to provide guidance to states on the elements to be included in national nuclear laws.

Technical Cooperation

Through the IAEA Technical Cooperation programme, states obtain support in establishing the infrastructures needed to prevent unauthorized use of nuclear material and other radioactive sources, including legislative assistance, technical advice and other support to establish systems for protection and control of radioactive sources. Under this programme, four significant projects of relevance to the prevention of illicit trafficking in radioactive materials have been established. The projects relate to nuclear legislation, protection of radioactive sources and physical protection of nuclear material.

OUTLOOK

The IAEA programme 'Security of Material' will continue to focus on the prevention of illicit trafficking. Nuclear materials need to be protected at all times, with improved international standards underpinning national efforts to provide adequate protection. Physical protection personnel at state authorities and at nuclear facilities will continue to require training and opportunities for exchanging views and experience with colleagues from other states.

The work to protect other radioactive sources will also continue. During the past year, radioactive sources have been confiscated (by states) that otherwise could have had serious impact on health and safety. States have, in their correspondence with the IAEA, indicated an increased awareness of the necessity to arrange for systems that would provide secure management of radioactive sources.

There is no room for complacency in the protection of nuclear material and radioactive sources. The IAEA programme will therefore be designed and implemented as a long-term commitment with activities aimed at preventing such unauthorized use of nuclear material and other radioactive sources that could result in illicit trafficking of these materials. When trafficking in these materials nevertheless occurs, the programme offers assistance in characterizing and handling material seized.

NOTES

1. Canada, France, Germany, Italy, Japan, Russian Federation, the UK and the USA.

Strengthening Cooperation Against Transnational Crime: A New Security Imperative

ROY GODSON and PHIL WILLIAMS

Transnational threats, by their very nature, demand responses that are novel in form, content and forum. National strategies are inherently inadequate for responding to challenges that cross multiple borders and involve multiple jurisdictions. The threats take several forms, ranging from the spread of exotic diseases to environmental degradation and illegal migration flows. Among the most serious at the close of the twentieth century is the rise of transnational criminal enterprises. Organized crime, fuelled by political, economic and cultural changes – including the globalization of trade, transportation and financial systems and the rapidly evolving technologies of communications and information – has ceased to be a domestic or local problem. It has become transnational.

Criminal enterprises have responded to global opportunities in much the same way as legitimate businesses. Transnational criminal organizations cross borders in search of lucrative targets, and also use this capacity as a means to elude or circumvent law enforcement by exploiting lacunae in criminal justice systems. Although they use borders for defensive purposes, as far as their criminal enterprises are concerned they operate, for all intents and purposes, in a borderless world. Governments, by contrast, are still confined by national borders, allowing antiquated notions of sovereignty to inhibit efforts to combat transnational crime. Few governments are able to cope effectively with organizations that can simply shift their activities to other locales to recover from losses or to evade pressure and scrutiny. Nor is this the only problem facing governments as they attempt to come to terms with a security challenge that has become pervasive. Governments are equipped and experienced in dealing with security threats from other governments. They are neither comfortable nor familiar with threats that are non-military in character, that jeopardize the economy and society rather than the state *per se*, and that cannot be dealt with through traditional state-centric policy options. Nevertheless, some important initiatives have already been taken in the effort to combat transnational criminal organizations. However, comprehensive strategies against transnational criminal organizations need to be based on a clear understanding of the kinds of threat they pose, a thorough assessment of their strengths and weaknesses and a clearer understanding of those countermeasures that have proved most effective.

Such strategies also need to encompass preventive measures, defensive or control measures and steps aimed at mitigating costs where prevention and control have failed. They should also go beyond law enforcement and traditional national security responses and focus on creating partnerships with the private sector and on strengthening civil society. In addition, there might well be ideas and approaches that can be borrowed from other areas. While transnational organized crime poses a security threat and not a military threat, some approaches that are familiar in military strategy, such as target hardening, centres of gravity, manoeuvre, surprise, and layered defence, could be applied in a social, political and economic context that infuses them with both new meaning and a high level of effectiveness. Similarly, concepts and approaches can be borrowed from the business world.

One of the main objectives of governments must be to put criminal organizations out of business. For example, they could restrict the business opportunities for criminal organizations through disrupting supply and demand, and by imposing barriers against the creation of new markets. The kind of competitive intelligence that is now so pervasive in the business world could usefully be applied to criminal enterprises. Such an approach would highlight both strengths and weaknesses, as well as opportunities and constraints. Insofar as the rise of transnational criminal organizations can be understood in terms of opportunities, incentives and pressures, and resources, then constricting opportunities, removing pressures and incentives, and degrading resources would go some way towards halting or even reversing the momentum of growth and development currently enjoyed by criminals. Unless this is done, transnational organized crime could prove to be a major security threat early in the twenty-first century. Without steps to dismantle and destroy criminal organizations, to disrupt their illicit markets and to isolate and neutralize those who collude with them, whether in government or the private sector, their power and wealth, and their capacity to inflict political, social and economic harm, can only increase.

This paper identifies key elements for comprehensive strategies to meet this challenge. After looking at the threat posed by transnational criminal organizations, existing approaches are explored. This provides the background to recommendations that build on best practices, especially in the law enforcement area. The need to extend the strategy to civil society and to engage in more creative efforts to change attitudes towards organized crime and corruption must also be recognized. There is also a clear need to expand programmes of state building, to establish effective and legitimate forms of governance. In addition, it is necessary to employ intelligence assets available to governments and to develop new and more effective modes of international and trans-state cooperation, bilateral, regional and global.

THE TRANSNATIONAL THREAT

Organized crime today is not the same as it was in the Prohibition era in the USA nor in Mario Puzo's *The Godfather* (1969). It has become a critical challenge to democratic governance, to transition and modernization processes in many parts of the world, and to national and international security.

Threats can only be properly understood in the context of vulnerabilities that abound in the post-Cold War era. Many states that once appeared militarily strong, politically and socially cohesive, and economically vibrant, now appear in a far different light. Others are undergoing difficult transitions to liberal democracy and free market economies. In some countries the new rulers appear to be not good democrats and legitimate businessmen, but a new breed of authoritarian criminals and illicit entrepreneurs. Consequently, one form of authoritarianism is simply being replaced by another.

A dark underside of globalization and interdependence is already emerging. Developments that have made it possible to move goods, people and money through the global economy and have traditionally been regarded by international political economy specialists as positive and benign in their effects have facilitated the movement of dirty money, as well as the transportation of drugs, arms, illegal aliens and nuclear material. Even though globalization and interdependence have made it more difficult to characterize the international system as purely a Hobbesian struggle among insecure states, they have facilitated the rise of a new breed of ruthless actors, willing to resort to violence. The fact that these criminal enterprises are, in James Rosenau's term, sovereign-free and rely predominantly on network structures only makes them all the more difficult to contain, especially for states that still conduct most of their activities through functional and geographic bureaucratic hierarchies. States have become almost outmoded organizations: in effect, we are attempting to deal with a twenty-first century phenomenon, using structures, mechanisms and instruments that are still rooted in eighteenth- and nineteenth-century concepts and organizational forms.

Typically, transnational criminal organizations have a home base where state authority is weak, corrupt or collusive. For example, Italian criminal organizations, especially La Cosa Nostra and the 'Ndrangheta carry out sophisticated operations worldwide. Similarly, Chinese criminal enterprises and Colombian and Mexican drug cartels have developed sophisticated regional and sometimes global operations of thousands of people that deal in billions of dollars worth of business. Russian criminal organizations, while less well-entrenched outside the former Soviet Union have also become transnational in scope, operating in Western Europe, the USA, Israel and the Caribbean. Nigerian groups operate in countries as diverse as Thailand, Brazil, Russia and South Africa. Organized crime groups exhibit important differences. Colombian drug trafficking organizations focus on a single, highly profitable product; Russian and Chinese criminal organizations maintain an extensive range of enterprises incorporating traditional criminal activities such as extortion and prostitution, as well as more novel ventures such as smuggling illegal aliens and nuclear materials.

Even allowing for national and regional variations, no state is immune from the threat posed by transnational criminal organizations. Historically, almost every society has had some form of localized criminal group, although they have seldom been a major threat to a state's survival or its ability to function. This is changing. Increasingly, criminal organizations are able to defy government authority, suborn or even partially supplant it. When the situation deteriorates to a point where criminal organizations can undermine a government's ability to govern, as in Italy, Russia, Colombia and elsewhere, then the problem goes beyond law and order and becomes a national and international security concern.

Why has organized crime been able to reach such a powerful position in some states? Where the state is weak, criminal organizations enjoy a congenial environment, operating with a high degree of impunity. They seek to perpetuate this weakness, using both corruption and violence. In other cases, criminal organizations can develop in strong states where there are too few checks and balances. Low levels of transparency encourage high levels of corruption. In such cases, the state might well license criminal organizations, albeit in carefully defined domains, while also exploiting them for its own purposes. In such circumstances, however, a loss of authority by state structures allows the criminal organizations to operate much more freely, and even to challenge the dominance of the state apparatus to the extent that they gain the upper hand. Even when they are not weak, corrupt or collusive states may have the capacity to act vigorously against criminal organizations but possess neither the will nor the inclination.

Using states that are weak, corrupt or collusive as their *home* bases, criminal organizations establish themselves in a variety of *host* states where there are large markets for their illicit products, and lucrative targets for other illicit activities.

Yet other states are drawn in as *transhipment* states, with criminal organizations using corruption to ensure safe passage of illicit commodities from drugs to illegal aliens. Mexico, situated between the drug-consuming USA and the drug-producing Latin American countries, as well as along some of the major alien trafficking routes, has seen the integrity and security of its political and economic systems deeply affected by criminal activities. Initially at least, drug transhipments merely passed through its territory. But links with Colombian drug trafficking groups have contributed to the rise of indigenous and powerful Mexican drug trafficking organizations. In the past, some states viewed their role as transit countries as marginally detrimental or perhaps even slightly beneficial. Increasingly, though, this view is being displaced.

Another category of states implicitly become *service* states for the criminal organizations, especially those with tight bank secrecy regulations. For most of these states, the benefits resulting from the inflow of bank deposits and the demand for financial services are still viewed as outweighing the costs. In the longer term, the corrosion of institutional integrity all too often emerges as a major problem.

As criminal organizations have become transnational, they have also developed connections with one another. Talk of a global Pax Mafiosa cannot be substantiated, but it is clear that criminal organizations have begun to establish links or alliances to improve their operational capabilities and to strengthen their ability to resist governmental control efforts. These extend from one-off deals at the low end of the spectrum to full-blown strategic alliances in which the participants cooperate systematically over the longer term. Cooperation among criminal organizations pre-empts competition, makes use of complementary expertise and distribution channels and ensures predictable supplier relationships.

Transnational criminal organizations have also become entrenched in the licit world. Symbiotic links to government officials protect their operations from law enforcement initiatives. Such linkages tend to be strongest in home states but also extend into host, transhipment and service states, contributing to what has been termed the global corruption epidemic.[1] Much corruption, of course, is self-generated by officials who place personal gain above the demands of public service. Stemming in part from the injection of capitalism into traditional patrimonial societies, corruption has pernicious consequences, leading in some cases to a failure of governance, with corrosive effects on both political and economic life. Even when the more drastic consequences are avoided, corruption undermines fairness and impartiality in the enforcement of rules, encourages incompetence and creates pervasive malaise in state institutions. Corruption has a distorting impact on the economy and can deter investment and stifle economic growth, consequences that are particularly debilitating in developing states and states in transition. If anything, corruption is even more dangerous and insidious when used as an instrument by transnational criminal organizations. In addition to the operational corruption that facilitates safe passage of illicit products, criminal organizations use systemic corruption to ensure the maintenance of a congenial, low-risk environment in the home state and, on occasion, in critically important host, transhipment and service states. Symbiotic relationships with political elites subordinate the purposes the state is intended to serve for the citizenry to the needs and demands of criminal organizations concerned with maximizing profit and minimizing risk.

Government and law enforcement officials, however, are not the only targets for transnational criminal enterprises. Banking personnel are sometimes recruited or co-opted to facilitate illicit activities such as money laundering. Criminal organizations try to dominate licit industries, such as construction and waste disposal. A willingness to use intimidation and violence, coupled with easy access to liquid capital, gives them a capacity to drive out legitimate entrepreneurs. As Jonathan Winer has noted, criminal organizations use the profits derived from their activities to purchase legitimate business. These in turn have a negative capital cost criminals do not need to borrow and can force out the competition through cut-rate pricing, until they control legitimate industries.[2] Extortion is another way in which criminal organizations impinge on licit business. The need to pay protection money puts an added burden on firms in the early stages of their development. Although firms in Russia find it preferable to pay what is, in essence, a form of criminal tax rather than the prohibitive level of government tax, criminals are more concerned with short-term benefits than long-term growth, making it difficult for enterprises to invest their profits in future growth.

The emergence of these groups and their increasing capabilities in a world of states is a broad and direct challenge to governability, national sovereignty and international security. The threat, however, lacks the highly visible, state-centric profile of a conventional military threat. This does not mean that organized crime is a marginal phenomenon. Like insurrectionists, members of transnational criminal organizations are largely indistinguishable from civilian populations. Their activities undermine the fibres of society, its economic and financial structure, its polity and its physical security but do so in ways that only become apparent when the process is well advanced and therefore more difficult to counter.

Legitimate entrepreneurs find it difficult to operate profitably in an environment in which criminal organizations are active, but criminal enterprises are flourishing in a world of global business. Estimates of the profits made by criminal organizations, of the amount of money that is laundered and of the size of illicit markets are inherently problematic, but huge sums are involved. A recent study by the United Nations (UN), for example, puts the total revenue of the illicit drug industry at about US$400 billion.[3] Drug money can benefit the economies of producer countries, providing foreign exchange and economic multiplier benefits. But it can also make the tasks of macroeconomic management more difficult. The huge profits also provide opportunities for those involved to buy political influence. For the consumer countries, of course, the costs are counted in terms of health, lost productivity and increased crime and violence.

One area where there are more precise estimates of the impact of criminal activities, is counterfeiting, which is believed to cost licit business somewhere in the region of US$200 billion a year. Reportedly, US automobile manufacturers and suppliers lose around US$12 billion a year through sales of counterfeit parts alone, and American job losses stemming from counterfeit goods run as high as three-quarters of a million.[4] Other areas where there are very obvious costs include ecocrimes ranging from toxic-waste dumping to the smuggling of fauna and flora. The latter has now reached a level where it poses a real threat to biodiversity. Trafficking in art and antiquities is robbing states of their cultural heritage; and trafficking in arms not only helps to fuel ethnic conflicts but also augments levels of violence in more stable societies.

There are also the less tangible costs associated with transnational criminal organizations. Drug trafficking, for example, is an inherently violent activity, whether the focus is on the opium fields of Southeast and Southwest Asia, the cities of Colombia or the streets of the USA. Violence is used by the organizations involved to protect turf and profits and to settle disputes. It is also used to eliminate or intimidate members of the government or the judiciary as well as investigative journalists. Not only do criminal organizations challenge the government monopoly of violence, but they also pose a threat at the individual level. If individual security is inversely related to the level of violence within society, the greater the violence – whether a result of civil strife, factionalism or criminal activity – the less security is enjoyed by citizens. Furthermore, violence is often perpetrated on individuals by criminal organizations that traffic in women and children – treating them essentially as products and fundamentally depriving them of their human rights.

As well as posing significant threats to governments and to individuals, transnational criminal organizations also threaten the integrity of financial and commercial institutions at both the national and the international levels. While criminal organizations are more likely to exploit than attack financial systems, the threat is a subtle one, involving a gradual erosion of trust as banking officials are co-opted to launder money or commit various kinds of fraud. Transnational criminal organizations also challenge efforts by governments to regulate the global political system and establish codes of conduct, principles of restraint and responsibility, and norms of behaviour. Regimes to inhibit the proliferation of nuclear, chemical and biological weapons, for example, are highly dependent upon cooperation among suppliers and the ability to isolate rogue states. Alliances of convenience between rogue states and criminal organizations willing and able to supply materials, components or precursors of weapons of mass destruction could drive large holes through these regimes. And for the criminals, using existing trafficking networks for product diversification is cheap, easy and potentially lucrative.

The implication of this is that organized crime poses a novel mix of direct and indirect challenges to security and stability. Simply because the threat is very different from those that have traditionally dominated the security agenda does not mean that it has been ignored. Indeed, states, international organizations and some private-sector groups have already adopted initiatives to combat transnational organized crime. The next section provides a brief survey of existing responses, as a preliminary to considering what more could be done.

THE EXISTING RESPONSE

As transnational organized crime has become ubiquitous and pervasive, devising and implementing effective countermeasures has become a security imperative. Independent national responses will not suffice. The logic is simple: so long as transnational criminal organizations capitalize on global processes to structure their operations in ways that limit the effectiveness of initiatives by any single nation, the response needs to be extensive in scope, multilateral in form and, to the extent possible, global in reach. An effective response requires, at a minimum, the coordinated participation of a significant number of governments and the non-governmental sector. As there is no global organization with the authority, responsibility and capacity to develop comprehensive strategies to combat transnational organized crime, the optimum has to give way to the feasible.

There has been a variety of initiatives based on cooperative approaches among states and some private-sector organizations with a cumulatively positive impact. A more critical assessment, however, suggests that these initiatives create confusion about roles and responsibilities and uncertainty about which measures work most effectively. Even so, they are an indication that the international community has begun to recognize the seriousness of transnational criminal organizations. Although no attempt is made here to consider all these initiatives, a brief discussion of the more important ones can help to provide a fuller sense of both the strengths and weaknesses of the existing approach, and to highlight the components that have to be put in place before a fully coordinated strategy can be devised and implemented.

One of the oldest examples of international cooperation against transnational crime is Interpol. Established in 1923, Interpol is based in Lyon, France, with National Crime Bureaus in member states. The official languages are Spanish, French, English and Arabic. The aims of the organization are to ensure and promote the widest possible mutual assistance between criminal police authorities within the limits of laws existing in the different countries and in the spirit of the Universal Declaration of Human Rights. Interpol is an organization of police and, as such, benefits from the professional trust police have in one another. At the same time, some view it as a policemen's club rather than a formal intergovernmental organization. Its regular budget of about US$30 million is hardly lavish for a global organization with 270 personnel.

Interpol clearly fulfils several important if modest functions, especially relating to the exchange of information. Interpol's system of notices covers requests for arrest of a suspect with a view to extradition (red notices), requests for information about a suspect, circulation of information about those who have committed or are likely to commit a crime, circulation of information about corpses, missing persons, stolen property and notification of criminals' methods of operation and places of refuge.[5] In recent years this system has become much more useful as a result of a computerized communication system designed to link the 176 National Central Bureaus. The Interpol database, with 120,000 records containing fingerprints and photographs as well as biographical data on criminals, about 6,000 of whom are subjects of red notices, can be accessed by member countries through the Automated Search Facility (ASF). The capacity to circulate this information quickly and easily facilitates capture of criminals. Interpol has extended its database capabilities to encompass stolen vehicles, increasing the chance of recovery even across national borders. It has also organized a series of conferences dealing with various criminal activities. The creation of an Analytical Section has enhanced the quality of intelligence provided to member countries about crime trends and large-scale criminal activity. Interpol has strengthened its relationship with the UN and has extended its interests to cover environmental crimes, child pornography and trafficking in women and children.

Interpol's automated search system and the communications network are important assets, and include a 24-hour 'one stop shop' for all international inquiries by law enforcement agencies. The services provided by the National Central Bureaus have been improved but their effectiveness varies. Some, such as the British Bureau located within the International Division of the National Criminal Intelligence Service, are reportedly highly effective.

In spite of the modernization of Interpol's technological infrastructure and the development of a forward-looking strategy, its global membership and uncertain status have made it difficult for the organization to extend its level of information exchanges and go far beyond the provision of useful if modest services. Consequently, some member states have begun to look for alternative institutions through which to develop international cooperation against transnational organized crime.

Partly because of the perceived inadequacies of Interpol and partly because of the momentum generated by European integration (which has had an inevitable spillover effect into law enforcement through the development of the Third Pillar dealing with justice and home affairs) the European Union created its own agency for police cooperation. Largely an initiative of Chancellor Kohl, Europol, as it is known, is designed to counter transnational crime within the boundaries of an enlarged European Union. A European-wide programme of information exchange is being developed. The focus is on illicit trafficking in drugs, radioactive materials, stolen vehicles, human beings and illegal immigrants, as well as associated criminal organizations and money laundering activities. Europol is also beginning to provide criminal intelligence analysis and support for investigations to counter criminal activities involving two or more member states. It also has a remit to develop both training programmes and build expertise.

With a 1997 budget of 5.6 million European Currency Units (ECUs), (plus ECU2.2 million for the Europol Computer System) and a limited number of personnel, Europol is still in the early development stage. Ratification of the convention on which it is based proceeds slowly. Member-nations are reluctant to give up any issues related to national sovereignty and they still wish to maintain exclusive control over national information. Relations with non-European police agencies and other international bodies, both in Europe and across the Atlantic, are also of concern given that criminal networks extend beyond the bounds not only of national law enforcement but also of regional law enforcement efforts.

Regional initiatives are also important. They include the Caribbean Financial Action Task Force on Money Laundering, Organization of American States, efforts to combat corruption and various initiatives to strengthen law enforcement cooperation in the Baltic region and in Southern Africa. In addition, to these regional initiatives, there are also sectoral initiatives to deal with particular kinds of transnational crime. The CITES convention, for example, prohibits trafficking in endangered species of fauna and flora. A 1970 United Nations Educational, Scientific and Cultural Organization (UNESCO) Convention on the Means of Prohibiting and Preventing the Illicit Import, Export and Transfer of Ownership of Cultural Property is intended to prevent illicit trafficking in art and antiquities.

Other relatively recent global initiatives include the 1988 UN Convention on drug trafficking whose signatories commit to take action against money laundering. In 1989, the G7 nations set up the Financial Action Task Force (FATF). FATF subsequently promulgated 40 guidelines for the prevention and control of money laundering. FATF membership has extended beyond the initial member states and further initiatives have been taken to develop more stringent guidelines against laundering the proceeds of criminal activities. These are important steps towards the development of a global anti-money-laundering regime, although effective implementation is uneven. Tightening provisions against money laundering in some jurisdictions has led criminals to relocate to others that place a premium on secrecy, and to states in transition and other jurisdictions where anti-money-laundering legislation is non-existent.

Although regional and sectoral measures are important, they necessarily provide a narrower range of responses to a much broader phenomenon. The need for the international community to respond more comprehensively and more energetically to transnational crime is increasingly being reflected in the work of the UN. The UN Crime Prevention and Criminal Justice Division (CPCJD) was created in 1975 at the Fifth UN Congress on the Prevention of Crime and the Treatment of Offenders. It has a very broad mandate, which includes organized transnational crime. During the late 1980s and 1990s, the UN has devoted increasing attention to this problem. On the recommendation of the Eighth Congress in 1990, the UN General

Assembly adopted Model Treaties on Extradition and on Mutual Assistance in Criminal Matters. The most important single initiative, however, was the World Ministerial Conference held in Naples in November 1994. This Conference led to a Declaration of Principles and a Global Action Plan against organized transnational crime. The UN initiative crystallized recognition of the problem and lent added momentum to the mobilization of the international community.

More specifically, the Declaration and Action Plan emphasized international cooperation and placed the possibility of a convention against organized crime on the agenda. The urgent need to increase reliable knowledge about the nature, scope and manifestations of the challenge, as well as about the capacity of criminal justice systems to respond effectively was also recognized. Assistance in both the legislative and regulatory areas, as well as technical cooperation and the provision of technical assistance, was deemed essential to increase and equalize the risks faced by transnational criminal organizations wherever they operate. The Declaration and Action Plan not only embodied a broad-based agenda to combat transnational organized crime but also, in the words of the subsequent report of the Secretary General, demonstrated that the international community has reached agreement on a basic set of common objectives and on the fundamental elements of the modalities required to attain them.[6] The report also acknowledged that considerably more work is necessary to operationalize this basic agreement by way of consistent and coordinated implementation.[7]

Part of the problem of implementation stems from the fact that the Crime Prevention Division is limited in resources and personnel. The Division's modest staff of 35 and small budget of US$4 million has been overextended. Like other international organizations it is dependent upon states for information and does not control the scope, pace or even the extent to which the provisions of the Action Plan are implemented. The Division provides needs assessments and technical assistance for specific countries as part of its focus on ways to enhance state capacity to combat these organizations. For all the problems surrounding its implementation, however, the Naples Declaration and Action Plan remain important as the first systematic attempt to develop an integrated global programme to combat transnational criminal organizations.

Another recent effort to develop a systematic global approach was launched by the G-7/P-8. In 1995 the G-7 Heads of State created a group of experts to counter transnational organized crime and prepare recommendations for the annual G-7/P-8 summits. This group, known as the Senior Experts Group on Transnational Organized Crime, followed the precedent of the FATF and developed a list of 40 recommendations, most of which focused on practical and operational matters rather than more conceptual issues such as definitions. Significantly, little attention was given to developing a strategic plan.

Drawing in part on the background papers for the 1994 meeting in Naples, the recommendations underlined the importance of mutual legal assistance and extradition, and emphasized the importance of cooperation even in the absence of dual criminality. They also highlighted the need for a central authority within states to coordinate cooperation; techniques for mutual education (such as secondments and personnel exchanges); witness protection including reciprocal arrangements; the need to criminalize technological abuses and the smuggling of persons; the importance of removing safe havens (or sanctuaries) for criminals; better firearms regulations; and the development of international cooperation on electronic surveillance, undercover operations and controlled deliveries. The group also urged that states consider adopting measures for asset forfeiture, as well as passing the necessary regulatory and legislative measures to combat corruption. It also added to the debate about the merits of a single convention as discussed at Naples and subsequently formally proposed by Poland.

As part of its enquiry, the group provided an inventory of instruments and practices of the P-8 member states. The conclusion was that although many practices of P-8 members overlapped or converged, dual criminality and extradition remained a problem as some states have criminalized membership in an organized crime group while others use the vaguer notion of criminal conspiracy. The overall implication, as the CPCJD has long argued, is the need for harmonization of national legislation.

The most significant aspect of the G-7/P-8's work lies not in the details of the Expert Group's recommendations, but rather in the fact that most major states have placed the fight against transnational organized crime high on their agendas, recognized the need for a vigorous response and developed a mechanism that could eventually assist in the formulation of strategies against transnational organized crime through a more comprehensive approach. The possible components of such an approach are discussed in the next section.

INTERNATIONAL STRATEGIES

A single comprehensive and coherent strategy to combat organized crime developed by a guiding authority would be the ideal approach. However, it is not attainable. A more incremental approach, if carried out carefully, could have very positive results. National, bilateral, multilateral, regional and global efforts, both governmental and non-governmental, should be complementary rather than contradictory, and reflect similar overall priorities and guiding principles directed towards feasible goals. Benchmarks for measuring progress toward these goals are required. The strategies proposed here reflect those needs and stem from simple but important questions. What exactly are we dealing with? What should be the specific objectives of the international community in responding to the challenge? What are the major components of overall, well-integrated strategies? Who needs to be involved in their development and implementation? What major obstacles and problems have to be overcome for such a programme to be effective?

Responding to these questions makes clear that the basis for a more coherent approach is a continuing series of global and regional assessments. Developing coordinated strategies against transnational criminal organizations also requires specifying objectives and the means to pursue them. Among the major components of these strategies are: mobilizing the international community and the private sector; intergovernmental cooperation; developing appropriate legal frameworks and methods for coordinating national efforts; the use of international law to bolster local activities; and establishing mechanisms to share information that both anticipates and targets criminal activities. Cooperative relationships among police organizations in different countries, for example, are critical to sharing information about the most effective techniques and technologies. Government partnerships with various private-sector institutions are another approach to countering organized crime. Educational programmes in schools and business, for example, can prevent or retard the growth of organized crime and corruption.

In addition to these measures, law enforcement and intelligence capabilities can be focused and strengthened and methods of disruption integrated into the strategy, with appropriate legal safeguards. Judicial and civic institutions in some states can be supported to eliminate safe havens or sanctuaries for criminal organizations. Where this fails, a more punitive approach might be needed in efforts to eliminate collusive relationships between a particular transnational criminal organization and members of the state apparatus. With these requirements in mind, this paper presents an initial strategic design for comprehensive international responses to organized crime. Growing understanding of transnational criminal organizations and the dynamics of illicit markets will lead to revisions and refinement and more effective strategy counteractions.

COMPREHENSIVE AND COMMON ASSESSMENTS

During the last several years, at the national and international levels, law enforcement agencies, intergovernmental bodies such as the UN and public policy analysts have all begun to focus their attention on transnational criminal organizations: the structures, operations, strategies and instruments of these organizations. Research and analysis, however, has been fragmented rather than cumulative. Carefully and sharply delineated threat assessments are required to facilitate prescription and to underpin policy. Elucidating the nature of the threat and its main characteristics and methods; analysing how transnational criminal organizations work; developing the methodologies best suited for understanding the particularities of both substate and transnational criminal enterprises; and identifying the key vulnerabilities of criminal organizations that can be exploited by national and international law enforcement efforts are essential components of this effort.

Such assessments could utilize criminological and social science theories concepts of globalization, theories of markets and migratory patterns, for example, to understand the overall scope of the transnational crime problem. Intelligence and law enforcement sources should be analysed to gain greater insight into and understanding of the specific activities engaged in by transnational criminal organizations, as well as the dynamics of the illicit markets in which they operate. Using such techniques and sources of information, an ongoing appraisal of transnational crime groups and their activities can be formed.

This could incorporate approaches not usually used by law enforcement. One would be a SWOT analysis, a common business technique that identifies the strengths and weaknesses of particular groups, as well as the opportunities and threats they face in their immediate environments. This could be applied not only to identification of the vulnerabilities of specific organizations but also to those of transnational criminal organizations *per se*. Opportunities for action must be identified in this stage with analysts exploring potential avenues for effective policies designed to undermine the strengths of the organizations, exploit their weaknesses, minimize the market and other opportunities available to them and maximize the threats. Discerning the vulnerabilities of criminal organizations in their structure, operations or other factors, is a critical component of informing the policymaking process, making it possible to identify opportunities for policymakers to advance national interests *vis-à-vis* criminal organizations.

States will produce their own assessments, based on specific national and regional circumstances, resulting in areas of consensus and areas of disagreement. While national and regional peculiarities and variations must be acknowledged, a similar framework of analysis would facilitate a more fruitful dialogue among nations and across regions. However, wherever transnational criminal organizations are active, certain critical areas need to be addressed.

- The home base of any organization and the scope of its activities in one or more host states.
- Range of activities pursued by the organization and an assessment of the contribution in each area to the overall profitability of the criminal enterprise.
- Structure of the organization and whether it is a hierarchical or a network style of operation. There is a tendency to equate hierarchy with organization and to treat networks more like *dis*organized crime. A network is, in fact, a sophisticated and resilient organizational structure – flexible and adaptable, rapid in responding to changed circumstances, whether the change emanates from threats or opportunities.
- Major bonding mechanisms that underpin the criminal enterprise. Bonding can be based on family, ethnic or tribal ties, or on shared experience in youth gangs or prison.[8] It is also a dynamic quality that can grow as the result of a series of criminal successes (or decline in the event that the criminal organization suffers a series of reverses), which encourage the members of the organization to develop a great deal of trust in one another's contributions to the criminal activities. Criminal organizations attempt to create or perpetuate bonding by developing a distinct ethos, initiation rites and rituals, and imposing discipline and identity. These procedures help to instil loyalty and

337

fear, thereby adding to the groups' security and maintaining secrecy.

- How criminal organizations disburse profits. Estimates of the scale of global money laundering ranges from US$200 billion to over US$1 trillion annually. Yet, relatively little is known about how criminal organizations actually use their proceeds. Some money is obviously spent to run and protect illicit enterprises through bribery and corruption, or the purchase of hi-tech equipment for intelligence and counterintelligence. Illicit funds also finance personal acquisitions such as luxury homes and cars, and some is secreted in locations beyond the reach of law enforcement. A portion is almost certainly reinvested in order to expand the criminal enterprise, while other funds are laundered for investment in legitimate business.

- Major links with other criminal organizations. Important patterns of cooperation appear to be developing among various criminal organizations. Why some are strategic and others tactical, the way they are created and maintained, their lifecycle and the distribution of benefits all require much more study. This would provide the basis for strategies intended to dissipate trust among criminal organizations.

- Connections with the upperworld. Criminal organizations cannot function effectively without collaborative relationships with the licit world. Identifying points of vulnerability that criminal organizations typically exploit, or that are exploited by political and economic elites, may help to track patterns of behaviour.

- Public relations strategies of criminal organizations. Transnational criminal organizations occasionally attempt to mobilize support among the legitimate population through paternalism and seemingly benevolent acts. Leaders of criminal organizations portray themselves as nationalistic entrepreneurs whose activities are beneficial to the society as a whole. Programmes to eliminate slums in Colombia and the provision of food parcels during the Kobe earthquake are just two examples. How widespread and successful such initiatives are, and whether they undermine law enforcement, requires study.

- Ways in which transnational criminal organizations penetrate the licit economy. The legitimate economy provides targets for extortion activities, markets for illicit products and the financial infrastructure for laundering the proceeds of crime. The banking sector and industries such as construction and waste disposal have become favourite targets for criminal activity. Exploring this more fully would help to identify the vulnerabilities of the licit economy and develop successful preventive strategies.

- Measures undertaken by transnational criminal organizations to manage the risks they confront from state authorities and rivals. All business enterprises contend with risk as a normal part of their activities, but criminal enterprises face distinct forms of risk from the efforts of law enforcement and their rivals. The more sophisticated organizations develop a variety of risk prevention, risk control and risk absorption strategies. Risk prevention, for example, through widespread corruption ensures that a criminal organization maintains a secure operating environment. Risk control defends the organization against law enforcement and other criminal organizations through counterintelligence and the use of violence. Risk absorption might include the transfer of assets from criminal leaders to their family members so even if the leaders are arrested and their assets confiscated, their wealth is protected. Developing a greater understanding of these risk management measures is a prerequisite for neutralizing or exploiting them.

- Cottage industries supporting organized crime. Transnational criminal organizations depend on certain services and products such as false identity documents, safe houses and legal assistance. These support structures have become indispensable to the success of activities such as alien smuggling or various kinds of fraud.

- Dynamics of illicit markets. Some markets are dominated by a few large organizations, but usually the participants are much more varied and include a mix of legitimate and semi-legitimate entrepreneurs. The relationship between these entrepreneurs and criminal organizations needs to be explored. Emphasis on organizations needs to be supplemented by analysis of market dynamics and trafficking patterns in products as diverse as drugs, nuclear materials, flora and fauna, CFCs, and art and antiquities. This should include both demand and supply side along with transaction flows.

- Extent to which cultural factors impinge on the structure, operations and activities of transnational criminal organizations. Many groups can be understood in terms of profits risk reduction, but there are also distinctive cultural factors (such as *guanxi* in the Chinese case) that influence or facilitate criminal activities. Just as the impact of cultural factors on licit business activities has become a topic of research at many business schools, the relationship between culture and transnational criminal organizations also needs to be examined.

- Major strengths and weaknesses of each organization. Criminal intelligence analysis should amalgamate the kind of net assessment used in military intelligence and military planning along with the SWOT analysis. These approaches could encourage focus on the criminal operating environment and analysis of how exploitable opportunities can be reduced.

This list provides a set of targets that could be pursued through both open source intelligence and more clandestine sources. A good deal is already known about certain criminal organizations and there are approaches to intelligence analysis such as the Organizational Attributes Strategic Intelligence System (OASIS) used by the US National Drug Intelligence Center that are imaginative in both concept and design. These could usefully be extended from drug trafficking groups to other criminal organizations. Good intelligence, however, is no guarantee of effective strategy. In the case of transnational organized crime it also has to be widely (if sometimes selectively) shared in order to have maximum impact.

INFORMATION SHARING ARRANGEMENTS

Using this set of categories, or something very similar, it should be possible to provide a variety of assessments that can be shared. Information sharing has several dimensions and there are critical tradeoffs between access and security. The first tier of information sharing, open sharing, would make analysis available to all interested and approved parties. The goal here would be to inform policymakers in several countries about the global crime problem and the activities of major criminal organizations. Some in the law enforcement community perceive that international cooperation on counter crime matters has been frustrated by a lack of understanding of certain types of crime. This is changing. There is growing recognition that no country is immune from becoming a home state, host state, transhipment or service state for transnational criminal organizations, and sharing information is essential to counteracting the growth and power of transnational groups.

Nonetheless, this is a sensitive area. For the most part, the information in first-tier sharing focuses on strategic, or macro-level, issues rather than tactical, source-sensitive law enforcement information. This has some shortcomings, but provides a basis for a much more comprehensive and effective diagnosis of the overall challenge. Indeed, the exchange of national assessments at this level would enable global institutions such as the UN as well as regional bodies to form and disseminate their own comprehensive assessments. This carries risk of disclosure, but the benefits of sharing at this level outweigh the potential risk. Not all states need to work together, but they should be aware of the general trends elsewhere. Such assessments could also be filtered for use in private-sector educational programmes, corporate and business awareness efforts and as an additional element contributing to national planning.

A second modality of information sharing would involve key secret information and/or intelligence about criminal organizations among governments and organizations. Some states might be excluded from this cooperation altogether because of internal corruption, criminal interests or governmental weakness. There are precedents for sharing sensitive information internationally, including the exchanges among NATO's Nuclear Planning Group, the contributions of national assessments to the International Atomic Energy Agency's (IAEA's) Action Team investigating proliferation activities in Iraq, and exchanges of intelligence on terrorism. When the interests of states coincide and those interests can best be achieved multilaterally, sharing sensitive information is not a major obstacle – up to a point. Since operational intelligence of this type could include sources and methods, sharing secrets among governments and organizations would likely be on limited basis. While selectivity could sometimes cause political problems, it is essential when a number of states suffer from systemic or institutionalized corruption. It is not always in the interests of opponents of criminal organizations to cast wide their net seeking international cooperation when some states have been corrupted at the very highest levels. For example, General Noriega's primary interests lay with criminal groups and activities, not in opposing them. A two-tier approach to the issue of information sharing is important to attempts to develop effective, well-coordinated international strategies. These strategies are the theme of the next section.

DEVISING STRATEGIES AGAINST TRANSNATIONAL ORGANIZED CRIME

Unlike transnational problems, such as environmental degradation and the spread of infectious diseases, criminal organizations present a *strategic* threat to the international community, not just a policy problem. Transnational criminal organizations are engaged in significant *dynamic*, *adversarial* relationships with governments worldwide, co-opting, corrupting even cooperating with some of these governments. These organizations adapt to their threat environment, restructuring and redirecting their operations along the path of least resistance, and developing new and sophisticated risk management strategies. Consequently, static or one-off policy responses to criminal organizations are unlikely to have more than short-term impact. Given the ability of criminal organizations to adjust to attacks against them, interested states must recognize that they are engaging cooperatively a set of strategic adversaries and that they must therefore regularly assess and react to the actions of these adversaries. Assessing the threat and readjusting strategy is an ongoing process in which governments try to emulate the qualities of flexibility and adaptability displayed by transnational criminal organizations themselves both in analysis and in response.

At the same time, governments need to ensure that there is accurate and timely assessment of *new* threats and appropriate recalibration of existing efforts to combat criminal groups and activities. Anticipating emerging crime threats provides opportunities for both preventive and pre-emptive actions that can have maximum impact, by allowing government and law enforcement agencies to be proactive rather than reactive. One innovation that might be effective in encouraging early recognition of emerging threats is to create small units within national intelligence and law enforcement agencies charged with monitoring illicit markets and other activities of criminal organizations and highlighting anomalies or novel forms of behaviour that could presage new trends. Such units should make it possible not only to react promptly and effectively to the activities of transnational criminal organizations, but also to attempt to divine their future efforts and to act pre-emptively against them.

Who should take the lead in developing an international strategy? Many governments now recognize that organized crime is no longer simply a law enforcement concern, but rather a national security threat. Boris Yeltsin, Helmut Kohl, Ernesto Zedillo and Bill Clinton, among others, have voiced strong concern about organized crime as a local, regional and global problem. The USA has now begun to take the most obvious leadership role in this area. President Clinton gave the organized crime threat unprecedented prominence in his UN 50th anniversary speech in October 1995. At the same time he issued Presidential Decision Directive 42, declaring organized crime to be a threat to global security and mobilizing the entire US government, rather than just law enforcement, in the fight to counter it. This initiative included the use of economic instruments against transnational organized crime with the invocation of the International Emergency Economic Powers Act to freeze the assets of Colombian cartel front companies. Impressive as these initiatives are, however, some view US leadership as overly reliant on legal tools and somewhat heavy-handed.

A likely evolution is that leadership in developing and implementing an international strategy against transnational criminal organizations will take place on an *ad hoc* basis, both regionally and globally, as interested and willing states step forward to carry out the necessary diplomatic work. Natural groupings for states seeking to collaborate against crime already exist with the EU and the G-7/P-8, prominent among them. With more states affected by organized crime and willing to dedicate some resources to countering the problem, opportunities for developing a more ambitious programme than anything that has yet been done now exist. International efforts will be most effective based on consensual arrangements, but leadership is important to mobilize this consensus and to establish some priorities.

THE MAJOR COMPONENTS OF THE STRATEGY

A strategy against transnational organized crime requires clear and unequivocal objectives. Unless there is agreement on what the international community is trying to achieve, the prospects for an effective, strategy are negligible. Law enforcement personnel tend to focus less on strategy than on reactive, parochial responses, especially on arrests of a few leaders of organized crime groups. While arrests are important and are the domain of law enforcement, overall strategy, with clearly enunciated and realistic objectives, as well as an explicit effort to relate ends to means is necessary to tackle today's organized crime. There is no prospect, for example, that transnational organized crime can be eliminated. Consequently, reduction and containment should be

343

the objectives. Strategy should incorporate not only measures to deter organized criminal activities but also initiatives to defend societies against organized crime by reducing vulnerabilities and opportunities. Action designed to harden societies and institutions, in both the public and private sectors, against infiltration by criminal organizations is essential. More aggressive measures to decapitate the leadership of criminal enterprises, undermine the integrity of their organizations and strip them of their assets are needed. Because the strategy is international, it must include setting norms, and increasing and equalizing the risk faced by transnational criminal organizations irrespective of their home base.

Strategies against organized crime have to be sustained over the long term. Some elements may be urgent, while other initiatives may take several years to devise and implement effectively. Initial successes against particular criminal organizations do not mean that these organizations are necessarily out of business. When criminal organizations are under pressure from law enforcement often they adopt a low profile until vigilance is relaxed. Then they gradually increase their activity level once more. Where law enforcement has become complacent, criminal organizations can often make inroads in infiltrating government and business before they again become targets. Also, in some cases, success against organized crime in one country can contribute to problems elsewhere, as developments in Colombia and Mexico have shown.

International Conventions and Establishing Norms

A regulatory approach to organized crime involves the creation of a policy framework that makes it both more difficult for criminal organizations to pursue their activities and easier for governments, either unilaterally or collectively, to take offensive actions against these organizations. Such an approach rests on states cooperating in order to achieve common interests. One of the priorities in developing coordinated international responses is for states to identify common, actionable values that are threatened by transnational crime. Once these national values have been clarified and placed in the context of other states' values, the process can move forward to forming strategies and designing policies.

The major mechanisms for establishing these values and codifying and coordinating international responses include international conventions. Given the subject matter, the requirement that participating states consent to proposed international responses, and the need for international legal instruments to which national and (possibly) international courts may have recourse, international conventions hold a promising place in the range of options available for coordinating policy internationally. In forming international conventions on criminal law and criminal activities, the problematic question of national sovereignty is sidestepped. Rather than weighing each international case individually and evaluating the merits of foreign claims against concerns of national sovereignty, accession to an international convention would signal a state's recognition that it is in its interest generally to cooperate with other states in this area. International conventions would eliminate much of the *ad hoc* nature of current international efforts, promote rationalization of the system and assure participating states of similar treatment.

In devising a convention, efforts should also be made to engage in what (for lack of a better phrase) might be termed anticipatory norm creation; that is, the establishment of international norms governing certain activities based on the assessment that organized crime *will* become a problem in this area, but enacted or emplaced *before* criminal organizations vigorously move in. For example, had the international community anticipated that transnational criminal organizations would begin to engage in large-scale alien smuggling five or ten years ago, it might have been possible to construct the outlines of a response such as repatriation agreements, special maritime search agreements and immigration exclusion laws before such a response was needed. This is not to suggest that every facet of life be regulated, as that would be as injurious to civil rights and quality of life as any threat from organized crime. In those instances where methods and techniques for anticipating organized crime indicate criminal opportunities, however, and where the cost of acting pre-emptively is relatively moderate, there might well be scope for action. For example, it is already clear that reducing opportunities for criminal involvement in cyber-payments and electronic financial transactions should be a high priority. Viewing this as a problem in the distant future can only lead to a situation in which government authorities and law enforcement agencies are playing a game of catch-up as criminals become adept at exploiting new technologies.

In short, conventions against transnational organized crime would have important symbolic value, help to legitimize national actions against criminal organizations and could have a pre-emptive impact. They would also provide a set of standards and expectations that the signatories would have an obligation to live up to and facilitate the exertion of peer pressure as a common effort of the international community in addressing the problem.[9] The signing of conventions would also provide opportunities for public education and for efforts by political leaders to mobilize those in the private sector whose support they need in order to be more effective.

Enhancing National Judicial and Legal Institutions

States with weak judicial and legal institutions are particularly vulnerable to transnational criminal organizations. Even where a state is sensitized to the threat, lack of institutional effectiveness can preclude the formation and execution of a robust counter-crime strategy. While the international community cannot build foreign institutions from the ground up, there are opportunities for education, training and technical assistance that make a difference in key areas. Functional assistance is especially important when it contributes to the development of functional cooperation between police agencies or customs services in different nations. The USA, the UK and France take this subject seriously.

Some states, especially those in transition and those deeply affected by transnational criminal organizations, might need assistance in developing a regime of criminal law upon which their courts can operate more effectively. Russia's struggle to devise and institute a new criminal justice system is indicative of the magnitude of the challenge in this area. It is not only underdeveloped states, however, that need advice and assistance. Some industrialized states also need to recognize that their current laws, for example those concerning asset forfeiture for criminal activities, need to be reformed. Laws that require asset forfeiture directly related to a single predicate offence such as drug trafficking are not enough, neither is a system of proportionality to social harm. Transnational criminal organizations adjust to such laws by separating their criminal activities from other assets potentially subject to forfeiture, for example by making cashless drug transactions where payments are made separately from the narcotics transactions. There needs to be a punitive element to forfeiture laws designed to deter criminal activities generally.

346

Harmonizing Regulatory and Legal Regimes Across State Boundaries

Similarly, both developed and underdeveloped states must improve their regulation of international and national financial transactions and bring their regulations much more into line with one another. International and national financial transactions offer not only opportunities for interdicting criminal activities, but also provide an avenue for law enforcement agencies to monitor, analyse and plan against transnational criminal organizations. States with more sophisticated financial regulatory systems need to rationalize their systems across international boundaries to deprive criminals of the ability to move funds in and out of certain countries according to their financial needs. Those states with less developed regulatory systems will need assistance to bring their regulatory regimes up to the standards of the more developed states. Rationalization and improvement of regulatory regimes governing international finance are imperative to any strategy aimed at countering transnational organized crime that hopes to achieve reasonable success over time. Since money is the foundation of most criminal enterprises, denying them the ability to move and use money as they please is a key objective for the international community.

National laws can also be brought more into line with one another. Standardization or harmonization is often held up as the ideal, but a more immediate goal should be to achieve greater interoperability. Many of the past problems in international law enforcement efforts have centred around differences in national legal systems and specific national laws. Although many of these were minor, the complications they caused were major. Simply eliminating the complications and creating a situation in which the dual criminality that facilitates extradition is relatively common would be a major step forward. In addition, achieving broad agreement among states in areas such as controlled deliveries would also enhance the capacity to attack criminal organizations. There are several good examples of international agreements that have harmonized national criminal codes or created international criminal law regimes. The 1962 Benelux Treaty on Extradition and Mutual Assistance in Criminal Matters is an early and far-reaching example of this type of deep international cooperation. The Shengen Conventions, adopted by most EU members, represent significant achievements by European states in their efforts to prevent and combat international crime while maintaining a concern for civil liberties. The Europol Convention, now under discussion in Europe, would go even further, harmonizing criminal law throughout Europe and bolstering international law enforcement within the European Union. It is important that regional cooperation of this kind is achieved in a way that does not preclude broader cooperation such as that between Western Europe and the USA. However, institutional change takes time, even if the aim is the more modest one of interoperability rather than harmonization of national laws.

Strengthening Law Enforcement

So long as national law enforcement capacities differ so markedly, making legal systems more congruent will not have maximum impact. An effective legal framework cannot achieve much unless it is accompanied by effective enforcement. Raising the overall effectiveness of law enforcement, therefore, should be another component of the international strategy being outlined here. As part of such an effort, law enforcement officers from countries where expertise is limited and training is poor could be afforded more sophisticated training by more developed countries. Should such efforts do no more than raise the morale of these police organizations, enable them to take advantage of global information systems and train them in the use of important technologies, they would be a success. The USA, France and Britain have long-established training programmes for foreign police from less developed areas and from countries in transition from totalitarian or authoritarian regimes to more democratic societies. In addition, countries such as Germany have provided training and assistance to customs authorities in the Commonwealth of Independent States. These efforts are designed to acquaint foreign law enforcement officers and middle management from these regions with law enforcement investigative techniques, methodology, the rule of law and standards of conduct in civil societies. They also fulfil a very important function in that they help to create effective transnational law enforcement networks. The importance of this is difficult to overestimate as it often takes a network to defeat a network.[10] Since transnational criminal organizations are often network-based, it is important to create parallel cross-border networks of law enforcement officers who also develop a relationship of trust with one another, and can therefore exchange tactical and operational information with a high degree of confidence.

348

In addition to international or unilateral efforts to aid specific states, the international community will need to enhance and empower intergovernmental organizations such as Interpol. Interpol has serious limitations but could well play an increasingly important role in coordinating relationships between Europol and non-EU members of Interpol. At the same time, a special organization comprising representatives of police and security services of a variety of states might need to be formed in order to institutionalize expertise in dealing with organized crime internationally and to produce and distribute analysis of criminal operations for tactical use by national police organizations.

International enforcement mechanisms are necessary because some criminal organizations have structured their operations so that only minor crimes are committed in any single national jurisdiction. The totality of their activities might constitute crimes of massive proportions. In laundering money, for example, the process may be spread across a number of national jurisdictions and specific actions (such as investing cash in legitimate businesses or the losing money at gambling establishments) may not be crimes. In some cases, crime must be considered not as a single act, but as *participation in a process*. Law enforcement organized along national lines, bounded by state boundaries and nationalist outlooks and sources of information, is not competent to meet this challenge.

Part of the answer could be the creation of an international criminal court and an international convention against transnational organized crime. Although states tend to resist the creation of an international criminal court as a trespass on national sovereignty, recognition that the activities of transnational criminal organizations are themselves a threat to sovereignty may encourage relinquishing some of the formalities of sovereignty to protect the underlying realities. Precisely which criminal activities would come under the jurisdiction of the court would depend on what was needed to be effective. This is not yet an idea whose time has come. However, it is a natural step to further progress towards a truly international strategic response.

Removing or Isolating Safe Havens

Unilateral or multilateral policy actions are needed as part of robust international strategies to deny transnational criminal organizations safe home bases from which to operate with relative impunity. This could include providing security assistance to imperilled governments on a bilateral basis. Destabilized states often fail to provide basic security for their own citizens. Colombia provides numerous examples of politicians, judges and policemen who died fighting the drug cartels. The US, French and other governments can play a role in helping to protect presidential candidates from shootings, judges from bombings and off-duty police from kidnappings. An American-trained group in Colombia, in collaboration with the USA, defeated the Medellín Cartel in 1993–94 and led to the capture of six of the nine Cali cartel leaders in 1995.

In some cases the problem is not so much weakness of the state as collusion between criminal organizations and state authorities. An international strategy for countering organized crime must incorporate both the will and the means to influence the behaviour of states that wittingly contribute to organized criminal activity. In the case of Panama under Noriega, after a period of negotiation and efforts to induce Noriega to leave office, the USA resorted to the use of military force.

Military force is a difficult choice, especially when the sanctuary state for transnational criminal organizations is large and powerful. There is a spectrum of available alternatives between large-scale military force and meaningless diplomatic demarches. Economic, political, intelligence-related, military, paramilitary and other instruments have roles to play in this regard. Intelligence, for example, can be used to foil assassination attempts or to guide foreign police operations, paramilitary forces can protect certain foreign persons. At the stage of strategy formation the specifics of how these various instruments might be used are not important; what is important is to recognize the range of instruments available to states and to conceptualize new methods of applying them.

Employing Non-Traditional Counter-Crime Methods

Pursuing traditional regulatory law enforcement strategies, even more intensively and efficiently than before, will not alone prevail over transnational criminal organizations. Disruption is also necessary. In practice, the law enforcement approach attacks a few individuals in an organization and puts them in jail; disruption activities, however, directly target the organization and its ability to operate, irrespective of whether the criminals are formally brought to justice. Compared with the traditional legal approach disruption activities can be much less expensive in terms of resources. Law enforcement efforts focus on criminal prosecutions, which can take years to develop, are difficult to execute and take time to bring to closure. Criminal organizations, however, are often vulnerable to efforts designed to sow confusion and distrust. Methods include strategic penetration of criminal groups, the application of disinformation through narrow channels to undermine confidence and trust among criminal leaders, and the employment of double agents and sting operations for long-term disruption. Such tactics can be particularly useful in undermining strategic and tactical alliances amongst criminal organizations, since these alliances depend ultimately upon trust for their effectiveness. At the same time, this goes beyond legal due process. Consequently, disruption efforts have to be used with care, and with supervision and oversight from parts of government other than the agencies directly involved in the operations. With that proviso, however, this is an area that promises significant payoffs.

Counterintelligence is also important. Just as governments try to infiltrate criminal organizations, so these organizations and their allies in government try to infiltrate and corrupt law enforcement in an effort to thwart or neutralize efforts to combat organized criminal activities. Criminals seek both information and protection. Consequently, protecting government assessments as well as maintaining the integrity of both intelligence and law enforcement services require measures to forestall or inhibit criminal penetration. This is particularly important in international collaborative efforts that involve participants of widely varying degrees of vulnerability to criminal penetration and influence.

Mobilizing and Incorporating the Non-Governmental Sector

Neither governmental nor intergovernmental efforts to combat organized crime can succeed fully without the participation of the private sector. Government action alone is neither feasible nor desirable in a civil society. Certainly it cannot solve the crime problem. Effective responses require the cooperation and creativity of the private sector, government–private sector partnerships and community education programs. There are large roles for the private sector in protecting itself, educating the public to the threat, developing civic institutions and civil behaviour in society, conducting research into the nature of the organized crime problem and developing means to deal with it, and cooperating with government initiatives.

Few individual companies have the capability to take on organized crime, but opportunities for collective action in particular industries and for public–private partnerships are considerable. Where such partnerships are put into effect they allow the resources and ingenuity of the private sector to be used to prevent organized crime from making new inroads. The banking industry, for example, has begun to make preventive education a priority. The OECD's Financial Action Task Force illustrates how to develop this type of government–private sector cooperation, as do some of the initiatives of the G-7/P-8. Governments can disseminate information to the private sector on the threat and how to deal with it, and the private sector can keep governments informed about their needs concerning organized crime and of changes in organized crime activities. Some measures have already been taken. Law enforcement agencies in some countries work with individual banks to sensitize them to threats. The security directors of many sophisticated banks have created a professional association, the International Banking Security Association (IBSA), that meets regularly to exchange information and to consider preventive measures that can be taken without the involvement of government. Some member banks in the British Banking Association have produced first-rate audiovisual training material for their employees, and for use in other countries. Similarly, the US Overseas Security Advisory Council of the Department of State, which represents American businessmen concerned about physical security and terrorism abroad, recently created a Transnational Crime Committee to address methods of improving private sector–government cooperation. In Britain, Customs and the freight-forwarding industry have a memorandum of understanding in which Customs promises to expedite movement of commerce in return for a commitment by the industry to provide information on suspicious activities. Such information can provide valuable and actionable intelligence and has led to some significant drug seizures. This kind of scheme requires minimal investment, has potentially significant payoffs and could easily be extended to other countries.

In addition to businesses, trade unions, educational organizations and other groups can be mobilized for educational and preventive purposes. Preventative educational programmes in primary and secondary schools throughout the world – what specialists refer to as legal socialization – might turn out to be an important ingredient in the overall global strategic mix. Already some regions have created civic education programmes to counter crime and corruption. For example, in Palermo, Italy, 25,000 children annually participate in a multifaceted educational programme that incorporates practical exercises, school projects and classroom lectures. The goal is to change the cultural norms that allow the Mafia to flourish. These programmes attack the clientilistic pattern of Sicilian life, in which corruption and the assistance of a Mafia boss to obtain a job, public housing or a hospital bed is accepted as a necessary part of everyday life. The Comitato dei Lenzuoli's Nine Uncomfortable Guidelines for the Citizen Who Wants to Confront the Mafia includes citizens learning to claim their rights from the state and not relying on the Mafia for assistance, and educating children about democracy and respect for law. Other programmes target what is perceived to be an exaggerated individualism that is at the heart of the Mafia culture. As part of this sense of individualism, defending one's turf is admired, and retaliation and vengeance are viewed as desirable masculine qualities. Civic education programmes for children, in contrast, promote self-help and dispute resolution through activities that stress the concept of team play and conciliation. Even broader initiatives have been taken in Hong Kong.

In addition, a new international non-governmental organization, CIVITAS, based in Strasbourg, France has been created to strengthen effective education for informed and responsible citizenship in new and established democracies. The members of CIVITAS recognize the need for civic education programmes to combat crime and corruption. Its statement of purpose notes that corruption, crime and violence all pose threats to the vitality of democracy.

These efforts are notable. Most of them are new, and are not yet systematically incorporated into the school curriculum, even in Italy. Civic education programmes that can be fully integrated into primary and secondary school curricula around the world and that draw upon the lessons learned from the current efforts are much needed.

Just as private companies and educational institutions can contribute to the success of a counter-organized-crime campaign, other types of non-governmental organizations (NGOs) and civic organizations can also make significant contributions. NGOs often have access to or develop their own sources of information, and they are particularly adept at monitoring certain activities in the field. Human Rights Watch and Amnesty International, which monitor human rights internationally, exemplify the type of information gathering and assessment role that NGOs might play. Examples related more directly to the activities of transnational criminal organizations include End Child Prostitution in Asian Tourism (ECPAT), which has succeeded in focusing attention on an extensive but long-neglected problem and which has had some success in pressing governments to impose criminal penalties on citizens who have sex with minors while overseas. Germany, the Netherlands and Australia have subsequently successfully prosecuted such cases. When it becomes clear that abusing child prostitutes overseas can no longer be done with impunity, this will affect market demand. Another NGO also making a contribution is Transparency International, which monitors corruption, producing international rankings of states that are widely disseminated and reported.

Greater transparency is also an area where there are opportunities for partnerships between governments and the media. Journalists in print and television, for example, should be encouraged to investigate and document transnational criminal organizations and their activities in an informed rather than sensationalist manner. They should receive not only government and law enforcement cooperation wherever possible, but also protection where necessary. While the press has an obvious adversarial role with government that is particularly important in emerging democracies, it should also be regarded as a partner especially for those governments committed to rooting out corruption and combating transnational criminal organizations.

CONCLUSIONS

The strategy outlined above is intended to be both realistic and comprehensive. Although the growing wealth of transnational criminal enterprises, their capacity to corrupt and co-opt governments and the adaptability and resilience of their structures make them extremely formidable adversaries, they are neither invulnerable nor invincible. It may be impossible to eliminate organized crime, but much can be done to combat it, and many important initiatives have already been taken. The mix of global, regional and bilateral arrangements we now have, has developed somewhat haphazardly. Cooperation has grown up in incremental steps and without any overall design, but is now at a point where some planning and regularization would be productive. There has to be a clear and sustained commitment to dealing with a long-term problem based on structural changes in global political, economic and social relationships.

Political will is critical both to mobilize support and resources against transnational criminal organizations and to ensure that resources are allocated more effectively. For example, we need to rearrange priorities in the balance of effort dealing with drug trafficking and with organized crime. At present, combating transnational organized crime is the poor relation of drug control in terms of overall resources devoted to the problem. An alternative approach would be to view the drug market as simply one of the illicit markets in which transnational criminal organizations are major players. In other words, the drug problem can be seen as a sub-set of the transnational organized crime threat. The other critical issue is to ensure that combating transnational criminal organizations remains high on the priority list of the major powers and is not relegated or sacrificed for the sake of political and economic convenience. Even if there were a commitment by governments to a long-term strategy that is proactive, comprehensive and involves extensive collaboration with the non-governmental sector, this is still no guarantee of success. But without such a strategy, failure in the struggle against transnational criminal organizations could well be inevitable.

NOTES

The authors wish to thank Joseph Trapple, Ph.D. candidate at Georgetown University, for his assistance in the preparation of this article.

1. See Robert S. Leiken, 'The Global Corruption', *Foreign Policy*, No.105 (Winter 1996–97), pp.55–76.
2. Jonathan M. Winer, 'International Crime in the new Geopolitics: A Core Threat to Democracy', in William F. McDonald (ed.), *Crime and Law Enforcement in the Global Village* (Cincinnati, OH.: Anderson, 1997), pp.41–64, at p.47.
3. *World Drug Report* (Oxford: Oxford University Press, 1997) p.124.
4. These assessments are provided by the International Anti-Counterfeiting Coalition (IACC) on its Web site (http://www.ari.net/iacc/economic.html).
5. See Malcolm Anderson, 'Interpol and the Developing System of Police Cooperation', in McDonald, op. cit., pp.89–102.
6. See Phil Williams and Ernesto Savona (eds.), *The United Nations and Transnational Organized Crime* (London and Portland, OR: Frank Cass, 1995), p.174.
7. Ibid.
8. Francis J. Ianni, *Black Mafia* (New York: Simon and Schuster, 1974), pp.282–90.
9. See Williams and Savona, op. cit. p. 180.
10. This is an important theme in John Arquilla and David Ronfeldt (eds.), *In Athena's Camp: Preparing for Conflict in the Information Age* (Santa Monica, CA: RAND, 1997).

Drafting the United Nations Convention against Transnational Organized Crime

DIMITRI VLASSIS

On the recommendation of the Commission on Crime Prevention and Criminal Justice, the General Assembly adopted in December 1998 a resolution by which it established a new intergovernmental Ad Hoc Committee. This body was charged with a dual task: to elaborate the convention against transnational organized crime and discuss the elaboration of three additional international legal instruments or protocols to the convention on illegal transport and trafficking in migrants, on illicit trafficking of persons, especially women and children, and on illicit manufacturing of and trafficking in firearms, their parts and components and ammunition. States undertook the commitment to see this process to completion by the year 2000 and did so. The General Assembly also accepted the Commission's recommendation to elect Ambassador Luigi Lauriola as the Chairman of the Ad Hoc Committee.

The adoption of the December 1998 resolution marked the beginning of a process that will lead to an historic action by the international community in the fight against transnational organized crime. However, for all practical purposes, this process had begun a few years before the formal action by the General Assembly. The idea for a global international legal instrument against transnational organized crime first surfaced at the Naples Ministerial Conference on Organized Transnational Crime, in November 1994. The scepticism of some of the developed countries about the feasibility of negotiating such an instrument were at the root of the rather conditional language that found its way into the Naples Political Declaration and Global Action Plan, which was the main product of that event. But the seeds had been sown. Two follow-up regional ministerial conferences, in Buenos Aires in 1995 and in Dakar in 1997, served as fora for a large number of countries to voice their political support for the new convention and strongly urge the expedient commencement of negotiations. In

December 1996, Poland submitted a first draft of a possible convention to the General Assembly in an effort to boost the process and demonstrate that many of the issues that countries feared would be difficult to tackle were in fact much more accessible. The Commission on Crime Prevention, with its annual sessions, provided the opportunity for countries to continue exploring the matter and helped nurture the political will required for action. In 1997, the Commission moved a step closer to the formal endorsement of the new convention and the authorization to begin negotiations, by recommending to the General Assembly the adoption of a resolution with which it set up a group of governmental experts and asked it to explore the contours of an international convention. This group was hosted by Poland in Warsaw in February 1998 and compiled a list of options, which was in essence the first rough draft of a new convention. The product of the group's work was reviewed by the Commission in April 1998 and, as mentioned earlier, the Commission recommended to the General Assembly the adoption of the resolution, by virtue of which the Ad Hoc Committee was established.

In order to prepare for the work of the Ad Hoc Committee, and to make the best possible use of the time between the recommendation of the Commission and action by the General Assembly (which normally makes decisions on matters related to crime prevention and criminal justice late in the year), an informal group of 'Friends of the Chair' was formed. This group held three meetings – in Rome in July, in Buenos Aires in August and in Vienna in November 1998 – to discuss mainly procedural matters in preparation for the establishment and formal sessions of the Ad Hoc Committee. Further, in order to ensure the uninterrupted continuation of the work on the elaboration of the convention, and to sustain the momentum towards the new instrument, the government of Argentina generously hosted an informal preparatory meeting of the Ad Hoc Committee in Buenos Aires from 31 August to 4 September 1998. That meeting completed the first reading of the list of options that had been compiled in February in Warsaw by the intergovernmental group of experts, and produced a new consolidated draft text, which was the basis for the Ad Hoc Committee's work when it held its first official meeting in Vienna from 18 to 29 January 1999.

With the negotiation of the new convention, the international community embarked on a challenging and demanding endeavour: to equip the world with a strong, functional and effective international instrument to fight organized crime. It is an instrument that will act as a shield for all countries of the world against the operations of organized criminal groups; an instrument that will strengthen the existing capacity of countries to counter organized crime and create that capacity for those countries that do not yet possess it; and an instrument that will ensure that there are no more safe havens for organized criminal groups to operate from, flee to or hide in and enjoy their ill-gotten gains.

Organized crime is a threat to all the values that the democratic world holds dear. There are fundamental changes that have brought this about. The traditional roles, activities and structures of organized crime are being reviewed and altered. The result is a new profile of organized crime. Diversification, flexibility, increased sophistication and modernization are its new characteristics. The old, well-known 'mafias' have revamped their structures and operations, while smaller and much more flexible groups have emerged and are operating all over the world. They, too, are shifting from country to country, region to region and activity to activity, depending on opportunity, profitability and the lack of capacity on the part of national authorities to place their operations at risk. Organized crime has become a global business with turnover and profits that very often dwarf the gross domestic product (GDP) of many nations. Recent findings suggest that the profits of migrant smugglers could be US$9.5 billion annually. Another US$6 billion is earned by trafficking in stolen, smuggled or looted art and US$5 billion by trafficking in flora and fauna. It is estimated that if trafficking in stolen motor vehicles were a legitimate business it would rank fifth in the Fortune 500. Two million women and children are estimated to be the victims of trafficking, an activity whose dimensions cannot be measured only in monetary terms, in view of the human suffering it entails. All this is additional to the more traditional activities of organized criminal groups, such as drug trafficking, arms trafficking and smuggling and numerous other illicit activities, with huge profits. These profits find their way into the legitimate financial systems and markets, placing their very existence in grave danger. It is a consensus view that the present scale of money laundering transactions ranges between two and five per cent of the global GDP. The potential implications defy imagination.

The point is that organized crime is no longer a merely national law enforcement problem, to be dealt with by local authorities, sometimes cooperating with each other. It is an international, indeed a global problem, requiring joint, concerted and sustained action by governments and the civil society together at all levels. The elaboration of the new convention must be done with all these facts and needs in mind.

The process did not start from zero. The international community had made several important steps forward in the effort to tackle the problem. The 1988 Convention against Illicit Drug Trafficking and the initiatives of organizations such as the European Union and the Organization of American States and influential groups such as the G8, have made the momentum towards the convention possible. They have also resulted in a body of work that can provide inspiration. The challenge facing states is to develop an instrument that will enable them to deal with transnational organized crime in all its forms and manifestations. To do so, they must try to go beyond the existing international instruments and guidelines, being resourceful and innovative.

The Ad Hoc Committee has held seven sessions so far. At the session in January 2000, the Committee began the finalization of the text of the convention. The discussions held so far, the texts under consideration, the vigorous pace kept until now and, most importantly, the commitment to complete the negotiation process by the end of 2000, which was achieved (that is a very short period for the elaboration of such a major international instrument), demonstrate that states have accepted this challenge. However, they should be encouraged not to shy away from it in the future, no matter what difficulties they encounter. And there still are, and will be, difficulties.

One of the issues that needs to be resolved concerns the scope of the convention. There are currently two views on the matter. One contends that the convention should include a definition of transnational organized crime and contain a list of offences committed by organized criminal groups. The other view, which appears to be shared by the majority of countries, is that the convention will achieve its goals if it is guided by an awareness that organized crime can be best attacked if the focus is not so much on the activities organized crime is engaged in at any given time but on its structures and operations. According to the proponents of this view, trying to cover in the convention all possible activities in which organized criminal groups are engaged, or may be engaged in the future, is an exercise in futility. Even if the text is as comprehensive as can be, the instrument will be limited already when finalized and signed. The convention should attack and seek to destroy criminal organizations, regardless of their activities. Only then will the new instrument withstand the test of time and help countries fight organized crime. The international community needs a convention with a broad scope, designed to be effective no matter how diverse and sophisticated organized criminal groups are or might try to become.

One of the issues related to the scope of the convention is criminalization. The new convention will be an efficient tool if it embodies the commitment of states to accept obligations to take specific legislative measures. Fighting organized crime in the present global setting requires compatible laws and national measures. The convention should bring about the desired level of compatibility in key areas of national legislation and regulatory regimes, especially with regard to participation in a criminal organization or conspiracy. This aspect of the convention is crucial. Criminalization provisions will ensure that all countries put up the same insurmountable obstacles to the operations of criminal groups, but also lay the foundations of meaningful and successful cooperation.

The convention's provisions on cooperation are equally important. The purpose of these provisions would be to deliver to national law enforcement and judicial authorities the tools they need to succeed in investigating and prosecuting organized crime cases. For this purpose, it is foreseen that considerable discussion will take place about the scope of these provisions. The view has been advanced that the convention should not only be a tool that national authorities can use to build and process cases of organized crime; it should enable authorities to determine at a very early stage whether the case that comes across their desk is one in which organized crime is involved. Very often, the first indications or scraps of evidence that surface are scanty and not enough for even the most experienced investigator or magistrate to have an accurate picture. With the transnational character of organized crime more and more prevalent, the competent authorities need information and evidence to complete their understanding of a case at a very early stage in their work. The convention should be there to help them get that information and evidence from other countries as soon and as early as possible and, in addition, with a minimum of effort. For all these reasons, the negotiations are characterized by flexibility and innovation to build into the convention the modalities that are essential for law enforcement agencies and the judiciary to do their job.

The financial aspects of organized crime and the potential implications of the funds that are laundered daily were mentioned above. The new convention would provide an opportunity, not to be missed, to put in place a set of measures that would essentially remove obstacles to investigating and prosecuting money laundering, regardless of the predicate offence. The provisions of the 1988 Convention and other international recommendations and regional instruments can serve as the point of departure. Many countries think that the new convention can and must go beyond and include obligations for states to make money laundering a criminal offence, and cooperate in its investigation and prosecution, without regard to the source of the illicit assets or income that is laundered. These provisions need to be supplemented and reinforced by provisions on confiscation of assets and on bank secrecy. Both issues are quite delicate and complicated. However, many countries believe that we cannot look forward to an instrument that can be successful in fighting organized crime without innovative measures designed to deprive criminal organizations of their lifeline and source of power: their wealth. We cannot hope to deliver effective blows to transnational criminal organizations while allowing bank secrecy provisions to stand in the way of criminal investigations. Therefore, we foresee that a lot of effort will be put into finding acceptable but also workable ways of dealing with both confiscation of assets and removing bank secrecy for the purpose of criminal investigations.

We are all aware of the maxim on the value attached to an ounce of prevention. That value is even higher when it comes to action against organized crime. Many countries believe that the new convention will make a long-lasting contribution to national and international efforts by including provisions designed to achieve two fundamental goals – to keep organized crime out of the legal economy and out of politics. In order to shield the legitimate economy from the efforts at infiltration of organized crime, it is necessary to include measures that would prevent organized crime from identifying and entering markets, one of its increasingly prevalent characteristics. Second, the convention should include measures designed to strengthen the culture of legality, which is the only way of ensuring that organized criminal groups do not forge links with the political establishment, or find support within society.

In addition to the negotiations on the convention, the Ad Hoc Committee was charged with the elaboration of three protocols against smuggling of migrants, illicit manufacturing of and trafficking in firearms, their parts, components and ammunition, and trafficking in persons, especially women and children. The elaboration of these instruments has been proceeding in parallel with the work on the convention and they are currently at various stages of development.

The achievement of the goals of the convention will hinge not only on the obligations and measures it will include, but also on the capacity of all countries to sustain their commitment and honour their obligations. There needs to be a conscious effort through appropriate provisions in the convention to achieve comparative parity in the capacity of states. That implies provisions on technical cooperation and the concomitant commitment by donor countries to make available the required resources. The new convention must mark the beginning of a joint effort in which there will be no weak links. Lack of capacity to fight organized crime domestically or to cooperate so as to fight it internationally is bound to create weak links that the international community cannot afford. Countries should, therefore, be encouraged to look upon technical cooperation as an investment in the future with the potential for very high returns.

Finally, considerable thought is already being given to the provisions on the implementation of the convention and its protocols. The premise for this is that the international community needs an instrument that is not only forward-looking and innovative, but also functions. Its implementation requires a mechanism of regular and vigorous follow-up so that weaknesses or lapses, and their reasons, can be quickly identified and corrected. The effort does not stop with the elaboration and ratification of the instrument. On the contrary, that is where it begins. There are now draft provisions, which will be thoroughly debated, to put in place a monitoring mechanism for the purpose of ensuring that this will not end up as just another international instrument that remains only in the books as a honourable effort.

The work before the Ad Hoc Committee continues to be complex and difficult. However, there are many reasons for optimism. Rarely has an idea matured and acquired the consensus of the international community so quickly, overcoming scepticism about the tendency to reduce international instruments down to the lowest common denominator. The decision to go forward and to do so in two years shows the determination of the international community to resist that tendency and will give states the tool to make a quantum leap in the fight against transnational organized crime.

POSTSCRIPT

This contribution covers the negotiations up to a certain point and is included for its historical value. The Convention and the two Protocols have now been completed, approved by the General Assembly of the United Nations (November 2000), and signed by 124 countries (Convention), 82 countries (Trafficking Protocol) and 79 countries (Migrant Smuggling Protocol), up to the end of February 2001.

Abstracts

The Dynamics of Illegal Markets *by Pino Arlacchi*

This study examines the nature and dynamics of illegal markets and suggests ways in which these can be attacked. It defines an illegal market as a place or principle within which there is an exchange of goods and services, whose production, selling and consumption are forbidden or strictly regulated by the majority of states and/or by international law. The analysis also argues that multilateral treaties on the protection of human rights, international conventions on slavery, narcotics and psychotropic substances, the outlawing of violence in inter-state disputes, more restrictive domestic and international regulations on the use and trade of arms, are some of the basic examples of legal provisions contributing to the creation of today's illegal markets. Differences between legal and illegal markets are highlighted and the role of criminal organizations in illegal markets is explored. The analysis also highlights ways in which criminal markets and criminal organizations can be attacked and suggests that governments have already succeeded in bursting the myth of the invincibility of criminal organizations. The Convention against Transnational Crime will facilitate even further inroads against illegal markets.

Transnational Crime: Definitions and Concepts *by Gerhard O.W. Mueller*

This paper examines the concept 'transnational crime'. It looks at the origins and development of the term noting that it was coined by the then UN Crime Prevention and Criminal Justice Branch, in the mid-1970s to identify certain criminal phenomena transcending international borders, transgressing the laws of several states, or having an impact on another country. In the 1990s it was refined to cover 'offences whose inception, prevention and/or direct or indirect effects involved more than one country' The author, drawing on the UN approach identifies 18 categories of activities that come under the rubric of transnational crime. Each of these categories is discussed in turn and the analysis discusses the ways in which many of them have been facilitated by globalization.

Globalization and Transnational Crime: Effects of Criminogenic Asymmetries *by Nikos Passas*

Although international white-collar crime and illegal markets, commonly described as 'organized crime', are no new phenomena, but have received increasing attention in recent years. All too often, however, their underlying dynamics are not fully explored. Accordingly, this analysis contends that the causes of corporate offences and illegal enterprises can be traced to 'criminogenic asymmetries', defined as structural disjunctions, mismatches, and inequalities in the spheres of politics, culture, the economy and the law. These asymmetries generate or strengthen the demand for illegal goods and services; (2) generate incentives for particular actors to participate in illegal transactions; and (3) reduce the ability of authorities to control illegal activities. The asymmetries are multiplied and intensified by globalization. At the same time, control capacities are seriously undermined. Ultimately, however, the asymmetries are the results of government policies. Recognition of this needs to be the starting point for developing more sophisticated responses.

Organizing Transnational Crime: Networks, Markets and Hierarchies *by Phil Williams*

In recent years, the scale, diversity, and range of activities pursued by criminal organizations has broadened significantly, while illicit markets and informal economies have also expanded. This paper seeks to provide some conceptual clarifications that might be helpful in understanding these developments, to identify both macro-level and micro-level factors that help to explain why criminal enterprises move from domestic to transnational activities, and to examine the way these enterprises are structured. It suggests that traditional models of criminal organizations that emphasize hierarchical or pyramidal structures are not particularly appropriate to transnational criminal organizations or transnational markets. Indeed, the key to understanding transnational criminal organizations and the markets they inhabit is through criminal networks that are active in criminal markets that are also populated by a myriad of other actors. The paper also considers the role of academic analysis and suggest that it might be particularly useful in assisting data collection, monitoring and early warning as well as in the creation of networks of knowledge and expertise.

Criminal Fraternities or Criminal Enterprises? *by Letizia Paoli*

This analysis focuses on those lasting large-scale criminal organizations, such as the Italian Cosa Nostra and 'Ndrangheta, the American La Cosa Nostra, the Chinese Triads and the Japanese Yakuza, that are usually presented as the archetype of organized crime.Although their members are heavily involved in illegal businesses today, neither the development nor the internal organization of mafia associations are the product of illegal markets dynamics. Far from resembling a modern business firm, the major associations in mafia organizations are founded on relations of ritual kinship. With the entrance into the mafia group, the novice is required to assume a new identity permanently and to subordinate all his previous allegiances to the mafia membership. The kin-like relations created with the rite of initiation are then further reinforced with symbols and codes drawn from the kinship language. To be effective, the ritual brotherhood that is created must be ready to use violence. The analysis concludes that this organizational formula - a mix between ritual kinship and violence - seems to be essential for the survival of large collectivities 'on the wrong side of the law', because all major illegal organizations resort to it. In addition to the mafia organizations the clannish model of organization is employed by terrorist groups and juvenile gangs.

Organized Crime and Ethnic Minorities: Is There a Link? *by Frank Bovenkerk*

Every time new signs of organized crime are discovered in modern, urban societies, with striking frequency some ethnic minority - either recent or still unassimilated immigrants or some indigenous minority like Native Americans in the United States or gypsies in Europe - is singled out as the source of the trouble. A description of the groups engaged in the Western world's drug trade, for example, reads like a list of foreign and local ethnic minorities. Yet, in twentieth century history, drawing a link between criminality and ethnic or national descent or the status of a minority has led to any number of theoretical and political miscalculations and misconceptions. Accordingly, the analysis here offers a critical assessment of this issue. It explores the reasons for posing the question of linkage, arguing that although the issue is sensitive it must not be taboo. It then explores three groups of factors related to the linkage: political and geographical causes, a sociological explanation, and the extent to which ethnic organized crime is culture-related. The analysis concludes that there are three good theoretical grounds for assuming there really is such a link: there are political and geographical factors that make such a linkage probable; following the logic of strain theory, it is clear that under certain conditions, some minorities run a heightened risk, and finally, illegal organizations can sometimes thrive within the seclusion of ethnic minority communities. The implication of all this is that the topic deserves to be on the research agenda.

Transnational Chinese Organized Crime Activities:Patterns And Emerging Trends *by Ko-Lin Chin Sheldon Zhang and Robert J. Kelly*

In recent years the increase of Chinese crime groups in heroin and human trafficking activities has been widely reported. Yet, only a handful of serious research studies have been conducted. This analysis clarifies the various Chinese crime groups that are often considered to make up the 'Chinese Mafia,' and then examines their two major transnational criminal activities – heroin trafficking and human smuggling. Based on a series of studies on Chinese organized crime groups covering four main areas: (1) a descriptive analysis of various Chinese crime groups in the United States and Asia; (2) problems of extortion in New York City's Chinese community; (3) the structure and activity of Chinese gangs; and (4) Chinese alien smuggling, the analysis highlights a new kind of different criminal subculture, be it for the sale of drugs or the smuggling of human or other illicit commodities, among the Chinese in the United States, Hong Kong, Canada, Australia, Europe, and other parts of the world. Members of this subculture include import-export businessmen, community leaders, restaurant owners, workers, gamblers, housewives, and the unemployed. It is extremely difficult to penetrate this subculture because members have no prior criminal records, no identifiable organization, and no rigid structure, or clearly defined deviant norms and values. They can conceal their criminal activities through their involvement in lawful business activities. Their participation in criminal activities is sporadic rather than continuous. It argues that law enforcement needs to take these modalities into account in its efforts to combat Chinese crime.

Maritime Fraud and Piracy *by Jayant Abhyankar*

The range of maritime fraud is startlingly wide and, as with other types of crime, is constantly being expanded in line with the ingenuity and imagination of the people who practice it. Indeed, today's maritime fraud can be defined as a combination of various criminal acts such as forgery, piracy, theft, arson etc, where one or more parties end up losing money, goods or even a vessel. Maritime crime and frauds can be classified into the following types: documentary; charter party; insurance; container crime; deviation; phantom ships; and piracy. The analysis not only looks at the mechanisms and modalities of the major maritime frauds but also identifies warning signs and highlights ways in which the chances of being a victim can be minimized. The phenomenon of phantom ships is also examined. The analysis also provides a discussion of six major types of piracy.

Crime in Cyberspace by P.N. Grabosky

The convergence of computing and communications has already affected most if not all of the major institutions of society. It has also created unprecedented opportunities for crime. Given the fact that cyberspace knows no boundaries, and that computer crime often transcends national frontiers, effective countermeasures will also require a degree of international cooperation that is without precedent. Information systems are being used to facilitate organized drug trafficking, gambling, prostitution, money laundering, child pornography and trade in weapons (in those jurisdictions where such activities are illegal). Such systems enhance the speed and ease with which individuals may act together to plan and to execute criminal activity. The main kinds of activities are discussed, along with emerging technologies of encryption and high speed data transfer that not only enhance the capacity of sophisticated criminal organizations but also place their communications outside the reach of law enforcement. The detection, investigation and prosecution of forms of criminality related to cyberspace pose formidable challenges. Overcoming the transnational issues of crime in cyberspace lies in developing cooperation between nations, and the various ways in which this has been done – and can be extended – are identified.

The Rise of the Modern Arms Black Market and the Fall of Supply-Side Control by R.T. Naylor

The volatile combination of a breakdown in the old oligopoly of power, the resurrection of ethno-religious identification in place of membership in a civil society, and the triumph of savage capitalism with its increasing disparities in the distribution of income, wealth and ecological capital goes far to explain the present-day epidemic of political violence. The other reason for much of the current carnage is the triumph of a 'free market' in the instruments for effecting political and social change by violent means.

Historically the control mechanisms were of two sorts: major power control and limited capacity of non-state actors to obtain the means of payment. Today, neither of those constraints seems operational. Weapons are easily available to all who have the ability to pay, and the global explosion of illicit activity has put the means of payment within the grasp of a remarkably diverse set of insurgent groups, paramilitary forces, militant religious sects and unabashed bandit gangs. This analysis develops the reasons for this availability, highlighting the disintegration of supply-side control and criticizing a narrow focus on control of light weapons. Supply side solutions have severe shortcomings. The real problem is the demand side. And attacking the problem of arms proliferation from the demand side requires efforts to shift loyalties back, away from clan, sect and tribe in favor of rebuilding civil societies.

Trafficking and Sexual Exploitation of Women and Children by Livia Pomodoro

This analysis starts from the premise that migrants may be considered in need of protection because of their extreme vulnerability, especially where there exists markets which encourage their exploitation. Recent classifications of persons in need of protection include women (who have been recruited with false promises of employment but who are destined, in practice, to be coerced into prostitution and unpaid labor) and children. The problems have been exacerbated by greater freedom of movement within the whole of Europe, east and west; the great gap in living standards between developed and developing countries; the virtual lack of serious penalties for certain types of crime; and the growth and internationalization of organized crime. The analysis identifies shortcomings in the responses of the international community and proposes a series of remedial measures.

Trafficking in People: The Human Rights Dimension by Office of the High Commissioner for Human Rights (OHCHR)

Starting from the proposition that organized trans-border criminality of all types is thriving, and trafficking in people for diverse purposes has been on the increase, generating huge profits for the traffickers and international crime rings, this analysis looks at both the dynamics of trafficking and the nature of the anti-trafficking regime, before identifying additional measures that urgently need to be introduced. It emphasizes the need for a comprehensive definition of trafficking, based on accepted international standards and more in keeping with modern manifestations of trafficking to include not only commercial sex work, but also manual or industrial labor (that amounts to slavery), marriage, adoption, domestic servitude, begging or for criminal purposes.

Another fundamental principle is that measures taken by states to combat trafficking must focus on the promotion of human rights, and must not further marginalize, criminalize, stigmatize or isolate victims of trafficking, thereby making them more vulnerable to violence and abuse. Among the additional measures needed are efforts to break the poverty cycle, better training of officials, and more opportunities for victims to press criminal charges or take civil action for compensation from the traffickers.

Money Laundering in Italy *by Alessandro Pansa*

The salience of money laundering reflects its incredible importance within the criminal world, especially now that economic related crimes are the most widespread. At the same time, money laundering is strategically important since its international scope obliges criminal organizations to develop transnational networks, as well as to connect with criminal environments of different origins. Although there are major gaps in knowledge about money laundering, analyses carried out as a result of specific criminal investigations Italy have provided important insights. They suggest that focusing on the financial system alone is not effective. In fact, the results of the fight against money laundering based on a repressive and preventive system, with a mainly financial approach, are not encouraging. The preventive system consists of prohibitions and control barriers confined almost exclusively to the financial sector. Most of the trade market is not included, yet this an area where real and effective transparency and efficient prevention mechanisms can be reached only by means of direct involvement of the participants themselves. In light of all this, there are three ways to respond more effectively: (1) strengthening the repressive system against money laundering by enhancing investigators' operative capacity at the international level and beyond the financial system; (2) increasing resort to the seizure and confiscation of assets whose origin cannot be proven by criminals; and (3) the involvement of the international economic system, making it feasible and favorable for legally operating subjects to reject dirty money by refusing to cooperate with money launderers.

Strengthening the International Legal System in order to Combat Transnational Crime by *Giuseppe di Gennaro*

Over the last 20 years there has been a growing preoccupation with transnational crime. This has mobilized various international authorities and numerous initiatives have been taken within Europe by the Council of Europe and the European Union, while comparable steps have been taken in other parts of the world, and most notably by the United Nations. The UN has studied the subject at a number of important meetings, and particularly at the Ministerial Conference on Transnational Organized Crime, held at Naples, 21–23 November 1994. Yet the criminal organizations have increased in quantity and type, the links between criminal powers and the management of the economy, conduct of business, and public and political authorities, have become ever more complex and shadowy. Accordingly, it is necessary to give greater vigor to the international legal system in combating transnational crime. In this connection, the lack of a common definition has been a problem. Beyond agreement on a definition, it is clearly necessary to improve judicial cooperation. Unfortunately, initiatives relating to judicial organization, however important they may be, do not have a direct impact on the control of this type of crime. The functioning of all such judicial machinery presupposes an investigative capability at an international level which can obtain the essential data for the discovery of crimes that have been committed and the identification of their perpetrators. Such a capability is possessed only by the police organizations. Although collaborative accords between the various national police forces are an important step forward, real efficiency can only be achieved by a genuine internationalization of the police.

Responding to Transnational Crime by *Raymond E. Kendall*

Starting from the premise that transnational crime is a major challenge facing the world community in general and the global law enforcement community in particular, this article looks at major trends in organized crime and the role of Interpol in combating transnational crime. The analysis emphasizes that investigations of transnational criminal organizations are much more complicated than investigations of traditional crime groups operating in one area or country. It suggests that Interpol has a critical role to play especially given that it has an efficient, secure and reliable telecommunications system which links each of the Interpol National Central Bureaus by e-mail and gives automated access to a central database of information on international crime and criminals. Another important initiative has been the creation of an analytical criminal intelligence unit to extract and analyze data from the organization's centralized database. By facilitating the exchange of not only investigative data but also law enforcement-related technology and forensic methods, Interpol will continue to act as a bridge which links the law enforcement agencies of the world.

Transnational Organized Crime and Institutional Reform in The European Union: the Case of Judicial Cooperation *by Cyrille Fijnaut*

In recent years, the European Council, the European Parliament and the European Commission have frequently emphasized the importance of police, customs, and judicial cooperation among the member states in controlling organized crime in the European Union (EU), particularly where protection of the financial interests of the European Communities (EC) is concerned. Differences have emerged, however, over the continued development of judicial cooperation in the EU versus the expansion of a communitarian or supranational criminal justice system. The analysis looks at both sides of this argument, while also following the laborious and complex progression of judicial cooperation as given shape in the EU, both in the context of the Third Pillar and in the context of the First Pillar. It also includes reference to the Action Plan to combat organized crime adopted by the European Council in spring 1997. Tensions between the two pillars are identified, but since 1995, judicial cooperation appears to have been boosted as much as police cooperation with the result that the 'espace judiciaire et policier européen' is finally becoming reality. Consequently, the argument concludes that a radical supranational approach should only be employed if it has both been clearly demonstrated that the problem of organized (economic and financial) crime is really so serious that a communitarian approach is called for and that intergovernmental, judicial (and police) cooperation, despite improvements, is no longer really suitable for bringing and keeping this crime under control.

Responding to Transnational Crime – The Role of Europol *by* *Emanuele Marotta*

The analysis identifies the new challenges presented by international organised crime and elucidates the response of the EU countries, with particular emphasis on the role, competencies and the activity of Europol. It suggests that new challenges can be understood in terms of novel elements in criminal behaviour often in relation to the use of new technologies, the spread of the criminal environment to new fields of activity; and a better understanding and assessment of existing criminal phenomena, that have been investigated and revealed more fully than in the past. The principal characteristics of the organized threat to the European Union are discussed in relation to fraud, extortion, illegal immigration and money laundering as well as the nature of Russian organized crime. The establishment of a European Police Office – Europol - is the European Union's answer to this threat and is a milestone in the effort to strengthen law enforcement cooperation in a Europe without frontiers. Having looked at the role, responsibilities, and limitations of Europol, the author suggests that Europol requires that national police agencies revise their organizational and functional schemes, look beyond national borders and cooperate more.

International Atomic Energy Agency Programme against Illicit Trafficking of Nuclear Materials and Radioactive Sources *by Anita Nillson*

Since 1995, the IAEA has implemented a programme called Security of Material aimed at assisting member states, through training, expert assistance, equipment and exchange of information in their efforts to protect nuclear and other radioactive materials against unauthorized (criminal) activities and provide them with the knowledge and tools for detecting and responding to incidents of illegal trafficking should they occur. An important element of the programme is the maintenance of the Illicit Trafficking Database Programme in which the IAEA continuously registers confirmed incidents of illegal trafficking in radioactive materials. It is generally agreed that the problem of illicit trafficking of nuclear materials and radioactive sources should be addressed first through prevention. The complexity of measures for safety, security, physical protection, accountancy and control (including the control of trans-border movements) of these materials constitute the protective system as a whole. Technical cooperation and legal and regulatory cooperation are also required.

Strengthening Cooperation against Transnational Crime: A New Security Imperative *by Roy Godson and Phil Williams*

Starting from the recognition that national strategies are inherently inadequate for responding to challenges that cross multiple borders and involve multiple jurisdiction, this paper outlines a comprehensive strategy against transnational criminal organizations, based on an assessment of the kinds of threat they pose, their strengths and weaknesses, and countermeasures that have proved most effective. It examines the existing responses, and in particular the role of Interpol, Europol, the G-8, and the United Nations and then contends that more comprehensive and coordinated strategies against transnational criminal organizations are essential. These require specifying objectives and the means to pursue them and include information sharing arrangements, international conventions and norms, enhancing national judicial and legal institutions, harmonizing regulatory and legal regimes across state boundaries, removing or isolating safe havens, employing non-traditional counter-crime methods, and mobilizing and incorporating the non-governmental sector particularly in developing a culture on which the rule of law can be based. In conclusion, it is noted that although a long-term strategy that is pro-active, comprehensive, and involves extensive collaboration with the non-governmental sector, is no guarantee of success, without such an approach to combating transnational organized crime failure is virtually guaranteed.

Drafting the United Nations Convention against Transnational Organized Crime *by Dimitri Vlassis*

The United Nations during the 1990s increasingly took initiatives against transnational organized crime. The World Ministerial Conference on organized transnational crime held in Naples in November 1994 resulted in a Political Declaration and Global Action Plan. It also sowed the seeds for the negotiation of a Convention against Transnational Organized Crime. This analysis highlights the negotiating process that took place until early to mid-2000. It highlights the contentious issues such as the scope of the convention, the concerns of certain nations and groupings, and the key differences that had to be overcome before agreement could be reached. Key milestones in the negotiating process are identified and the critical role of the Ad Hoc Committee is also discussed.

Notes on Contributors

Jayant Abhyankar is the Deputy Director of the International Maritime Bureau (IMB) – a specialized division of the International Chamber of Commerce. Founded in 1981, the IMB takes a leading role in countering maritime fraud, piracy and related problems. Abhyankar is a master mariner and holds a Master of Science degree in International Shipping from Plymouth where his thesis was on martime crime. He has been with the IMB sice its inception and was in charge of setting up the piracy reporting centre in Kuala Lumpur.

Pino Arlacchi was appointed Executive Director of the United Nations Office for Drug Control and Crime Prevention (ODCCP) on 1 September 1997,with the rank of Under-Secretary-General. He was also named Director-General of the United Nations Office at Vienna (UNOV) where he lives and works. Pino Arlacchi was a member of the Italian Senate from 1995 to 1997 and of the Chamber of Deputies from 1994 to 1995. During this period, he was elected Vice-President of the Parliamentary Commission on the Mafia, on which he had served as an adviser from 1984 to 1986. As Senior Adviser to Italy's Ministry of the Interior in the early 1990s, Mr Arlacchi established the Direzione Investigativa Antimafia (DIA), a law enforcement agency createdto fight organized crime. In 1989, he became President of the International Association for the Study of Organized Crime. In 1992 Mr Arlacchi was appointed Honorary President of the Giovanni Falcone Foundation, in recognition of his commitment to fighting the Mafia. The Foundation was named after Mr Arlacchi's close friend, the Italian Prosecutor Giovanni Falcone, who was assassinated by the Sicilian Mafia in 1992.

Frank Bovenkerk, PhD is Professor of Criminology at Willen Pompe Institute for Criminology and Criminal Law. A cultural anthropologist by training and a Professor of Criminology at the Faculty of Law at Utrecht University, Dr Bovenkerk has published extensively on matters of migration, discrimination and racism, ethnicity and crime and is an expert on international organized crime. Most of his books (on Colombian organized crime in Europe, Turkish Mafia) are in Dutch, but the results of a Parliamentary Enquiry into organized crime in the Netherlands was published in

1998 by Kluwer International as *Organized Crime in the Netherlands* with Frank Bovenkerk as one of the authors.

Ko-Lin Chin who received his PhD in sociology from the University of Pennsylvania, is Associate Professor at the School of Criminal Justice, Rutgers University-Newark. He is the author of *Chinese Subculture and Criminality* (Greenwood Press, 1990), *Chinatown Gangs* (Oxford University Press, 1996), *Smuggled Chinese Immigrants in America* (Temple University Press, forthcoming), and co-editor of *Handbook of Organized Crime in the United States* (Greenwood Press, 1994).

Cyrille Fijnaut is a Professor of Comparative Law at the Schoordijk Institute of the Faculty of Law of Tilburg University, the Nettherlands. Since 1996 he has also been a visiting professor of law at the New York University School of Law within the framework of the Global Law School Program. His research concerns predominantly problems of policing and organized crime at a national, European and international level. In the last ten years he equally served as an expert to four parliamentary committees of inquiry in Belgium and the Netherlands. He is one of the editors of the *European Journal of Crime, Criminal Law and Criminal Justice* and of the *International Encyclopaedia of Criminal Law*. Some of his most relevant publications in English are; *Organized Crime in the Netherlands* (together with F. Bovenkerk, G. Bruinsma and H. van de Bunt; Kluwer Law International, 1998) and *Undercover: Police Surveillance in Comparative Perspective* (together with G. Marx; Kluwer Law International, 1995).

Giuseppe di Gennaro is Counsellor of the Italian Minister of Justice for Albania and chairs the Steering Committee for the Pact of Stability in the Balkan Region against Corruption. As a magistrate he has acted in several judicial functions including Section President of the Penal Cassation Court of Italy. He is a former Director-General of Penal Affairs, former Under-Secretary-General of the United Nations for the fight against crime and drugs, former Chairman of the UN Commission for Crime Prevention and Criminal Justice and former President of the European Committee for Criminal Affairs.

Roy Godson is a Professor of Government at Georgetown University and President of the National Strategy Information Center, at Washington DC – based research, education, and training center concerned with security issues. His current work focuses on

375

identifying nontraditional security challenges and developing strategies to combat them. Over the last two decades, he has written and edited 20 books and numerous articles on a variety of security related subjects. His most recent books include *Dirty Tricks or Trump Cards* (Transaction Publishers, 2001) and *Organized Crime and Democratic Governability: Mexico and the US-Mexican Borderlands* (University of Pittsburgh Press 2001; Spanish Edition, Editorial Grijalbo, 2000). He is also the editor of the quarterly journal *Trends in Organized Crime*. In 1998 and 2000 he organized the Georgetown Executive Leadership Seminar on Strategic Approaches to Countering Transnational Crime.

Peter Grabosky is Director of Research at the Australian Institute of Criminology. He was a Russell Sage Fellow in Law and Social Science at Yale Law School. He has published widely on white collar crime, regulatory systems, and related issues. He has published (co-authored with Dr Russell G. Smith, *Crime in the Digital Age: Controlling Telecommunications and Cyberspace Illegalities* (Sydney: The Federation Press; and New Brunswick: Transaction Publishers, 1998).

Robert Kelly is Professor of Social Science and Criminal Justice at Brooklyn College and the Graduate School of the City University of New York. His published works include studies of minority youths in higher educational institutions, societal reaction to the AIDS phenomenon, studies of racketeering in toxic waste industries, nature and operation of organized crime in America, and various monographs on the impact of bilingual policies in the United States. He is co-author of *Handbook of Organized Crime in the United States* (Greenwood Press, 1994). His most recent book is *Upperworld and Underworld* published by Kluwer.

Raymond E. Kendall graduated in Modern Languages from Exeter College, Oxford University and, after completing his military service in the early 1950s with the Royal Air Force, mostly in Malaya, he joined the Ugandan Police as Officer in charge of Crime, Kigezi District, Western Province. In 1962 he joined the Metropolitan Police, New Scotland Yard in London, spending most of his service in the Special Branch and rising to Deputy Assistant Commissioner. In 1971, Raymond Kendall became Assistant Director, Drugs at Interpol Headquarters. Promoted to Director, Liaison and Criminal Intelligence in 1976, he was first elected Secretary General in October 1985, at the 54th session of the Interpol General Assembly in

Washington DC, USA. He was re-elected in 1990, and again in 1995 for a further term of five years and retired in 2000. Raymond Kendall holds numerous awards for merit and distinguished service from many countries, including the Queen's Police Medal for Distinguished Police Service from the UK and he was appointed a *Chevalier de la Légion d'Honneur* in the French 14th July Honours list in 1997. His professional interests are the coordination and promotion of efforts to combat and prevent international crime; the promotion of cooperation between all criminal police authorities in member countries; and the development of all institutions likely to contribute effectively to the prevention and suppression of ordinary law crimes.

Emanuele Marotta has been Deputy Director of Europol since 1 July 1999 and in this function is responsible for the Intelligence Analysis Department. He first joined Europol in 1994 having been a senior officer in the Italian National Police (including responsibility for border police controls) From 1987 to 1994 he was Director of the International Affairs Division of the Central Directorate for Antidrug Services (Ministry of Interior) in Rome. In this capacity he was a member, sometimes head of the Italian delegation in main international fora dealing with illicit drug trafficking, diversion of chemical precursors and organized crime, such as Interpol, Trevi Group III, Schengen, Chemical Action Task Force, Pompidou Group, CELAD. From 1992–93 Marotta was Scientific expert of the Council of Europe for drafting the Convention on Illicit Drug Trafficking. In 1987–88 he was a member of the drafting committee of the UN Convention against Illicit Drug Trafficking.

Gerhard O.W. Mueller is Distinguished Professor of Criminal Justice, Rutgers University, Newark, NJ, USA. After earning his JD from the University of Chicago he went on to receive the LLM degree from Columbia University. He was awarded the degree of the Dr Jur (hc) by the University of Uppsala, Sweden. He has been teaching criminal law, criminology, criminal justice and international comparative criminal justice since1953. From 1974 to 1982 he served as Director of the United Nations Crime Prevention and Criminal Justice Branch. In the past he served also as President of the American Society of Criminology and Chair of ISPAC.

R.T. Naylor is a Professor of Economics at McGill University, Montreal, Canada. His research concerns include: international black markets, smuggling, money laundering and enterprise crime. He consults for and lectures to goverment agencies involved in tax and criminal justice enforcement issues and to forensic accounting firms involved in investigating financial fraud. His work appears regularly in, among other journals, *Crime, Law and Social Change*, of which he is also a senior editor. He has recently been appointed Senior Fellow of the University of Toronto Centre for Peace and Conflict Studies and Visiting Research Associate at the York University Nathanson Centre for the Study of Organized Crime and Corruption. He is the author of *Hot Money and the Politics of Debt* and most recently of *Patriots and Profiteers*.

Anita Nilsson (Swedish) is Senior Co-ordinator, in the Office of the Deputy Director General, Department of Safeguards, at the International Atomic Energy Agency. Her major responsibilities consist of being Chair of the Information Review Committee and Co-ordinator of Programme M: Security of Material (including illicit trafficking and physical protection).

Office of the United Nations High Commissioner for Human Rights
The mandate of the Office of the United Nations High Commissioner for Human Rights derives from Articles 1, 13 and 55 of Charter of the United Nations, the Vienna Declaration and Programme action and Assembly resolution 48/141 of 20 December 1993, by which the Assembly established the post of United Nations High Commissioner for Human Rights. In connection with the programme for reform of the United Nations (A/51/950, para. 79), the Office of the United Nations High Commissioner for Human Rights and the Center for Human Rights were consolidated into a single Office of the United Nations High Commissioner for Human Rights as of 15 September 1997.
Functions and organization
The Office of the United Nations High Commissioner for Human Rights:
(a) Promotes universal enjoyment of all human rights by giving practical effect to the will and resolve of the world community as expressed by the United Nations;
(b) Plays the leading role on human rights issues and emphasizes the importance of human rights at the international and national levels;
(c) Promotes international cooperation for human rights;
(d) Stimulates and coordinates action for human rights throughout the United Nations system;
(e) Promotes universal ratification and implementation of international standards;

(f) Assists in the development of new norms;

(g) Supports human rights organs and treaty monitoring bodies;

(h) Responds to serious violations of human rights;

(i) Undertakes preventive human rights action;

(j) Promotes the establishment of national human rights infrastructures;

(k) Undertakes human rights field activities and operations;

(l) Provides education, information advisory services and technical assistance in the field of human rights.

The Office is headed by a High Commissioner with the rank of Under-Secretary-General.

Alessandro Pansa is at present Direttore Centrale della Polizia stradale, ferroviaria, di frontiera e postale (Director of the Highway, Border and Postal Police). He graduated in law at the University of Naples. He entered the Italian Police in 1975 and his first assignment was in Calabria where he fought against organized crime and terrorism. In 1982 he was transferred to Rome and the Narcotic Drugs Department. Since 1985 he has tackled organized crime, specifically money laundering. He is a former Director of the Central Operational Department of the Police; and was a Prefect.

Letizia Paoli has worked since 1998 in the Department of Criminology of the Max Planck Institutute for Criminal Law in Freiburg, Germany. In 1997, she obtained her PhD in political and social sciences at the European University Institute in Firenze with a thesis on the Italian mafia (*Fratelli di mafia: Coso Nostra and 'Ndrangheta*, Bologna, Il Mulino, 2000). Paoli has been consultant to the Italian Ministry of the Interior, the Direzione Investigativa Antimafia, the UN Office for Drug Control and Crime Prevention in Vienna (UNODCCP) and the UN Interregional Crime and Justice Research Institute in Rome (UNICRI). Among her most recent publications there is a volume on illegal drug use and trafficking in post-Soviet Russia (*Illegal Drug Trade in Russia*, Freiburg, edition iuscrim, 2001). The book stems from a research project which was commissioned by the UNODCCP and entailed field research in nine Russian cities, including Moscow and St Petersburg. Paoli is currently conducting a study on local drug markets in Frankfurt and Milan, which is partially financed by the European Monitoring Centre for Drugs and Drug Addiction in Lisbon.

Nikos Passas is Associate Professor of Criminal Justice at Temple

University, Pennsylvania, USA. His degrees are PhD (Sociology of Deviance), University of Edinburgh, DEA, (Criminology), University of Paris, LLB, University of Athens. Passas has an abiding interest in theoretical criminology. He has written extensively on anomie theory. His elaborations of the original statement of this theory have made it possible to apply it to deviance and crime by upper-class individuals, professionals and organizations. Dr Passas also specializes in the study of white-collar crime, organized crime and international crime. His empirical studies have focused on cross-border crimes and frauds committed in the European Union (especially in connection with agricultural subsidies); bank-related offenses and the Bank of Credit and Commerce International (BCCI) scandal; political and commercial corruption at the national and international level; and crime and deviance within and by new religious movements. Dr Passas has authored several research reports and acted as a consultant to various bodies, including the United Nations Center for International Crime Prevention, the Commission of the European Union, and the German Parliament.

Livia Pomodoro is President of the Juvenile Court of Milan; Secretary-General of the Centro nazionale di prevenzione e difesa sociale; Secretary and Standing-Coordinator of the ISPAC Functional and Resource Committees. She graduated in law. Her previous posts include magistrate, Court of Cassation, Italy; Deputy Chief of Cabinet and Chief of Cabinet, Minister of Justice; and deputy-prosecutor, Court of Appeal of Milan.

Dimitri Vlassis holds a law degree from the University of Athens (Greece) and an LLM (Master of Laws) from the University of Miami (USA). He has pursued postgraduate studies in international law at the George Washington University. He is an attorney, licenced to practice law in Greece and member of the Athens Bar Association, and was recruited by the United Nations in 1989 following the successful completion of a United Nations National Competitive Examination, working with the Center for International Crime Prevention of the Office for Drug Control and Crime Prevention of the United Nations Office at Vienna ever since. Since 1998, he has been Secretary of the Ad Hoc Committee for the Elaboration of the United Nations Convention against Transnational Organized Crime. His responsibilities at the Crime Center also include action against organized transnational crime, money laundering, corruption, and other forms of economic crime. He was principally responsible for the organization and servicing of the Naples World Ministerial Conference on Organized Transnational Crime (November 1994), as well as for the International Conference on the Prevention of Money Laundering and the Control of the Proceeds of Crime (Courmayeur, Italy) (June 1994). In addition to these tasks, D. Vlassis has been actively involved in the technical cooperation programme of the Center, leading or participating in needs assessment and advisory services missions in numerous countries, including Cambodia and Somalia (in the context of UN peacekeeping missions).

Phil Williams is Director of the University of Pittsburgh's Ridgway Center for International Security Studies and Professor of the Graduate School of Public and International Affairs. Williams has written extensively on transnational organized crime and on international security issues and has consulted for a variety of organizations including the United Nations and the United States government. He is also consultant for Veridian/PSR and for Centra. In summer 2000 he was a Visiting Scientist at CERT/CC at Carnegie Mellon University.

Sheldon Zhang received his PhD in sociology from the University of Southern California. He is Associate Professor at the Sociology Department, California State University, San Marcos. His research areas include Chinese organized crimes, Asian gangs, juvenile corrections, informal social control, and program evaluation. His papers have appeared in journals such as the *British Journal of Criminology, Crime and Delinquency, Journal of Criminal Justice,* and *Crime, Law and Social Change.*

Index